Practical Politics

in the United States

Editor

CORNELIUS P. COTTER

Practical

Contributing Authors

HERBERT E. ALEXANDER	DONALD B. JOHNSON
EDWARD F. COOKE	CONRAD F. JOYNER
CORNELIUS P. COTTER	JAMES B. KESSLER
SVEN GROENNINGS	KARL O'LESSKER
STANLEY J. HINDEN	DOUGLAS ROSS
ROBERT J. HUCKSHORN	MARK SPROULE-JONES

NEIL STAEBLER

Politics

in the United States

ALLYN AND BACON, INC.   Boston

Preface

In December 1965, The Robert A. Taft Institute of Government, a bipartisan foundation concerned with propagating interest in political participation, approached the editor and offered to underwrite the costs of compilation of a series of essays on aspects of practical politics. It was quickly agreed that the essays should be prepared by persons whose intellectual interest in politics had been complemented by participation. The focus should be political organization and campaigning. This book is the result.

Each of the authors has attempted to infuse his chapter with the ring of authority that comes from close personal experience with the subject at hand. Indeed, some of the chapters were designed as recountals of personal experience. Yet none would counterpoise "practical" politics and the academic study of politics. They can go hand in hand, as demonstrated by the backgrounds of the contributors to this study.

Full biographies are given; and it suffices here to point out that all of the contributors have demonstrated intellectual interest in politics, whether evidenced by participation in the work of presidential study commissions, by foundation, newspaper or academic appointments, or some combination of these. Each has had practical political experience of the kind which does not merely breed anecdotes, but sharpens insight and informs his sense of what it is important to discuss and what can be passed over.

The Robert A. Taft Institute of Government, and particularly Mrs. Preston Davie, Chairman of the Board of Trustees, and Miss Marilyn Chelstrom, Executive Director, have been instrumental in bringing this work to fruition, but at no time has anyone at the Institute sought to influence the selection of participants, to set topics, or edit. In short, the editor and authors must be held responsible for the content of this book, not the Institute.

While the individual authors enjoyed help from sources too numerous to acknowledge here, the final manuscript results from the patient and Herculean efforts of Miss Rose Isom at Wichita State University, Wichita, Kansas, and Miss Joyce Beilke and Mrs. Gilda Malofsky at the University of Wisconsin—Milwaukee.

CORNELIUS P. COTTER

Introductory Note

The writings contained in this book were undertaken at the request of The Robert A. Taft Institute of Government. The purpose of the Institute, which is non-partisan and educational, is to bring about among American citizens an understanding of the principles and processes of government in the United States, an awareness of individual political responsibility at every level, and the importance of the two-party system in providing responsible government.

The Taft Institute's principal program is one of seminars for elementary and secondary school social studies teachers. The Taft Seminars are designed to give background and to assist teachers in their classroom treatment of the American political system. Experienced politicians, Republicans and Democrats, as well as political scientists are called upon as instructors. Of these Taft Seminars, the *Cincinnati Enquirer* stated in an editorial after the seminars were held a second year for teachers in that city, "There hardly could be a more fitting memorial to the late Senator Robert A. Taft, who believed with all his heart that a knowledgeable electorate is the surest route to good government."

A part of the Institute's political education program is the publication of materials. In December 1965, Dr. Cornelius Cotter, a distinguished political scientist at Wichita State University, and later at the University of Wisconsin, was asked to serve as editor for a series of writings on the two-party system and practical politics in the United States. Dr. Cotter secured a number of persons, many of whom were political scientists who had also actively participated in the political system by running for office, managing campaigns, serving as Republican and Democratic Party leaders, to prepare materials on various aspects of practical politics. This book results.

The Taft Institute is indeed grateful to Dr. Cotter and to the 12 authors who contributed the thoughtful and meaningful studies that make up the chapters of this book. In accord with the Institute's non-partisan nature, there are many points of view expressed by the individual authors. Their statements are their own and the individual members of the Taft Institute's Board of Trustees, Education Committee and

Advisory Council may or may not concur with them. It may be expected that no one person will agree with all ideas set forth. The Institute hopes, however, that exposure to various opinions will contribute to the understanding of many Americans concerning the principles and processes of government in the United States and that further they will serve as a stimulus to active participation in the political system.

MRS. PRESTON DAVIE, CHAIRMAN
THE ROBERT A. TAFT INSTITUTE OF GOVERNMENT

Introduction

We are interested in political parties from three principal vantage points: (1) As parties provide auspices for candidacy for public office. (2) As parties contribute toward dividing the politically participant public into majority and minority groupings for purposes of selecting public decision-makers at all levels. (3) As parties express the centrifugal and centripetal forces of localism and nationalism which constantly seek new adjustment in a federal political system.

(1) In the United States candidates for public office tend to be self-designated rather than recruited by the political parties. And, in general elections, even incumbents lack expectations of substantial party help. Insofar as the presidential candidate can be regarded as heading a ticket, the myriad of other members of that ticket are as likely to be actively working to dissociate their campaigns from the presidential campaign as they are to be seeking a ride on the ticket leader's coattails. It is convenient, even essential, as an aspirant office-holder to be a Democrat or a Republican, and to gain party nomination, which can be achieved without the consent of the officialdom of the party. But the convenience is to be defined in terms of having a position in one of the two major party columns on the ballot, and whatever ticket-voting benefit may accrue, more than in terms of active support by an integrated party machine.

(2) American political parties, in short, do not do much for their candidates and have little control over their selection or campaigning. Likewise, there is little or no party discipline—in comparison, at least, to other western democracies—to bind party office-holders together after the election. This means that parties are unable to translate into public policy the evanescent and frequently platitudinous statements which comprise the platforms upon which their candidates supposedly run. These characteristics of American politics invite depiction of the system as chaotic and have been the basis for recurrent urgent calls for eleventh-hour reform. Putting aside for the moment the merits of an alarmist view of the conduct of politics in the United States, let us look at a few functions which the two major parties do perform.

Each party has reserved for it a place on the ballot in every partisan election (some local elections are or purport to be nonpartisan in nature). If one secures a major party nomination he is assured of having his name placed on the ballot. This is no mean feat. It means that he has narrowed competition for the desired office from some indeterminately large number of persons thinking of seeking or actively competing for the nomination to another nominee or two and himself. It means also that while he is guaranteed no mobilization of professional party management, financial resources, and the like, to engineer his election, he is likely to find the party officers more inclined to help than impede his election. It is necessary to say "likely," for on the one hand, if he is a gubernatorial or presidential candidate, he may be able to take formal control of the party mechanism, appointing his own officers and staff. At the other extreme, if he has won the party nomination without party benediction and continues to face active hostility, the party leaders may not only sit on their hands, but also offer discreet help to the opposition, perhaps as part of an agreement on distribution of patronage after the election.

What are some of the tangibles and intangibles which a party can offer to its nominees beyond an assured place on the ballot? The parties maintain precinct organizations which vary in strength from area to area and time to time. The candidate may be able to enlist such existing strength or to recruit selectively from it. Although he must count on securing the bulk of his own campiagn funds independently (and without irritating party leaders by diverting funds from traditional patterns of giving), he may receive some financial help from the party. There are strong traditions of regional, demographic, and other identification with the major parties, which persist election after election. The parties continuously seek to purvey images which hold onto and intensify the traditional allegiances of these groupings, while making inroads on group allegiances to the opposite party. In doing this they provide their candidates with a bonus or deficit vote, something to build upon or to attempt to dig one's way out of.

(3) Lord Bryce found in 1889 that the federal system resembled "a great factory wherein two sets of machinery are at work, their revolving wheels apparently intermixed, their bands crossing one another, yet each set doing its own work without touching or hampering the other." An exponential increase in the number of governmental units through which we seek to accomplish social purposes, and the growing complexity of the relations between various levels of government, makes this simile seem more apt today than in Bryce's time. Yet there are countervailing factors—increasing intimacy of national-state governmental relations, direct patterns of relations between the national and local units of government, the tendency toward specification of uniform national policies enforceable in each state through cooperation or national fiat—which make clear the inapplicability to contemporary federalism of a simile evocative of crossing governmental bands which do not meet.

It is not feasible to avoid relating party behavior to the system of federalism and the tradition of regionalism and localism which prevail. Indeed, the notion of a "winning party" is necessarily ambiguous in the United States, where one party can carry the White House but not the Congress, or the Congress can turn at midterm; where one party can dominate nationally, and another, regionally entrenched, make informal treaty with factions of the former to accomplish policy objectives.

Social scientists sometimes speak of the danger of "reifying" institutions—that is, thinking of institutions in terms of concrete existence as "things" rather than as stable but always changing sets of relationships. There is some question, given the limited purposes ascribed to American political parties in this introduction, and given the kaleidoscopic nature of political parties within the federal system, whether, in terms of "is" and of "ought" it is not reifying political parties to speak of "national" parties, with all that the term conjures concerning physical trappings of existence.

Yet in the parts which follow, we shall argue that political parties are discernible phenomena at the national level—one can put one's hand on them—while simultaneously, it is consistent to say that parties, such as we have them are diffuse, contingent, "sometime" entities.

It is the process and tradition of contesting for office through the electoral mechanism, rather than any single victory or defeat in an election, which is of decisive importance to the perpetuation of the democratic political system. We do not mean naively to invoke the famous "unseen hand" of classical economics which supposedly, through the market mechanism, translated the selfish calculations of numerous economic actors into a pattern of activity which cumulatively accorded with the public interest. Yet we suggest that in a democracy, the pursuit of office—that is, of public decision-making power—by thousands of candidates, whether independently or in various alliances, whether for selfish or altruistic purposes, is essential to the preservation of the political system.

In this limited and vital sense we seek to imbue the reader with a comprehension of, and even a sense of vicarious participation in, party activity and campaigning.

The thirteen chapters of this book fall into five parts. In Part One, we speak of the development of political parties, various propositions concerning their appropriate functioning, and their efficacy in the American democracy. Here, too, we acquaint the reader with the most tangible emanation we have of national political parties, the national party committees which have responsibility for arranging the quadrennial presidential conventions. In Part Two, we move to where the votes are and review party organization at the state, city, and suburban level. In Part Three we deal with political campaigning for state and national legislative office, seen from the vantage points of the campaigner, the campaign manager, and, through a survey study, the chastened eyes of all defeated candidates for Congress in 1960. In Part Four, we describe the development of national convention politics in the United States, the selection of the delegates who select the presidential candidates, the conduct of national conventions, and the financing of presidential elections. In Part Five, we offer a basis for comparative analysis by looking at campaigning in Britain and Scandinavia and conclude the book with an evaluation of American parties today.

Contents

part one

NATIONAL PARTIES

UNWANTED *by the constitutional framers, regarded as a distinctive threat to the plan for government which was beaten out compromise by compromise in Philadelphia, political parties have become integral to the functioning of American democracy. We have been schooled in the paramountcy of the two-party system of politics. When we seek evidence of this phenomenon, we find both confirmation and refutation. Even in an era of mass media, national politics are predominantly conducted at the local level. Congressmen come from local constituencies, convention delegates are selected and frequently instructed locally. The election of the President is still, at least formally, confirmed by the tally of state electoral votes. We obviously lack "responsible party government"—a term defined in Chapter 1. Yet in a physical sense, and in popular imagery, we have two national parties, even if they lack sharp ideological delineations.*

Chapter 1 discusses the development and function of parties in the United States. Chapter 2 provides information on the two national party headquarters and their relations to their local and state party units.

CORNELIUS P. COTTER

Cornelius P. Cotter studied at Stanford University (A.B. 1949), Harvard University (M.P.A. 1951; Ph.D. 1953), and the London School of Economics (1951–52). He has taught at Columbia University (1952–53), Stanford University (1953–61 with leaves), and Wichita State University (1963–67), prior to assuming his present position as Professor of Political Science at The University of Wisconsin-Milwaukee.

Cotter has been active in California and Kansas Republican politics, and has served in staff positions of a political and governmental nature in Washington, D.C. In 1959 he was Republican National Committee Faculty Fellow, and for the first half of 1960 Assistant to the Chairman, RNC. From 1960 to 1963, with a three-month intermission teaching at Stanford, he was Assistant Staff Director, United States Commission on Civil Rights.

His books include *Government and Private Enterprise* (1960), *Powers of the President During Crises* (with J. Malcolm Smith, 1960), *Issues of the Sixties* (edited with Leonard Freedman, 1961), and *Politics Without Power: The National Party Committees* (with Bernard C. Hennessy, 1964). He has contributed to learned journals and books of readings, including the chapter "Legislative Oversight" in Alfred de Grazia, *et. al.*, *Congress: The First Branch* (1967). In addition, Cotter has supervised the production of numerous government documents and RNC materials.

CORNELIUS P. COTTER

1. American Political Parties*

The first observation of note about political parties in the United States is that the founding fathers not only did not foresee the eventual form that political parties would take, but they believed they had built into the Constitution positive barriers against parties.[1] The President, the Senate, and the Supreme Court were placed beyond direct election. The doctrine of separation of powers seemed certain to keep any one "faction" (a term used almost interchangeably with "party") from gaining control over the government. J. Allen Smith, whose work *The Spirit of American Government* profoundly influenced a number of subsequent critics of the Constitution, has pointed out that the American government was patterned after the British government of the day.[2] The British government, like our own colonial political systems, had not yet been introduced to party responsibility. It was characterized by control by the property-owning classes and a positive distrust of party. The very existence of party, as a matter of fact, would endanger the system by resulting in the generation of pressures for expanded suffrage as the parties competed for power at the polls. The Reform Bill of 1832 marks the point at which parties began to assert superiority over the Crown and the Cabinet in Great Britain, making the latter responsible to a majority in the House of Commons.

---

* This chapter has benefited from the generous contribution of Professor Robert L. Peabody of The Johns Hopkins University, who participated in its final revision.

[1] See, e.g., Arthur N. Holcombe's discussion of "The Unplanned Institution of Organized Partisanship," *Our More Perfect Union* (Cambridge, Mass.: Harvard University Press, 1950), Chapter IV.

[2] J. Allen Smith, *The Spirit of American Government* (New York: The Macmillan Company, 1907). Smith, an unabashed majoritarian, advocated a number of constitutional reforms which would make the American political system more like the British strong two-party system as it had evolved in the last half of the nineteenth century.

Madison, on faction, is representative of the attitude of the framers of the Constitution. His position, stated in the *Federalist Paper* No. 10, warrants extensive quotation.

> Among the numerous advantages promised by a well-constructed Union, none deserves to be more accurately developed than its tendency to break and control the violence of faction. The friend of popular governments, never finds himself so much alarmed for their character and fate, as when he contemplates their propensity to this dangerous vice. . . .
>
> By a faction, I understand a number of citizens, whether amounting to a majority or minority of the whole, who are united and actuated by some common impulse of passion, or of interest, adverse to the rights of other citizens, or to the permanent and aggregate interests of the community.

But Madison goes on to admit that factionalism cannot be eliminated without surrendering liberty which, "is to faction what air is to fire." Thus the purpose of the framers was not so much to eliminate factionalism as to control and minimize it. Madison saw the system of representation set up in the Constitution, which he distinguished from pure democracy, and the system for electing the President as at least confining "factionalism" to the State level: "The influence of factious leaders may kindle the flame within their particular States, but will be unable to spread a general conflagration through the other States."[3]

This characteristic determination of the framers to have politicians and political office without political parties resulted in a historical contretemps which ushered in lasting changes in the system of nominating and electing presidents. Under the original form of Article 2, Section 1, presidential electors equal to (but not including) the number of Senators and Representatives of each State were to be selected in a manner to be prescribed by the State Legislature. They were to assemble in the State and cast votes for two persons, at least one of whom must be from another State. The person receiving a majority of the total electoral votes cast was to become President of the United States. The person receiving the next highest number was to become Vice-President. The electors, however, were not required to distinguish between the two offices in their ballots. If no one were to receive a majority or if the vote were evenly split, the election was to go to the House of Representatives, where each State delegation was to have one vote.

No opposition was expressed either to the election of Washington in 1788 or to his re-election in 1792.

---

[3] Alexander Hamilton, John Jay, and James Madison, *The Federalist: A Commentary on the Constitution of the United States* (New York: The Modern Library, 1937), pp. 53–62, 53, 54, 61. These papers were first published at regular intervals in the New York press in 1787–88.

For a brief period Congress deliberated as a group of individual members. With the introduction of Secretary of the Treasury Alexander Hamilton's fiscal program, however, the first party organization came into existence among national officeholders.[4] On the one hand there arose a combination of congressmen supporting a strong federal government and particularly favoring the manufacturing, commercial, and financial interests. Their program aroused the opposition of Southern and agrarian interests, organized around such political leaders as Thomas Jefferson and James Madison of Virginia. Their opposition came to be known as the "Republicans," a name that implied that their party enemies, the Federalists, favored a monarchy. They were also called "Democratic-Republicans" and toward the end of the Federalist period, simply "Democrats."

Party elections began in the United States in 1796, when George Washington declined to run for a third term. In his famous Farewell Address of 1796, deeply disturbed by the developing split between the Hamiltonians and the Jeffersonians, the outgoing President warned against "the baneful effects of the spirit of party."

> It serves always to distract the public councils and enfeeble the public administration. It agitates the community with ill-founded jealousies and false alarms; kindles the animosity of one party against another; foments occasionally riot and insurrection. It opens the door to foreign influence and corruption, which find a facilitated access to the government itself through the channels of party passion. . . .
> A fire not to be quenched, it demands a uniform vigilance to prevent its bursting into a flame, lest, instead of warming, it should consume.[5]

In 1796, Federalist John Adams was elected to the Presidency, narrowly defeating the Democratic-Republican candidate, Thomas Jefferson.

It was not however until the presidential election of 1800 that political parties made a full-fledged effort to secure the support of the electorate, with Jefferson supporters being particularly active through extra-governmental party organizations called "Democratic Clubs." When in 1801 the ballots were counted for the 1800 presidential election, it was found that Jefferson and Burr, Republicans, each had 73 electoral votes; the incumbent Federalist President, John Adams, had 65; Charles Cotesworth Pinchney, his Federalist running-mate from South Carolina, had 64; and John Jay of New York, another Federalist, had one vote. Party discipline had held firm; the scattering

---

[4] Joseph Charles, *The Origins of the American Party System* (New York: Harper Torchbooks, 1961).
[5] "Washington's Farewell Address," *Documents of American History*, Henry Steele Commager, (ed.), 5th ed. (New York: Appleton-Century-Crofts, Inc., 1949), pp. 169–175, 172.

of votes for the Vice-President which had occurred in 1796 had been eliminated. "Every elector who voted for Jefferson in 1800 also voted for Burr, and every Federalist elector but one (in order to assure Adams a lead) gave his votes for both Adams and Pinckney."[6]

Despite the apparent understanding that Jefferson and Burr were running as a team, Jefferson as President and Burr as Vice-President, the election went to the House of Representatives under the provision of Article 2, Section 1. It was up to a "lame duck," Federalist-controlled Congress to choose between the two Republicans. In the House of Representatives it took 36 ballots to select Jefferson as President and Burr as Vice-President. The result of this experience was the adoption of the Twelfth Amendment in September 1804. The Twelfth Amendment provides that electors will vote for President and for Vice-President, one of whom may not be from the same state as the electors. The Twelfth Amendment, coupled with the development of the practice of statewide rather than district selection of electors, which meant that the whole slate went to the statewide majority, sealed the practice of party government in the United States, as we understand it.

De Toqueville has described the ideological basis of the rise of parties in the early decades of the United States:

> When the War of Independence was terminated and the foundations of the new government were to be laid down, the Nation was divided between two opinions—two opinions which are as old as the world and which are perpetually to be met with, under different forms and various names, in all free communities, the one tending to limit, the other to extend indefinitely, the power of the people. The conflict between these two opinions never assumed that degree of violence in America which it frequently displayed elsewhere. Both parties of the Americans were agreed upon the most essential point; and neither of them had to destroy an old Constitution or overthrow the structure of society in order to triumph.[7]

If, indeed, parties did arise in America in part to pursue alternative ideologies, it seems to be the consensus of subsequent students of American government that they survived almost solely as mechanisms for electing people to office.[8] It frequently has been pointed out that if the Constitutional framers did not prevent the rise of national parties, they at least prevented the development of responsible party

---

[6] William N. Chambers, *Political Parties in A New Nation* (New York: Oxford University Press, 1963), p. 158.

[7] Alexis De Toqueville, *Democracy in America*, Vol. I, Bradley Edition, (New York: Alfred Knopf, 1946), pp. 175–76.

[8] However, it can be argued persuasively that the two major parties do differ on their advocacy of the rate of change that should take place; the degree of governmental intervention that is desirable; and the kinds of economic, religious, and ethnic groupings which make up their base of support.

government in the United States. By "responsible party government" we mean to invoke a number of notions:

- A political process characterized by central party control over the choice of nominees for office.
- A system of government in which party nominees when elected to office work in unison with one another in the legislature and with the executive, thus making it possible to translate party electoral victories into policy and program.
- As implied, above, a system in which it is not possible at the polls to elect a chief executive of one party and national legislature dominated by another.
- A system in which the elected chief executive leads his party, and in which it is the norm for the leader of the minority party to become chief executive upon their victory at the polls.

The implicit, if not the explicit model, for most advocates of "responsible government" is the British two-party system.

In a review of contemporary efforts to evaluate the functioning of political parties in the United States, E. E. Schattschneider suggests: "The greatest shortcoming of the party system results from the failure of the system to convert politics into party government. This deficiency is related in terms of the whole problem of the local power in the party system."[9] Schattschneider goes on to charge that, "the parties function effectively in electing candidates to office but govern badly because they do not mobilize effectively the men they elect to office."[10] Merle Fainsod contends that: "The disciplined political power necessary to integrate public policy on a party basis has been lacking." This is caused by the "heterogeneous membership and . . . amorphous character" of the parties. "Cautious party leaders faced with the challenge of achieving an electoral majority seek to keep their disparate elements together by blurring the issues rather than by emphasizing them. This strategy necessarily makes each party an instrument for the reconciliation of group and sectional conflicts.[11] This tendency toward diffusion, pointed out Fainsod, is reinforced by our federal system of government.

Criticism of our parties reached a peak with the publication in 1950 of a report by the Committee on Political Parties of the American Political Science Association.[12]

Time does not diminish the spate of literature critical of the blurring of ideological differences between the two major parties. It

---

[9] *The Struggle for Party Government,* (College Park, Md., University of Maryland, 1948), p. 29.
[10] *Ibid.*
[11] "Consolidating Party Control," *American Political Science Review*, 42, (1948), pp. 316, 318.
[12] "Toward a More Responsible Two-Party System," *American Political Science Review*, Supplement, September 1950.

has become the fashion to apply elements of framework for analysis of political parties developed by the French political scientist, Maurice Duverger. He distinguishes between parties which come into being from external sources (outside the parliament) and those of parliamentary origin. Parties originating outside parliament are more disciplined and centralized ("In fact, their development begins at the top whereas that of the others starts at the base."); parliamentary parties are less coherent. Duverger finds "a certain more or less open mistrust of the parliamentary group" in parties of external origin.[13] Duverger goes on to apply other sets of distinctions between parties, based upon structure and process, but these are not of immediate concern here.

Recently the argument has been made, and buttressed with considerable evidence by way of recital and analysis of American political history that, in effect, we have "four-party politics in America." We have, speaking loosely, an internal Democratic and an internal Republican party (the "congressional parties") and, we have external Democratic and Republican parties (the "presidential parties"). Presumably, for the party out of power, the party's national committee represents the presidential party, such as it is.[14] This situation is not merely observed, but is deplored, by James MacGregor Burns, who argues for a candid realignment of members of the congressional parties into a liberal party and a conservative party, each willing to, and presumably capable of, taking leadership from its president when it commands the White House.

Burns' book invites comparison with an impassioned plea for party reform, published in 1932 by a University of Chicago economics professor who was destined to become a distinguished member of the more liberal wing of the congressional Democratic party—Paul H. Douglas.[15] In The Coming of a New Party,[16] Douglas argued that the

---

[13] Political Parties, (New York: John Wiley & Sons, Inc., 1954), quoted matter from p. xxxiv.

[14] James MacGregor Burns, The Deadlock of Democracy, (Englewood Cliffs, New Jersey: Prentice-Hall, Inc., 1963).

[15] Douglas illustrates the difficulty of applying Burns's classification of four-party politics to individuals in Congress. While voting more liberally than most Senators, he has also established a record of considerable independence from the leadership of both parties in Congress and the White House. Douglas, himself, described the four-party politics of Congress: "We have a group of liberal Democrats from the North and West, virtually all of the Democrats from the North and West, and we have a group of conservative Democrats, largely, though not entirely, from the South. The Republicans have two political parties, a large number of conservatives, . . . and a small, but gallant, group of liberal Republicans." Congressional Record (daily ed.), May 26, 1961, p. 9130.

[16] (New York: Whittlesey House, 1932). Douglas won his third and last term in the Senate in 1960 by over 400,000 votes. At the time of his 1966 defeat by Charles Percy, Douglas had built a solid reputation in the Senate as a crusading reformer and independent.

two major parties of that day purveyed a philosophy of individualism, and of laissez-faire; and that they propagated the Horatio Alger myth that thrift, intelligence, and perseverance suffice to insure success. The parties offered, said Professor Douglas, "a strange compound of frontier traditions, the Protestant ethic, and 18th century rationalism." In voting for either party, the average farmer or working man who has most to gain from collective action permits those who hold economic power to retain the reins of government. Professor Douglas had a prescription for action: It would not be possible to capture the old political parties from within, for their domination by capitalists was too great; thus, it would be necessary to found a new party. In states in which a non-Communist Socialist party was strong, this might be used as a vehicle.

Douglas addressed himself to the question why a national third-party movement might be expected to succeed in 1932, whereas previous efforts generally had failed. There were two principal reasons for failure in the past. First of all, these efforts had not been timely. The 1932 effort would be. Secondly, earlier efforts had failed because the parties were hastily built national organizations instead of organizations which had been built from the ground up. The new party which Douglas heralded would develop at the local, county, and state, as well as the national level, and would develop in that sequence. Douglas conceded that the American Federation of Labor undoubtedly would oppose such an attempt, but he thought that the help of local unions could be enlisted.

Professor Douglas failed to take heed of a principal obstacle to such a third national party. Some people claim this is the constitutional requirement of a majority in the electoral college. People do not want to take the chance of throwing the election to the House of Representatives. Others attribute partial responsibility to the character of the states as single-member electoral districts for the selection of Presidential electors, the entire slate of electors being given to the party which gains a majority or plurality vote. A third party, it is said, is likely to drain votes principally from one of the two major parties, leading the dissentient elements of that party who might have sentimental ties to the third party, to remain regular in their voting behavior for fear of throwing the election to the opposite major party by plurality.

Both conjectures are plausible, but they do not hold up under close scrutiny. With respect to the first, some elements of the population or parts of the country may, on occasion, have eminently practical reasons for founding a third party. The purpose would be to throw the presidential election to the House of Representatives, with the expectation that the House would be more likely to pick a satisfactory candidate than would the nation as a whole. Indeed, this was part of the motivation for the founding of the Dixiecrat party in 1948 and the fielding of the States-Rights party in 1956. The very people

who adduce the second reason, namely, a rational calculation by a
person that to cast his vote for a third party might weaken the party
which he regards to be the lesser of two evils among the major parties
and throw the election to the party which he opposes, tend to regard
our political parties as "built not on the rock of Faith but rather on
the broad mudflats of popular desires and individual ambitions."[17]
And this, of course, is not as much a contradiction as it may, at first
blush, seem. Some people may make rational calculations in voting;
others are guided by passion. Still others—perhaps most members of
the electorate—struggle to effect a compromise between reason and
passion as they frame a party choice in an election. In spite of all the
inhibitions to third party movements, however, as many as a half-
dozen or more third-parties are fielded at the state and sectional
level in every presidential election.

   Returning to Professor Douglas' proposal for the founding of a
new party on a national level, and the principal obstacle to such an
effort, it is simply this: state statutes today collectively embody
Madison's determination that if political parties cannot be avoided in
a democracy, their number shall be restricted and they shall be ex-
tensively regulated. That is to say, political parties are not voluntary
associations which can be formed with the ease with which one may
create neighborhood clubs. Curtis D. MacDougall, a citizen of Illinois,
discovered this fact in 1948.[18] He and others sought to establish the
Progressive party in Illinois, in order to compete in the Presidential and
Senatorial elections of that year. They found that the only way to get
on the Illinois ballot was to secure 25,000 signatures of qualified voters
including the signatures of at least 200 qualified voters in each of at
least 50 of the State's 102 counties. The Progressive party leaders
could easily have secured 25,000 signatures in Chicago, but they could
not get the 200 signatures in each of 50 counties. It is relevant to
point out that at that time 52 per cent of the State's registered voters
were residents of Cook County (Chicago). MacDougall and his associates instituted suit claiming that they were being deprived of due
process and equal protection of the laws and of their privileges and
immunities under the Constitution. The case was carried to the
Supreme Court of the United States, which responded to their plea
as follows: "To assume that political power is a function exclusively
of numbers is to disregard the practicalities of government. . . . It
would be strange, indeed, and doctrinaire, for this Court applying such
broad Constitutional concepts as due process and equal protection of
the laws, to deny a State the power to assure a proper diffusion of
political initiative as between its thinly populated counties and those

---

[17] E. Pendleton Herring, *Politics of Democracy*, (New York: Rinehart and
Company, 1940), 225–26.
[18] *MacDougall v. Green*, 335, U.S. 281 (1948).

having concentrated masses. . . . The Constitution is a practical instrument. . . ."[19] The Progressive party did not get on the ballot in Illinois.

What is a political party in the United States today? Since the introduction of the Australian ballot* in Massachusetts in 1888 and its adoption by all of the states in the next two decades, a political party has become what a state defines it to be. States define "political party" in stipulating by statute the conditions of getting a party designation on a publicly-printed ballot and participating in a publicly-financed primary, if such is provided by law. Howard Penniman in *Sait's American Parties and Elections* has said, " 'Party' may be defined as an organized group that seeks to control the personnel and policy of government. This definition views party from the standpoint of function. State election laws, however, adopt a different criterion— that of demonstrated voting strength. Thus, in Massachusetts a 'political party' is a party which at the preceding state election polled for Governor at least 3% of the entire vote cast for that office. . . ."[20]

In order to get on the November 1962 ballot in New York State, the newly formed Conservative party required 12,000 petition signatures by registered voters. Providing they polled at least 50,000 votes for Governor, they would stay on subsequent ballots automatically. The Conservative party was formed in part to counter the effect of the Liberal party in New York, a party whose 200,000 to 500,000 votes have often been instrumental in throwing an election from one party's candidate to the other's.[21]

Furthermore, while the provisions for defining party membership vary considerably from state to state, their common characteristic is that the citizen elects himself to membership in the party by formally registering his choice with public officials where this is possible, or by merely identifying himself as a Democrat or Republican. As Robert A. Horn points out in his review of constitutional decisions reflecting the changing nature of the political party from private clubs to publicly-controlled associations:

> . . . The astonishing fact is that the states have deprived the parties of almost all right to determine who may become a member, and on what conditions, or to expel a member, and on what conditions. Yet these rights seem to be of the very essence of a voluntary association, and their infringement by government would be deeply resented by most other types of associations. Still more astonishing,

---

[19] The effect upon this reasoning of *Baker* v. *Carr*, 369 U.S. 186 (1962) and succeeding decisions establishing the "one man one vote" rule for Congress and for both houses of state legislatures has yet to be tested.

* A ballot printed and distributed at public expense, with provision for insuring secrecy in voting. First adopted by Victoria in 1856, hence "Australian ballot."

[20] (New York, Appleton-Century-Crofts, Inc.), 4th Ed. 1942, p. 161.

[21] *New York Times*, (February 16, 1962), p. 17.

then, is the fact that these laws were devised and passed by the
party leaders in the legislatures.[22]

With several important exceptions—the right of Negro voters to
participate in Democratic party primaries in the South, the protest of
Communist party members of their exclusion from the ballot, and the
MacDougall v. *Green* case—political parties have not objected to the
loss of these rights, for the laws regulating parties have been devised
by the state and local leaders of the two major parties, with the result
if not always the intended purpose of preserving the two-party system.

It has been said that "Power in America . . . [is] situational and
mercurial; it resists attempts to locate it the way a molecule, under
the Heisenberg principle, resists attempts simultaneously to locate it
and time its velocity."[23]

This is especially true of the political parties which we depend
on to give us the approximation of party government that we enjoy.

In one of the early textbooks on political parties, Charles E.
Merriam attempted to cope with the problem of indicating to his
readers the locus of political power in the party systems. He discovered that the best he could do was to list some agencies of the
parties, including national state and local party committees, the
campaign committees in Congress which concern themselves with
electing their partisans to the House and the Senate, the party leaders
in executive positions such as the President and governors, party
leaders holding no official position, and party conventions, national
and state. "Somewhere in these various agencies," he concluded, "may
be found the control and direction of the party. . . . The President is
practically the only agency through whom they are all united, as
there has never been a national boss who could claim sovereignty
over all these various domains of party power."[24]

It is easy, but not instructive, to draw pyramidal charts showing
a symmetrical and articulated party organization ranging from the
precinct captain, upon thousands of whom the national party structure
rests, through ward, county and township committees, state committees and culminating, at the apex, in the national committees of the
two parties. It is not instructive for three principal reasons: (1) Such a
chart would not necessarily indicate the pattern of relationships which
characterize the various units of the American party systems. (2) The
chart would not accurately reflect the structure, much less the process,
of the two parties. There are congressional district committees, campaign committees, finance committees erratically distributed but which

[22] Robert A. Horn, *Groups and the Constitution* (Stanford: Stanford University
Press, 1956), p. 101.
[23] David Riesman, *The Lonely Crowd* (New York, Doubleday & Co., 1950),
p. 257.
[24] *The American Party System* (New York, Macmillan, 1923), pp. 298–99.

function on a relatively stable basis, and then there are innumerable ad hoc committees brought into being for special purposes and limited periods of time. Any combination of these may be of more importance than the traditional county, state, and national committees at any given time. (3) Such a chart would be inaccurate in that the locus of power, such as it is, within the party at any given time, might well lie outside the chart, reposing in a combination of people holding no political office, or being a function of an uneasy truce among a number of competitors for party power.

Let us return to the problem of defining standards for judging the performance of political parties in the United States. The adequacy of performance of our political parties depends on what is expected of them. Recall Edmund Burke's definition, "Party is a body of men united for promoting by their joint endeavors the national interest upon some particular principle on which they are all agreed."[25] Burke relates party to the function of dispassionate espousal of public policy which is regarded to be in the national interest. Recall, also, the criticism of American parties cast by contemporary political scientists in terms of their failure to prove responsible party government. If one applies these standards, the American political parties must be regarded as failures.

However, there are some who will boldly assert that the lack of clear-cut issues dividing the parties is a positive asset, and one to be valued. E. Pendleton Herring, for example, in his book *Politics of Democracy* has suggested, "The present party system helps to preserve existing social institutions by blurring sharp issues and ignoring others. Party rule discourages the alignment of economic differences through political channels. Much of the impatience and even disgust with our existing political parties stems from dissatisfaction with this tendency."[26] In effect, what Herring is suggesting is that we have avoided the dangers of factionalism in the United States, as defined by Madison, by having parallel factionalism within each party. We depend upon third parties and non-party interest groups to attempt to precipitate radical new approaches and programs which, when they have become respectable, may be taken over by one or both of the two major parties.

Herring's thesis finds support from political sociologists and historians. Seymour Martin Lipset employs the term "crosscutting bases of cleavage," to describe the process whereby, in the United States, factionalism is moderated and compromised in many areas and at many strata, thus preventing the development of two ideological

---

[25] *Thoughts on the Cause of the Present Discontents,* 1770. A convenient abridgment may be found in *Burke's Politics, Selected Writings and Speeches of Edmund Burke,* edited by Ross J. S. Hoffman and Paul Levack, (New York, Alfred A. Knopf, 1949), p. 3 ff., and p. 41.

[26] *Op. cit.,* p. 131.

parties, diametrically opposed to each other on an issue and class
basis:[27]

> If crosscutting bases of cleavage make a more vital democracy, it
> follows that, all other factors being constant, two-party systems are
> better than multi-party systems, that the election of officials on a
> territorial basis is preferable to proportional representation, and
> federalism is superior to a unitary state.

Stressing the need of "conflict or cleavage" in society in order to
produce the competition for power and the efforts to defeat the party
in power, which are essential to the existence of democracy, Lipset,
nonetheless stresses the simultaneous, and, as usual, seemingly contradictory, need for consensus, i.e., agreement at least on the rules
of the game, and perhaps upon a limited set of fundamental value
propositions.[28] The proper balance of conflict and consensus is aided
by "a situation in which all the major political parties include supporters from many segments of the population. A system in which the
support of different parties corresponds too closely to basic social
divisions cannot continue on a democratic basis, for it reflects a state
of conflict so intense and clear-cut as to rule out compromise."[29]

The theme is re-echoed by historian Alan Nevins in these terms:

> The greatest disaster that ever befell the nation in the past resulted
> from a temporary division of parties along sectional lines. The worst
> disaster that could possibly happen to it in the near future would
> be a division along economic and class lines . . . [I]f we did have
> a Conservative party of the propertied and a Radical party of the
> unpropertied we might at last be within sight of the day when the
> losers in an election would begin throwing up barricades in the
> streets.[30]

Nevins' invocation of the spectre of barricades in the streets is redolent
of one of the most elemental, and perhaps profound, justifications of
party, yet made. This was offered by the British legal historian, Sir
Henry Sumner Maine. In effect, Maine takes the position that the
fundamental function which political parties perform in a democratic
society is to sublimate the process of conflict for political and economic
power, diverting it from warlike channels into peaceful channels.
Having cautioned that nothing is "more menacing to popular government, than the growth of Irreconcilable bodies within the mass of the
population,"[31] Maine went on to say:

> . . . Party is probably nothing more than a survival and a conse-
> quence of the primitive combativeness of mankind. . . . The best

[27] *Political Man, The Social Bases of Politics,* Anchor Book Edition (New York:
Doubleday & Co., 1963), p. 80.
[28] *Ibid.,* pp. 1–4.
[29] *Ibid.,* pp. 80–81.
[30] Alan Nevins, "The Strength of our Political System," *New York Times
Magazine* (July 18, 1948), pp. 5, 31.
[31] *Popular Government* (New York: Henry Holt & Company, 1886), p. 25.

historical justification which can be offered for it is that it has often enabled portions of the nation, who would otherwise be armed enemies, to be only factions.

. . . Party feeling is probably far more a survival of the primitive combativeness of mankind than a consequence of conscious intellectual differences between man and man. It is essentially the same sentiment which in certain states of society leads to civil, intertribal, or international war; and it is as universal as humanity. It is better studied in its more irrational manifestations than in those to which we are accustomed.[32]

In the introduction to his book on Political Parties, Maurice Duverger notes that[33]

. . . In 1850 no country in the world (except the United States) knew political parties in the modern sense of the word. There were trends of opinion, popular clubs, philosophical societies, and parliamentary groups, but no real parties. In 1950 parties function in most civilized nations, and in others there is an attempt to imitate them.

Amorphous in ideological profile, diffuse in locus of power, and seemingly incapable of translating electoral victory into legislative and administrative programs, American political parties yet perform more vital functions, and perform them more adequately, than their denigrators are prepared to concede. Restricted in funds and authority, powerless to define party policy, frequently shunted aside in time of election crisis, the two national committees contribute importantly to the capacity of the parties to perform these functions.

At least four such functions merit mention: (1) The parties do contribute to the generation of ideological alternatives for the American voter. Their differences tend to be in degree, emphasis, and method. But there are definable differences between the two parties on many vital issues even though they usually incline to seek the same goals with varying methods.[34] Their ideological differences are nuances, rather than alternatives, perhaps, and it takes a highly sophisticated electorate to appreciate them. (2) The parties, largely through the national committees, seek to project images favorable to the voter. The party of big business today, was the party of the full dinner pail and of prosperity during the McKinley and the first Roosevelt administrations. The party of the common man today, may bear a different imprint a few generations hence. Each party strives for a favorable public image, and to saddle its opposition with one which is less than attractive. It is characteristic, and possibly a defect, of our

[32] *Ibid.*, pp. 101, and 31, respectively.
[33] Duverger, *op. cit.*, p. xxiii.
[34] See, e.g., Julius Turner, *Party and Constituency: Pressures on Congress* (Baltimore: The Johns Hopkins Press, 1951); David B. Truman, *The Congressional Party* (New York: John Wiley & Sons, Inc., 1959).

party system, that the party images in the United States are much less blurred than the ideological differences between the parties.

Much has been written on the subject of majority rule, and much stress has been placed upon the majoritarian premises of a democratic political system. Yet it cannot accurately be said that American political parties provide an agency for effecting majority government. The single member electoral district system makes it possible for a party to poll more aggregate votes for congress than its opposition, and still garner but a minority of the seats in the House of Representatives. The electoral college system makes it possible for a presidential nominee to receive a majority of the electoral vote and the presidency, even though he received a minority of the popular vote. Within any state those who cast their vote for a presidential candidate either capture a unanimous electoral college vote for their candidate, or see their vote cancelled, in consequence of the provision that the entire electoral vote of a state goes to the candidate winning a majority of the popular vote in that state. (3) The political parties of contemporary America may not be mechanisms for the invariable assertion of majority rule, but they do provide opportunity for those who wish to and can qualify to participate. The participation ranges from the negative of nonparticipation to the extreme of running for public office. It is true that the parties do not effectively select or screen candidates and that, in Duverger's terms, both parties are parties of notables (i.e., individuals can independently assert candidacy and seek to capture not only the party nomination, but also the party machinery itself, such as it is), but they do provide a framework for securing candidates and contribute to the polarization of candidacies. (4) Finally, the American political parties, much criticized by those who measure them against the standard of "responsible party government," do contribute to the maintenance of responsible government in the United States. Here, too, the national committees are particularly active and particularly effective.[35] The staff of the national committee of the party which does not have the presidency devotes itself to a full-time scrutiny of the president's behavior and that of his administration, ranging from the ridiculous to the sublime. It is the job of the national committee staff to focus attention upon any behavior which can be exploited to partisan advantage, whether it be President Eisenhower's golf game, President Kennedy's almost single-handed effort to roll back steel prices, or President Johnson's Texas ranch-house mannerisms.

The question remaining and which at this point we must leave open is: Can we afford to be satisfied with these justifications of existing party institutions in an age in which "the primitive combativeness of mankind" threatens his eradication?

---

[35] Cornelius P. Cotter and Bernard Hennessy, *Politics Without Power:The National Committees and American Politics* (New York: Atherton Press, 1964).

CORNELIUS P. COTTER

2. The National Committees and Their Constituencies

INTRODUCTION

An organization chart would depict each of the two national committees at the apex of a pyramidal structure of party units. The base of the pyramid would be precinct organization and intermediate layers would include county and township committees, congressional committees (in some states) and state central committees. It would be difficult to fit all party units within the rigid hierarchical structure leading to the national committee apex, and therefore, ambiguously situated off to the side would be senatorial and congressional campaign and policy committees, and many auxiliary and ad hoc party organizations.

Yet, in a significant sense, the national committees symbolize the two-party system in the United States, and party government, such as we have it. Virtually unrecognized by law, unincorporated bodies, entities which must be brought into being afresh with the adoption of resolutions at each quadrennial presidential nominating convention, the national committees are deeply grounded in American history and indispensable institutions in our political system.

This chapter is about the national committees, what functions they perform, how they are composed and staffed, and their problems of relating to the multitude of other groups which form the mosaic of each party. Primary attention will be given to the Republican National Committee, with which the author has served, although frequent allusion will be made to Democratic National Committee experience. In essence, the story of one national committee is the story of both.

FUNCTIONS OF THE NATIONAL COMMITTEES

Writing over sixty years ago, Jesse Macy in *Party Organization and Machinery*, probably capsulized as well as anyone the formal duties of the national committees:

> To the national committees are assigned many practical matters of business. They arrange for a place of meeting for the national convention and supervise the details of plans for its suitable entertainment. The disbursing of the vast sums of money collected for party purposes pertains to them, and for unlimited judgment, discretion, and political sagacity. More delicate and important is the committee's task of providing for the organization of the convention by selecting the temporary chairman. Ordinarily the chairman so named is accepted by unanimous consent; but this rule has been subject to . . . notable exceptions. . . .[1]

Technically, as Macy points out, once "the national convention has been organized, the authority of the national committee is at an end, though the chairman retains his office until the new national committee has been organized." A 1964 study, while suggesting considerable turnover of membership in the national committees, also suggests elements of stability. It showed that some 376 people had served on the Republican National Committee, 1948–1963—of whom 120 were state chairmen qualifying under the 1952 change of rules— and 309 members had sat on the Democratic National Committee. Records of continuous membership were set by a RNC member who dated his service from 1928, and a member of the DNC tracing her service to 1942.[2]

A further vital function of the national committee, in theory at least, is the conduct of the presidential campaign for the convention

---

[1] (New York, The Century Co., 1904), pp. 74, 78. Although no formal provision is made in the Rules, the national committee appears to have the additional authority to fill vacancies on the ticket which occur between the adjournment of the National Convention and the elction. There is but one instance, since the inception of the national committees, when this power became relevant. That was when Vice-President James S. Sherman, who was on the slate with William Howard Taft for re-election in 1912, died the Saturday night before the election. George H. Mayer states in *The Republican Party, 1854–1964*, New York, Oxford University Press, 1964, p. 333, that "the Republican national committee replaced him with Nicholas Murray Butler of Columbia University."

Letters in the RNC file suggest that what happened is that after the election, Republican electors in the only two states won by Taft, Utah and Vermont, expressed a desire to cast their vice presidential ballots for Butler, and received the concurrence of the RNC: "After the election, the electors in Utah and Vermont expressed a desire to vote for Nicholas Murray Butler—a right which was theirs without consultation. The officers and the Executive Committee of the Republican National Committee concurred in the choice but it was not deemed to be necessary, in the circumstances, to assemble the full Committee."

[2] Cornelius P. Cotter and Bernard C. Hennessy, *Politics Without Power: The National Party Committees*, (New York: Atherton Press, 1964), p. 20 ff.

nominee. However, as we shall see, a number of factors combine to make the national committees' campaign role, for the party out of power, at least, conjectural.

PARTY CHAIRMAN AND STAFF

In January 1967, the RNC Executive Committee approved plans to move into a Republican Center to be constructed on Capitol Hill across the street from the Cannon House Office Building. The building is to be erected by Capitol Hill Associates, Inc., which presently operates the Capitol Hill Club, a Republican social club. The interior is to be constructed to the satisfaction of the National Chairman, and the Committee will occupy the building on a lease-purchase arrangement. Also in the building will be the Congressional Committee, the Capitol Hill Club," and perhaps the Senate Campaign Committee."[3] Mid-year, the Democratic National Committee moved from its K Street offices to rather plush facilities overlooking the Potomac in the Watergate section of Washington. "The new location is a $1.15 cab ride from the center of Washington and the Senate-House complex," reports the *Chicago Daily News*.[4]

This seeming bit of trivia is appropriate introduction to a discussion of the relationships which exist between the national committees and their parties. Compose a group, equip them with a quadrennial set of seemingly *pro forma* duties which are pregnant with opportunity to influence the political scene, call them the national committee of a national party, and, in a pluralistic democracy, they are likely to try to act like the directors of a national party 365 days in the year. As long ago as 1911 a historian of the Republican party complained:

> The quiet and almost unnoticed extension of political power by the Republican national committee during the past forty years has been truly remarkable. This simple agency of party activity of little more than a generation ago has silently assumed functions and privileges undreamed of at the time of its creation. It aims today to dictate to the very party which created it, to control conventions, prescribe candidates, distribute party rewards and to consolidate and perpetuate the power which has fallen into its hands.[5]

He goes on to raise the spectre of great national party bosses such as DNC Chairman Arthur P. Gorman who served during Cleveland's first administration, and RNC Chairmen Matthew S. Quey and Marcus A. Hanna, who served Harrison and McKinley. These were men

---

[3] *Republican Congressional Committee Newsletter* (January 30, 1967), p. 3.
[4] (July 5, 1967), "Democrat Chiefs Move to Ritzy Neighborhood."
[5] Gordon S. P. Kleeberg, *The Formation of the Republican Party* (New York: Moods Publishing Co., 1911), pp. 222–23.

who dominated a party in a position subordinate to the President or approaching equality with him. Patronage, policy preferences, and money were the elements of their work. In modern parlance we would add "party image" to the list, but it is doubtful if men like Mark Hanna thought so much in terms of the appeals of a party as in terms of its "proper" function and role—a near perfect correlation existing between these and the welfare of the country.

Powerful as these men may have made the national committees in their day, it was a tentative and episodic assertion of power. It is no secret today that the national committees aspire to a more sustained and pervasive influence, looking not, perhaps, toward the responsible party government model but toward as much internal union as parties can reasonably hope to achieve within a political system which by constitution and custom foredooms party unity. They pursue this end in two principal ways: (1) They attempt to bring greater integration and coherence to party organization at the state and local level, tying them to the National Committee with the gossamer bonds of service and exhortation, which must suffice when the kind of party organization described in Chapter 12 is beyond achievement. (2) They attempt to make less discrepant the relations between them and the party organizations which have been brought into being to service the campaign and policy-formulating needs of partisans in Congress. This is one reason for the significance of the impending RNC move to Capitol Hill, where propinquity may reduce staff frictions between various party committees, and a reason for newspapers comment on the distance of the new DNC headquarters from the Hill.

Strategies suited to the pursuit of party integration vary depending on whether the party has the presidency. It would be erroneous to assume that because a national committee was of the same party as the President, its relations with the Hill would be easy sliding. But the influence of the White House, not to mention patronage, can be of great help in establishing a modicum of cooperation between the party at the state and local level, and the National Committee. A certain amount of cajoling and bargaining between White House and Hill, and of head-knocking, if necessary, at the National Committee can bring about at least the appearance of harmony.

Who speaks for the *Party?* The answer depends upon many factors. Does the party have the White House? Does it have a self-aware "titular leader"? Has the pre-convention nominating campaign been launched? What are the character and talents of the national chairman? How does he conceive his role? Certainly one of the dilemmas of the National Chairman is that he cannot, at times at least, avoid speaking for the party. Either he cannot avoid doing so, or he cannot avoid having the mass media impute the effort to him.

Thus we have the example of Meade Alcorn, chairman during a portion of the last Eisenhower years, pressured by the President to create an RNC policy-formulating committee—which he did in 1959.

Sensitive to the dangers of creating dissonant voices within the Party, Alcorn sensibly preferred to let the Republican Administration's record speak for itself and depict party program and policy. But the Chairman follows the bidding of a President. A few months later, in early Spring 1959, when he was compelled for personal reasons to resign the chairmanship, the mass media erroneously alleged he did so in protest at Eisenhower's supposed refusal to permit the National Chairman to participate in Cabinet meetings as the voice of the party.

Alcorn probably had no more desire to attend Cabinet meetings on other than an invitational basis than did his successor Thruston B. Morton. As an Assistant Secretary of State under the peripatetic John Foster Dulles, Senator Morton could recall the boredom of the Cabinet meetings, which he frequently attended for his absent boss, and as Chairman did not covet the opportunity to attend. But rumor fed on his supposed disgruntlement at being excluded from White House policy-making. In short, a Chairman can avoid policy-making, but he cannot avoid policy. Perhaps the Coordinating Committee, founded in 1964–65 and discussed later in this chapter, is as much an effective mechanism for Ray Bliss, a desk politician whose interest and forte lie with tactics rather than TV performance, to share policy responsibilities he cannot eschew, as it is a "natural" mode of behavior of a party out of power.

It would be erroneous to say that national chairmen do not take an interest in policy. Paul M. Butler as Chairman of the DNC when the presidential Democrats were out of power and the congressional Democrats intent upon going their own way independently of the national committee, sought to make that instrument the policy organ of the Party. Not only did he bring into being and nourish the Democratic Advisory Council, but also he spoke out on issues and, eventually, candidates.

> I have been told that the sole duty of the National Chairman is to maintain the unity of the Party. The Chairman, in this view, should behave like the proverbial good child, to be seen but not heard.
>
> Unity is a pretty word, and I am all for it, but what does it mean in this case? Does it mean unity without regard to conviction, without regard to the ideals which already have been the life-blood of this party?
>
> I submit that unity on these terms is only a synonym for sterility and death . . .
>
> I have tried to make the National Committee a clearing-house for the ideas which we as a responsible people must champion or, failing, perish as human beings. I have seen it as our duty to listen to the many voices which speak to us, the voices of all Democrats, of citizens who know that when they catch our ear that they catch the official ear of our Party. I have seen it as our duty to express their views as widely and vigorously as we can. I have assumed as an obligation of the Democratic National Committee not the mere

maintenance of unity, but rather a renewed dedication to principle. Unity is founded upon principles rather than upon men.[6]

A national chairman may covet a policy-influencing or formulating role. It would seem that he should do so in full awareness that it is a role, the playing of which makes a man expendable. For unless he is an ideological chameleon and a consummate personal political tactician, it is unlikely that he will outlive his ideas. But then, a national chairman must regard himself as expendable anyway!

The elements of the job, like the vigor with which it is invested, are determined by the occupant—a man who while likely to be intensely political in background, is equally likely to have had little anticipation of ever holding down the party chairmanship. It is a position to which it is not practicable to aspire and to which there are no established avenues of advancement. This is not to suggest no pattern of activity by chairmen can be discerned. Cotter and Hennessy identify five major roles which chairmen may assume. Ordered in terms of importance, they are "image-maker, hell-raiser, fund-raiser, campaign manager, and administration."[7] An active chairman will be preoccupied with party "image." He will be a public relations man of sorts, although he may have a deep personal aversion for public display and may play his role behind the scenes. We have already noted the difficulty, if not impossibility, of the task of the chairman who is determined to avoid responsibility for the party's public image and thereby avoid stepping upon toes of other elements of the party. The chairman is expected to be an unmitigated and uncritical party enthusiast. At the risk of weakening his image-making efforts—that is those activities which strengthen the public facade of the party—he must in conclaves of the faithful recite with enthusiasm the phrases appropriate to evoking emotional response. Hell-raising is ritualistic image-confirmation within the ranks of the faithful. Not only does it take millions (see Chapter 11) to run a presidential campaign; it requires about $1 million a year merely to keep open the doors of the national party headquarters. The chairman must raise money or go out of business. Particularly for the out-party chairman, and for both chairmen in non-presidential election years, this task is difficult and thankless. Sources of money seem to believe the national committees should go out of business after each quadrennial election. In this view they are supported by party members in Congress.

Regardless of the opinions they may offer of their national committee, party members in and out of office expect each headquarters staff in Washington to be a service agency. The chairman may seek to improve its performance as such. On occasion, as with John Hamilton in the years following the 1936 Republican debacle, and Ray Bliss after 1964, a politician with administrative talents and drive

---

[6] Opening remarks at 1960 Democratic National Convention, pp. 3–4. Mimeo. July 11, 1960.
[7] Op. cit., p. 67.

may accept the challenge of rebuilding such internal organization as the party has.

The national committees exist not merely to stage the quadrennial presidential nominating conventions and to work at burnishing the party image during the interim. Presumably the staff is composed of campaign experts and the party's headquarters unit has a vital role to play in presidential campaigns.

When the Convention has adjourned and while the workmen are still in process of dismantling its facilities, the nominee has probably already come to a few basic decisions concerning the operation of his campaign. Who will manage it? Where will campaign management be located (physically as well as institutionally)? Then come questions of grand strategy and tactics, fund-raising and so on.

Herbert Hoover, wishing to run his own campaign in 1928, chose his close friend and Coolidge-administration Cabinet member, Dr. Hubert Work as National Chairman. In 1932, occupied with official business, he turned the campaign management over to National Chairman Everett Sanders, operating out of Chicago. For the decade of the 1930's the DNC headquarters moved back and forth between Washington and New York, as suited the convenience of Chairman James A. Farley. Stevenson, in part to reduce appearance of White House control of the campaign, installed an old Chicago friend, Stephen Mitchell as DNC Chairman in Washington, and located the campaign staff, under Wilson Wyatt of Louisville in Springfield, Illinois.

The vital question is whether the campaign will be run out of the National Committee or from a separate and discrete campaign organization. This is not to be confused with the question—conceding their inevitability—how many "independent" campaign organizations of limited scope will be set up, encouraged, or tolerated. Richard Nixon resolved this question in favor of a separate campaign organization which virtually ignored the existence of the National Committee and was largely redundant of it. John Kennedy coopted the Democratic National Committee, quickly made it into a sprawling, throbbing, seemingly confused personal campaign vehicle, which was grinding out work while its counterpart was stalemated. Barry Goldwater took over the RNC in 1964, fired those who did not meet his test of loyalty, brought in a new breed of political-managers, and stationed security guards at the doors. After the 1968 convention, Hubert Humphrey designated Lawrence F. O'Brien Democratic National Chairman. The appointment promised to revivify a DNC which had suffered steady attrition of morale and prestige during the Johnson presidency. Richard Nixon retained Bliss as chairman (there was doubt, until the very end, that Bliss would consent to stay on), but maintained direction of the campaign from New York.

The argument is straightforwardly presented by some that it is desirable for American political institutions and generally in the interests of the candidate to take over the National Committee and employ it as his campaign vehicle. The Committees need the strengthening which comes with assurance of a significant campaign role. The candidate, so the argument goes, really does not have time to do much other than tinker with the traditional campaign machinery.

While offering the argument, it is only fair to indicate some factors that militate against merely turning the campaign over to the National Committee. They are principally two in number: (1) By the time success has been achieved in the Convention hall, the candidate has a core staff which has all of the we vs. them *esprit de corps* of a group which has fought shoulder to shoulder through thick and thin in the pre-convention campaigning. He is prone to use this as his elite managerial group. (2) By this time also, the National Committee, either in its very neutrality prior to the Convention, through detectable bias as in selection of Convention city or temporary chairman, or through public comments by the chairman is likely to have made itself *persona non grata* to the candidate. Staff neutrality during the pre-convention period is easily translated into hostility. The tendency in the midst of battle is to dichotomize between those who are for, and those who are against. The purportedly neutral are against. Where the Committee has shown overt bias, as, perhaps, was the case at the RNC prior to the Eisenhower nomination in 1952 or the Willkie nomination in 1940, it may take considerable effort merely to persuade the candidate the Committee is worth cleaning out and making usable. Where, as in 1960, DNC Chairman Paul Butler speaks about the candidates with relative freedom, it is difficult to assess what seeds of suspicion concerning the National Committee have been sewn and where. In March, Butler was chided by *The Denver Post* for offering the opinion that Kennedy was far ahead in the quest for the Democratic nomination. Debating Senator Hugh Scott in May, he offered the opinion that "the one man in this country best qualified to be President" was Adlai Stevenson.

Regardless of the validity of distinctions between "in" chairmen and "out" chairmen, and between chairmen selected by the candidate or incumbent President, and those actually selected by the National Committee, it is possible to advance two seemingly contradictory arguments with respect to the locus of power in the National Committee. The first is to the effect that the Chairman *is* the National Committee. The second is that the staff *is*. The arguments can be cogently made, with effective marshalling of facts and anecdotes because at various times, with both committees, either has been the case and is likely to be again. Another reason for the plausability of the argument in favor of staff is, of course, that the Chairman is likely to be as strong as his staff.

> . . . Ideally stated, the position (of National Chairman) seems one fit only for supermen. Because no supermen have been party chairmen, however, the ideal has not been reached. Some chairmen have been very inept indeed—badly prepared for the job, indifferent, and insensitive. Some of the chairmen have considered the job quite unimportant. It is said that Rep. Joseph Martin (R., Mass.)

visited the national committee office only twice in the twenty-eight months he served as chairman. Some chairmen, at the other extreme, have been imaginative, energetic, and much in the public eye. Only a few have appreciated even the small opportunities a chairman has for bringing order, articulation, and responsiveness to a national party system which is un-national by design and experience. Chairmen who have made an effort to understand their job and to apply their talents often find their lot to be frustration, opposition, and derision.[8]

The transiency of the chairmanship necessitates heavy reliance upon staff. It is a rare chairman who will, upon assuming office, undertake a large-scale housecleaning. He is dependent upon the experience and recollection of the staff in part for a conception of the functions of the national committee, and certainly for awareness of how to go about performing them. The staff may have an anachronistic conception of the committee's functions or how to best go about discharging them; inevitably it will vary in competence, talent, and experience. But collectively it can lay strong claim to being as much as we have by way of functioning national party apparatus in the U.S. At the same time, the very tenure which differentiates the staff from the chairman, has contributed to the breeding within the staff of a kind of veneration for the office of chairman. This, loyalty to party and national committee, and the awareness that there is no guaranteed tenure, combine to increase the likelihood that any staff will be predisposed to respond with alacrity to the wishes of a new chairman, given the presence of Neustadt's vital elements:

1. That his personal involvement be certain.
2. His orders are unambiguous.
3. The orders are widely publicized so that attention focuses upon compliance.
4. Those responsible for carrying out his wishes have the resources to do so.
5. They also have no doubt of his authority to issue them.[9]

Neustadt, of course, wrote of presidential power. His determinants of effectiveness, however, are as relevant for a national chairman as for a President. And national chairmen, who, like most Presidents, go into office without previous experience in it, have given orders which have turned out to be non "self-executing" in part because of the absence of one or more of these factors.

PARTY COMMITTEES IN CONGRESS

James MacGregor Burns in *Deadlock of Democracy* has popularized the terms "congressional parties" and "presidential parties." His thesis

---

[8] Cotter and Hennessy, *op. cit.*, p. 63. Reprinted by permission of the Publishers, Atherton Press, Inc. Copyright © 1964, Atherton Press, New York. All rights reserved.

[9] Richard E. Neustadt, *Presidential Power* (New York: John Wiley & Sons, Inc., 1960), p. 19.

is that the two parties in Congress are so distinctive from the parties "downtown" as to make it realistic to regard them as separate entities whose identity of name is not to be taken as identity of interest.

When we speak of "The Capitol Hill Committees" today, we refer to seven, and possibly eight groups, between the two parties. We take into account the six which Hugh Bone identified in 1964—the Senate and House campaign committees (four) and the Senate policy committees (two)—plus a now well-established House Republican Policy Committee and an emerging Democratic equivalent.[10]

Immediately following the Civil War, hardly a generation after the Congressional caucus had been shorn of its presidential nominating function, and the National Conventions with their interim National Committees had come into being, members of the two parties on the Hill formed committees to seek such campaign strength as can be found in numbers.

> The origin of the congressional campaign committees remains somewhat obscure. Simeon Fess sees their birth in a committee of correspondence appointed during the presidency of James Madison. The *Democratic Manual* attributes the origin of the Democratic Committee to a joint House-Senate committee formed in 1842 to publish "a declaration of principles for General Harrison's administration." If these dates are accepted, then the Democratic congressional committee was formed before the national committee, which was officially organized in 1848. In 1860 and 1864 the Republicans in Congress used a joint campaign committee to assist their House candidates.
>
> Most textbooks, however, give 1866 as the date of origin of both the Republican and Democratic congressional committees. Until 1912 they were little more than sporadic campaign committees. . . . In 1916, when senators became popularly elected, both parties recognized the need for a separate campaign committee for senators, and the senatorial committees became the recognized agencies for this purpose.
>
> In both parties the House and Senate campaign committees function independently of each other and of the national committees. The *Democratic Manual* specifically states that the Capitol Hill committees have "no organic connection with either the Democratic National Convention or the Democratic National Committee". . . .[11]

The Republican campaign committees on the Hill now tie-in their finance appeals with those of the RNC. There would appear to be increasingly fruitful relationships between the Republican policy committees and the RNC.

---

[10] See Hugh A. Bone, *Party Committees and National Politics* (Seattle, University of Washington Press, 1958) and Charles O. Jones, *Party and Policy-Making: The House Republican Policy Committee* (New Brunswick, N.J., Rutgers University Press, 1964).

[11] Bone, *op. cit.*, pp. 127–28. Reprinted by permission of University of Washington Press.

The policy committees in the Senate go back to the Congressional Reorganization Act of 1946. They are staffed by employees who are paid by the Senate. Their functioning varies from party to party and from time to time. At times the Democratic Policy Committee staff has been little more than an augmentation of the staffing available to the floor leader. The Republican Policy Committee staff has prided itself upon the impartiality of its work, and its ability to provide Republican Senators with arguments and data supporting either side of any issue. In recent years, in recognition of the party's diminished membership in the Senate, all Republicans have been welcomed at the Wednesday noon meetings of the Policy Committee.

Reputedly Sam Rayburn and Joe Martin wanted no part of a policy committee setup, and for that reason the Reorganization Act's provisions in this regard were restricted to the Senate. However, by 1959 a group of "young Turks" had bootlegged into operation a reasonable facsimile of a House Republican Policy Committee, drawing staff from individual members' allowances and relying upon volunteer effort. The committee has issued position papers and its members have called attention to its activities and their views with carefully publicized floor speeches. The Democratic Study Group not only has signified a purpose similar to that of the Republicans working with the Policy Committee, but also in its Tuesday luncheon meetings has brought together Democrats on the Hill and those in the agencies downtown.

Although we shall allude shortly to recent events in the Republican Party which may auger change of attitude between party members on the Hill and at the national committee, it remains true that political scientists of Democratic and Republican persuasion, actively involved in their party's work in Washington, uniformly have been impressed by the tenseness of relations, if not the active hostility, between the congressional party and the national committees. This is partly bred of ignorance. Persons now on the national committee staffs, who formerly occupied positions on the Hill, freely confess that while in a congressional or senatorial office, they knew more about, and related more readily to, the state chairman than to the national chairman. They had few if any contacts with the national committee staff and merely indulged the popular presumption of their ineptness and incompetence.

But there are objective and enduring reasons for continuing strain between the congressional party and the national committee. The people on the Hill consider themselves engaged in the realities of mid-term politics, while the "Downtown Democrats and Republicans" serve as minions of the administration or as agencies for the production of vaporous releases and frivolous programs aiming at improvement of that mystical essence, party image. And, insofar as the national committee represents the presidential party—and it does—the constitutional separation of powers which makes for legislative-executive friction, makes for friction between the Hill and the national committee.

The congressional committees are frankly vehicles for helping incumbents to get re-elected. They offer only incidental assistance to challenger candidates. The presidential party seeks repudiation or endorsement of the office-holding party at mid-term and therefore takes great interest in the care and feeding of challenger candidates who are generally ignored on the Hill, and given inadequate service. Thus, to the extent to which the National Committee concerns itself with congressional elections, whether in marginal districts or otherwise, it tends to do so in ways which are not of great practical concern to incumbents in Congress, and not likely to earn appreciation and more cordial relationships.

The congressional party and the presidential party operate in two distinct, but roughly parallel, political systems.

THE REPUBLICAN COORDINATING COMMITTEE: A MOVE TOWARD PARTY INTEGRATION

After the 1960 presidential campaign, months of speculation concerning Nixon's coming role in the national party were followed by additional months of guessing whether he would run for Governor of California. The September 1961 announcement of his candidacy for Governor in the 1962 race at least temporarily removed the former Vice-President from National Republican leadership. William E. Miller, the New York congressman who had succeeded Senator Thruston B. Morton in the Chairmanship of the RNC was quoted by the UPI in October 1961 as suggesting the " 'real leadership' of the GOP is up for grabs." Later that month, the *Washington Star* (October 18) reported in effect that the Chairman "believes Richard M. Nixon has 'renounced his position of titular head' of the party. In fact, former President Eisenhower is the party's national leader, he told a news conference. . . ." Hardly more than a month later the Chairman drew the pall of confusion further over the party by a statement "that he did not know who was head of the Republican Party." He suggested there might not be one at all.[12]

A party in this state is susceptible to infiltration and control—perhaps toward influencing the membership and conduct of its next Convention, the character of its next nominee, or for less ulterior purposes. Organized and latent groups intervene at times of confusion such as this.

One such group was the short-lived Republican Citizen's Committee, representing a belated effort by former President Eisenhower and his associates to keep the control of the Republican party in its

---

[12] *The New York Times* (December 1, 1961).

Eastern, internationalist, and moderate wing. The former President's influence in his party was more vigorously asserted in his early retirement than it was during his incumbency, but with little practical success. Born at an "All Republican Conference" held at the Gettysburg farm in June 1962, the Committee had but grudging support from the Hill and the RNC, and while it did maintain offices in Washington for a period, it quietly folded in the wake of the Goldwater campaign for the Republican presidential nomination.

The Goldwater convention victory and subsequent Republican electoral debacle of 1964 set the stage for bloodletting and reorganization in the national party. During the period between November 1964, and April 1, 1965, when Ray Bliss of Ohio took over the RNC chairmanship from Goldwater's Dean Burch, numerous power groupings within the party began to assert themselves, in an effort to insure their influence in any Republican leadership coalition that might develop to fill the vacuum created by Goldwater's renunciation at the polls, and subsequently by Republican leaders at the state and national level. These tendrils Bliss proceeded to gather together, coopting the efforts of many divergent groups into the Republican Coordinating Committee.

Bliss had been instrumental in forging one influence group within the party, and did not lack awareness of their potential as vehicles for disruption or accommodation. In March 1963, while Ohio State Chairman, he had convened a Republican State Chairman's Conference in Washington, D.C. In two days of closed meetings the Chairmen held presentations on fund-raising, the use of field men, labor and the Republican party, the use of party publications and surveys. The lasting results of this meeting were not immediately discernible—but apparently it did not fall into that pattern of activity which is to be dismissed as ephemeral.

Following the National Governors Conference in Miami in mid-summer 1963, at which a political split developed on the civil rights issue, the Republican governors formed a Republican Governors Association and Governor Robert E. Smylie (Idaho) called a meeting to be held in Denver, September 14, 1963.[13] The news release on the meeting was put out by the Republican National Committee, and Chairman Miller was reported to "see the Association as a promising vehicle for improving liaison between the Governors and other elements of the party."[14] The release indicated that the Governors Association would "function also as an advisory body to the National Chairman." The participation in the Governors' meeting of National Chairman William Miller, Senate and House Campaign Chairmen, Thruston Morton and

---

[13] *The Washington Post* (August 18, 1963) A-6, "GOP Governors to Aid Party Image Buildup."

[14] *Ibid.* The Press Release was issued for August 16, 1963 and captioned, "GOP GOVERNORS TO MEET IN DENVER."

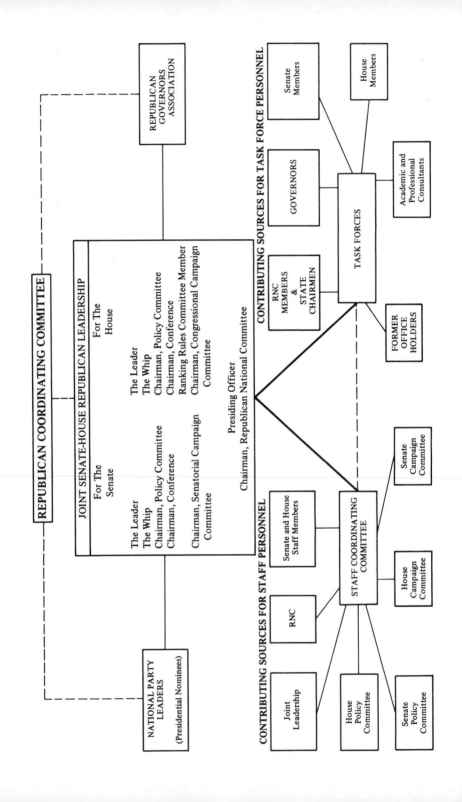

REPUBLICAN COORDINATING COMMITTEE

REPUBLICAN GOVERNORS ASSOCIATION

JOINT SENATE-HOUSE REPUBLICAN LEADERSHIP

For The Senate

The Leader
The Whip
Chairman, Policy Committee
Chairman, Conference

Chairman, Senatorial Campaign Committee

For The House

The Leader
The Whip
Chairman, Policy Committee
Chairman, Conference
Ranking Rules Committee Member
Chairman, Congressional Campaign Committee

Presiding Officer
Chairman, Republican National Committee

NATIONAL PARTY LEADERS

(Presidential Nominees)

CONTRIBUTING SOURCES FOR TASK FORCE PERSONNEL

Senate Members

House Members

GOVERNORS

Academic and Professional Consultants

RNC MEMBERS & STATE CHAIRMEN

TASK FORCES

FORMER OFFICE HOLDERS

CONTRIBUTING SOURCES FOR STAFF PERSONNEL

Senate and House Staff Members

RNC

Joint Leadership

House Policy Committee

Senate Policy Committee

STAFF COORDINATING COMMITTEE

House Campaign Committee

Senate Campaign Committee

Bob Wilson, and State Chairmen's Association head, Ray Bliss, gave promise that the new group might form a part of an increasingly articulated structure of Republican organization.

Republican party leadership was changed in the House in December 1964, Representative Gerald R. Ford, Jr. of Michigan replacing Charles M. Halleck of Indiana as minority leader. In early January 1965, it was thus Senator Everett Dirksen and Gerald Ford who announced the formation of a group which incubated during the tandem regime of "Ev and Charlie." This was the Republican Coordinating Committee, to be composed of eleven congressional leaders, the five living men who were Republican presidential nominees, five Republican governors, and the Chairman of the RNC.[15] Earlier news stories to the effect that Goldwater recognized the primacy of the congressional Republicans for policy-making under the circumstances then existing, and that Dirksen, at least, would do nothing to challenge Dean Burch's job, suggested an informal pact between the losing candidate and the Hill.[16] The Sunday, January 24 meeting of the Republican National Committee erupted with demands for strengthened RNC representation on the Coordinating Committee—which had yet to function.[17]

The Republican Coordinating Committee has proved to be a viable means of keeping Republican leaders in the public eye, and offering them opportunities to work toward harmonious "policy" expression. Ray Bliss as National Chairman has been the "Presiding Officer" of the group which now includes twelve members of Congress (seven Representatives and five Senators), the five presidential candidates and five representatives of the Republican Governors, six officers of the National Committee, and the President of the Republican State Legislators Association. Its staff work is performed by the Republican National Committee, whose Director of Research doubles as Staff Coordinator for the group.

> The Republican Coordinating Committee has unique aspects which differentiate it from previous efforts and proposals therefore, including:
>   1. Representation of all elements of a party—the former President and all party Presidential nominees, Senators, House Members, Governors, State Party organizations, and State Republican Legislators.
>   2. Regularity of meetings and continuity of research activities.
>   3. Appropriate staffing.
>   4. Public and party acceptance of its position papers.
>   5. Institutional, as opposed to what might be termed "ad hoc," existence—i.e., a nonemergency operating pattern.

---

[15] *The New York Times*, January 12, 1965, p. 1; January 13, 1965, p. 24.

[16] *Ibid.*, December 15, 1964, p. 25.

[17] *Ibid.*, January 29, 1965, p. 19.

Because of the differences the Republican Coordinating Committee has so far proven more successful than comparable groups. Unlike its predecessors, the Republican Coordinating Committee was not designed for one objective or one election, but is far more generalized in nature and application.

The Republican Coordinating Committee has issued 18 position papers and almost a score of shorter policy documents. Over 100 experts have assisted the Coordinating Committee in the preparation of its policy declarations. It has been staffed with professionals. Its activities have not been characterized by exclusion of any element of the Party, or by dissents. As it approaches its third year it is clearly a unique experiment in American government and political science.[18]

NATIONAL COMMITTEE AND LOCAL PARTIES

The State Party Apparatus. The 50 State Republican Chairmen were asked to report on their budgets for 1961, and on staff augmentation for the preceding presidential-election year. Forty-six responded. The purpose of the line of questioning was to acquire information concerning the substantiality of party organization at the state level.

The data susceptible to quantification is tabulated on Pages 34–35. The first thing which strikes one, from the tables, is that eleven State Chairmen report they give full time to their political work. Eight of these reported they were paid.

As of the time of the poll, the record for continuous paid staff service at the RNC was 30 years. However the Rhode Island Republican State Committee reported one secretary employed for 32 years; Massachusetts reported staff continuously employed as long as 22 years, and New York had staff members continuously employed up to 28 years. Iowa, Montana, and New Hampshire reported that members of the State Committee clerical staff had from ten to fourteen years' tenure. While most State Committee Chairmen reported clerical staff tenure ranging from less than one year to four years, it is apparent that state party headquarters are not ephemeral operations. New York State reported executive staff with tenure ranging up to 17 years; Washington, 10 years; and Missouri, Delaware, and Minnesota with 9, 8, and 7 years respectively. As one would expect—and in the tradition of American politics—executive tenure in political management tends to be of brief duration. However, it is significant that 28 states reported the employment of full-time executive staff by the State Committee, the number ranging from one to nine.

New York reported an increase of about fifty clerical and eleven professional staff during the 1960 campaign; Nebraska augmented its staff by 19 professionals and 3 clericals; and Ohio reported increases

---

[18] *The Development of National Party Policy Between Conventions, op. cit.,* pp. 1–2.

of 13 and 15 respectively. Other State Committee staff increases for the campaign are erratic. They do not fall into patterns related to state population, or the strength of the Republican vote in the state. Illinois and Indiana, for example, reported staff augmentations (clerical) of 2 and 6 respectively for short periods during the presidential campaign, which compares with the hiring of 4 clerical and 2 professional staff members by the South Dakota Committee, or, more significantly, perhaps, of 3 clerical and 8 professional staff members by the Texas State Committee.

Responses were received from all but one of the seventeen Southern and Border States.[19] Of the sixteen respondents, only four failed to employ clerical staff (one on a part-time basis). Eight of the seventeen reported the services of paid executive staff (and to this should be added Virginia, whose State Chairman, I. Lee Potter, at that time headed the Republican National Committee's "Southern Division," and was considered a full-time staffman). We have already seen that there is almost a perfect negative correlation between full-time and paid chairmen, and Southern or Border State Republican Committees. Oklahoma is the significant exception on both counts, and Florida boasts a full-time unpaid chairman. Maryland's State Chairman, when queried as to his full-time or part-time status responded: "I sometimes wonder"—which is probably par for the course.

Eleven out of 46 reporting states planned expenditures of $100,000 or above in the non-election year of 1961. In order of magnitude of budget, these are listed below:

Indiana	$495,000	(1960 deficit	$300,000)
New York	391,000	(	289,695)
Minnesota	251,000	(	200,000)
New Mexico	250,000	(	38,200)
Pennsylvania	240,000	(	8,000)
Ohio	200,000	(	)
Washington	170,000	(	)
Connecticut	124,000	(	25,000)
Wisconsin	120,000	(	38,000)
Illinois	100,000	(	)
Texas	100,000	(	)

Texas, which reported a planned budget of $100,000 for 1961, also reported a State Committee clerical staff of three full-time and one part-time person, each with eight years tenure (thus going back to the first year of the Eisenhower administration). The party had been resuscitated in 1952.

---

[19] Alabama, Arkansas, Delaware, Florida, Georgia, Kentucky, Louisiana, Maryland, Mississippi, Missouri, North Carolina, Oklahoma, South Carolina, Tennessee, Texas, Virginia, West Virginia

FINANCES AND STAFFS OF REPUBLICAN STATE COMMITTEES, 1961

State	1961 Budget	1960 Deficit	Chairman Full-Time	Chairman Paid	Clerical Full-Time	Clerical Part Time	Professional Full-Time	Professional Part Time	1960 Campaign Extras Cler.	1960 Campaign Extras Prof.
Ala.	None								3	
Alas.	$10,000									2
Ariz.	$18,000		Yes		1		1			1
Ark.	No information									
Calif.	No information									
Col.	$38,000		Yes		2	1	1			3
Conn.	$124,000	$25,000	Yes	Yes	6		3		8	11
Del.	None				2		1		5	
D.C.	$18,000				1				7	
Fla.	$38,000		Yes		2		1			2
Ga.	$30,000				1		1	2	1	1
H.I.	No information									
Id.	None				1					
Ill.	$100,000				2		2		2	4
Ind.	$495,000	$300,000	Yes	Yes	5	1	2		2	
Ia.	$75,000			Yes	1	1	1		6	
Kan.	$36,000				1	1	2		3	1
Ky.	None								2	
La.	None					1			2	
Me.	$63,855				1					2
Md.	None			Yes	1		2	1	3	6
Mass.	None	$103,000	Yes	Yes	9		2	1		2

Mich.	No information	Yes	Yes	4		9		2	3
Minn.	$251,000			1		1		2	
Miss.	$50,000			1		1		3	7
Mo.	$65,000					1		3	
Mont.	$26,786			2	1			3	19
Neb.	$35,000							1	1
Nev.	$10,000								2
N.H.	$50,000			1				6	4
N.J.	None	Yes		4					7
N.M.	$250,000			2		5		5	7*
N.Y.	$391,000			21		1		50*	7*
N.C.	$10,000			1		7			1
N.D.	$49,000			10	5	2	7	3	15
Ohio	$200,000	Yes	Yes	3	1	9	1	13	7
Okla.	$50,000	Yes	Yes	1		2			5
Ore.	$81,000			9		1		2	5
Pa.	$240,000	Yes	Yes	1	2	4		5	3
R.I.	$40,000	Yes	Yes			1		2	2
S.C.	None				3			4*	3*
S.D.	$63,000		Yes			1	1	4	2
Tenn.	None							2	
Tex.	$100,000			3	1	5		3	8
Utah	$35,000			1	1			1	2
Vt.	$12,000				1	1		1	1
Va.	$8,000				1				2
Wash.	$170,000			3			2	1	
W.Va.	$25,000			1		1		8	7
Wis.	$120,000			2	1	4		4	3
Wyo.	$15,000				1	2		1	2

* Estimated

There is, then, viable party apparatus in the states and counties, measurable by number and tenure of staff, expenditure made and programmed. How should these party units relate to the national party apparatus—the National Committee?

The State Chairman's Views. Twenty-one state chairmen responded at some length to the question: "In what ways could the National Committee staff be helpful to you and your staff?" The responses fall into three categories, and are reproduced below for the convenience of the reader. Some chairmen emphasized the role of the National Committee in providing each of the fifty state party apparatuses with information on policy issues, thus helping to inform the local party and to point out for it party positions which might be presented to the electorate. A number of chairmen emphasized the responsibility of the National Committee to provide organizational leadership— spurring the state parties to effective campaign organization and providing them with instruction and aid toward that end. Here it is significant to note that only one of the forty-six respondent chairmen suggested the desirability of tightening national-state party organization to the point at which an effective chain-of-command relationship would run from the National Chairman down into the field. The Washington State Chairman suggested

> . . . I am strongly in favor of the stressing of 'organization procedures' and further development of a tie to the national chairman and organization which recognizes their responsibilities and accept their leadership. It is my hope that every-area-candidate-finance-party organization has its direct tie, by chain of command, to national. Even as I hope to achieve the same relationship from the county organization in Washington state to the state organization.

The third emphasis was on the provision of such services as the speakers bureau by the National Committee, in order to accommodate the local party organizations.

The ambivalence of county and state chairmen toward the National Committee is clear. The RNC and the national candidate, provide a convenient scapegoat for local leaders in a presidential-campaign year, where the party has not won the White House. If the party lost locally, it went down to defeat in consequence of national mishandling of the campaign, or in consequence of the party's preceding administration. If the party won locally, the causes of victory tend to be attributed to local candidates, leadership and issues.

The National Committee is not popular with county party leaders. Yet it is considered essential by county and state leaders. National Committee hegemony over local and state party organization is not wanted, yet the representatives of these organizations suggest the sense of need for more by way of national party leadership and meaningful contact with the National Committee.

These reactions may spell the need for a more systematic effort at national headquarters to ascertain the kinds of communications which are regarded as helpful and meaningful at the local level, and the need for significantly increased, although carefully formulated, field work by the National Committee.

The County Chairman's Views. A questionnaire was also sent out to all Republican county and township chairmen and vice-chairmen on behalf of National Chairman Meade Alcorn. The attitudes which the respondents expressed probably are typical of those which persist today among party workers in the field. These attitudes are indicative of the magnitude of the tasks which the national committees have taken on in attempting to build more coherent party apparatus.

A great many respondents to the Republican County Chairman questionnaire complained of national committee neglect and indicated hostility to the committee. Characteristically, this took the form of expressing surprise, sometimes coupled with appreciation, that the national committee should evince interest ("at this late date") in the opinions of the county chairmen. To the consternation of the national committee staffer, however, these complaints were interspersed with such advice as "I think the National Committee should cut down on its mailing. It sends out more material than any of us have time to read." The two lines of criticism are not necessarily in conflict. In effect, respondents complained of a mechanistic, one-way, flow of communication from the National Committee to the field, and averred that reciprocal relationships and personalized follow-up were desirable. A woman co-chairman from Massachusetts, responding to a question concerning Meade Alcorn's speech to the National Committee in Des Moines, expressed her hostility in these terms: "Did not read Des Moines address [mailed out with the questionnaire], as I do not like thinking of national committee."

Asked what should be done toward rehabilitating the party in anticipation of the next presidential elections, most respondents cast their advice in terms which suggested reliance upon the national organization. They called for professionalization of the party apparatus and indicated a lack of confidence, based on personal experience, in voluntary organization and staffing. "It is no longer possible to rely upon volunteer help to organize and keep the party active on a year-round basis. We must have paid professional directors who will be responsible for keeping alive political and financial organizations of the party. Probably these directors should be responsible for an area no larger than a Congressional District." This advice came from a Minnesota county chairman and must be considered in the light of a statewide trend toward professionalization of that party. From Pennsylvania came the advice that the party look into the organization of the March of Dimes, Heart, Cancer, and Easter Seal drives, as a pattern for organization, and a Kansan reiterated the need to "es-

tablish year-round full-time offices in every state and larger counties."
Bay County, Michigan reported "Every county of our size should have
a year-round office staffed by at least one *competent* worker to keep
files current, do publicity, check poll lists, etc."

Inconsistent with the stereotype of the cigar-crunching political
boss, the county chairmen who responded to the questionnaire seemed
to regard politics as the pursuit of ideals and policies. They volunteered
comment on party ideology, in response to questions which did not
invite such an emphasis at least as frequently as they indicated concern
with organization, staffing, finance, and candidates. In balance, they
projected an image of an ideologically lost group—some questing
blindly for a code by which to politic, some counselling a return to
the old verities, and others stressing the need for change. A Michigan
respondent complained that "the precinct worker can work his head
off and not get anywhere unless we have . . . a well developed campaign showing our ideals and the why of said ideals and also show
where the nation is headed by this socialistic, inflation, boss-controlled
program of the Democrats." A Pennsylvanian counselled, generally,
"You must get across that we have something to offer." From Texas
came the advice, "Cut out spending wherever possible, cut out oil
imports, and do something to emphatically curb labor, particularly the
teamsters." An Oklahoma chairman saw "a crying need for the Republican Party to take a definite and firm stand on honest conservatism
and states rights."

Counterposed to these expressions of implied criticism at the
party's tendency to drift from its old values, were injunctions to "Get
us off the hook with Labor. Refute the Party of the Rich." (Illinois)
"Make the Republican Party the peoples Party." (North Dakota)
"We desperately need to devote more effort, ingenuity and money to
the job of convincing people that the Republican Party is in fact the
party which most nearly reflects the hopes and aspirations of the
average American." (Connecticut).

But, if ideals, policies, and a sense of direction and purpose were
linked to organization and effective electioneering, so was patronage.
The sense of need for patronage was surprisingly well distributed
geographically. From Maryland, Tennessee, Massachusetts, Illinois,
Montana came the cry for federal jobs. The Clay County, Illinois
chairman advised:

> Get rid of Democrats. I'm informed 80% of the federal employees
> are Democrats and no effort has been made to move them. The
> ASC office in our county is the worst thing ever. They have about
> half the county Dem. farmers working. They have been known to
> measure the same field of corn 3 or 4 times. The Republicans are
> burned up with such things.

From a county chair*man* in Montana came the complaint, "our
workers do not feel important or effective, no influence or prestige in

patronage—we feel like we are just good girls but are not being dated." From Kentucky came the stark advice: "Get rid of New Deal Civil Service Commission so we can get some Republicans jobs."

Indeed the comments on patronage tie-in with the expressions of dissatisfaction with the party's "image"—for what it stands for, presumably, is reflected in the people it appoints to office.

Thus, when asked for advice toward winning the next election, the county chairmen tended to reply in terms which suggested a responsibility at the national level—a responsibility to provide local workers with more recognition, to professionalize the party apparatus and enlarge it, placing it on a full-time basis, a responsibility to find an ideological formula which would make for party cohesion and incentives to work, and finally, a responsibility to translate victory at the polls into jobs for the faithful. These were things which, in the eyes of the county chairmen, the national party organization should have done, and had significantly failed to do. Little was said by way of criticism or advice, concerning the problem of financing the next election. As assessments of national Republican leadership were volunteered, much was said concerning the failure of presidential political leadership. If Ike proved a vote-getter for the Republican party, he did not thereby ingratiate himself to his flock of county chairmen.

Commenting on the alleged lack of national leadership, a West Virginian complained "We have lost our real politicians in the Republican Party." From Ohio: "I agree we need workers, but we also need a Captain, who talks like a Republican. The President does not try to sell the party to the people." An Illinois respondent advised that "Eisenhower, in press conferences, speeches, etc. should lead the way in openly attacking Democratic programs or lack of programs." A Pennsylvania chairman expressed the feeling that "From a political standpoint he has not been out there working with us. We need, in fact want, political leadership at the top." The county chairmen of the party in power would seem to expect leadership and partisan behavior, not merely from the officials of the national party apparatus, but from the man who they helped place in the White House.

A good deal of insight into the vigor, source of leadership, and adequacy of organization of the local party can be gleaned from responses to the question, "How were funds raised in your county?" Consider the following: "I am the only one who put on anything and I did it at my own expense." (South Dakota) "Left mainly to the county chairman." (Michigan) "All that was raised I did personally." (Nebraska) "I put up $2000 and my friends another $1000 so we have all we needed." (Missouri) "Personal contact with the few steady contributors." (Colorado) "We received none, from any source." (Tennessee) "Major contributions were from candidates and office holders." (Maine) "One of the best qualifications for running for office was if you could afford to." (Massachusetts) "Money was raised from state job holders and loyal Republicans." (An Illinois county) "If we have no jobs for Republicans in this county how can we expect to get funds?" (Kentucky)

The respondent from Worcester, Massachusetts reported, "The towns raise it for the State Comm., and if we're lucky we get a portion back—we must, somehow, see that the candidates get what they need—without each of them having to beg from the same people." From Tulsa, Oklahoma came the opposite complaint: "The State finance committee raised *all* the money, then gave back a small amount to Tulsa County. This is a very poor arrangement. Tulsa Co. practically financed the State—yet we have practically *no* money for Tulsa Co. candidates."

Many county chairmen reported effective programs for raising funds at the county level and in cooperation with the state committee. Perhaps the most consistently positive reports came from Minnesota respondents: "All money used in county was raised by the County Committee. Under our system we retain 25 per cent of what is raised and the balance goes to the state organization." From Marion, Ohio came the report that funds were raised by "an advisory committee made up of interested persons, members of the Executive and Central committee to work with candidates and with the public."

After all of the attribution of fault to national organization, personalities and issues, to lack of leadership, to lack of funds, to Democratic strengths, to Republican weaknesses beyond the power of the county chairman to correct, "What, if anything is being done in your County" toward 1960? The response from Livingston, Missouri comes close to summarizing that of respondents around the country:

> Nothing. In the first place the Congressional Committee is, as it now stands, *useless*. The State Committee members as far as we can see do nothing in their respective districts. The State Committee flounders around with exception, possibly, of the Chairman.

Note the consistency of the trend to lay the problem at another door, simultaneously heaving a sigh of frustrated surrender. From Middlesex, Massachusetts: "Nothing—an old tired worn out machine which can no longer do the work and is reluctant to give an inch to the younger people." From West Virginia: "Nothing as yet as we are waiting to find just what the Republican party will offer the voters."

The foregoing appraisal is harsh, for the questionnaires evoked a significant number of responses from chairmen who already were vigorously at work on forthcoming state and local campaigns, who had established screening committees to find attractive candidates, and who were initiating action toward rejuvenating party leadership at the local level, improving organization and fund-raising. But the responses to the questionnaire would suggest that the national party may, if it is guilty of offering something less than clearly directed and vigorous leadership, have a somewhat amorphous and indolent collection of troops in the field, to whom to offer leadership.

STABILITY AND CHANGE

The picture of the Republican National Committee and of its constituency which has been presented here is relatively dynamic. Republican organization today is in many ways vitally different from what it was a decade ago, and Republican activity since 1960 is in marked contrast to the relative somnolence of the RNC during the Eisenhower presidency. George Mayer complains in the preface to his party history, earlier cited, that most histories "give the misleading impression that the party exists nine months every four years to conduct a campaign for the Presidency." The activity described in this chapter may be a part of a long-term trend on the part of each party, toward improved organization, closer ties between the various units within the party, and full-time, year in, year out, party work aimed at enhancing party prospects for electoral victories.

On the other hand, it is equally likely that a presidential victory is all that would be required to dissolve whatever semblance of integrated party organization exists among Republicans today. In short, we have yet to see persuasive evidence that either party has accomplished a level of integration that is other than a reflection of its vicissitudes at the polls—the out party being preoccupied with organization and effectiveness of functioning, the in party being complacently sprawling and loose-knit.

part two

WHERE THE PRECINCTS ARE

TODAY *we transact our public business through 91,186 units of government exclusive of the national government and the fifty states. These include 3043 counties, 18,000 municipalities, 17,142 townships, 34,678 school districts and 18,323 special districts. In the basic units of electoral politics (some 166,072 precincts in the United States) the votes are cast which determine who will transact this business, whether it be at the levels of a sewage district, the governorship, Congress, or the presidency.*

Politics is the process whereby candidates are recruited to seek these offices (more frequently than not a process of self-recruitment), and the processes whereby they pursue electoral victory. For most offices of any significance, political parties, at some point or other in the political process, come into play as recruiting, sponsoring, campaign management, and vote-mobilizing mechanisms.

In Chapters 3, 4, and 5 we gain understanding of the political process at the state level and in the city and suburbs. (The reader who wishes acquaintance with problems of campaigning in a rural constituency will find it in Kessler's account of campaigning for the state senate in Indiana, Part III, Chapter 6.)

NEIL STAEBLER

Neil Staebler studied at the University of Michigan (A.B., 1926) and is the recipient of Honorary Doctor of Laws Degree, University of Michigan (1962); was visiting professor of practical politics, University of Massachusetts, 1962. Staebler is a business man, president of Michigan Capital and Service, Inc., and partner in Staebler and Son, a building and land development company, now in its 82nd year of business in Ann Arbor.

Staebler is a former chief, Building Materials Branch, Office of Price Administration (1942–43); Consultant to Federal Housing Expeditor (1946); Member, President's Commission on Campaign Costs (1961–62); U.S. Representative-at-Large, Michigan (1963–64); delegate to County, State and National Conventions; Michigan Finance Director for National Committee (1949–50); Chairman, Democratic State Central Committee of Michigan (1950–61); Democratic National Committeeman from Michigan (1961–64), (1965–); Chairman, Democratic National Advisory Committee on Political Organization (1955–60); director, Special Projects Division, Democratic National Committee (1960); Democratic candidate for Governor (1964); director-at-large, National Training Laboratories National Board (1965–).

Staebler authored *How to Argue with a Conservative* (1966).

DOUGLAS ROSS

Currently a student at the Woodrow Wilson School of International and Public Affairs at Princeton, Douglas Ross is a more recent recruit to the political wars. Besides having served as Mr. Staebler's aide, he was formerly Legislative Aide to Representative John D. Dingell (D.–Mich.) A former student of the London School of Economics and graduate of the University of Michigan (A.B. and M.A. in economics), he has spent a good deal of time in teaching and working in Detroit's inner city.

Ross co-authored *How to Argue With a Conservative* and has just completed *Robert F. Kennedy: Apostle of Change* for Simon and Schuster.

NEIL STAEBLER AND DOUGLAS ROSS

3. The Management of State Political Parties

What can we believe about the nature of political parties? Newspapers often refer to them as "political machines" capable of "crushing" the opposition. Party officials are "bosses" or "powers behind the scenes." Is this editorial exaggeration, headline writer's shorthand, or fact?

What explains the sudden shifts in the status of the parties? After the 1964 elections, some said the Republican party was dying, others called it already dead. Two years later this dead or dying Party suddenly came to life and registered spectacular victories coast to coast. How does this happen?

A more basic concern of many people is the question of political power. How does it arise? Who exercises it? How is it used to win elections? Is political power a sinister thing? Is it affected by special interests, by campaign contributors? Can an ordinary individual, by working for a party or a candidate, get to share in it?

We must continue to ask these questions. Insight into the internal workings of our parties is indispensable to an understanding of the American pattern of politics and our form of democracy. To describe politics only in terms of its forms and general purposes, or only in terms of its derelictions and shortcomings, is to paint a caricature. Since many people tend to do one or the other, there is a great gap between what many Americans believe about party politics and the political system as it operates. This lack of knowledge is not healthy. Political parties are an essential element in self-government. As Clinton Rossiter puts it:

> Parties and democracy arose together; they have lived and pros-
> pered in a closely symbiotic relationship; and if one of them should
> ever weaken and die, the other would die with it.

The management of the state political parties provides a convenient window to politics. An examination of how state party leaders
affect decisions on policies and personnel can tell us much about the
source and use of political power, the nature of the parties, and the
role of individuals in them.

In this kind of study, a particular effort must be made to distinguish the descriptive from the normative—the "is" from the "ought."
This means describing state politics as actually practiced by politicians,
rather than state politics as we might wish to see it.

First, we need to know a little about the context in which this
political management takes place—the state party itself. The subject
is discussed elsewhere in this book, but general observations about the
structure and function of state parties are called for here.

TYPES OF POLITICAL PARTIES

> Decentralization of power is by all odds the most important single
> characteristic of the American major party; more than anything else
> this trait distinguishes it from all others. Indeed once this truth is
> understood, nearly everything else about American parties is greatly
> illuminated.   —E. E. SCHATTSCHNEIDER

The first step toward the understanding of the structure and
functioning of state political parties is the realization that *there are no
national parties*. There are Democratic and Republican National Committees which coordinate the activities of the 50 Democratic state
parties and Republican state parties. In the minds of most voters,
there are national candidates, national issues, and overall national
parties. People think of themselves as Republicans and Democrats in
national affairs. But what we actually have in the operating field of
politics are collections of loosely-federated state parties with the pre-
ponderance of political power centralized in them. The adhesive that
tenuously binds these state parties together, on those occasions when
they behave in concert, consists of a largely ceremonial national committee, the party's members of Congress, the Administration if it is the
Presidential party, and the prospects of success or failure in the up-
coming election.

Expecting monolithic party organizations on the state level is
usually not realistic. Each state party, in its turn, is likely to be decentralized down to the city, county, town, and even precinct levels.
V.O. Key said, "an American party is not a 'hierarchy' but a 'system of
layers' in which each layer—local, state, and national—is independent
of the other."

While the degree of independence varies greatly, many local party
officials would agree with the County Chairman who, when asked why
he did not respond to inquiries from the State Chairman, said, "When
I see by the postmark it's a letter from you, I don't bother to open it; I
just throw it in the wastebasket right away."

Nevertheless, the state party, despite its decentralization, is most often a relatively autonomous organization with a direction and continuity of its own. The country as a whole with its great physical span, its sectionalism and state's rights, its remoteness of the grass roots from Washington, lends itself poorly to comprehensive, centralized control of national party behavior; the state is the largest political unit in which a unified party organization can be created and commanded by a single personality or group. If state parties harbor heterogeneity approaching the national scale, they are at least geographically manageable.

State party organization usually is centered around the office of governor. The lines of influence from a governor's mansion are more visible and personal, and hence more impelling, than those which crisscross the continent from the White House. A governor can hope to know and effect the party leaders of every county, city, and hamlet in his realm; the President cannot. Of course, the "out" party of the moment, i.e., the state party which does not have the governorship, is forced to operate without this valuable cohesive and rallying element. Such a party obtains what unity it can muster from the realization that concerted action provides the best chance of wresting this nerve center of power from the opposition.

To the extent that they are successful in charting a discrete course, and are somehow able to fashion a limited unity of purpose and action out of the greatest imaginable diversity, political parties must be regarded as minor miracles in social cohesion. No other voluntary organization—no club or civic group—embraces a comparable breadth of membership. In every state, the parties include men and women from every socioeconomic stratum, every ethnic group, every religious commitment. Parties represent a complex and often contradictory collection of different positions on the same issue, different styles, different long-term philosophies and objectives, and different traditional and historical allegiances.

Splits and differences are a continuing phenomenon within every state political party. Yet out of this almost infinite variety, at any given time there usually emerges a dominant party philosophy, a dominant coalition of forces, and dominant personalities which impose upon the party at least a transitory direction and force. Somehow—and this will be the central point of our discussion—each party is able, as is no other voluntary organization, to bring together into working relationship the diverse and often conflicting aspirations of cross-sections of the populace. For example, a Democratic candidate in a big city district may find himself attending a coffee hour in a home where the springs are protruding from the sofa, followed by a coffee hour in a home where the guests are admitted by a butler.

Interparty competition is another important determining variable in state party behavior. Politics, stripped of issues, is a battle to gain and maintain power. When one party succeeds in winning majority support, the other party will do everything it can to cut into the winner's

appeal, to slow down and capture its momentum, and to replace it as
the party in power. If the "out" party fails in one attempt, it will regroup
and on another tack work to take over a winning majority.

This incessant and often bitter interparty competition does more
than merely satisfy the sporting instincts of Americans. Folklore and
appearances aside, state elections are not the twentieth-century counterpart of the Roman spectacle or the medieval joust. Party competition
is a crude yet compelling means by which information and meaningful
discussion of issues can be injected into politics. In attempting to
depose the "in" party, the "loyal opposition" becomes a vigilant if
sometimes irresponsible observer and critic of the operations of government. Rossiter is correct in citing the party in opposition as "one of the
most effective checks in our enduring system of checks and balances."
Whatever a state party conceives to be its functions, this constant drive
for power in the face of an equally determined opposition does much
to shape the manner in which that state party is managed.

Of course, no two states are alike. To avoid having to treat each
of these one-hundred parties as a special case, we will apply two party
characteristics as a basis of classification: (1) the principal motivation
of the party, i.e., whether the party is *issue-oriented* or *job-oriented*;
(2) the distribution of power within the party, i.e., whether the party
is subject to centralized ("boss," if you wish) control or whether power
is shared to a considerable extent by the rank-and-file. There are, of
course, no pure representatives of these categories; all state parties fall
somewhere on a spectrum of situations differing in degree.

An excellent discussion of party categorization according to motive
is developed in the introduction to John Fenton's *Midwest Politics*.
Fenton characterizes programmatic or issue-oriented parties as those
dominated by individuals who "come together out of some common
concern with public policy and a desire to do something about it." The
LaFollette-led progressives of Wisconsin were such a party, as are some
of the current Democratic and Republican parties of Maine, Michigan,
Wisconsin, Minnesota, Washington, Oregon, and California.

"Traditional" or job-oriented parties, on the other hand, are those
whose members are "primarily concerned with obtaining government
jobs and privileges." A notorious example of this type of party was the
Tammany-controlled New York Democratic party of the turn-of-the-
century. State Senator George Washington Plunkett eloquently elabo-
rated Tammany's *modus operandi*, declaring from his throne, the
bootblack's stand in the county courthouse, in 1905:

> This civil service law is the biggest fraud of the age. It is the
> curse of the nation. There can't be no real patriotism while it lasts.
> How are you goin' to interest our young men in their country if
> you have no offices to give them when they work for their party?
> . . . How are we goin' to provide for the thousands of men who
> worked for the Tammany ticket? It can't be done. These men were
> full of patriotism a short time ago. They expected to be servin'

their city, but when we tell them we can't place them, do you think their patriotism is goin' to last? Not much.

In short, the important distinction between the two types of parties, according to Fenton, is that,

the people in the traditional parties are active in politics because they want a job, and issues are perceived as tools by which to secure the jobs, whereas the people in the programmatic parties are in politics not for the job as such, but because the job is seen as the means of securing the policy goals they regard as desirable.

Locus of party power, our second classifying variable, is defined along a spectrum bounded by "bossism" and manipulation on one end and participatory politics on the other. In practice there is no state party in which some grass-roots participation is not necessary; however, an imbalance in one direction or the other is usually discernible.

Looking back over this brief introduction to our study of state party management, we find four basic factors: (1) intraparty diversity; (2) interparty competition; (3) predominant party motivation; (4) distribution of power within the party. Recognizing that the unique interaction of these four factors in each state party does much to form the context and set the limits within which political management must take place, we move now to our main topic: the exercise of political power by the party leadership.

WHAT IS POLITICAL POWER?

The closest we can come to a general theory of state party management is to say that a party leader's every action and pronouncement, be it his motivation program or patronage, must be measured in the light of his natural desire to preserve his position of leadership. His concern may be simply to hold on to his prestigious title. In most cases, however, a party leader, like anyone else, takes pride in his work. Whatever plus or minus values society may put upon his programs and procedures, he has an investment of time and talent to protect. If he is primarily patronage-oriented, the careers of others are often dependent on his maintenance of power; if he is issue-oriented, he sees loss of power as a setback to his programs.

To explain that a party leader leads in order to keep leading may seem obvious. Yet even our most informed citizens often express bewilderment at "why the party by-passed the best man to run a party hack," or "why that issue was suddenly dropped in the campaign," or "why this incompetent was appointed to an important position." In most of these cases, the answer must be cast in terms of the fight for political survival by a particular leader or group, *even if it means losing the election*. In more than a few instances state parties have remained almost permanent minorities because an intransigent leadership has refused to relinquish or share power with those whose support might bring the party victory at the polls.

At the county level this desire of the leadership to maintain power sometimes verges on the ludicrous. Under a former Michigan statute, the officers of the party county committee were selected by the nominees for county office. In one small county where Democrats had no early prospects of election, the Democratic county chairman several times discouraged all nominees for county office, except one mentally retarded fellow who, upon nomination, dutifully selected the slate of party officers handed to him by the county chairman.

Like most general theories, this theory of state party political management probably raises more questions than it answers. Not the least important of these is, "What is political power?" Everyone reads in the newspapers about "power politics," "the balance of power," "the power of the office," but few pause to ask themselves what these phrases really mean. In the broadest sense, power can be defined as "the capacity to oblige others to take a particular action." In the area of state political management we can define power as "the capacity of individuals and groups to determine the policies and actions of their respective state parties." But this still does not tell us very much about state political power. How are we to recognize it? The "capacity to oblige" is not often worn on the lapel.

In a state political party, power can take many forms. The most visible is the ability to command voter loyalty, which explains why power in a state party is sometimes so decentralized. Rossiter writes:

> The essence of political organization is loyalty that runs in both directions, and the higher one moves up through the layers of our parties, the harder it becomes to keep such loyalty blooming with the fertilizer of personal contact.

If the voters in a state were willing to cast their ballots as their respective precinct leaders counselled, regardless of the directives of the "higher-ups," we would have to conclude that power in that party was held by the collective precinct leaders. Power can be centralized only when direct voter loyalty is given to a statewide figure or group, or when those who shape the voters' judgment feel tightly bound to such a figure or group.

This hold over the voters, whether based on confidence, charisma,* coercion, or whim, constitutes political power, because it is a means of getting people elected to government or party offices—which in turn

---

* *Charisma* is a word taken from the writings of the German political sociologist, Max Weber. It refers to a self-appointed leader who exerts a kind of magnetic pull upon others to follow him. As Weber used the term, charismatic leadership was most likely to occur in times of stress when the populace looked for "heroic feats of valor." H.H. Gerth and C. Wright Mills, *From Max Weber: Essays in Sociology*, New York, Oxford University Press, 1946, p. 52 ff.

yield the prizes of our political process: legislative programs, or patron-age and money, depending on the party's motivation. Thus a figure like Huey Long, who was personally able to command the loyalty of a majority of voters in Louisiana, was far more powerful than the Gover-nor or Senator in a state where such loyalty is more widely dispersed. This also explains why the heads of private interest groups are some-times party powers of the first magnitude. To the extent that a leader of the United Auto Workers or the Pennsylvania Manufacturers Associa-tion or the American Medical Association is able to deliver the votes of his membership, and to the extent that state party people view the support of that membership as vital to their own success, that leader will possess "capacity to oblige" in that party.

A related, though usually more subtle, form of political power is money. Power can be bought through campaign contributions, by the purchase of ads in party publications, through overpaying for public contracts, through bribes and a myriad of other financial ex-changes, both honorable and corrupt. At the heart of most of these dealings lies the irresistible political truth that money buys votes. By this we are not referring to the former "machine" practice of giving voters cash to go to the polls and mark the right ballot. Today's politicians are more sophisticated, and, in all fairness, usually more scrupulous. But they must have money to carry on their work. Ela-borate election campaigns created by high-powered public relations firms, involving extensive television exposure, billboards, bumper stickers, buttons, brochures, and paid professional staff, are the current vogue for gaining the voters's support. And they are expensive. A recent candidate for the Governorship of Pennsylvania reportedly spent $1.5 million in the primary alone!

While the skyrocketing costs of getting elected—already as high as $1 per registered voter for some state parties—has led to increased party reliance on independently wealthy candidates like the Kennedys and Rockefellers, the vast majority of politicians still are men of modest means. The parties and most of their candidates depend on contributions to win. Therefore, in state parties where the campaign coffers continually are replenished by the large offerings of a relatively few men, these contributors may acquire considerable influence owing to their ability to cripple the party financially if their wishes too often go unheeded.

Perhaps more important than the individual giver is the effective asker: the fund-raiser who knows how to get large contributions. Somewhere in or near the cabinet of a national administration, near every governor, and high in the national and state committees of both parties, is a person whose specialty is fund-raising. At the county committee level fund-raisers are even more important.

A strictly intraparty but nonetheless potent form of power is a reputation for accurate judgment in matters of strategy and organiza-tion. A party member enjoying widespread confidence for these qualities can wield a great amount of influence. At the national level, a good case in point is James Farley who was able to garner political power in the Roosevelt Administration, not because he swayed any group of voters or was a lucrative source of campaign contributions, but because his far-reaching network for gathering pertinent information and his political intuition made him a valued advisor to the President. Another is Ray Bliss, the former chairman of the Ohio Republican party and subsequent national GOP chairman, who wielded the power of confidence in a state and is now developing it nationally.

The principal drawback of this type of power is that it is by nature ethereal, lacking any tangible base beyond the faith and favor of those who hold power more directly. A poorly concealed bluff or a bit of disastrous advice can evaporate a carefully accumulated reservoir of goodwill and confidence overnight, leaving its owner virtually without influence.

Another form of power is that of influencing appointments. Despite the development of state civil services founded on the merit system, many offices still are filled by appointment, from state supreme court justice in some states to county truant officer. The power of appointment is roughly proportional to the competition for the open office. If a job is demanding and its salary and prestige small, the Governor or whoever is authorized to make the appointment might even be forced to relinquish some of his own power in order to induce someone of stature to assume the post. However, in the more common case where a number of individuals and groups express a strong interest in a position, a prudent appointment is a traditional technique for enhancing the influence of the benefactor.

It is no mere coincidence that the police review board appointed in 1966 by New York's Mayor John V. Lindsay included two Negroes, a Puerto Rican, a Jew, an Italian, and an Irishman. Appointments are an effective device for creating and strengthening ties with different groups in the community as calculated to win votes in coming elections. Appointments within a political party, made by the state chairman and lesser officials, frequently are distributed with similar intent.

The power to command publicity through access to the mass media is a final aspect of state political power which should be mentioned. Holders of high office, such as governors, senators, and mayors of large cities, usually can count on TV, radio, and newspaper coverage of their activities and pronouncements—though the degree and kind of coverage they get may depend more on the newspaper's editorial policy than on the importance to the public of the activities and pronouncements themselves.

The owners and major advertisers of many newspapers and TV stations exercise enormous political power, particularly in areas where they enjoy a monopoly on news reporting and editorial comment. Given the uninformed state of our electorate—a recent poll in Michigan revealed that only 10 per cent of the voters knew the name of the present Lieutenant-Governor—a newspaper's endorsements often can make the difference between victory and defeat. This has caused state politicians to develop a healthy respect for those who dictate editorial policy, granting them more than a little "capacity to oblige."

The power of the mass media is not monolithic; there are discernible layers. Most reporters tend to be Democrats, most managing editors and owners tend to be Republicans. The rewrite men, usually reflecting the opinions of top management, are on the watch to correct any apparent overfriendliness toward Democrats or underrepresentation for Republicans. They do this by rewriting the lead of a story, by deleting or changing other passages, and by determining the length of the article. Rewriting, condensation, and position in the paper are devices used by the management to rebuke or reward reporters. An overly zealous Democrat on a Republican paper quickly learns management's view of him by observing what happens to his stories. Beyond the rewrite man is the magic of the headline writer, who also reflects management opinion. A twist of phrase in the headline may totally change the impact of a news item. Compare "LBJ Yanks Dogs By Ears" and "President Relaxes With Pets."

When the student of politics looks at a political news story and its headline, he should ask himself, "What is the real content of this story?" Then he should analyze what the newspaper did with it. Is the story played up or down? Is it actually a rumor made to appear fact, or a fact which the paper is trying to impugn by undermining the credibility of the sources? Is the whole story given? If the article is part of a series, is the paper attempting to minimize the importance of the issue by dropping out portions of the story? Is it a set of allegations and surmises which the paper is trying to build into a story? The student soon learns that the kernels of hard fact are mixed with media chaff, and that the newspaper's point of view is as great a component of what he reads as any element of objective reality.

By now it should be apparent that many different people hold power in a state political party. However, in defining "party leaders," for our purposes, as those few men who either personally possess or represent the predominant power in the party, it is not always obvious to which specific individuals we are referring. In most states, a glance at the party's organizational chart can be very deceiving. The party chairman may be enormously influential, or he may be little more than a figurehead for the Governor, a party faction, or the managers of the dominant industry or union in the state. Usually he operates on some middle ground, having a limited say in most matters, absolute authority in few.

Because, as we pointed out earlier, the American party is not a disciplined "hierarchy" but a system of relatively independent "layers," power may reside where we least expect it. The virtual political boss of one Midwestern Republican party for many years was the State Treasurer. He dictated the recipients of government contracts, and arranged for a kickback of 2 per cent—which went into Republican campaigns—at his discretion. In some states, the head of the highway department exercises an influence unexplained by his constitutional authority. Out of the large budget with which he staffs his department he may employ several assistants, who don't know an overpass from a forward pass, to labor as political organizers.

Sometimes the purchasing agent of a public works commission is a formidable party power, working in collusion with influential government suppliers. Often an assistant who controls the Governor's daily calendar develops power by determining who will get to see the Governor and who will not. Such unlikely personages as the county coroner and county auditor have been known to attain party leadership.

In short, attempting to identify the real leaders of a state party can be an involved and complex task. The more programmatic and broad-based the party, the more likely that its organizational chart will approximate the actual distribution of power.

Having stated a general theory of party management, defined the different forms of political power, and described a few of the ways in which this power can be distributed within a state party, we are ready to analyze some of the techniques politicians use in the day-to-day direction of their parties. Here, especially, theory is not enough. Political leaders are the last people to operate by the book, preferring to fall back on the eighteenth-century dictum: "What exists is possible."

THE UTILIZATION OF POLITICAL POWER

Most state parties have more than one legitimate leader. They often have a large number of individuals and groups who carry weight within the party. While theoretically comrades-in-arms united in a common cause, these individuals and groups more often than not operate at limited cross-purposes stimulated by personal and factional feuds. However, we will ignore this multiplicity temporarily and focus on the activities of the state party chairman. For even in states where the chairman is not the repository of considerable political power, he normally does the bidding of those who do hold power, and hence operates as though he held it himself.

The party chairman's tasks—as representative of the activities of all who have a hand in the party's management—can be divided into eight basic functions: (1) recruitment of secondary leadership and rank-and-file workers; (2) nomination of candidates for public and party office; (3) patronage and party appointments; (4) formulation of issues, and public education; (5) publicity; (6) conduct of the election campaigns; (7) money-raising; and (8) post-election implementation of the party program.

Recruiting. Nearly everything a state chairman does is undertaken ostensibly to strengthen the party's prospects for victory at the polls. All but the most cynical of us would probably agree that most chairmen regard their duties as a means for promoting effective operation of our democratic processes and a better life for all. But, as we have noted, underlying these usually altruistic intentions there exists the deep-rooted drive to keep power and a position of leadership. Nowhere can this dual motivation be viewed more clearly than in the function of recruiting.

To win elections a party needs people, and lots of them. County, district, and precinct organizations have to be led and manned; workers are needed to identify and register potential party supporters; candidates require volunteers to distribute literature, arrange meetings, solicit funds, and carry out the thousand-and-one other tasks that are part of a successful election bid.

Unfortunately, in this country, party workers traditionally have been about as scarce as understatement in campaign speeches. According to recent polls, only about 10 per cent of the electorate ever contributes time or money to a party or candidate. And there is a high attrition rate among those who *are* politically active; fatigue, frustration, disillusionment, or plain disgust, result in a constant turnover of party people.

Party recruitment is one of the continuing functions of a chairman. While he does not corral personally every doorbell-ringer and envelope-stuffer, he must devote a great deal of time to the discovery and development of the secondline leadership that will recruit and direct the rank-and-file. The state chairman normally centers his efforts in areas with no party organization or in those with ineffectual or "paper" parties, i.e., chartered groups with membership lists and little else.

In counties, townships, cities, and districts where there is no party activity, building permanent organizations usually involves finding a few capable people to get the ball rolling. A chairman can accomplish this in a number of ways. He may obtain names of possible leaders from other party people with contacts in the area; often a man or a woman who has been successful in nonpartisan civic affairs or in a field such as law, business, journalism, or teaching, and who is thought to possess the right party leanings, makes a good prospect. An individual who enters politics briefly to aid a particular candidate may be persuaded to accept a continuing commitment.

One of the great contributions of Adlai Stevenson was the attraction he exerted on people to become active in politics. His enthusiasts may have provided the crucial margin in the subsequent campaign of John F. Kennedy.

The state chairman's approach to a would-be leader is a product of both the prevailing motivation of the party and the personality of the individual approached. In an issue-oriented party the chairman might challenge his listener to join the party fight to develop candidates and programs to cure his community's social and economic ills. Where patronage and privilege are the dominant motifs, the conversation is more likely to turn on questions of job opportunities and influential connections. Assuming success, the chairman must see that his recruit is trained in the fundamentals of party organization, and that he survives the political gestation period to become a vital and vigorous addition to the party.

In an area with an ineffectual organization, the local leaders often protest loudly that they would produce results for the party if only there were some competent and willing workers to aid them. Here the state chairman will quietly locate potential leaders and extract commitments from them. The next step is an informal meeting with the remiss local leader at which the new recruits are introduced as individuals who would like to help. Inundated with talent, the local leader must either produce or run the risk of displacement by the newcomers.

Sometimes the problem of party personnel rests on simpler factors. One county committee in Michigan that complained about the difficulty of finding good party workers, particularly women, finally discovered the source of its trouble: the committee held all its meetings in a bar. By moving to schools, public buildings, and homes, the committee found it could attract a large circle of women workers and members.

Successful recruitment serves the chairman's needs in another respect. Local organizations directed by personnel he has recruited represent his best insurance against the loss of power and party control. As Rossiter has put it, loyalties cultivated with personal contact are the "essence of political organization." The greater the number of key party people who feel beholden to the state chairman for the time and attention he has lavished on them, the surer that chairman's grip on the party.

Nominations. The nominating process is the "crucial process of the party." As E. E. Schattschneider observed:

> the nature of the nominating procedure determines the nature of the party; he who can make the nominations is the owner of the party. This is therefore one of the best points at which to observe the distribution of power within the party.

Why is the nominating process closely related to party control? In the first place, if a nominee wins his bid for public office, he automatically acquires influence within the party through his command of the loyalty of a large section of the electorate. What interests the party chairman primarily is how that power will be used. It may be withheld from the regular party as the basis for an independent voice in state politics, as was the case with Robert Kennedy's nomination and election to the Senate in New York in 1964. Or it can redound to the advantage of the party organization, strengthening the chairman's hand.

This explains why party leaders usually prefer candidates who are of, by, and for the party, and why a state chairman often will battle bitterly to secure the nomination of those who are friendly to the regular organization. Only when winning appears essential to the survival of the party, and thus to the chairman's position and power, can he be expected openly to encourage an attractive candidate with whom he has little or no political leverage.

Second, since a nominee symbolizes the party's style and stance on issues during the campaign, a state chairman who favors a specific program is greatly abetted by a congenial candidate who can win support for it among the voters. In factional feuds, whether over personalities or issues, the group that can get its people nominated clearly enhances its chance to prevail.

The nominating process may also be used in other ways. Nominating a particular candidate may placate a dissident group within the party, avoiding a threatened power struggle. A nomination may be rammed through by the chairman of a boss-run party as a show of strength, or to rebuke an individual or group. Occasionally a candidate will be selected solely to get him out of the way. The Democratic machine in Illinois chose Adlai Stevenson and Paul Douglas to head its ticket in 1948, convinced that their certain defeat would remove them permanently from the political scene—at the same time strengthening future liberal support for party regulars. Only one flaw marred this ingenious scheme—the unexpected victory of Stevenson and Douglas.

Preserving personal political power is not, of course, the state chairman's sole consideration in promoting the nomination of certain candidates; usually he also wants candidates who can be elected. A candidate without "political sex appeal" will fail to function as a magnet either for workers or voters. Unfortunately, high respect for the party and strong public appeal are a rare combination in a candidate, and the nature of the necessary compromise will largely be determined by the motivation of the party's leadership, the relative strength of the opposition party, and the available candidates.

The avenues of intervention in party nominations open to a state chairman are limited by the legal formula in his state. In some states, nominations are made by party convention, in others by direct primary, in still others by a combination of both. The primary, as "an alternative means to power other than winning support of the organizational leaders," theoretically places serious restrictions on the party chairman's ability to control the nominating process.

However, as we have noted, theory and practice often diverge. While we would expect a chairman to have a considerable say in nominations made by the party convention, we find he also can exert substantial influence over nominations by primary. He may do this by bringing about a pre-primary endorsement by a convention. In states where such endorsements are considered to be inconsistent with the image of the party as an open and democratic vehicle, the chairman may operate behind the scenes. Sometimes he may choose not to invoke his influence, either because he believes there is little from which to choose among the available candidates, or because he is convinced his man cannot win. But when the chairman does decide to back or oppose a candidate, he can bring a considerable array of political weapons into the battle.

Fortunately, everywhere except in certain bitterly segregationist sections of the deep South, these weapons have become more subtle and more civilized than they once were. Reminiscing over a hard-fought party primary in New York just before the turn of the century, the Tammany tiger, George Washington Plunkett, wistfully recalled:

> It was wonderful to see how my men slugged the opposition to preserve the sanctity of the ballot . . . They not only slugged our opponents but threw them in basements and rolled ash cans on them.

The notorious Al Capone obtained victory for his primary candidates in Cicero, Illinois, through the silent but firm persuasiveness of thugs with leveled machine guns at critical polling places.

Today the most effective means by which a state chairman can influence a primary outcome is quietly and unofficially to mobilize the party faithful behind the favored candidate. Where the party is unified, relatively strong, and responsive to his directives, the chairman can by his influence provide the favored candidate with precinct workers, campaign contributions, easy access to the public, and local endorsements (unlike most state organizations many local party units do endorse). The impact of such an effort is intensified by public indifference toward primaries—less than 35 per cent of the electorate normally bother to vote—which throws the nominating decisions largely back into the hands of the party faithful, who constitute a majority of the voters in a primary election.

Many chairmen attempt to insure a continuing supply of cooperative and appealing party aspirants by grooming their own candidates, i.e., by picking people to run for lesser offices and, if successful, encouraging them to run for progressively higher positions. This enables the party to take the measure of the man over a period of time while he develops basic political skills and increased public recognition.

This was the approach used in Michigan to develop Negro candidates for statewide office. By appointing highly qualified men to appointive positions, where they earned the respect of the public, the Democratic leadership made their nomination to higher office feasible.

Six statewide elections involving Negro candidates have now occurred in Michigan, in each instance with a white opponent, with the result that three Negro Democrats were elected.

The grooming technique can enhance the chairman's power in another way. Whenever he can present a candidate who is regarded both inside and outside the party as the "logical" choice for an office, the chances of stiff primary opposition are minimized. However, despite these techniques, it is not unusual for an individual with resources of his own to defeat the regular party's candidate in a direct primary, thus shifting some political power away from the party leadership.

Appointments. In most state parties, the chairman, with the advice and consent of his central committee or executive board, is authorized to appoint people to serve on standing party committees, to head special fund-raising projects, to arrange dinners and other party rites, to publish the party newspaper, to staff the headquarters, and to fill other permanent or temporary positions. The chairman's guidelines in making these appointments are generally the same as his considerations in wishing to control nominations for public office: a stronger position in the party and a stronger front against the opposition.

Appointments also can be manipulated for less obvious purposes. When a party holds the governorship, a chairman concerned with the party's image may convince the governor to make a series of appointments to public office calculated to convey the party's commitment to pure merit. This may take the form of a conscious selection of several non-party persons of high repute.

Party appointments made directly by the chairman often are open rewards, designed to emit a signal to others that if they will help the party and work with the chairman, they too may benefit. Often the selection of a member of a particular ethnic, religious, social, or professional group is a means of courting the allegiance of that group.

A special case is that of women, who perform more than half of the work in political parties, yet are woefully under-represented in public office. Because most women subordinate professional careers to their family attachments, comparatively few are available for appointment. When it is possible to appoint a woman to high public or party office, there is the strongest possible incentive to do so.

Party appointments frequently are tendered to major financial contributors, not as a reward so much as to put the person under obligation to make further contributions. An ingenious chairman will think of other ways to turn the appointive power to his own and his party's advantage.

Issues and Voter Education. Before exploring the role of the state chairman in formulating party issues and educating the electorate, we should note first the basic lack of ideological commitment in American political parties, even in those we have classified as "programmatic." This is not because our politicians are any less thoughtful or courageous than those of other nations, despite the cries to the contrary from spokesmen of the far Left and Right in this country. It is rather a result of the nature of our two-party system.

Each of our parties, unlike those in nearly every other nation, attempts to gain the support of the entire populace, aiming its appeals at every segment of society. Whatever a party leader's principal motivation—program or patronage—he cannot realize his goal without winning elections. In most states, a victorious coalition demands "programs and candidates having as nearly universal an appeal as the imperatives of politics will permit."

In Europe, where nearly every significant—and some not so significant—ideological position and socioeconomic class commands a political party of its own, the majority needed to govern the country is formed by a post-election coalition of parties whose interests are similar enough to permit accommodation in an alliance. By contrast, in this country the accommodation takes place prior to elections, in the broad coalitions that are the national Democratic and Republican parties. The ideological boundaries between these two great pre-election coalitions naturally are often blurred and there is frequently a substantial overlapping of beliefs, programs, and even voters.

Rossiter has aptly characterized our parties:

> They are creatures of compromise, coalitions of interest in which principle is muted and often even silenced. They are vast, gaudy, friendly umbrellas under which all Americans, whoever and wherever and however-minded they may be, are invited to stand for the sake of being counted in the next election.

It is therefore surprising that issues play as large a part as they do. Let us take a look at the perspective of the political leader with regard to issues.

The party chairman views issues as susceptible to exploitation to the party's interest in various ways. Formulated and publicized by the party, issues can be used to attract specific groups needed to win an election, to improve the party's cohesion by refreshing its sense of direction, to resolve an intraparty power struggle, to stimulate the enthusiasm of party workers, to attract attention in the mass media, and to promote realistic solutions to pressing public problems. Of course, in many instances the issues that titillate the voters' interest are the product of outside forces over which the chairman and his party have little or no control; in this case, the chairman works to handle these issues so as to serve the objectives outlined above.

Vietnam, for instance, is precisely the kind of issue that troubles the chairman of the party in power nationally and delights his opposition. Like the Korean War, it is only dimly perceived and understood by the electorate. The party in power—in this case the Democratic party—attempts to treat the matter so as to maximize support from the opposition while at the same time minimizing intraparty criticism and defection. The Republicans, simultaneously, can offer criticism from every angle and can gain recruits among those dissatisfied from totally opposed points of view—in this case, the doves who want to pull out of Vietnam and the hawks who want to end it quickly by dropping the bomb.

Issues also serve a much broader function, that of creating in each party a reasonably constant psychological appeal. In Graham Wallas' words, this is the function of transforming an impersonal organizational chart into "something which can be loved and trusted, and which can be recognized at successive elections as being the same thing that was loved before." The form and texture of this appeal will vary depending on the sectional mores, belief systems, and socioeconomic conditions of that part of the electorate from which the party is drawing its basic sustenance. We are talking about bundles of ever-changing issues which somehow convey a congenial and constant presence to the "little" man, the property-owner, the man of means, the underdog, the rugged individualist, the intellectual, or to whatever self-image a particular group cherishes.

Major party issues and programs usually emerge from an extended process of trial-and-error in which a strong state chairman can play an influential part. When he senses or suspects that a large number of people have a common attitude which would fall within the purview of legitimate party concerns, the chairman may "float a trial balloon" at a meeting or in an interview in order to test public reaction. Usually the reaction is varied. The chairman then explores this mixed bag in an effort to identify a pattern; that is, what kinds of individuals and groups are in favor, are opposed, are neutral.

If this initial experiment uncovers the possibility of substantial popular support for a new party plank or campaign appeal, the chairman probably will consult office-holders and party officials to determine their appraisal of the issue in terms of its effect on the party's image and chances for victory at the polls. Out of this evaluation and what other party people and the newspapers have to say will come the final decision on how to treat the issue and what priority to give it.

When the chairman has a pet issue or program he would like to see the party adopt, he has recourse to a number of techniques: the establishment of party educational projects and workshops designed to win support for the proposal; the dispatch of sympathetic persons to speak at party gatherings; the appointment of like-minded individuals to party resolutions committees; the inclusion of a discussion of the favored topic on the agenda of party meetings; and his own direct advocacy of the issue or program in speeches and official party publicity. In these ways, a state chairman can exercise considerable influence over the programmatic content of the party.

There is a crucial intermediate step between selling the party faithful on a program and winning elections with that program: the task of educating the electorate. This is a function many parties neglect until just before elections, and then are dismayed to find that opposing interest groups have moved into the informational vacuum, weakening the party's influence on the electorate and its political power in the state.

"Educating the electorate" can be carried on for a variety of reasons. From the political scientist's detached perch, Clinton Rossiter regards political education as a national necessity, explaining that "the citizens of a free nation must be instructed in the practices of democracy and kept informed on the issues of their times, not merely to become more forceful agents of public opinion and more skillful voters, but also to live more satisfying lives." Practicing politicians tend to take a somewhat less abstract view of their educative function.

The perceptive party chairman, particularly if his orientation is programmatic, recognizes that party issues and platforms can help win elections only if the voters have been prepared in advance to understand and accept them. New ideas planted in an uncultivated context will yield indifference at best, often fear and misunderstanding. When Adlai Stevenson, late in the 1956 campaign, made his proposal for a limitation on atomic testing, he threw the campaign into great confusion. His program was misrepresented by the opposition, and his supporters had the double task of trying to make clear what he proposed and convincing people that the idea was desirable. Even the patronage-inspired politician must confront this problem: at least one group of supporters will insist on a commitment to some program or principle, compelling the leader to explain this intruding issue to the rest of his coalition.

The chairman must try to broaden the outlook of "one-issue" individuals and groups. Every party harbors people with exclusive and often fanatical attachments to a single issue such as disarmament, civil rights, or conservation. The chairman must try to head off crippling collisions between power groups in the party by promoting acceptance and support by these people of a wider range of party programs.

These forms of political "education," which are propaganda in either its best or worst sense, call for techniques similar to those by which the chairman influences the party's acceptance of particular issues. Speeches, public hearings and debates, party seminars, coverage by the mass media, letters to the editor, and campaign slogans and brochures are among the devices used.

In recent years some politicians have come to believe that the effort to generate broad understanding of pertinent issues is largely a

waste of time. Operating on the assumption that voters really are not
interested in the specifics of state and local government, these leaders
tend to rely on a TV blitz, just prior to the election, designed to
project a favorable "image" of the candidate. If candidates can, in
fact, be "sold" to the people much like cigarettes—and there is some
evidence that this may be so—the traditional party function as a crude
adult educator will atrophy and eventually be abandoned.

Publicity. A function of state party management that pervades
nearly every aspect of the state chairman's job is that of publicity.
Particularly in situations where a member of the chairman's party
does not occupy the governor's mansion, it falls to the chairman to
become the party's official spokesman. He must take the lead in
issuing statements condemning the opposition for its failures, both
real and imagined, while singing the praises of his own party. Because
this activity is by nature partisan, much of the public tends to regard
an outspoken chairman as a hack chained to the party machinery.

State chairmen rely primarily on press releases and press conferences to make their views known to newspapers, radio and TV
stations. This is usually facilitated by the development of special
relations with a few key journalists through whom exclusive stories
and "leaks" can be channeled. The "leak"—an informal and con-
fidential suggestion that a reporter might find a story by checking out
this rumor or by investigating that nominee's financial background—is
a particularly useful device. It enables the chairman to draw widespread attention to an activity likely to embarrass the opposition or
compliment his own party, which, if publicized directly from Party
headquarters, would lose much of its credibility.

Other facets of the chairman's publicity powers, such as gaining
support for his own ideas, putting pressure on obstreperous party members, and wooing the economic, social, and ethnic groups needed for
a victorious coalition, have been alluded to in earlier discussions.
Suffice it to say that the manner in which the chairman exercises these
powers will be a significant determinant of the chairman's success
and that of his party.

Campaigns. All the functions of the state chairman—recruiting
party members, nominating candidates, making appointments, formulating and explaining issues—combine to have a powerful impact on
who the candidates are and on the nature of their campaigns. The
campaign, more than any other activity, will bear the chairman's
imprint.

In those states where a "lone-wolf" operation is standard, with
each candidate creating his own independent and self-contained organization, no single voice can be heard very clearly in the cacophony
of several hundred separate campaigns. The most a chairman can do

here is try to establish personal contacts with individuals on as many campaign committees as possible, getting information and giving advice through them.

In states where the various campaigns are centrally coordinated to some degree and an effort is made to present a united front against the opposition, the chairman can enter the picture more directly. As a first step, he will map a comprehensive strategy to mobilize party workers from the state to the precinct level. Except where a party has no serious opposition, this battle plan will be built around two basic objectives: identifying probable party supporters and seeing that they are registered to vote; getting them to the polls on election day. This grass-roots activity is both traditionally and actually the *sine qua non* of politics. How well registration and get-out-the-vote projects are conducted may make a difference of from 5 to 20 per cent in the final returns—the margin of victory and defeat in most elections. Ironically, while this is a crucial aspect of party management that political leaders are willing to discuss frankly, its importance is consistently underestimated by the party rank-and-file and the voting public. It is too "simple" and too devoid of back-room intrigue.

Depending on the degree of central coordination possible, the chairman will attempt to allocate the party's workers, money, personalities, and publicity so as to promote the best interests of the party as a whole. This is not always easy. For example, the visit of a national party dignitary frequently is the occasion for much internal party pulling and hauling. In the 1966 campaign in Michigan, four visitors—Johnson, Humphrey, and the two Kennedys—were the star attractions. Every section of the state wanted them and built up the most elaborate cases for having them campaign in their area.

The state chairman may feel that for the best interests of the party as a whole, scarce political resources should be concentrated in marginal contests, where a little extra may mean victory, at the expense of those campaigns which seem either safe or hopeless. But this can be done effectively only in the most centralized of state parties. Even there, every candidate from governor to drain commissioner can be expected to clamor for his fair share, and more.

Of all candidates in an election, the gubernatorial candidate is of the greatest importance to the state party and its chairman. In most states, his name heads the ticket. Major attention and publicity are centered on his campaign. In the perspective of history, U.S. senators are probably far more important than governors, but a governor is generally far better known and attracts much more concern in elections. His role as head man, the frequency with which he is quoted in the media, and the prevalence of the "housekeeping" functions of state government, all combine to give him a preeminence in the political structure and in the campaign. In many states, there is the additional factor of state patronage which may include, as in Indiana and

Pennsylvania, thousands of jobs ultimately under the governor's determination.

The style and behavior of the gubernatorial candidate will greatly affect all other candidates in the party. If he runs with the party and helps other candidates, the whole ticket is strengthened and party workers everywhere get great encouragement. If he disavows his party or ignores it, for instance by omitting the party label from his literature, he may win election himself at the expense of other candidates. Few candidates go so far as George Romney, who in the 1964 election permitted his committee to publish ads in all principal newspapers pointing out, with illustrations, how the voter could split his ballot for Romney alone.

Whether a gubernatorial candidate stresses the issues, blurs them, or ignores them has an effect on the campaign and the party. A candidate who cooperates with the party in soliciting funds helps to strengthen it; one who goes his own way in solicitation may greatly disorganize other candidates, and of course one who seeks or accepts contributions from unsavory sources may wreak great damage on the whole ticket and the party.

The state chairman in working with the gubernatorial candidate tries to get the candidate and his committee to pursue the course which offers the greatest combination of strength to all the candidates on the ticket. If it is evident that only the governor can be elected, so that funds had better be concentrated on his behalf, the chairman then tries to "keep happy" other candidates and their supporters with an eye both to their immediate cooperation and their longer-term adherence to the party.

It is a rare campaign in which there are not many misunderstandings and frictions among the enthusiasts for the numerous candidates. One of the state chairman's most important functions is to reconcile these differences and clear up misunderstandings wherever possible. A favorite ploy of the opposition party is to start a rumor to the effect that one candidate is "cutting out" other candidates in his campaign speeches. The state chairman finds it wise to run down such a rumor and either lay it to rest or correct the practices of the offending candidate.

The function of the state chairman is to see the campaign in its entirety and to see it whole, from the viewpoint of the public. If friction is visible, if inconsistencies occur, he will try to see that they are eliminated. If a candidate is obscured, he will try to get him more attention. If in the chairman's opinion the gubernatorial candidate or other major party voice is not coming through to the electorate, he will work with the campaign managers to try to solve the problem.

The methods a chairman uses to lead his workers into the field are largely determined by where the party stands on the other spectrum, that of principal motivation. In a job-oriented party, the chairman can marshal his people to the tattoo of blunt directives; he possesses weapons of persuasion, even coercion, in the form of paying positions and other patronage. By contrast, the leader of the primarily programmatic party must cater to his workers, struggling to motivate and excite them; he has little with which to cajole them, except the prospect of improving their government and thus the state of society. Should he fail to make this prospect sufficiently vivid, attractive, and attainable, the organization may evaporate from under him.

Motivation differences will also affect other aspects of the campaign. In issue-oriented areas, party workers will be provided with literature and bumper stickers; the emphasis will be on many small meetings and maximum contact with the electorate. Such workers must be prepared by the party to discuss at least the basic issues with their friends and neighbors. Patronage parties by contrast are hesitant to rely on the rank-and-file as a medium of persuasion, using instead the mass appeals of billboards, newspaper ads, large rallies, and TV appearances. In practice, some mix of these two approaches is usually adopted.

Money Raising. Every state political party must have money— and lots of it—if it is to be successful. In 1964 alone, the bill for political activities in the United States at all levels of government came to $200 million.

It is no longer a subject for headlines when a contest for a governorship or a U.S. Senate seat costs in excess of one million dollars. A candidate for governor in Pennsylvania reportedly spent $2.5 million in his campaign in 1966, and lost! The typical Congressional race in a two-party district costs between $10,000 and $50,000 per candidate; a contest in a New York District in 1964 found one candidate spending more than $180,000. In short, American politicians apparently have adopted the principle promulgated by a British campaign agent many years ago: "Win the election; never mind the expense; a defeat is the most expensive of all contests."

On what do candidates and parties spend these astronomical sums? A relatively small portion—about $125,000 annually by the Michigan Democratic party—goes to maintain the operations of the permanent party organization: staff salaries, party headquarters, telephone, postage, and usually a party journal.

Campaigns are by far the largest consumers of political funds. During its transitory but explosive existence, each major campaign not only bears the same kinds of expenses as the permanent party organization, such as rent, salaries, postage, and printing, but today's well-run campaign demands in addition TV and radio time, billboards, bumper stickers, buttons, brochures, public opinion surveys, transportation and baby-sitter allowances for volunteers, and, in some instances, hourly wages for precinct and poll workers.

While this list is not long, each item on it is costly. One-half hour of prime time—between 8 P.M. and 11 P.M.—on a statewide network in Michigan runs about $12,000; five 30-second spots sell as a package for $4500. A good-sized billboard overlooking a busy Detroit freeway rents for roughly $1000 a month. To cover the state of Michigan with a candidate's bumper stickers costs $30,000—300,000 stickers at a dime each. Nearly all statewide campaigns currently make some use of public opinion surveys—at a cost of at least $6000 for each poll—even though many candidates say they are not quite certain what to do with the results. And so the budget runs.

Where does this money come from? In patronage states, percentage assessments on the salaries of all those who owe their jobs to the party are an effective way of replenishing campaign coffers. A similarly simple strategy is sufficient where the party is amply financed by a small number of extremely wealthy patrons. However, in the more common case where money must be extracted from a multitude of sources, it becomes a principal task of the party chairman to devise a comprehensive blueprint for raising money.

From the politician's point of view, there are four classes of contributors: the very small contributor who gives $5 or less; the middle contributor who donates from $5 to $100, the range over which the most money is raised; the large contributor who gives $100 to $1000; and that very small but influential group of givers who can be convinced to part with $1000 or more.

Over a period of time, each chairman develops a number of methods for reaching these four classes of contributors. Generally, very small contributions are best obtained by indiscriminate solicitation, often through a house-to-house canvass such as Dollars for Democrats or a street-corner project of the tag-day type.

Mail solicitation has been used with some success on middle-level contributors, but is impractical for very small contributors and fails to maximize the yield from larger givers. The rate of return for even good mailing lists rarely runs above 5 per cent. An especially effective way of reaching the $5 to $100 contributor is the committee drive, in which the names of potential givers are assigned to specific party members who systematically call on them. Another technique for this middle group is the fund-raising dinner or cocktail party with an admission charge from $10 to $100.

The large and extremely wealthy contributors are the subjects of very careful planning. They may be visited by a high-ranking party official, invited to an exclusive dinner at which time their support is requested by the party luminaries, or proffered a membership in a select group such as the President's Club in the Democratic party at the rate of $1000 per annum.

Whatever the technique employed, two broad principles underlie all solicitation: (1) the solicitor must be committed to the party

cause and (2) the solicitor should be the financial peer of the people
he solicits, i.e., he should already have donated, in the same dimension
in which the potential contributor is expected to donate.

A chairman gets spread quite thin over the many aspects of party
activity, but one field which he can never neglect is money-raising.
A disproportionately large amount of his time is inescapably committed to meeting the need for funds. It should not be assumed, of
course, that he does all the work himself, or that he is the most
active party worker in the field of finance. Every chairman finds one
or more trusted lieutenants to work in this field and encourages the
formation of a finance committee to give them support and assistance.
Sometimes the chief finance role is borne by the party treasurer, sometimes by the chairman of the finance committee, often with the
assistance of one or more paid employees.

The task of the finance committee is not only to raise funds for
the state party but also to reconcile the competitive and conflicting
demands for funds from the national committee, the national senatorial and representative campaigns, the state legislative campaigns, and
the needs of all statewide and local candidates. No one has yet found
an answer to unified political fund-raising analogous to the United
Fund. The dominant party in Indiana, Pennsylvania, and a few other
states has a ready-made solution in patronage contributions, but in
most states political contribution is a chaos of competitive contests.
Since contributors have a natural inclination to give to a candidate
rather than to an impersonal party organization, in the welter of
conflicting requests for individual candidates, the state committee is
in some danger of being "starved." One of the main roles of the state
finance chairman is to make sure that this does not occur.

The fact that fund-raising is complex does not mean in most
state parties that the activity is haphazard. Over time, the efficient
party chairman comes to know from whom he can expect contributions, and in roughly what amounts. However, since the sources and
dimensions of political donations vary greatly from state to state,
we can make no meaningful generalizations except to point out that
political contributors are a minority group in this country, constitut-
ing less than 10 per cent of the voting-age population.

Implementation of the party program. As Clinton Rossiter explained:

> . . . one of the basic functions of a party in a democracy [is] to
> make concrete promises to the electorate and then, if invited by
> the electorate to govern, to make good on these promises.

Mr. Rossiter notwithstanding, American political parties at all levels
are notoriously delinquent in keeping their campaign promises to the
voters. And this indictment of our party system applies not only to
the victors of our annual and biennial contests for office, but also to the

losers as well, who it is hoped will provide an opposition consistent with their own pre-election platforms. Why do our parties have so much difficulty doing in December what they vow in November?

First, there is the fact of the coalition which each party represents. When a party is victorious at the polls, the various constituent groups of the coalition often begin struggling over priorities and the manner in which the party program should be implemented. If the party controls the state legislature by only a narrow margin, some legislators can be counted on to blackmail the party for support on critical votes, causing the program enacted to depart from the program promised. On the other hand, if the party in control enjoys a substantial majority, party discipline often is difficult to maintain, enabling special-interest groups to move effectively into the resulting chaos and compromise the party's pre-election pledges. Finally, the decentralization of most state parties enables many running on the party ticket to campaign without committing themselves to the statewide platform, or even to campaign in opposition to portions of that platform.

In the face of all these difficulties, a state chairman committed to the consistency of party position is forced to draw on every available device of party control: manipulation, intimidation, assertion of party responsibility, and development of party morale.

If the chairman possesses great personal power within the party, a direct telephone call to the Governor or to the maverick legislators may be enough to enforce adherence to the party platform. Failing this, a chairman can quietly approach individuals and groups from the constituencies of the legislators in question, asking them to put pressure on their respective representatives in the form of resolutions, phone calls, letters, or personal visits. Party conferences and workshops which focus attention on issues in danger of being compromised or abandoned is another way of re-enforcing programmatic consistency and quelling potential revolts. If none of these techniques succeeds, a determined chairman can publicly prod recalcitrant party members in speeches and through the press—a practice most chairmen prefer to avoid because of their desire to keep intraparty differences from the public eye.

It should be pointed out, however, that even the most tenacious and outspoken chairman employing all of the above devices may fail to convince or coerce the party's members in the government to make good on the party's pre-election promises. Thus, implementation of party programs remains one of the great problem areas in the performance of our state political parties, and one of the most difficult tasks of those state party chairmen who concern themselves with it.

Edward F. Cooke

4. Big City Politics

PROLIFERATION OF LOCAL OFFICES

The importance of local politics and local governments in the development of our democratic system cannot be overemphasized. The United States is a nation built from grass-roots politics. Our country originated in the small settlements: the towns and villages of New England and the Middle Colonies, and the plantations of the South. As a people spread across a continent, they settled new towns and villages which, over time, formed themselves into states. The backbone of the entire American system is still these local units of government. Local citizens —our friends, neighbors, even relatives—operate these local governments and give a distinctive character to local politics.

The tremendous scope and variety of local governments in the United States is shown by Table 1.

TABLE 1.   LOCAL GOVERNMENTS IN THE UNITED STATES

Government Type	Number
Counties	3,043
Municipalities (Boroughs, Cities, Towns, Villages)	17,997
Townships	17,144
School Districts	34,678
Special Districts	18,323
Total	91,185

Source: Census of Governments, Governmental Organizations, Vol. I., 1962.

The pattern of politics will vary among the different units of government or among the separate regions of the country. Within the same state the politics of a large city, Chicago, Illinois, for example, will differ in several significant respects from the politics of a rural county such as McDonough County in Western Illinois; Pennsylvania's suburban Bucks and Montgomery counties, adjacent to Philadelphia, have a political game quite distinct from rural Tioga County which borders upstate New York. And even counties of similar size, population, and perhaps economic base, will have marked varying political processes. The courthouse politics of the Byrd organization in Virginia is much more disciplined than county politics in Maine and Montana.

Over 500,000 individuals are elected by their fellow citizens to man and operate the 91,000 units of local government. The vast majority of these public offices are filled by part-time, non-salaried politicians—men and women who give their cities, towns, boroughs and school boards many hours of their time, though their primary occupations may be in business, the professions, or managing a family. A small number, about 11 per cent of the 500,000, are full-time, paid public servants. For some of these politicians, service at the local level is the starting point of a career in public office that may well lead all the way up the political ladder to the White House. Former President Harry S. Truman, it will be remembered, began his political career as an elected county official in Missouri.

Although we do not have a complete picture of the pattern of political careers throughout the United States, nevertheless sufficient evidence exists to reveal the value of local politics as a training ground for higher public office. Studies of state legislators in Wisconsin, Ohio, New Jersey, California, and Tennessee show a high proportion of those legislators in the samples had held a local office before election to the state assembly.[1] Professor Matthews's research on the backgrounds of United States Senators also revealed that a significant number had served their local governments in such capacities as judges, prosecuting attorneys, school boards, and other elective positions.[2] A similar pattern of career experience was discovered by Professor Schlesinger in his study of state governors. About 20 per cent of the 995 governors who served between 1870 and 1950 had, at some period in their life, been elected to a local public office.[3]

It would be misleading to leave the impression that there is one, established, overall pattern for political advancement in the United States. One does not move lock-step up the political hierarchy from local to state to national public office. Yet many Americans do begin

[1] J.C. Wahlke, H. Eulau, W. Buchanan and L.C. Ferguson, *The Legislative System* (New York: John Wiley & Sons, Inc., 1962), p. 96.

[2] Donald R. Matthews, *U.S. Senators and Their World* (Chapel Hill, N.C.: University of North Carolina Press, 1960), p. 283.

[3] Joseph A. Schlesinger, *How They Became Governor* (East Lansing, Mich.: Michigan State University, 1957), pp. 10–12.

their political careers at the local level and attribute much of their later political success to this earlier experience. Moreover, thousands of citizens find service in their local governments not only interesting and stimulating, but also personally rewarding in itself.

URBAN POLITICS

Politics of urban America is generally more organized than the politics of rural, or even suburban, areas of the country. Great concentrations of people packed into a relatively small territory with their diverse ethnic, racial, national, and religious backgrounds, and compounded by the impersonal nature of city living, are among the factors which brought about the need for a more systematic and continuous method of handling a city's political life. In fact, some cities became notorious in American politics because of the ruthlessly efficient manner in which the party organizations controlled their politics and governments. These were the "political machines," run by the "bosses," who have become so much a part of America's political folklore.

Political Machines. The old style city "machine" was pictured as a corrupt, tightly knit organization, headed by a furtive "boss" who had fought, bribed and manipulated his way to the top of the party. The machine was credited with almost unlimited power and venality. It controlled voters, rigged elections, milked the public treasury, granted all sorts of favors and privileges (for a price), fixed the laws, and fostered crime and corruption. A few machines were this powerful, most were not; yet all tended to be lumped together under this stereotype. Although this type of city machine, real or imagined, has largely passed into history, it is important for an understanding of today's urban politics to have some knowledge of what these organizations were like, how they operated, and how they adjusted to new conditions.

Machines developed in the cities during the post-civil war era because a number of events occurred which necessitated political leadership capable of making decisions affecting the lives of hundreds of thousands of people and the economy of the community. First was the tremendous migration of people to the cities. In 1850 only 15 per cent of the country's population lived in urban areas, but by 1890 over 40 per cent were city dwellers.

The bulk of the newcomers was from foreign countries, primarily from eastern and southern Europe. However, a significant number were native-born Americans from small towns and farms attracted to the city by the vision of fame and fortune it might bring. Such a surge of humanity requiring all kinds of services from government practically overwhelmed cities. Business and industry flourished and made demands upon government—paved streets, fire protection, side-walks, franchises, enforcement (or non-enforcement) of laws.

Municipal governments in this era were weak and disorganized. Their structures divided power among a large number of popularly elected officials who served short terms. City officials, whether capable or not, were unable to cope with the population and business explosion and the resultant demands generated by them. In such a chaotic system where a power vacuum existed, it was relatively easy for a strong political leader to organize his forces within the party, put his men into the various public offices, and make the deals and cut the red tape to get things done. Thus a businessman would merely have to see the boss or one of his henchmen to gain a favor or to get the city to do, or not to do, something. All for a price, of course. The immigrant laborer would see his precinct or ward leader to obtain a job or loan. The price, in this case, was the worker's loyalty and vote on election day.

The boss and his machine were able to stay in power through inducements, corruption and force, if necessary. Thousands of immigrants were assimilated into city life and were beholden to the dominant machine for favors, jobs or charitable acts. In exchange for these material inducements, the machine expected, and generally obtained, the vote of the worker, his family, and relatives. Moreover, some members of these immigrant groups viewed the political machine as a means of obtaining social recognition and as a vehicle for advancement in the American system when barriers were raised in other areas. Thus the Irish, Italians, and others found city politics a means of social and financial, as well as political, advancement.

Merchants, businessmen, utilities, and in fact, practically anyone who had to deal with the city government, were often silent partners in the machine's operations. Contributions and donations, voluntary or involuntary, from these sources provided the funds that supported the political organizations and their many activities. In addition, the machine was often silently allied with the underworld elements of the community. Police, city and party officials would be paid off by the criminal interests for lax or non-enforcement of the laws.

Although machines came under repeated attack from reform groups—newspapers, writers, even the courts—nevertheless, they were able to survive until the 1930's when a series of events took place which, cumulatively, either destroyed or badly mangled the old style political machine.

The passage of a new immigration law in the 1920's drastically reduced the number of foreign-born coming into the cities. Since machines had traditionally appealed to these people, their absence was sorely felt. Moreover, the older immigrant and the Negro were becoming less dependent upon the organization as they became accustomed to urban life. New groups, particularly labor unions, were arising in the cities and were claiming a loyalty and allegiance which formerly was given only to the political party. Then, too, reforms in election procedures were enacted in state after state, thus making it much more difficult for machines to rig elections. In many cities, election reform was coupled with the adoption of non-partisan local elections which had the effect of eliminating the major political parties from the ballot. Newspapers, often the originators of non-partisanship, reinforced the idea of political independence by stressing a "vote for the man, not the party" concept.

More important, yet supplementing the impact of these other factors, was the adoption during the 1930's of the New Deal social welfare programs. Social security, unemployment compensation, wages and hours legislation, aid to dependent children, public assistance, and many more measures had the effect of reducing the dependency of city people on the machine for charity, jobs or the dole. Instead, these laws tended to foster the attitude of looking toward *government* rather than the political party for services and help. As a citizen, one was entitled to these benefits as a matter of right. He need not trade off his vote for a favor handed out by the local political leader.

By themselves, the various social welfare programs might not have broken the hold machines had on their supporters. However, the prosperity engendered by World War II and maintained in the post-war era permitted thousands of city dwellers to escape from the poverty that kept them dependent on the machine. Prosperity, combined with all the travelling of war time America, gave large numbers of people the means and the mobile experience to sever old patterns of living. And thus, from the late 1940's down to the present day, we have seen the steady migration of city dwellers to the suburbs.

In retrospect, many of the conditions that made the political machine so successful and powerful have disappeared from the American political scene. Political organizations in the cities had to either adjust to these new environments or face extinction. In the 1940's and 1950's we saw the last of the Crump machine in Memphis, the Hague machine in Jersey City, Curley in Boston, Kelly-Nash in Chicago, and Prendergast in Kansas City. Yet political organizations still operate in some of our greatest cities headed by such men as Daley in Chicago and Barr in Pittsburgh.

In our metropolitan politics, candidates rarely get elected on their own. There is the need for professionals: in this case, professional politicians. But the professionals who control the city organizations today are a different breed of leaders because politics in the mid 1960's is different from that of the 1930's or at the turn of the century. Political organizations are more complex, more business-like in their procedures and operations in order to cope with the greater sophistication of the voter and with the new issues and problems. Urban renewal, mass transit, school desegregation, air pollution, housing discrimination, and industrial redevelopment are contemporary problems that do not lend themselves to old style patronage politics. Party leaders increasingly have to hire pollsters and statisticians to find out voter wants and public relations experts to plan campaigns. Moreover, outsiders are often consulted to obtain expert advice and assistance in drafting programs and policy stands dealing with these new issues. Personal popularity is still important, as the successes of Mayor Lee in New Haven, Mayor Lindsay in New York, and Mayor Cowger in Louisville bear witness, but the trend appears to be away from the old-time personal machines exemplified by Hague in Jersey City or Thompson in Chicago. Yet, mayors, councilmen, and other local officials have to be elected; therefore, parties have to organize to win these elections.

Organizational Politics. The extent and scope of the organized effort will vary from city to city. In most metropolitan communities, one or both of the major political parties will control the politics, exercising what amounts to a monopoly over the political process. Yet within the parties, power may be factionalized, divided up among a number of leaders, each with his own following. In other cities, the Republican and Democratic parties share their political influences with non-organizational political clubs such as are active in New York and California. They vie with non-party groups such as civic leagues or business associations which, in some cases, are as well organized for political action as any party. In many of the smaller cities, by contrast, politics is a sporadic, part-time activity, centered on a five or six week campaign, and emphasizing individual or small group effort.

City parties, like American parties in general, are organized so as to carry out their prime function—to win elections. Parties are structured to concentrate their strength and influence at the points in the governmental system where public offices must be filled by election. In essence the party structure runs parallel to the governmental structure.

At the citywide level there usually exists a party committee, headed by a chairman, and composed of a varying number of members representing the different sections of the community, called wards. The main job of this city committee is to select candidates for citywide office, plan the campaign, raise the money and coordinate the efforts of subordinate party units. In some cities, a small group, variously called the central or executive committee, will share in the decision-making under the chairman's guidance. Or the chairman himself, in some places, will run a "one man show," rarely consulting the executive or even the city committee.

Below the city committee in the party structure are the ward organizations and then the precinct committeemen and committeewomen. In each of the election districts, or precincts, one man and one woman are appointed by the party leaders, or elected by the party members, to represent the organization in that area. The job of the committee member has no set boundaries, but generally it is expected that he (and she) will be the direct contact between the voters in the district (especially those registered in his party) and the party organization. Precinct members circulate petitions, implement registration and "get out the vote" drives, pass the word among the party faithful, keep the leaders informed of events and opinions in the district, do favors for the people and act as their intermediaries with the party and government. The objective of all this activity is to round up as many votes for their party's candidate as possible. To facilitate the work of the precinct committee men and women in the larger cities, a loyal party member is assigned one or two blocks of houses. These "block workers" report to the precinct committee and thus provide a close contact with the rank and file voter.

All the precinct men and women in the ward comprise the ward committee which is generally led by a chairman or ward leader. The ward organization is most concerned about ward politics such as the selection of councilmen, justices of the peace or other offices whose constituency encompasses the ward. The Ward Chairman coordinates the citywide campaign with the ward and precinct activities.

The theory of party organization is to have a party worker in direct contact with as many voters as possible and to have a definite chain of responsibility. This is the ideal situation, but very few city organizations have ever achieved this level of perfection. More often than not, the party has trouble filling all its precinct committee posts. In 1964, some 18 months after the time for filling committee positions had passed, the Republican party in Pittsburgh still had over 300 vacant precinct assignments. Moreover, the turnover of personnel at this level of political action is extraordinarily high. Again, using the Pittsburgh area as an example, the Democratic party, in power for over 30 years and noted for its organizational strength, installed 38 new chairmen out of 165 in the county and 700 new committee members out of 2500 when it met in 1966 to reorganize. This turnover occurred in a two-year period.

To the outsider, and perhaps, to the minority party, the organization may appear to function smoothly and efficiently. However, internally there may be a considerable amount of bickering and fighting for power and advantages within the organizations. Sometimes these intra-party battles carry over into the primary and leave deep wounds that fail to heal by general election day, thus causing the defeat of one or two of the organization's candidates. Parts of the organization, though not openly contesting for leadership, still may give only lip service to the orders from the city leader.

In short, the locus of power within the party organization varies from city to city. In the Philadelphia Democratic party, under the leadership of the late Congressman William Green, the important decisions, the real power, was concentrated at the top of the organization. In other cities, such as Boston, power may rest at the ward or regional level. The Democratic organization in Pittsburgh exhibits a different pattern with power dispersed at various party levels, but key decisions were made by the late Mayor and Governor David L. Lawrence.

Non-partisanship. In a number of communities, elections are conducted without reference to national party labels. In these so-called non-partisan elections, candidates run on their own, with just their names and, perhaps, addresses on the ballot, or, as in some cities, with the labels of local political groups. Over 60 per cent of cities in the United States with populations over 5000 have non-partisan local elections. Although non-partisan elections are found in all sections of the country, the highest concentration is in the Mid-West and Plains states and the lowest in the Middle Atlantic and New England areas. Non-partisan elections are also associated with the council-manager form of government, some 85 per cent of the manager governments having them. It is not surprising that such a close relationship exists, since both non-partisan elections and manager government were a part of the reform movement which had a significant impact on local politics during the first two decades of the twentieth century.

The absence of national party labels on the ballots does not necessarily mean the elimination of partisan politics. In some localities that operate non-partisan systems, there is no real difference in the manner of campaigning. In fact, one astute observer of local politics, Professor Charles R. Adrian, has identified four types of non-partisan elections.[4]

In the first type, the local candidates run without the Republican or Democratic party labels. However, it is well-known by the citizens that the regular party organizations are supporting local candidates and they associate the various candidates with the regular parties. In such cities—Chicago is a good example—only candidates identified with the major parties stand a chance of winning. There is no substantial difference between this type of non-partisan election and an openly partisan system. Candidates and office-holders are recognized by the voters, and behave in their public activity, as a part of the regular party organization.

Under the second type of non-partisan election the candidates run without party labels, but are supported by various political groups which may or may not include the local wings of the major parties. Open campaigning is engaged in by the groups who stand a degree of responsibility for the candidates they back. Cincinnati presents a current example of this type. The Republican and Democratic parties contest for power, but the dominant political force is the City Charter Committee of Cincinnati, usually called the Charter Party.

In the third type, local candidates are supported by local groups—businessmen's associations, chambers of commerce, civic groups, citizens' organizations—often in alliance with the local newspaper. The

---

[4] Charles R. Adrian, *Governing Urban America* (New York: McGraw-Hill, Inc., 2nd Ed., 1961), pp. 101–102.

regular party organizations have little to do with the local campaign, primarily because the voters are indifferent or even hostile to their efforts. The local groups take the lead in organizing slates of candidates, electioneering for them, providing money and manpower, yet these groups assume little or no responsibility for the actions of the endorsed candidates who win. In fact, these groups may shift their support from election to election, perhaps actually opposing candidates supported in a prior election. Dallas, Fort Worth and Cambridge, Massachusetts are examples of this type of system.

The fourth type of non-partisan election probably comes closest to the ideal the reformers had in mind when they introduced non-partisan elections. No party labels appear on the ballot and neither political parties nor interest groups play an important role in the elections. Candidates are "self-starters," pushing their own qualifications for office. They organize their own supporters, depending upon friends, relatives, neighbors, or acquaintances for financial and campaign help. Whatever organized effort evolves is strictly for campaign purposes and it hardly survives the one campaign. If the successful candidate runs for re-election, he generally has to go through the same organizing process and headaches again, starting from scratch. This type of non-partisan politics is quite common throughout the country, especially in smaller communities.

Non-partisan elections were a reform injected into local politics to curb some of the abuses of political machines, but behind the immediate objective was a philosophy of local government. In its simplest form, this philosophy likened city government to a business. The Council was the Board of Directors; the City Manager, the operating head; and the voters were the "customers." Therefore, city government should be run like a business—efficiently, economically, quietly. Partisan politics just didn't fit into this scheme because parties were considered a source of corruption, a cause of inefficiency and a center of contention. The solution was to eliminate parties from local politics. "Vote for the man, not the party" became the rallying cry of the reformers and removing party labels facilitated this ideal.

It is difficult to assess the impact of non-partisan elections on local politics. The fact that almost two-thirds of our cities have one form or another of these elections is proof that they have altered the older pattern of politics. However, sufficient evidence exists to demonstrate that by and of itself non-partisanship is no cure-all for corrupt or even inefficient government. Merely to switch from partisan to non-partisan politics will not automatically change the character of local government.

Except in the smaller communities, a candidate "completely on his own" is rare; thus some group takes the lead in recruiting persons to run for public office. In partisan cities, the party leaders perform this function, but in the non-partisan cities, the task is taken on by civic clubs, businessmen's associations, newspapers, or unions. The

backing of one or another of these organizations is often essential to
success at the polls.

SIGNIFICANT ELEMENTS IN URBAN POLITICS

One of the persistent questions making the rounds of the local taverns,
luncheon clubs, fraternal societies, and even women's bridge clubs is
"who really runs this town?" To be sure, the taproom patrons, businessmen, and country club set know that there are such local officials as
mayors, councilmen, supervisors, and commissioners. Also they are
reasonably well-informed of the law and practice which gives these
public officers the authority to make decisions. Yet there is that nagging
suspicion that the real, crucial decisions are made by someone, or
some small group, operating behind the scenes.

The same question is asked by social scientists who specialize in
studying local politics. Only in their case, they talk about "community
influentials" who play a significant role in the "community power
structure." Whether the question is asked in the local barbershop or
in the scholarly journals, the purpose is the same—to identify those
persons whose opinions and desires carry the greatest weight in the
making of governmental decisions.

At the outset we should remember that local officials are part of
an ongoing political and social system. They do not exist or make
decisions in a vacuum, shut off from outside influences or information.
To the contrary, public officials belong to a multitude of groups—
political, social, religious, fraternal, and business. They have a variety
of backgrounds, experiences and associations which tend to affect their
judgments, consciously or unconsciously. Moreover, there are individuals, as well as groups, who deliberately try to influence governmental decisions.

As we stressed earlier in this study, public policies often emerge
out of the competition among groups and individuals. But this does
not necessarily mean that some "unseen hand" pulls the strings behind
the local officials. The real problem for the interested citizens or re-
searcher is to identify those groups and individuals active in local
politics and then attempt to measure how much influence they exert
over a community's affairs. Equally important is a determination of
why these influentials, as they are often called, want to exercise this
influence over the making of public policy.

It may be easier to find the reasons why people want to influence
governments than to actually measure their influence. A person may
try to convince the local authorities of the wisdom of a certain course
of action because he will directly benefit from this policy. Thus a
local contractor may urge the city to build a water or sewer line to
a particular section of the community where he owns property. He
will argue that it will be good for the city—improve fire protection,

stimulate home-building, add assessments to the tax rolls. Unmentioned, of course, would be the possibilities that he would build the water line and the value of his property would be increased.

Of course, the motives of those most interested in many of the local government issues are not so easily identified.

LOCAL GROUPS IN LOCAL POLITICS

One of the distinguishing characteristics of American politics is the number of private groups which share political influence with political parties. Private associations which in some way attempt to influence public officials or the course of public policy are called political interest groups or pressure groups.

A wide variety of interest groups exist at the local level. Some are branches of state or national organizations, such as the Chamber of Commerce or the local union. Others are purely local creations, such as the Crescent Hills Improvement Association. These groups vary in the size of their membership, financial resources, the quality of leadership, objectives, and, of course, in the influence which they exert on local decision-makers. Some of the more significant local groups would include the following.

Business Groups. Although a diversity of business associations characterizes our state and national politics, this is not the situation at the local level of government. Generally, the Chamber of Commerce, the Board of Trade or Merchants' Association acts as the spokesman for local business interests. Usually such groups are dominated by the local merchants and real estate dealers, especially in the smaller communities. In the large cities, such organizations will have a much broader membership.

The business interests are primarily concerned with such policies as zoning, keeping the tax rate down, cutting government expenditures, sprucing up the downtown shopping area and attracting new residents and businesses into the city, provided, of course, this activity won't cost too much money. In communities with non-partisan elections, business groups play an important role in local politics, even to the extent of recruiting and supporting candidates for local office. For many years the business groups in Los Angeles and Detroit were major factors in the local politics of these two cities.

However, businessmen or business groups, are not in total agreement on what they want from government. In a large city, for example, the merchants in one section may be agitating very strongly for the construction of a city stadium in their locality, whereas other business groups may be just as intensely opposed to such a plan. Or the downtown Chamber of Commerce may try to convince the city fathers of the need for high speed, limited access highways emptying into their shopping district while chambers of commerce on the fringes of the city may not take too kindly to this proposal, if it would draw customers away from their stores.

A few specific types of business merit special mention. Contractors are an active force locally not only because they might be interested in contracts for paving or building, but also because of the manner in which the local authorities enforce plumbing, safety, zoning, and building regulations. Real estate dealers are another group which keeps a watchful eye on the town hall. They are concerned about taxes, zoning, keeping out "undesirable" elements and generally maintaining or improving the so-called "image" of the city. As an aftermath of the riots in Watts, Detroit, and other cities, real-estate interests are concerned over riot control, fair housing and slum rental legislation.

Another local business group that takes a continuing interest in local affairs is the liquor dealer—tavern owner, beer distributors, liquor retailers, hotel and restaurant owners. Whether liquor will be sold in the community is a decision frequently left to local voters or officials. Moreover, the enforcement of liquor regulations such as closing hours or serving minors comes under the jurisdiction of the local police. Liquor interests generally have most to fear from local authorities and local public opinion; thus, they are constantly alert to changes in opinion or in public policy.

Labor Organizations. Labor's role in local politics is hard to assess. Basically, labor's political efforts are focused on national and state politicians and policies. Most of the issues that affect labor directly and deeply are fought out and decided at these levels of government. Moreover, a unionist as taxpayer, homeowner, demander of services is undistinguishable from his neighbors. Nevertheless, labor organizations do attempt to influence local politics and are particularly active in the larger cities.

In the main, labor's objectives at the local level tend to be broad and general rather than specifically labor-oriented. Thus they support such programs as public housing, expansion of social services, public transportation, recreational facilities and equal job opportunities. Within their own ranks, support for such policies at the local level is often lukewarm since, as taxpayers, they would have to pay for these services. Perhaps the only distinctly local labor issues would be support for the unionization of municipal employees and the placing of limitations upon the local police in labor-management disputes.

In smaller communities, labor groups, if any exist, appear to have only minimal importance, unless the community is a workingman's suburb where union politics is taken seriously. In the metropolitan cities, labor leaders and their organizations may be key members in the political power structure because of their vote potential. Labor groups endorse candidates for mayor, council, county commissioner, and other local offices. They supply financial and manpower assistance to their favored candidates. Since the 1930's, labor unions have become closely allied with Democratic party organizations in most of the big cities. In fact, for a number of years in Detroit it was difficult to determine any difference between the United Automobile Workers organization and the local Democratic party organization. The close ties of labor with the Democratic party tend to give labor leaders an important voice in party circles, especially in making nominations. Yet this advantage has its drawbacks since it reduces labor's influence in the Republican party and handicaps its policy goals whenever Republicans gain control of the government.

Government Employees. The men and women who work for local governments are among the most aware and active groups in a community. Since their jobs depends upon the wishes of the city fathers, they must be attuned to local politics.

If the patronage system is the accepted practice, then municipal employees tend to be essential cogs in the dominant political organizations. They are expected to do all that is typical of political activists—persuading friends and neighbors, electioneering, and contributing to the party treasury. If a merit or civil service system is in vogue, then municipal employees are expected to refrain from any overt political action. These laws, however, do not prevent them from making known their views in a private, personal, informal manner. Moreover, the employees have regular, or irregular, means of bringing their demands to the attention of the mayor and council. Increasingly local government employees are joining unions, either of their craft specialty, such as plumbers and electricians, or the general municipal governmental employees unions. Government employees, whether unionized or not, are interested in wages, working hours and conditions, fringe benefits, pensions, and promotion policies. If the employees can achieve their goals through the regular grievance channels, union negotiations or enlightened management decisions, they will probably stay out of open politics. If none of these channels are available or prove inadequate, they may try direct political action by supporting candidates, holding demonstrations or even going on strike.

Service, Social, and Veterans Organizations. The number of fraternal, service, social and veterans groups is almost beyond description. Lions, Elks, Masons, Knights of Columbus, American Legion, Rotary, Odd Fellows, Veterans of Foreign Wars, Moose are a mere sampling of such organizations. Not all are active politically. In fact, most of these groups make a point of proclaiming their non-political nature. Yet the very fact that they are organized and led by human beings sometimes involves them in local politics.

A service organization may take on a project such as beautifying the town or adding fluoride to the water. Knowingly or unknowingly, members may find themselves in the middle of a political controversy when another group, candidate, or officeholder takes the opposing view. Service and social groups do not like to be placed in this position, and, if caught in the middle, try as gracefully as they can to extricate themselves. More frequently local organizations may use bingo, lotteries, raffles, or even pinball and slot machines to finance part of their activities. Necessarily such groups are concerned about public and police attitudes toward these activities.

Often local organizations get dragged into local politics unwittingly. For example, politicians tend to be joiners, belonging to three, four, even five local groups. It's perhaps second nature for a politician to do a little politicking among his fellow club members and it is equally natural for a member to give his colleague a vote. Also bear in mind that there is a high degree of overlapping membership among fraternal, social, service and veterans' organizations. A person may belong to the Rotary, Legion, Elks, and Masons. He may be an officer in one or more groups. Thus a relatively small group of men may run practically every organization in town.

In small communities, one frequently hears that a potential candidate must belong to this or that organization before he will get anywhere in politics. Or that you must be a Rotarian, Elk, or Knight because that particular organization controls things. Sometimes these statements are true for a particular community, but it is difficult to generalize for all communities, since we know so little about the actual influence of these groups.

Racial, Ethnic and Religious Groups. Big cities are notorious in their manipulation of minorities for political ends. In cities such as New York, Boston, Philadelphia, Chicago, and Los Angeles, all sorts of national, church, and racial associations exist, and most become involved in politics in one way or another. Sons of Italy, Hibernian Society, Polish Alliance, Urban League, Holy Name Society, Ministerial Association, National Association for the Advancement of Colored People, B'nai B'rith, CORE, Council of Churches, Knights of Equity are merely a few of these groups which are sometimes active on the local scene.

Campaigning among minority groups is a necessary but questionable activity in cities. One has to attend the various affairs, but is never quite sure how many votes he picks up. I recall sitting through a long, two-hour program of a national group merely to get a five second introduction. Or on another occasion, we had more candidates at an ethnic picnic than picnickers. Like party affairs, a picnic may not gain votes for the candidate when he attends, but he may lose votes by not showing up.

Many ethnic and racial groups are interested in such public policies as equal job opportunities, civil rights, fair housing, adequate services, and police protection. Church organizations are often concerned with these same problems. In addition, the Local Ministerial Association may press for strict enforcement of the gambling and liquor laws or the Sunday closing of retail stores.

Political parties have long recognized the value of large blocs of potential voters represented by these minority groups. Leaders of nationality or racial groups were absorbed into the party hierarchy and were consulted in the arranging of local tickets. It is common practice for the parties in New York City to slate an Irish-Catholic or Italian, Negro or Jew for the top offices of Mayor, Controller and President of the Council. A student at the University of Pittsburgh composed the following doggerel to describe the ticket-making for City Council by Pittsburgh Democrats:

THE COUNCIL
Our machine is Catholic, effective, and strong
But answer we must the Protestant throng.
Five seats for us, one for a Jew,
Two for the WASPS, add a Negro, too.

The purpose of slate-making is to get as many groups as possible behind the entire ticket in order to win the election. Smaller cities and towns may not have such diversity of groups as exist in the core cities. Yet one or two ethnic or church organizations may play an important role in certain kinds of public decisions.

Reform Organizations. A persistent and colorful feature of American local politics is the frequency with which reform groups rise to challenge the dominant political organizations. Reform groups are composed of well-meaning, interested citizens, usually from the middle class, with a scattering of representation from the prominent citizenry echelon. Reformers usually want to throw the rascals out of city hall, obtain new leadership and institute certain changes in the administration of local affairs.

What arouses the reformer's ire varies from town to town. It may be a gradual deterioration of services over a period of years or the declining caliber of the people running the community's affairs. The fuse that sets off a reform movement might be an election fraud or city scandal. Citizens may become angered at evidence which suggests that graft and corruption are rampant within the local government. Under such circumstances the chances are that criminal interests—gambling, vice, narcotics—are in collusion with the local authorities, perhaps paying them off for lax law enforcement. Down through the history of local government, various cities have had a sorry chapter of graft and corruption and Phenix City, Alabama and Newport, Kentucky are but two recent examples.

Whatever touches off the reform movement, citizens organize, mount a publicity campaign, try to enlist the help of local communications media, persuade prominent men and women to run for local office and wage the campaigns. If conditions are right and ripe, the reformers may defeat several incumbents in the next election. Usually, it takes years before the reform group is able to topple the dominant organizations. Sometimes the reformers work within one or the other major parties, usually the majority party because they have the power.

The downfall of reform movements comes from their lack of staying power. Unless the group achieves a few successes early in the game, interest on the part of the rank and file tends to waver, leaders drop out, financing becomes more difficult, newspapers become bored, and recruitment falters. Even if the group is successful and captures control of the city administration, it may have trouble keeping up the drive and enthusiasm over a period of years. Leaders die or return to their businesses, people lose interest, officeholders become ambitious and the old guard politicians keep up a constant pressure. Philadelphia provides a good example of the short tenure of reform administrations. of its leaders, Joseph Clark went on from Mayor of Philadelphia to the U.S. Senate, James Finnegan became Adlai Stevenson's campaign manager and Richard Dilworth resigned as Mayor to run for Governor. In the matter of a few years, reformers were displaced in the Democratic party and the late Congressman William Green built one of the most effective and powerful city political organizations on the foundations laid by the reformers.

Reform groups, however, have left a lasting imprint on local government. Their successes in the past, and the relative ease in forming new groups pose sufficient threat to the parties and public officials as to set limits upon their indiscretions. In addition, some reform organizations have institutionalized their activities as sort of watch-dog research agencies. Taxpayers leagues, municipal leagues, civic clubs are examples of these groups. The Committee of Seventy has had a long career in Philadelphia as a watch-dog of City Hall. Though not exactly a reform organization, the League of Women Voters often times performs this function in many small communities. The heritage of good government left by reform groups is long and impressive—honest election procedures, civil service, council-manager form of government, direct legislation, competitive bidding and many other reforms in local administration procedures.

Communication Media. Communications are important to the political process. Leaders of all organizations have to use the various communication channels to reach their audiences. Newsletters, pamphlets, telephone, or bulletins may suffice to carry information and orders to the activists, but to reach the general public these leaders must turn to the commercial communications media. During a campaign, political groups can buy space in newspapers or buy time on radio and television. But to purchase publicity on a year-around basis would be outrageously expensive and beyond the means of practically all groups.

Thus the commercial communications media perform a vital role in bringing to the citizen body news, facts and interpretations of political events. Yet the media differ in their impact. Television and radio have become key campaign tools for political parties and candidates, even at the local level of politics. The brief 15, 20, or 30 second "spot announcement" is featured in these campaigns. However, as molders of public opinion, radio and television generally have little influence. Their role here is that of a purveyor and narrator of facts, usually brief.

Newspapers are a different story. Political ads placed by candidates and parties carry little weight, yet as the disseminator and interpreter of news, newspapers may have great influence in a community. Editorial endorsements in themselves are not influential, unless they are reinforced by a constant campaign of praise or criticism in the other pages of the paper. Publishers and editors can help or hurt a candidate (or party) according to the way they treat him in the paper. They can play up or tone down a particular event; they can give one candidate more and better coverage (first page, pictures, features) and ignore or bury his opponent in the back pages; they can distort or slant the news by the choice of headlines, adjectives, photographs. Of course, not all newspapers do these things; many give fair treatment to all sides and candidates; yet there is sufficient evidence from the entire country to document the charge of favoritism.

The effectiveness of newspapers in the political process is difficult to measure. In national and state elections over the past 30 years, newspapers have generally favored the Republican party, yet their opposition has not greatly damaged the Democrats. Local politics is another thing. With the emphasis on personalities and the concentration on one or two specific issues, local newspapers can affect the result of an election. The continual harassment of a local official or party may, in time, swing public opinion. Also newspapers are great propagandists for "vote for the man, not the party" concept, thus fostering split-ticket voting. Occasionally a newspaper will support a reform group and use its substantial power to defeat the incumbent machine. Newspapers, perhaps, have their greatest impact in influencing the public on issues. Here the average voter may have very little to guide him since the issue may be complex, his party has not taken a clear stand, or he has not bothered to learn about the issue. A newspaper campaign for conservation, elimination of stream pollution, or reform of the local courts may generate widespread public support. Also the voter may look to the newspaper for guidance in voting on a bond referendum or proposed city charter.

IMPORTANCE OF URBAN POLITICS

Americans live under several levels of government—national, state, county, city or town, and a multiplicity of special districts. The politics at each level of government is important in its own right, but in addition, each is interrelated with the politics and political outcomes of the other systems of authority. The politics of a particular city or suburb may be unique, yet that community's politics becomes an essential element in state and national politics.

Although urban politics has long been recognized as a factor on the national political scene, its role has assumed significant proportions since the 1930's Professor Samuel J. Eldersveld, in a detailed analysis of urban voters, emphasized the crucial part which they played in the Democratic presidential victories from 1932 through 1948.[5]

The Democratic coalition under Franklin D. Roosevelt during the 1930's had as one of its mainstays the heavy turnout of voters in the urban communities. It was the urban areas, combined with certain farm states, that accounted for Harry S. Truman's victory in 1948. In response to this overwhelming support, both Roosevelt and Truman initiated a number of programs which benefited cities and the people living in them. Direct aid to the cities hard pressed by the depression, WPA, PWA, CCC, housing and mortgage assistance, public works, and many more programs helped urban areas.

The importance of urban politics was further demonstrated in the election of Republican Dwight D. Eisenhower to the presidency in 1952 and 1956. It was the defection of large numbers of urbanites, from the cities as well as the suburbs, that gave General Eisenhower substantial majorities.

The 1960 presidential election probably provided the most dramatic example of urban influence on national politics. John F. Kennedy outpolled Richard M. Nixon by the small margin of 112,803 votes out of a total of some 69 million cast, yet Kennedy accumulated 303 electoral votes and Nixon only 219. The key to Kennedy's victory was his winning the urban states, especially New York, New Jersey, Pennsylvania, Illinois, Massachusetts, and Michigan, in some cases by rather small majorities. Further analysis reveals that Kennedy's winning margins in these states came from the large turnout of voters in New York City, Chicago, Detroit, and other cities. The importance of urban areas in Kennedy's election is typified by the electoral behavior of voters in Pennsylvania's two great cities, Philadelphia and Pittsburgh. Kennedy's state majority was 116,326 while carrying 15 of the 67 counties. Philadelphia gave him a majority of 331,544 votes and Pittsburgh 91,470 votes.

The Congress has also felt the impact of urban wants, demands, and aspirations. Unlike many state legislatures, (at least until recent times) the national legislature has reacted more quickly and positively

---

[5] Samuel J. Eldersveld, "The Influence of Metropolitan Party Pluralities in Presidential Elections Since 1920: A Study of Twelve Key Cities," *The American Political Science Review* (December, 1949), p. 1206.

to population shifts. As urban areas grew in size and population, they were allocated more representatives, often at the expense of rural counties. With greater representation there came a greater urban influence in party councils and in the attention paid to urban problems. The close liaison that developed between cities and the federal government during the 1930's in the fight against the hardships of the depression was strengthened during the war years, and became firmly established in the 1950's and 1960's as the emphasis shifted to minority group politics. The congressional response to urban politics has been the passage of legislation dealing with schools, mass transportation, pollution, housing, redevelopment, health, and civil rights.

Local governments have always had a large stake in the politics of their states. Simple self-protection is often the motivating force behind their concern, since local governments are legal creations of the state. Within broad limits set by state constitutional provisions, state governments possess almost complete authority over local units of government. Legislatures confer powers and duties and, in turn, may restrict or limit the activities of these localities. Thus a law passed by the state legislature, or an action, or even omission, by the governor could have a serious and lasting impact on any community.

In the past, especially during the latter part of the nineteenth century, state legislatures often abused their powers over local governments. Special laws were passed which singled out a particular town or city for preferential treatment. In several states the legislature changed the form of a city's government even over the objections of local officials and citizens. The worst of these abuses were corrected by reform legislation and constitutional amendments prohibiting the legislature from passing special acts affecting only one or a few towns.

Considerable power over local governments still is vested in the state legislatures. Recently the Pennsylvania state assembly passed a law requiring all Third Class Cities in the state to pay their policemen a specific minimum salary, regardless of a city's ability to finance such salaries.

In order to protect themselves and to keep themselves informed of what's going on at the state capitol, the cities, towns, townships and counties have formed state-wide associations. League of Cities, State Associations of Townships Commissioners, State Association of Boroughs are the names of some of these groups which have lobbyists representing their respective interests before the legislature and administrative agencies. The largest cities in a state, such as New York City or Philadelphia, often have their own lobbyist working full time.

In addition to the state legislature, the various state administrative departments—health, education, highways, labor, industry—have authority to make decisions, rules and regulations that vitally affect local governments. To cite a few common examples—a state department's decision to construct an expressway through the best residential section of the city or its decision to have a new highway by-pass a town; or the health department's order to a local community to build a sewage treatment plant.

Urban communities are particularly concerned about what transpires in the state capitol because in many states the government was dominated by the rural segment of the population. Urban dwellers often felt that their problems were ignored and their needs rejected without adequate consideration. A major breakthrough for increased urban influence in state affairs came from the voting strength concentrated in cities and suburbs. In the election of statewide officers, particularly governor, urban political organizations could exact promises and commitments in exchange for their support. As the urban vote became critical, governors and prospective governors tended to gear their programs to the demands and needs of urban inhabitants. Though the state's chief executive could not initiate legislative policies without the legislature's cooperation, nevertheless, he had certain weapons, such as the veto or threat of a veto, to prevent the more flagrant anti-urban laws. Moreover, as head of the administrative branch, an urban-oriented governor could direct his subordinates to administer or interpret the rules and regulations in a favorable manner toward cities and suburbs.

However, it is only in the 1960's that urban areas have secured the measure of influence and power in state legislatures to which their populations would entitle them. Many legislatures were controlled by representatives and senators from rural counties. Rural domination reflected the fact that the United States was once a rural nation. State constitutions and legislative apportionments passed in the nineteenth century, perhaps fair then, became imbalanced as people flowed into the cities and suburbs. State legislatures refused to reapportion themselves so as to give the developing urban centers their fair share of representation. As time passed, the population gap between legislative districts became greater and greater. Urban districts often had three, five or even ten times as many people as resided in some rural districts. In Tennessee, for example, one urban district had 23 times as many people as did the smallest legislative district which was rural.

Unless the legislature reapportioned itself, there appeared to be no legal way to force them to do this task. Governors were without power and the many attempts to have state and federal courts intervene met with failure. The situation was reaching crisis proportions, since some states were operating under apportionments based on the populations of 1910, 1900, or even earlier. Finally, in 1962 the United States Supreme Court decided the case of *Baker* v. *Carr*, which became a landmark in American government. In brief, the Supreme Court said that federal courts would now hear suits involving state apportionment laws and those which were unreasonable, arbitrary, or discriminatory would be declared unconstitutional. Immediately the federal courts were flooded with cases from all over the country. In a series of decisions, federal courts, led by the Supreme Court, struck down state apportionment laws and ordered new constitutional and legislative apportionment procedures. State courts also began to insist on fair and equitable apportionments. In 1964, in the case of *Reynolds* v. *Sims,* the U.S. Supreme Court added another important requirement—that both houses of the legislature be apportioned according to population.

It is too soon to predict the long range impact of recent state legislative apportionments. The immediate effect has been to increase urban representation which should, in time, give the legislature more influence in determining state policies and programs.

The importance of local politics to local citizens is almost self-evident. At the outset, the extent of citizen participation in the political processes creates a climate within which public business will be conducted. A high degree of apathy and disinterest could lead to low levels of turnout and create political conditions tolerant of machine rule. If a widespread feeling of disinterest prevails, then political parties or citizens groups may experience difficulties in recruiting candidates to run for public office. The people who do offer themselves may not be the most competent or able. An active, aware and interested electorate, though not necessarily guaranteeing good government, nevertheless forces parties and groups to recruit candidates of above average ability.

The outcome from local political struggles is to give certain individuals and groups vast power and wide discretion in the use of this power. Some have used the power unwisely; a number, corruptly; many others, incompetently. We have mentioned how some city leaders used their control to build up powerful political organizations based on patronage to party workers and favors to selected supporters. In some communities, primarily small towns, the political environment allocates to the town's elected officials a monopoly over public policy decision-making. In the larger communities, this function is shared with a variety of private groups or individuals who are concerned with different aspects of urban living—schools, housing, zoning, civil rights, renewal, and redevelopment.

Indirectly through the political process, and sometimes directly through the initiative and referendum, the local citizen may give direction to his community's future. In some localities there is little to be done. The townspeople are satisfied with the way things are and there appears to be no public sentiment for change. Maintenance of the *status quo* is the dominant theme. Local experimentation or innovation is discouraged, but where a demand must be met, there may be a tendency to "buck" the problem to another level of government. Social scientists Arthur J. Vidich and Joseph Bensman noted this inclination in their study of a small town in upstate New York.[6]

---

[6] Arthur J. Vidich and Joseph Bensman, *Small Town in Mass Society* (Princeton, New Jersey: Princeton University Press, 1958).

In contrast, other local officials may come to a decision to deliberately upset the established order for the purpose of moving the community ahead. Thus in Pittsburgh in the post World War II era, city leaders in cooperation with civic and business leaders, initiated and implemented what became known as the Pittsburgh Renaissance. In a continuing program that has been going on for two decades major sections of the city have been completely transformed. The people of Pittsburgh expressed their approval of the direction the city was taking by giving their political and social support to the leaders of the Renaissance movement.

In conclusion, we repeat one of the themes of this essay. The quality of government that Americans receive in their cities, towns, or villages reflects the kind of politics and politicians the community's political traditions nurtured and now tolerate. No institution or law can guarantee quality government. However, the odds are high that the people's business will be transacted fairly, honestly, and competently when there is an alert, interested, and involved body of citizens.

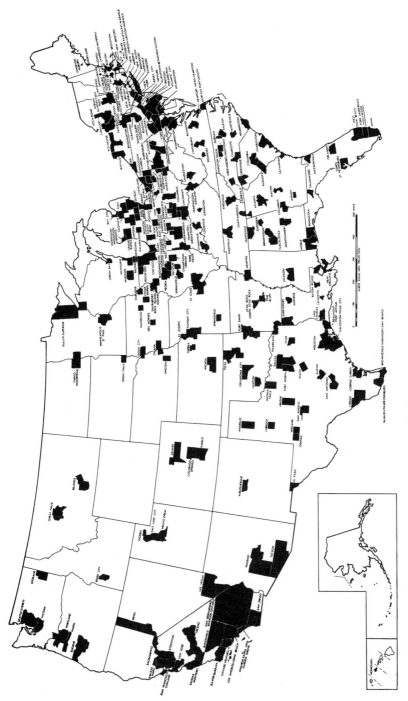

Source: U. S. Department of Commerce, Bureau of the Census.

STANDARD METROPOLITAN STATISTICAL AREAS: 1966

STANLEY J. HINDEN

Stanley J. Hinden is a former political editor of *Newsday* and chief of the *Newsday* bureau in the State Capitol, Albany, New York during annual legislative sessions. He has been on *Newsday's* staff since 1952 has covered political news in Nassau and Suffolk and at state and national levels. He has covered local, state and national political conventions and campaigns (1955–65).

Hinden wrote the twice weekly column "Inside Politics," and numerous news and analytical stories.

Hinden is presently Editor of Editorial Pages, *Newsday*, Garden City, Long Island, New York.

STANLEY J. HINDEN

5. Politics In The Suburbs

THE POLITICAL ACTION MOVES TO SUBURBIA

At night, the lights tell the story. Once they clustered tightly around the cities, small patches of brightness and color on the darkened countryside. Then, they began to spread, ever farther and farther out. Now, their glow lights the once empty farmlands; linking cities and towns and transforming whole regions into a single panorama of light. We call it Megalopolis, U.S.A.

The airline passenger or pilot sees it best. Fly from Washington to Boston on a clear night and the lights are unbroken for 450 miles—from Virginia to New England. Along the way, the cities of Washington, Baltimore, Philadelphia, New York, and Boston have all but lost their boundary lines in the neon glow that has mushroomed between the cities.

It is the same in many parts of the nation. Fly between San Francisco and San Diego; from Madison, Wisconsin to Detroit; from Syracuse, New York to Cleveland or from Dallas to San Antonio; and everywhere the countryside is alive with lights and life.

The lights are the symbol of America's biggest boom—the boom in people. In 1940, we were 132 million Americans. By 1950, we numbered 151 million. In 1960, the census was up again and we were 179 million people. In only 20 years, we grew by 47 million—a population explosion, and well-named.

Americans, by and large, have been going to those places outside the big cities, where once there were quiet villages or small cities, or perhaps just a few farms—to Anaheim, California and Syosset, Long Island—to Hollywood, Florida and St. Louis Park, Minnesota to Enfield, Connecticut and Englewood, Colorado.

95

We call it suburbia. But it also is a new frontier in American life. Like the old frontier, it offers an unusual array of challenges and opportunities to seek a better mode of life and build better communities.

Good government thrives on good politics and in the starting-from-scratch atmosphere of suburbia there is an unparalleled opportunity for Americans to encourage the intelligent conduct of our two-party system. With the old ways of both the city and country left behind, political parties can become what some persons claim they were always meant to be: the forum for all citizens to make the political decisions which eventually determine both the caliber of our office holders and the quality of our government—all the way from school boards to the White House.

The growth of suburban areas has taken place at an astonishing rate. Between 1950 and 1960, the population of America's cities increased by 22 per cent. Our rural population went up by 10 per cent. But the population in the suburbs jumped by 79 per cent. Suburban growth continues at this pace. Some 31 per cent of the people in the United States—55 million—now live in the suburbs.

Suburbia today offers the biggest open door in American history for citizen participation in politics. The proof is in the story of what happened outside of New York City, in the granddaddy of the nation's suburbs, Nassau County, Long Island. Here, a revolution of growth transformed a once sleepy country area into the sixth largest "city" in the nation and a once rock-ribbed Republican county into a political battlefield with a huge, swing-voting population.

On the map of New York State, Nassau County lies across the center of Long Island, the Atlantic Ocean to the south, Long Island Sound to the north. The western half of this fish-shaped island is occupied by the boroughs of Brooklyn and Queens; while the counties of Nassau and Suffolk occupy the eastern half. (See map.)

Brooklyn and Queens are part of the City of New York. Nassau is independently governed, as is Suffolk, one of the original counties of the state. Only a handful of signs mark the line where Queens divides from Nassau, and where New York City divides from the Nassau-Suffolk suburbs—sometimes called "the real Long Island."

The signs are hardly needed. The boundary is far more than a line on a map. It is a state of mind. To a Nassau resident, "the city" represents the standard image of crime-in-the-streets, racial violence, human and vehicular traffic jams; and a daily diet of dust and pollutants. Suburbia, to be sure, has an ever-increasing share of all these problems, but somehow to a Nassau resident, it all seems "different" in the suburbs.

It was in 1899 that Nassau's founding fathers decided they did not want any "entangling alliances" with the city and proceeded to divorce themselves and incorporate a separate county covering 274 square miles. Years later, many of the one million persons who joined the rush to suburban Nassau felt that they, too, no longer wanted any "alliances" with the city. They traded their apartments for six-room "ranch" homes with expansion attics on 60 × 100 plots and willingly accepted big mortgage and tax bills for a bit of grass, a few trees, and the "country" air.

They came to a county which, while small in population, had three important traditions: (1) it was the site of many major developments in the history of aviation, (2) it was the residence of many top society figures and, (3) it was a bastion of basic American Republicanism.

The friendly Republican climate of Nassau which the Morgans and Vanderbilts enjoyed was not of their making. It was the tradition, if not the heritage, of the Nassau "clamdiggers," that group of Anglo-Saxon Protestants who made up the bulk of Nassau's population for more than a half-century. They settled in small villages, along the line of the Long Island Rail Road and many commuted from what was called the "bedroom of the New York City" to Manhattan for business. So firm were the early Nassau residents in support of the Republican party that in the 1932 and 1936 landslides for Democrat Franklin D. Roosevelt, Nassau stayed in the GOP column with barely a waver. Indeed, before the suburban boom years, the Democrats had carried their last countywide offices in 1913.

The tide of change began to wash across Nassau as early as 1940, when the aviation industry, which had been largely dormant during the depression days, began tooling up and expanding for the war that lay ahead. The U. S. census in 1940 set the Nassau population at 406,748. It was still a "country" area. Each neat village had its shopping area, movie theater, and soda shop. Between each village were the woodlands and marshes and farms.

The flood gates opened in 1945. World War II veterans began returning. With them came a huge demand for new housing for their young and growing families. The sound of the bulldozer clearing trees and digging foundations became the theme song for the nation's first and biggest post-war housing boom. For the next 15 years, housing developments sprang up faster than crabgrass. In 1947, under the magic touch of builder William Levitt, 4000 acres of potato farms became the first Levittown, a community of 18,000 homes, 82,000 people, and several huge shopping centers.

The influx brought many crushing problems, none more severe than that of schools. One district, the Island Trees School District, had 26 students in a one-room school house in 1946. In 1966, it had 5860 students in six schools. Not all of Nassau's 62 school districts faced such staggering growth. But virtually every district became familiar with the controversy, bitterness, and intra-community warfare which accompany fast-rising school tax rates. All of Nassau's school districts operate under local control and the school budget remains about the only major item of governmental expense on which the citizen has a direct vote of approval or disapproval.

As the school boards struggled to provide classrooms for the vast influx of students, the battle of the spenders and the savers waxed even hotter. Although school board elections and budget votes are conducted on a non-partisan basis, the school board battles each year have engaged the attention of thousands of citizens—drawing as many rooters and workers as many major political campaigns.

Where the people came, the merchants followed. Macy's told Gimbel's about the big boom and they both headed for Nassau. Soon every New York City department store and chain store had a branch in Nassau.

Light industry grew and some 2100 industrial plants now occupy space in Nassau. The Long Island Rail Road, the world's busiest commuter railroad, still carries 90,000 regular passengers a day to and from work in New York City. But now about 58 per cent of Nassau's residents live and work in Nassau and nearby Suffolk County. "The bedroom of New York" became an integral community. Indeed, almost 100,000 people who live in New York City now come to work on Long Island. Today, if it were a city rather than a collection of incorporated and unincorporated areas, Nassau County would constitute the sixth largest city in the nation, ranking behind only New York, Chicago, Los Angeles, Philadelphia, and Detroit. The 1966 population of Nassau County—1,400,000—put it ahead of Baltimore, Houston, Cleveland, and Washington, D. C.

The word "staggering" perhaps best describes the impact of the suburban boom on the political complexion of Nassau County. The tripling of the county's population over a 25-year period created thousands of new governmental positions, hundreds of new political party positions, and candidates for dozens of new public offices. In this climate of ferment and reorganization, many who came into politics as amateurs stayed to become professionals.

The boom in politics opened the doors to thousands of Nassau suburbanites. For example, in 1940, Nassau County was divided by the county board of elections into 302 election districts or polling places. Under the election law, each election district is served by two Republican and two Democratic committeemen. Thus in 1940, the Republican and Democratic county committees, which are the basic political organizations in Nassau, were each composed of 604 committeemen. By 1967, Nassau County had grown to 903 election districts. With two committeemen for each district, the Republican county committee thus had grown to 1806 members—1202 more than in 1940. The Democratic party registered the same increase—which meant that 2,404 new county committee posts alone have been created, by the Nassau population boom.

In addition, the new political force which swept into Nassau has also created Liberal and Conservative parties in recent years. While neither has a full slate of committeemen, their activity has added another 1,386 committeemen as of 1966. Thus, some 3658 new jobs for political workers have opened.

This figure does not include, of course, such unofficial jobs as block captains, assistant committeemen, junior committeemen, and just plain door bell ringers—all of whom help the regular party committeemen. The normal yearly turnover of political workers also contributes to keeping the political ranks wide open. In addition, political leaders estimate that there are at least five of these workers—mostly during campaign time—for every committeeman—or about 17,000 people serving the Republican and Democratic organizations in each campaign.

Although there is some natural overlapping in functions, the yearly job of manning the polling places on registration and election days is handled by a four-man board at each polling place (two Democrats and two Republicans at about $25 a day each). This means that 3612 polling place jobs are open for loyal party workers three days a year.

In Nassau, the Republicans and Democrats have organized their parties along community lines. Thus, there is a Rockville Centre Republican organization and a GOP organization in Port Washington, in Garden City and every other major community. The committeemen in each community elect a leader or leaders. The Republicans call their leaders executive committeemen. The Democrats call theirs zone leaders. In 1940, the GOP had 62 executive leaders. The Democrats, who were far poorer in manpower, had 24. The 1967 figures show the GOP with 99 and the Democrats with 79. Thus, the political boom opened the door for 92 new key political leadership positions.

The population boom has had its inevitable effect on the number of public offices. In 1942, Nassau County had one congressional seat, which was shared with the adjoining counties of Suffolk and Queens. One state senator represented Nassau and Suffolk together. And

Nassau had two state assemblymen. Thus, the total congressional and state legislative delegation was four men, of whom only two were Nassau residents. In the 1966 elections, Nassau elected five congressmen, five state senators, and 12 assemblymen, for a grand total of 22. For a man or woman interested in seeking congressional or legislative office, suburbia has become a fertile field.

Politics has boomed on all fronts. In 1937, the first important Democratic dinner at $25 a head attracted 400 people. At their 1966 dinner, the Nassau Democrats attracted 1200 people at $100 a head and, together with an advertising journal, grossed $200,000. The Republicans, who had been well enough fixed financially so they had been able to forego the usual county political dinners until recent years, attracted 2000 people to their 1966 dinner at $100 a head, for a $200,000 gross.

Opportunity beckoned, too, for those seeking to work in government. In Nassau County, government workers rose from 4200 in 1940 to 20,000 in 1967, a small indication of the government needs and responsibilities in a growing community.

The story of Nassau County's civic and political growth is being repeated outside of big cities all across the nation. The 1950–1960 population increases in many suburban counties were astounding. Outside of Los Angeles, in Orange County, the population went up by 225 per cent. Arapahoe County, which adjoins Denver, Colorado, increased by 117 per cent. In Florida's Broward County, which includes Ft. Lauderdale, population was up by 297 per cent. Outside of Minneapolis, suburban Anoka County increased its population by 141 per cent in 10 years.

This type of suburban growth has not only opened the doors of politics to millions of Americans, but also it has confronted suburban political parties with a grave challenge. The challenge is the rise of the swing voter, the man or woman who holds no loyalty to any political party and who rapidly is beginning to represent the most important segment of the American electorate. How political parties face up to this challenge will be crucial to the future of the two-party system.

POLITICS IN SUBURBIA—
THE CHALLENGE OF THE SWING VOTER

Most suburbanites are homeowners. Indeed, the house is the basic symbol of suburbia. In Nassau County, 84 per cent of the families own their own homes. But owning a house can be expensive, and it takes a fairly good income for a man to provide his family with a home in the suburbs. There are the monthly mortgage payments: taxes, interest charges, and amortization; bills for heat, electricity, water, and general upkeep. Then, there is the cost of getting to and from work each day by rail or road. Inevitably, the suburbs have become communities populated by middle and upper-middle class Americans who can afford to live there.

Nassau County offers a fairly typical profile of the suburban community. Its population is heavily laced with professional men, business executives, white collar and skilled workers. They bring a touch of affluence to the county. The median income in Nassau in 1960 was $8515 per family, the highest in New York State and one of the highest in the nation. There is one car for every three persons, which means that there is at least one car in almost every family and two cars in 31 per cent of Nassau households. Nassau residents have multiple telephones and a dog in every other home. The county is one of the world's largest markets for baby food, gasoline, grass seed, and crabgrass killers.

Nassau's population is youthful. The median age is only 30.8 years and 34 per cent of Nassau's families have children under six years of age.

The religious and ethnic complexion of the county has undergone great changes. Once populated almost completely by white Protestants, Nassau today is estimated to be 45 per cent Catholic, 27 per cent Jewish, and only 28 per cent Protestant or unaffiliated. But the county is still predominantly white. Negroes make up only 3.2 per cent of the county's total population, a measure of both the economic and racial barriers facing Negroes who seek to move to the suburbs. Nassau residents also are distinguished by relatively high educational levels. Some 55 per cent of Nassau's adults have completed high school, while another 25 per cent have gone on to college. Thus, the average Nassau suburbanite is self-reliant economically and educationally and —as a result—politically as well.

One great irony is that while suburbia has been opening more political doors for average citizens than ever before, it also has been closing many of the traditional doors to political party control. Historically, political parties in the United States have served at least two roles: as the salesmen of ideas and philosophies—and as service organizations.

The bedrock strength of Democratic machines in the big cities such as New York and Chicago long rested on the ability of their political leaders to serve as unofficial—but highly effective—social service agents. It was in the party clubhouse, with the district leader presiding, that the unemployed could find jobs, the unlettered were given legal advice, the poor could find food and clothing and, in an emergency, even a bail bondsman could be located.

Economic progress and the growth of social welfare programs have diminished the demand for political parties to deliver the buckets of coal and Christmas turkeys so popular in the melting-pot era. But in a city of tenants, such as New York, the crush of humanity is still great enough to permit a district leader ample opportunity to serve as a buffer between many citizens and the problems of city life.

By contrast, in the suburbs, the political party is barely needed as either a buffer or as a dispenser of social services. The average Nassau resident is likely to know both his neighbors and some community leader. If he has a problem that cannot be solved by a phone call to a local official, he can find his way to the town or village hall without difficulty. For legal advice, he is generally able to retain a lawyer, and if he changes jobs, it is more likely to take place under the aegis of an employment agency than of a political club.

With few ties or debts to a political organization, and with the economic and educational background to make his own decisions, the suburban voter often swings around on the ballot, picking and choosing among the candidates in a manner which has confounded political scientists and unnerved professional politicians.

This swing-voting, however, is heavily tempered by a brand of suburban conservatism which is partially produced by the voter's role as a homeowner. The man who becomes a homeowner, as millions of Americans have discovered in the last two decades, suddenly becomes a voter with a changed interest in taxes and services, especially if he previously had been a city dweller.

This mood of conservatism, even among Democrats, helped Nassau Republicans maintain their traditional iron grip on local offices for 15 years after the suburban rush began. But the Republicans found that these votes were not as reliable as their old "hard-core" organization votes. Moreover, at the state and national levels, the new suburban voters were almost uncontrollable.

Political life thus became hazardous for many Republican office holders in Nassau who had grown used to decades of total GOP control. One Republican state legislator who had been moving toward an increasingly independent position observed, "I've been getting ready for the day when there won't be any majority party in this county. So I've got to broaden my appeal."

The reason for his concern is explained by a brief look at how Nassau, which once advertised itself as "the banner Republican county in the nation," became a two-party battlefield and a "swing" county. This is a step by step narration of how it happened.

1952—Nassau Republicans were still riding high behind the first-term candidacy of Dwight D. Eisenhower. Nassau voters responded by giving him 70.1 per cent of the vote, for a plurality of 175,000.

1954—Some nine years after the rush to suburbia began, the Republicans began to see the first signs of political trouble. Republican Senator Irving M. Ives ran a lack-luster race for governor against Democrat Averell Harriman, who scored a narrow victory. In the process, Nassau voters, for the first time, showed that they were willing to leave the Republican line in large numbers. Even so, Ives got 63.8 per cent of the vote in Nassau, for a plurality of 99,000.

1956—President Eisenhower scored well again in Nassau, getting 69 per cent of the vote and a plurality of 205,000. The big Eisenhower wins, however, were tending to obscure the steady growth of swing voting power.

1957—Democrats began to show unusual strength in selected local contests. This year, 20,000 voters who voted the normal Republican line "swung" back to vote for a popular Democrat for the State Supreme Court. He won his upset victory with the help of adjoining counties in the judicial district.

1958—The "swing" was becoming more and more apparent. Governor Nelson Rockefeller, in defeating Averell Harriman, for the governorship, took Nassau by 62 per cent with a plurality of 123,000 votes. But 77,000 voters "swung" back to the Democratic line to vote for a well-known candidate for the Children's Court bench who narrowly missed winning.

1960—The strategists of John F. Kennedy's campaign against Republican Richard Nixon, decided to try to neutralize the normal GOP strength in Nassau. Nixon, on the other hand, was counting on the traditional Nassau GOP plurality. Kennedy and Nixon both made several tours of Nassau. When the Republicans finally began to smell trouble, they brought President Eisenhower into the county for a last-minute campaign rally. It did not help.

Nassau, in the biggest top-of-the-ticket "swing" in history, went toward Kennedy. Kennedy did not carry Nassau—but out of 592,000 votes cast—Nixon got only 55.1 per cent—for a relatively weak plurality of 61,000 votes. Nixon's lag in Nassau put him well on the road to his loss of New York State.

1961—The Democrats made history. After waiting 48 years to win a countywide election, the Democrats elected Eugene H. Nickerson as the first Democratic county executive. The independent voters of Nassau "swung" 50,000 votes off the normal Republican line to give Nickerson a narrow, but historic win.

1962—The voters in Nassau made history again. Governor Rockefeller, while winning re-election to his second term, won 68 per cent of the votes in Nassau and a 150,000 vote plurality. But, in an all-time record for switch voting, 86,000 voters crossed back over to the Democratic line to give State Controller Arthur Levitt 52 per cent of the vote and a plurality of almost 28,000. Levitt thus became the first Democratic candidate for state office ever to carry Nassau County.

1964—The Republican dam in Nassau County broke completely. President Johnson took Nassau as he took the nation. He won 60.5 per cent of the votes in the county for a plurality of 133,000 votes over Republican Barry Goldwater. In the wake of the Johnson landslide, congressional seats, legislative seats, the county executive's office, other high county posts, and even a town supervisor's job, the toughest of all GOP prizes, tumbled into the hands of the Nassau Democrats. The county that had resisted Democrat Franklin D. Roosevelt and supported Alf Landon in the Democratic landslide of 1936 had turned around 28 years later and rejected Republican Goldwater to give its backing to President Johnson in the Democratic landslide of 1964.

1966—Significantly, the swing voters in Nassau again showed their power in the 1966 state elections. Governor Rockefeller, fighting an uphill battle, won a third term with a margin of 392,000 votes over Democrat Frank O'Connor. Some 140,000 of these votes came from Nassau County. Nassau thus gave Rockefeller 35.7 per cent of his winning margin.

The impact of what happened in Nassau County during some 20 years was felt far outside the borders of the County. The creation of a "swing" county introduced a new—and highly significant—element into the traditional balance of power between a Democratic city and Republican rural areas. Now there was a third force—which, with its huge chunk of votes could "swing" state or national elections either way.

This was true of New York State. While Nassau's political complexion had been changing, similar changes were taking place in the smaller suburban areas around New York City. As the suburbs multiplied, the established political patterns in state politics began to crumble. New York's traditional balance had always been between New York City, controlled by the Democrats—and upstate counties, controlled by the Republicans. (Nassau and Suffolk had always been considered "upstate.")

In the 1940 presidential election, Democratic New York City cast 51.1 per cent of the total vote in the state. Republican upstate counties cast 48.9 per cent of the vote. By the 1964 presidential election, the population shift to suburbia had dramatically changed the figures. In 1964, the Democratic city cast only 41.7 per cent of the vote. Upstate GOP areas cast 38.4 per cent of the vote. Suburbia cast 19.9 per cent of the vote—which was now the controlling bloc.

It was the old equation: people equal votes and votes equal power. In 1940, the four counties surrounding New York City—Nassau, Suffolk, Westchester, and Rockland—had been small, rural, safely-Republican counties. Together, they accounted for only 10.2 per cent of the total vote in the state. By 1964, they were big, suburban, "swing" counties with nearly 20 per cent of the vote in the state. The lesson was clear. The day when the state could be controlled by either the city or the rural areas was over. It was now the voters in the suburbs who carried the balance of power in New York State.

CLIMBING THE LADDER OF COUNTY POLITICS

The man at the bottom of the ladder is the committeeman. The man at the top of the ladder is the chairman. There are 1806 committeemen. But there is only one chairman.

It is a long way from the bottom to the top—but a man can make it if he is willing to work, to fight, and to sacrifice, and if the fates are kind. What follows is the fictionalized story of how a man might rise from committeeman to chairman. The story is placed in the framework of the Nassau Democratic party, although with only a few variations, it could be the Nassau Republican party, as well.

The year is 1956. Richard Campbell, a young lawyer, has moved to Levittown with his wife and two young children. Three years out of law school, Campbell has come to Nassau County after accepting an offer to join a large law firm in Mineola, site of the county courthouse.

Seeking to establish himself in Nassau, Campbell soon accepted a neighbor's invitation to join the civic association in Levittown. Campbell found that he liked the people he met in the community and he became active in civic association affairs. About a year later Campbell received a telephone call from the Democratic leader of Levittown, Wendell McGill. The leader came right to the point.

"Mr. Campbell," he said, "one of our two committeemen in your election district is moving to Suffolk County soon and I'm going to need a new man to take his place. I understand you've done some good work in the civic association and I am wondering whether you would be interested in becoming a Democratic committeeman."

Campbell was interested. He talked with McGill for a while and was told that the job would require at least several hours of work a week, considerably more during campaign season. McGill suggested that politics was a good field for a young lawyer, that it would help him make contacts which could improve his law business and that, if he were interested in running for office eventually, that this would be a good way to get started.

Shortly after Campbell agreed to become a committeeman in the 27th Election District, Fifth Assembly District, he was contacted by Steve Harper, who lived only three blocks away and who would be his co-committeeman. Harper had been elected two years earlier as part of a slate of rebel committeemen (two from each district) which had ousted the old leader and had elected McGill as the Levittown leader.

The McGill victory had come after a stormy battle in the Democratic party primary in which the McGill slate won a majority of the Levittown committee seats. The committeemen, in turn, voted for McGill as the new leader. As usual, the primary battle had been fought door-to-door among the enrolled Democrats in the district. There were charges that the old-timers had been do-nothing committeemen and there were counter warnings against the newcomers.

Two Sundays after Campbell signed on as a committeeman he was out on the streets with Harper, going from house to house, collecting signatures on petitions for Democratic Party candidates. They had a variety of petitions, some for candidates for countywide office, some for candidates for town office. They also had a petition listing their names. This one would put Harper and Campbell on the primary ballot for the positions of Democratic committeemen.

Using a card file which contained the names and addresses of the enrolled Democrats in the district, they worked their way down the streets. They needed only 25 signatures on their own petitions but they had been asked by the leader to get at least 50 signatures for each one of the other candidates. All of the latter would be forwarded to county headquarters in Mineola to be packaged into one petition containing several thousand names.

That was the beginning for Campbell. During the next three years, he was a working committeeman, a foot-soldier for the political wars, tramping from door to door on registration days, on election days, meeting the new voters, visiting the old voters, soliciting campaign funds, delivering literature, getting people to the polls, acting as the eyes and ears of his party on local community issues, and on voter attitudes toward state and national issues.

Then, in 1959, the Levittown leader, Wendell McGill, a professional engineer, was transferred to Boston. He had come to like the energy, interest, and enthusiasm demonstrated by Campbell. Two other committeemen who had seniority said they were too busy to take McGill's place as leader. So, McGill recommended Campbell. There was a bit of tugging, pulling, and persuading involved but the committeeman's council went along, electing Campbell as the new leader of Levittown.

This made Campbell the head of an organization covering 33 election districts, with 66 committeemen. He also found he had an amazing number of new problems.

One of his chief problems, Campbell found, was that a good portion of his private life had suddenly disappeared. His days in the office and his evenings at home were filled with a steady flow of phone calls and visits from friends and strangers alike, seeking information about everything from where to get a marriage license to who to ask about fixing a traffic ticket. Campbell and his wife found that their living room was constantly full of people: committeemen coming to get instructions or to bring a choice bit of local political gossip. ("Politics must have the fastest grapevine in creation," Campbell once told his wife.) At other times, there were local residents trying to convince Campbell to use his influence on behalf of some civic endeavor such as a new swimming pool, a new park or a new school. But always, there were people.

As the leader of Levittown, Campbell was permitted to attend a monthly meeting of zone leaders or Democratic community leaders in the Fifth Assembly District. This was Campbell's introduction to the policy-making machinery of the party, for it was this group which gave a first screening to potential candidates for office.

The Assembly district itself was the creation of the Legislature, and used for the purpose of electing an assemblyman. Democrats used the districts as a handy way of dividing the county Democratic organization into manageable units. Moreover, the State Democratic committee rules called for the election, in the primary, of a state committeeman and state committeewoman from each assembly district in the state. Under their by-laws, the Nassau Democrats simply made the state committeeman the assembly district leader.

In 1960, almost before he knew it, Campbell found himself involved in a primary fight over the state committee post in the Fifth A. D., which meant that he was also fighting for the leadership of the Fifth. The struggle had begun over a candidate for the State Senate. Campbell was convinced that the man supported by the leader was the poorest choice. He knew, moreover, that the leader had pressured some zone leaders to go along. One word led to another. The leader threatened to dump Campbell from the Levittown title and the fight was on. Campbell had the backing of only four of the 12 zone leaders and he was quietly opposed by the county chairman. By a vote of 1289 to 1102, Campbell carried the district. He was now an assembly district leader.

During this period, Campbell's life began to change in several new respects. His wife began to think fondly of the days when the living room had always been full of people. For once Campbell had gotten into the battle for the assembly district leadership, he was out almost every night making speeches, campaigning at various Democratic clubs, attending meetings of committeemen's councils, going to strategy sessions with his supporters. His law practice also began to boom, largely in the wake of the increasing numbers of friends and contacts he had made, many of whom liked him and brought law work to his office. Politics was becoming a mixed blessing for the Campbell family.

Winning the leadership of the Fifth Assembly District now gave Campbell control of an area with 124 election districts, 248 committeemen, 51,565 enrolled Republicans and 28,370 enrolled Democrats. As the A. D. leader, Campbell was responsible for both screening candidates and overseeing the implementation of party strategy in his district. And it was up to Campbell to see to it that his zone leaders did all the chores that he himself had once done. Campbell also helped to make party policy. He did this as a member of the small but powerful Policy Committee, a group which met weekly with the County Chairman Samuel Waters. Usually meeting at dinner, Campbell found that the group hammered out party policy, sometimes taking Waters' recommendations, sometimes balking. Waters, for his part, maintained a respectful relationship with the Policy Committee. The group which consisted of the six A. D. leaders, and several other party officers, were both Waters' strength and his weakness.

The Policy Committee gave the Nassau Democratic party a strong built-in element of democratic self-government. Yet, its operations, Campbell found, depended in large part on the relative strengths of personality of the chairman on one hand, and the men on the Policy Committee on the other. A strong chairman could dominate the committee. A weak chairman could be ruled by the committee. In any event, to have the support of the committee members was to control the party organization. And Waters had it.

The next four years were crowded with activity for Campbell and his wife. There were state conventions and county conventions, political and charitable dinners galore, and always the telephone ringing daily and nightly with politicians and newspapermen, candidates, and favor seekers. During these years, he had quit his Mineola law firm, opened his own office and expanded it first to one, then to several partners. As his political activity increased, his law business grew busier. But as he grew busier, he found himself devoting more and more time to politics and less and less to his law firm, which he was leaving to his partners.

It did not come as a shock that Waters one day announced his retirement for reasons of health. The leaders had known this was coming, although they were not sure when. Nor did it shock Campbell that there were other members of the policy committee who opposed his own bid for the county chairmanship. What did shock Campbell was the extent of the bitterness which the fight engendered on both sides, the fever and fervor with which the two sides fought for support among the committeemen, and the sheer exhaustion of it all.

On a September 28, the Nassau County Democratic Convention met in the Garden City Hotel ballroom amidst the hoopla of all such conventions, and the allied pandemonium of several demonstrations. It took two ballots, several fast behind-the-platform conferences, in which Campbell agreed to put some of the opposition supporters on the list of executive officers, and it was all over. The various switches were arranged, and the committeemen voted to elect Attorney Richard Campbell as county chairman.

It had been a long, hard road to the top. It would be just as hard to stay on top.

THE SOUND AND THE FURY—
CAMPAIGNING IN SUBURBIA

No one can quite remember the first time that a Nassau Republican took a drawing of a vicious-looking tiger, slapped it up on a signboard, and wrote underneath, "Keep Tammany Out of Nassau." This custom, some old-timers figure, started back in the 1920's when Manhattan's Democratic organization, Tammany Hall, began acquiring a national reputation for big-city bossism and political wheeling and dealing.

Some 40 years later, Republicans still put up signs that read,

"Keep Tammany Out of Nassau." Whereas the signs once infuriated Nassau Democrats, these days the signs merely irritate them. Moreover, Nassau Republicans, who once were deadly serious in their warnings of the Tammany menace, now look upon the slogan more with humor than fervor. But old habits are hard to break, and so each election, somewhere in the county, some Republican will put up the traditional Tammany Tiger sign.

Like many other bits of political foolishness, there are some serious undercurrents to the business of the Tammany Tiger. It has long been the dominant theme of Republican politics in Nassau that Republicans stand for a neat, clean, truly democratic form of local government, where the magic potion of "home rule" guarantees every man a real voice in his county, town, village, or school district government. All this, the Republicans are quick to point out, is in happy contrast to the graft, corruption, and bossism of traditionally Democratic cities such as New York, where the citizen's voice in his government supposedly is strangled by the octopus of a mammoth, centralized, partisan bureaucracy.

The Republicans are quick to rise in anger at any suggestion originating in New York City that the only way for the city to survive is to annex the nearby suburbs. From time to time, such suggestions have been made by city officials or political scientists who view with alarm the continued flight of middle-class families from the city to the suburbs—and the simultaneous migration to the city of low-income minority groups. Great anguish and dramatic cries of civic horror have greeted all such proposals.

Visions of apartment houses springing up in Salisbury Park and an elevated subway running down Old Country Road spring to GOP minds when they contemplate the "threat" of annexation. They see Nassau as another borough of the city metropolis with dirty streets and cracked pavement and rutted highways and—worst of all—the Tammany Tiger gaining political control.

To the Nassau Democrat, all of the above is pure fantasy. He sees it as a package of political scare tactics that has been cleverly disguised, and unbelievably successful in frightening Nassau County voters for many decades. The Nassau Democrat sees himself not as a suburban puppet of New York City Democrats, but as independent and free-thinking. If he is an old-timer in the county, he thinks of himself as a long-suffering member of the loyal opposition, who worked and fought and struggled for his cause for many years, although always outnumbered and outvoted. If he is a newcomer to the county, he tends to think of himself as a new breed of Democrat who can help to create a truly representative organization—one without bosses.

Moreover, the Nassau Democrat views the Republicans not as experts in responsive local government, but as patronage-hungry clam-diggers who turned local government into an endless series of feudal domains. The Nassau Democrat looks at the governmental structure of Nassau and sees one county, two cities, three townships, 62 school districts, 64 incorporated villages and 224 special districts. He sees nearly 356 in all and he is angered at the inefficiency and the high cost of such fragmentation.

He counts the number of political jobs involved in the Nassau governmental structure and soon becomes aware of the solid hard-core Republican vote which is rooted to the public payroll and has helped bring in overwhelming GOP majorities year after year after year. He decided that the way to more efficient government in Nassau is through centralization and consolidation—which in turn will help to break the GOP stranglehold on the county. He thought this way about the county until the Democrats won the county government in 1961 and still thinks this way about the GOP-controlled townships.

The Republicans, taking note of these conclusions, nod sagely at the mention of centralization and big government and say, "That's just what the Democrats in New York City do."

Then they go out and hang up another sign that says, "Keep Tammany Out of Nassau."

While the political parties, their leaders and their candidates try to sway Nassau voters with this mixture of philosophy and shibboleth, party success in local elections still depends heavily on the shoe-leather brigade—the men and women who work in the neighborhood election districts throughout the county.

It is an ancient, unwritten rule of politics that the simplest and most effective way to get a man's vote is to knock at his door and ask him for it.

It is a rule that dates to early days of politics—to the era before television brought the candidates into the living room, to the era when party was more important than personality, to the era when the local political worker knew the cradle-to-grave story of every family in his district.

But times change and politics changes, too. It would, for instance, have been of little use for the average Nassau committeeman to go house-to-house during the 1960 Kennedy-Nixon presidential contest. Long before the average committeeman could have arrived at the home of the voter to sing the praises of his candidate, the contenders would already have been seen on television.

The voter probably looked in on their nominations, watched their debates and caught the daily TV news films of their campaigns. Having personally watched and listened to the candidates, he felt perfectly able to make up his own mind about which man would do the best job of running the nation. There was, therefore, little room left for the committeeman to do much persuading.

The circumstances would vary a little bit if the committeeman were trying, instead, to "sell" a candidate for the governorship. Here, too, the voter is likely to have seen the candidates on television, or to have read about them, and may have made up his own mind about the candidates long before the committeeman arrived.

The circumstances, however, would vary a great deal more if the committeeman were trying to "sell" a candidate for state senator or for the county board of supervisors. There is rarely any television campaigning involved in these contests and the voter may not even know the names of the candidates who are running.

It is an ironic aspect of politics in the United States that most citizens have a far better idea of what the President is doing from day to day than what their local councilman is doing in his office a mile away, from month to month. This is, in part, because of the great amount of news coverage devoted to national events by the mass media, including network television. It is also true that most citizens find it easier to hold a strong opinion on whether Red China should be admitted to the United Nations than they do on whether a local sewage treatment plant, costing several millions of dollars, should be built on land in community A as against community B.

Thus, when the committeeman comes to talk about a man running for President, the voter believes he already knows all the issues. He may not be so sure about the governorship, and the committeeman may have a chance to argue that a great deal of his state tax money is coming back home to help keep the local school taxes down. But the committeeman's biggest chance to win some votes comes when he is "selling" local candidates.

While the day of the district worker who could "deliver" large blocs of voters is long since gone, especially in the suburbs, the shoe leather brigade still has many opportunities for important political services to the parties they represent. The handbook issued by the Nassau County Democratic committee for their "shoe-leather brigade" describes the basic functions of a committeeman in this way:

"1. To reach every person eligible to vote, but not registered, to let him know how to register, and to encourage him to enroll and vote Democratic.

"2. To see to it that every enrolled Democrat and every 'hidden' Democrat (registered to vote, not enrolled in the Democratic party—but leaning our way) votes on Election Day."

A Republican committeeman has exactly the same tasks. Indeed, in Nassau, because of the ever-increasing competition between the political parties, great emphasis has been put on finding the "hidden" voters. In recent years, both parties have become extremely conscious of the importance of every single vote.

On a national level, as political leaders frequently remind their workers, the 1960 Nixon-Kennedy presidential race was won by John F. Kennedy by a margin of less than one vote per precinct or election district. The Kennedy-Johnson ticket won by 112,801 votes, polling 49.71 per cent of the total vote. (There were, in 1960, 166,072 precincts in the U. S.) In 1954, Averell Harriman won the governorship of New York State by a similar margin. In Nassau County, with its big swing vote victory, margins have dropped consistently and the value of every vote has gone up. Congressional, legislative, county and town candidates have been squeaking into office by incredibly narrow margins. One recent contest for a Nassau District Court judgeship involving almost 107,000 votes ended in an absolute tie.

There have been many approaches to digging out "hidden" voters. One of the most highly organized and most ambitious was mounted by Nassau Democrats under the name "OPERATION DWOC." DWOC was the abbreviation for "District Worker's Organizing Committee" and it was an operation mounted above and beyond the regular committeemens' organizations. DWOC was dedicated to the proposition that the split-levels and ranch houses of Nassau were full of "hidden" Democrats who were ready and willing to work for the party if only someone would come and ask them to help.

The DWOC was directed by Attorney Marvin Christenfeld, who later became a Democratic elections commissioner in Nassau County. The teams began their work in heavily-Republican areas of the county and it took some time for Christenfeld's flying squad to work out its techniques.

"We discovered," Christenfeld said, "that the best system was for two people to work together. They'd give each other courage. And besides, one man going around looks like a bill collector. We wore big buttons saying, 'I represent the Nassau Democratic party.' And we'd say to the man or woman who answered the doorbell—after we identified ourselves—that we had come to ask their advice."

"We found," Christenfeld continued, "That nobody wants to work and nobody wants to give money but everybody is ready to give advice. People always ask, 'What would you like to know?' And we asked them who among their neighbors seemed like good prospects to become active Democratic workers—people who would be interested in addressing envelopes, going to Democratic meetings, walking with the candidates through their neighborhoods, collecting dollars-for-Democrats or holding kaffee klatsches."

"Since we weren't asking them for anything but advice," Christenfeld added, "We were able to develop a rapport with them. They would begin to think about people in their neighborhood who might be interested and they would give us some good names. Then, after a while, we had a chance to say, 'How about you? Will you work for us?' Sometimes they would say, 'Sure, I'll be glad to do some work.'"

"Well, we found," concluded Christenfeld, "that a two man team could canvass about 20 homes in two hours and out of that 20 homes we would find three or four willing to work as block captains, making phone calls, doing registration work and election day work. Then, out of 60 homes we would find someone who would be a crackerjack committeeman."

In the beginning, Christenfeld admits, the DWOC was suspect among many zone leaders and committeemen who didn't like the idea of a headquarters team descending on their bailiwicks. "They thought we were a hatchet squad. But when they discovered we were not there to knock off any leaders, they began to welcome us. Now we have a waiting list for zones that want a DWOC campaign."

What did the DWOC campaign prove? Basically, Christenfeld thinks, after some eight years of trial and effort, DWOC proved that the old rule of politics is true—the knock on the door is, indeed, the road to political success. The communities which were canvassed, and infused with new and energetic workers, responded favorably to the Democrats in the next election and the several elections which followed. In time, however, the districts began to drift back to their previous political strengths.

One of the reasons was that, although DWOC helped pump new block captains and new committeemen into local district organizations, the interest span of committeemen averages only a few years. They become busy with other matters, grow tired of politics, or move, change jobs, and for various reasons leave the ranks. The effort to find the "hidden" voters and "hidden" workers had to be continuous, if it was to be a sustained success.

It was almost as though the voters of these communities were saying to the Democrats, "What have you done around here lately?"

PAYING FOR POLITICS IN SUBURBIA

As other chapters in this book emphasize, the basic ingredient of politics is money—bushels of money.

There is money for banners and bunting and balloons, money for billboards and buttons and bands. There is money for posters and photographs and printing, money for postage and parties for the press.

Money is the fuel that powers the engines of politics. It pays for the ink that goes into the mimeograph machines, for the coffee and sandwiches that go into the campaign workers, and for the telephone calls that go out to the voters. Without money, there would be no torches for the torchlight motorcades, no halls for the hoopla and, perhaps, no campaigns for the candidates. Without money, the political race would soon grind to a walk.

In Nassau County the wonder is not that politics requires money —but that politics seems to require so much of it. It is still somewhat difficult for many politicians who remember the sleepy days of Nassau politics to believe what has happened in recent years. They are astonished to hear that a candidate for Congress has spent $200,000 on his campaign, to learn that a candidate for a local judgeship has spent $30,000 or that a town council candidate has spent $10,000 on a campaign for a job that only pays $15,000 a year.

The "old-timers" are really shocked, however, to find out that in 1964 the Nassau Republicans and Democrats spent more than one million dollars on their county campaigns! That was the year, of course, that saw three major races in progress in Nassau. Lyndon B. Johnson was running for President, Robert F. Kennedy was running for U. S. Senator, and Eugene H. Nickerson was running for Nassau County Executive.

And where did most of the one million dollars go? It went to the county executive's race. The first law of politics is the law of self-preservation. The Nassau Democrats would have been sad had Johnson lost the White House, and disappointed if Kennedy failed in his bid for a Senate seat. But the Democrats could survive those defeats. Not so with the race for Nassau County Executive. A Nickerson defeat would have been disastrous for Nassau Democrats, who had first captured the office only a few years earlier.

"Power is where power lies" according to the familiar adage and both parties knew it.

The county executive is the highest official of county government, chairman of the board of supervisors and the leading public figure in the county. He appoints the heads of departments and county agencies, establishes the fiscal policy of the county and supervises a work force of 13,000 persons.

To the Nassau Republicans, who held the county executive's office for many years, the post meant power and prestige. It provided scores of patronage jobs for lawyers and for laborers, jobs that in turn provided the GOP with workers and campaign contributions, and the cement with which to build a powerful organization. When the Republicans lost the office in 1961, they lost all that goes with it.

To the Nassau Democrats, who had suffered decades of political famine, their capture of the county executive's office provided a dazzling political feast. One day, the Democrats had been a party that was poorly-organized and poorly-housed—just plain poor. Almost the next day, it seemed, the Democrats had become a party that was over-organized, comfortably housed, and financially successful. What the Republicans had lost, they wanted back. What the Democrats had won, they were determined to keep.

It was understandable, therefore, that the Republicans and Democrats would be tempted to cheer for Johnson-Goldwater and Kennedy-Keating but to spend most of their money for Eugene H. Nickerson and his unsuccessful challenger John J. Burns.

CONCLUSIONS

Two decades have passed since the suburban boom began its sweep across Nassau County. Looking back across these years, it is evident that the massive migration was both a blessing and a burden to the two-party system.

The surge of one million new residents into Nassau activated a long-dormant Democratic party and forced it into strenuous competition with a long-dominant Republican party. Out of this struggle emerged a new balance of political power in which one-party rule was replaced by two-party competition—and two-party government.

The struggle gave Nassau two parties which were far more vigorous and vibrant than ever before. The doors of politics were opened to thousands of new political workers—from committeemen to congressmen. But ironically, as the ranks of the parties grew stronger, the ability of the parties to rely on voter loyalty grew smaller and smaller.

The men and women who moved to suburbia tended, increasingly, to vote for individual candidates rather than for party labels. The swing-vote became the dominant fact of suburban political life and left the parties with little old-fashioned control over the electorate.

Not surprisingly, the fickleness of the voters spurred Republicans and Democrats to step up their battle for election support. This meant more workers at all levels, more strenuous campaigning, ever-greater spending, close attention to issues and a determined search for attractive, intelligent candidates.

Essentially, what happened was that the business of politics prospered while the traditional hard-core strength of the political parties diminished sharply. Today in Nassau County, it is an accepted fact by both major parties that every vote, for every candidate, must be earned.

American life has changed a great deal in the past two decades, and many of our national institutions have changed as well. Politics, too, has undergone vast changes. Many of the old molds and traditions have been discarded; and there is a new look to the old game. In suburbia, especially, politics has become an increasingly competitive and fascinating endeavor that still offers a welcome to newcomers everywhere.

part
three

POLITICAL CAMPAIGNING

IT IS ARGUABLE *that the American form of democracy is extravagant. The costs, in terms of money and personal effort probably are greater than those of any other political system. The arguments for curtailing the number of elective offices and imposing limits upon campaign expenditure are hoary and trite. We have yet to find a way to conduct a cost-benefit analysis of our particular form of democracy.*

Comments on the money cost of politics are to be found in many chapters of this book. One cannot talk about any aspect of politics without talking about money. Part Four, Chapter 11 deals specifically with the costs of presidential elections. In the three chapters on political campaigning, we are concerned principally with the human costs of democracy—the manner in which the American political system satisfies a voracious hunger for candidates, without any seeming lessening of sacrificial offerings.

JAMES B. KESSLER

James Kessler studied at Stanford University (A.B., 1946, Ph.D., 1958). He has taught at Indiana University since 1958.

Kessler was Director, Indiana General Assembly's Tax Study Commission (1958–63); precinct committeeman; technical advisor in several state-wide and congressional political campaigns (Republican candidates); narrowly defeated by an incumbent State Senator in 1964 election; sought Republican nomination for Congress (1966); Kessler is presently a member of the Indiana General Assembly's Constitutional Revision Commission.

JAMES B. KESSLER

6. Running For State Political Office

PROLOGUE

Participation in a campaign as a candidate drives home the fact that a working democracy is the most demanding of political systems. It consumes huge numbers of candidates, large sums of money, and enormous amounts of energy.

I decided to run for the Indiana State Senate in 1963 with full knowledge of the grubbing hard work it takes to run a successful political campaign. No group of leading citizens knocked on my door to ask me to run. I decided to run because I like politics; because I feel it is the duty of every qualified American citizen to make himself available for public service at some time during his life; and because I thought I could win even though I had never held elective public office before.

I have always been fascinated with politics. When I was a boy, my father ran as a Republican for a seat in the Oklahoma House. He lost by a narrow margin.

I remember Alfalfa Bill Murray haranguing the country crowds from the concrete bandstand in Ardmore's Central Park as he campaigned for governor of Oklahoma on hot summer evenings. The speeches, parades and conventions were glamorous to a small boy; they have never lost their excitement for me. But my image of a campaign has changed.

For four years preceding my decision to run, I served as Director of the Indiana General Assembly's Bi-partisan Commission on State Tax and Financing Policy. Since determination of tax policy is one of the most important and difficult tasks of legislators, I got to know most of these men well and acquired first-hand knowledge of the formal and informal operations of the legislature. In this position, I developed respect for the ability, integrity, and dedication of most of Indiana's legislators on both sides of the political aisle.

DECIDING TO RUN

Why choose the State Legislature instead of some other elective office to start a political career? There were several reasons:

1. As a professional man, I had no desire to abandon my profession. The Indiana Legislature meets only sixty-one calendar days every other year. Therefore, I could afford to take a leave of absence without pay from my teaching position to serve in the legislature.
2. County and city offices provide interesting opportunities to participate in the determination of public policy, but most of these positions were occupied by members of my own party, or were full-time positions with salaries considerably less than my salary at the University.
3. As a professional student of politics and an employee of the legislature during two important sessions, I knew that the opportunities for service, for leadership, and for political advancement as a member of the State Legislature are substantial.

The question was whether to run for the House or the Senate. Monroe County's incumbent in the House was a friend of mine and a member of my own party. The legislative session immediately preceding the coming election was a hectic one. George McDaniel, the Republican State Representative from my home county (Monroe), told me during the last days of the special session which followed the regular session, that he didn't think he would run again after such an experience. His comment was fresh in mind as I considered the possibility of running for office.

The Indiana House has one hundred members. There are only fifty in the Senate. The turnover is higher in the House; consequently, it is easier for freshman members of that body to attain positions of leadership. Before the recent court-ordered reapportionment, House districts, except in the case of some multi-member districts, were smaller than Senate districts and thus campaigns for seats in the lower chamber were less expensive. On the other hand, Senators must seek re-election only once every four years, while House members must do so every two years in Indiana. If George meant what he said about retiring, I was certainly tempted to run for the House. This House district consisted of a single county (Monroe), while there were three counties in the Senate district (Brown, Greene, and Monroe). The Senate seat was occupied by a Democrat, also a friend of mine. Senator David Rogers had the advantages of incumbency and an old and honored name in the community. On the other hand, he won his first and second terms by the narrowest of margins, a circumstance which always encourages opposition.

The three counties in the Senate district, if they were considered as a unit, consistently supported Republican Presidential and Congressional candidates. The Democratic Presidential ticket lost these three counties by substantial margins in 1952, 1956, and 1960. Assuming that Republicans nominated strong state and national tickets, opportunities for Republican success in the state senate race seemed reasonable.

After carefully analyzing potential costs of a campaign for the House vis à vis those likely to be incurred in a campaign for the Senate, I chose the House, providing that the incumbent retired. After all, Monroe County was traditionally Republican, and the Republican nominee should be elected with a minimum of expense and effort. As a prelude to making a final decision, I talked to a number of acquaintances in my home town, Bloomington.

Bloomington is the county seat of Monroe County, and the location of Indiana University, my employer. I sought the advice of many people for a number of reasons. In at least some university towns there are real or fancied tensions between members of the university community (many of whom are transient) and native residents. Furthermore, it was my initial impression that the image of a college professor is unpopular among inhabitants of the rural townships surrounding Bloomington. Although my friends agreed that there is some basis for such apprehensions, without exception they thought I could overcome the negative aspects of this stereotype and were emphatic in their encouragement. One of my advisors was a local attorney, a former Monroe County prosecutor, and at one time a power in Republican state politics. His wife was also active in politics as Monroe County Republican Vice-Chairwoman, Vice-Chairwoman of my party's congressional district committee, and as the most recent Republican candidate for the state senate. These people clearly knew a great deal about Indiana politics. They told me some things I already knew about local political traditions—knowledge absolutely essential to the conduct of a successful primary campaign.

Indiana's political party structure is very complex. Precinct Committeemen are elected at the primary. In theory, and often in practice, precinct committeemen elect county chairmen and vice-chairmen who, in turn, elect the congressional district officers who form the state committee. Indiana is a patronage state. All political appointees must be cleared or endorsed by their precinct committeemen, and their county and district chairmen. Once a county chairman is elected, patronage and apathy make it possible for him to control the election of future precinct committeemen. Thus, the county chairmen can become powerful and they tend to stay in office for a long time. Many county chairmen are exceedingly jealous of their prerogatives.

HOW TO START A CAMPAIGN IN INDIANA

It is expected that a prospective candidate will call on his own county chairman first and then on the other county chairmen in his district *before* he announces his candidacy. If he fails to do this, he will be labeled as an anti-organization man. As such, any candidate is highly vulnerable in a contested primary.

I was also told that there are numerous factions in my party in Monroe County, and, in case I decided to run for the state senate, factions existed in the other two counties which are in the state senate district. These factions were created by bitter struggles for patronage during the administration of Republican Governor George Craig, by local political rivalries, by ideological differences, and by a variety of personality conflicts. I was told to see the county chairman first and then to see the factional leaders. I was also told to be very careful not to identify myself with any of these factions but to try to establish friendly relations with all of them, if possible.

The County Chairman in Monroe County, at the time, was an extremely wealthy, self-made industrialist noted for his extensive philanthropies. The chairman was popular as a man, but was so busy and difficult to see that most of his contacts with precinct committeemen were made through a young administrative assistant. This assistant was politically sophisticated, was active in raising funds for the party, and acted as the chairman's deputy in supervising local party activities, such as polling and registration. In these capacities, he became the focal point for all the accrued dissatisfactions of the precinct committeemen. I had to see this young man to get an appointment with the County Chairman. Dick was friendly. I soon found out, however, that he was ambitious to run for the House himself. When I talked to the County Chairman, he strongly advised me to run for the Senate since he thought the incumbent would probably seek re-election. This conversation created some indecision on my part. I called George. He said he hadn't made up his mind, but he urged me to run for the Senate. The longer George delayed his decision, the greater the possibility that others would be tempted to enter the state senate race. George didn't delay long. He announced his candidacy a few days later. The die was cast. It is almost impossible to unseat an incumbent in the primary. If you try and are successful, the bitterness caused by the ensuing intra-party battle can destroy your chances even before the campaign for the general election commences.

During the delay occasioned by George's indecision, there were rumors that Felix J. (Star) Brown might enter the race for the state senate. At that moment Star was a resident of Indianapolis and a member of the House from Marion County. He was a property owner in Brown County, however, and had been for years. He made many friends throughout the State in his position of authority and influence in the American Legion. The Legion is a power in Indiana politics. Its national headquarters is in Indianapolis.

Star was born in Ellettsville, Richland Township, Monroe County. He was a former Monroe County Treasurer and his large family had close political and personal ties with Monroe County's controversial former Republican Chairman, Fritz Ryan. Fritz was ousted two years earlier at the biennial county reorganization meeting by a coalition spearheaded by a young Republican professor. Fritz, noted for his anti-university views, was a natural ally for Star.

Many of my friends advised me to see Fritz in spite of the circumstances noted above. One of these friends was a man named Rodney Brown, the County Auditor, a native of Monroe County and past president of the Indiana County Auditor's Association. I got to know Rodney at the time my Commission recodified the property tax laws of Indiana. Since county treasurers, Auditors and Assessors are all deeply involved in the administration of the property tax, officers of their state associations were consulted about the recodification. Had they not been consulted, many unnecessary errors would have been incorporated in the recodification bill, and these men, who are political powers in their own counties, could have killed the measure in the General Assembly.

Rodney and I had some knockdown-dragout arguments about the responsibilities of County Auditors under the proposed legislation. Although we didn't always agree, he received a fair hearing. I grew to have great respect for his outspoken integrity. Little did I know during these confrontations that he would become one of my valuable friends and allies. Rodney was a Fritz Ryan man. Fritz was the one who urged Rodney to run for county office and Rodney was dedicated in his loyalty to the former County Chairman. Rodney told me that Fritz held court every Saturday morning in Republican Headquarters overlooking Court House Square in Bloomington. I called on Fritz at the earliest opportunity.

The former County Chairman is an elderly, tall, handsome man with a pronounced Hoosier accent. Since Fritz held patronage jobs in the State Highway Department under Republican Governor Handley and in the Republican Secretary of State's Office during Democratic Governor Welsh's Administration, I had seen him around the state house often and knew him quite well. During legislative sessions, county chairmen often act as doorkeepers for pay. As an employee of the Legislature, I had the privilege of the floor in both the Senate and the House. On a number of occasions my lobbyist friends got Fritz to deny me entrance to the floor as part of their strategy to delay action on some aspect of tax legislation. I mention this to demonstrate that Fritz knew who I was and knew that I had powerful friends in the Party, since these men always countermanded Fritz's orders (without reprimanding him).

When I went to see Fritz, one of the township trustees was in his office discussing a poor relief case under the trustee's jurisdiction. When

the trustee finally left, Fritz and I talked politics. It was clear that
Rodney had already mentioned my possible candidacy. Fritz was
friendly. He always was, even when he was ready to stick a knife in
my back.

Fritz told me that Star Brown was going to run. He advised me to
inform the Monroe County Clerk of my intentions as soon as possible.
In Indiana, all candidates for local office must file with the County
Clerk. Fritz's theory was that if the clerk knew and approved of an
impending candidacy, he would spread the word. As a consequence,
others would be discouraged from filing for that particular office.

After our meeting, I acted on this suggestion immediately. While I
was in the clerk's office, Mr. James Cotner, Bloomington City Attorney,
came in to transact some business. I told him he was high on the list of
persons I wanted to talk to before becoming a candidate. He was
enthusiastic in his support.

In the next week or so I sought the advice of at least twenty people
whom I considered to be leaders of the party in Monroe County. I got
a list of precinct committeemen and began calling on them. I also went
to see Mr. Doris Fleetwood, the Brown County Chairman, at his home
near the country crossroads called Belmont, and Mr. Irvin Pryor, the
Greene County Chairman, at his country newspaper office in Worthing-
ton. Both gentlemen were friendly but very noncommittal. County
chairmen are usually noncommittal in a primary unless there is no contest. They now expected a contest. I secured lists of precinct committeemen and vice-committeemen for Brown and Greene Counties and
listened eagerly to the comments of the county chairmen about political
affairs in their own counties.

Before I began the active phase of my campaign I went to Indianapolis to inform Republican Lieutenant Governor Richard O. Ristine
of my intentions. As a candidate for the gubernatorial nomination,
Ristine was deeply preoccupied with his own campaign to secure delegates to the state convention. In Indiana's hybrid nominating system
candidates for all offices elected by the state at large are nominated in a
state convention, which convenes a few weeks after the primary. At the
primary, of course, candidates for all other elective offices are selected.
When I arrived, Lt. Governor Ristine was conferring with some district
chairmen who were in a position to influence large delegations. After
waiting for an hour or so, I got to see Dick, and told him about my
plans. He encouraged me because he knew I was a strong supporter
and because he thought I would help the ticket in Monroe County.
He then gave me the names of some people to see in Greene County.

Having carefully observed the necessary protocol, I was now ready
to plan the formal announcement of candidacy. There were nine newspapers in the state senate district. The announcement, to be effective,
must be released at a time convenient to the publishers of weekly newspapers. An appropriate campaign photograph was selected; zinc cuts
and mats were ordered for the newspapers. So that all precinct com-

mitteemen would be informed in advance of the news release, I sent letters to each one. Monroe County had 29 precincts, Greene 59, and Brown 12, for a total of 100 precincts in the district. Since the vice-committeemen are likely to be as sensitive of their political positions as the committeemen, this meant 200 personal letters had to be sent out prior to the announcement.

While these letters were being prepared, I called on all the newspaper editors in the district. The owner of the Brown County paper, Mrs. Robert Wyatt, is the wife of the Executive Secretary of the politically powerful Indiana State Teachers' Association. I was informed by Mrs. Johnson, Mrs. Wyatt's assistant, that if I wanted an announcement in the Brown County Democrat, I would have to buy an ad, place my name on the political calendar each week, and pay in advance!

I saw John Waton, a former Democratic Lt. Governor and editor of the principal newspaper in Bloomfield, the county seat of Greene County. Bruce Temple, then editor of the Bloomington Herald Telephone, was especially helpful. I asked his advice on numerous matters. As a consequence, my home town newspaper helped me in many ways.

CAMPAIGN STRATEGY AND FINANCE

Before making the formal announcement I did some serious thinking about campaign finance and strategy. To help me in this respect, I invited some friends to my home one evening. I was careful to include people identified with all the major factions in Monroe County. To avoid any possible embarrassment, I told everyone who else was coming so that no one would be surprised. The approved list was a good one. There was Rodney Brown, representing the Ryan Crowd and the courthouse politicians; Robert McCrea, representing the Republican attorney; Dave Derge, a newly elected member of the City Council and one of my colleagues in the Political Science Department at Indiana University, representing City Hall. There were several others, including Georgianna Mitchell, a former national officer and organizer of Republican workshops, who encouraged me to run and offered financial support.

The agenda for this meeting contained a schedule of proposed activities for the month preceding the primary, together with an estimate of the cost of pursuing these activities. The proposed budget included such items as newspaper advertising, placards to staple on telephone posts, candidate cards, campaign gimmicks (matches and combs), travel expenses, postage for mailing several thousand letters, and an allowance for miscellaneous items. The budget for printed matter took into account, of course, the necessity for placing the union trademark (bug) on all campaign literature. Everybody was satisfied with the agenda.

However, when I asked how to raise the money, a good friend replied that the candidate is on his own in the primary! People would be offended if I solicited funds from persons other than my personal friends. This opinion was somewhat shocking to me, although it made sense. To put it bluntly, I had to be prepared to spend somewhere between $1200 and $1500 of my own money on a primary contest. Despite this setback, the meeting was a success. I now took steps to see more friends and to meet more people.

By the end of the campaign, some thirty-eight people contributed about $1500. The largest contribution was $500 and the smallest was $5. The list of contributors includes only three people I didn't know personally. Most of the contributions were unsolicited. It is interesting to note that no one even suggested that financial support was contingent on my having political views compatible with his nor did anyone try to make me promise to do anything for him after the election.

A few days after the meeting noted above I went to Greene County. There are two small towns and a number of lesser communities in the county. Bloomfield, located in the eastern part is a Republican stronghold. Linton, in Stockton township on the west side, is notorious as a Democratic stronghold. These towns are rivals in everything from basketball to politics. Linton has always been jealous of the fact that Bloomfield is the county seat, despite its smaller size. There is a river dividing the county and the river roughly separates most Republicans from most Democrats. Unfortunately for me, there were more Democrats on the west side of the river than Republicans on the east side. In order for a Republican to carry Greene County, he must win large numbers of Democratic votes.

In 1964, Greene County was a paper-ballot county. It was easy for people to "scratch" tickets.* Proof of the fact that they frequently do so is evident in the large vote cast for Eisenhower in 1952 and 1958, and for Nixon in 1960. Republican Congressman William G. Bray, soon to become a candidate for Governor, carried Greene County a number of times in his several successful efforts to win re-election in Indiana's Seventh Congressional District. But Bill Bray and his wife Esther are extraordinary campaigners. The Democratic vote for Bray was a personal vote carefully cultivated over the years and should not be used to estimate the possible vote for other Republican candidates.

In 1964, county commissioners and township trustees would be elected. In Indiana's rural counties, these offices are often hotly contested. A heavy vote means predominently a Democratic vote in Greene County. If I intended to carry this county, I would have to find out all I could about its political culture and its power structure. One thing I learned quickly about the culture is that country people like to meet the candidates. I would have to make as many personal acquaintances as possible.

---

* In Hoosier terms, a person who "scratches" his ticket votes for some candidates of each party instead of voting for all candidates of one party.

It soon became apparent to me that Star Brown, my primary opponent, was well known in Greene, Brown, and in the rural portions of Monroe County. He was well known and generally well liked. The only adverse comments I heard against him were that he was too old and that he lived away from the district too long. Since there was some question in my mind whether Star was really a resident of the district, I got some of my friends in Marion County to do some investigating. They secured an affidavit to the effect that Star voted in Marion County in the previous election. It was our opinion that this fact would make him ineligible to vote in Monroe or Brown Counties unless he re-registered. Obviously, this information could be damaging to Star's candidacy. Although I thought seriously of causing public disclosure of this fact, the more I thought about it, the less attractive the idea became. If I won the primary on a technicality, Star's friends might well desert me in the general election and I needed every vote I could get.

CAMPAIGNING IN GREENE COUNTY

The first time I went to Bloomfield, I went armed with a few names that Lt. Governor Dick Ristine had given me. But before I saw Dick's friends, I took a walk around courthouse square and shook hands with everyone I saw. One of these people was a policeman. He was friendly, as most Greene County people are. When he discovered that I was a Republican, he squinted his eyes and said, "Say, I want you to go right down the block there to Kenny Wellborn's place." I hadn't gone over my list of Greene County precinct committeemen yet, so I didn't know that Kenny Wellborn was a committeeman.

Mr. Wellborn was a very slightly built gentleman, with shrewd eyes. I introduced myself, gave him my card, told him I was a candidate and that I would appreciate an opportunity to talk to him. He invited me in. We sat down, and we talked. He asked some very penetrating questions. He wanted information about my personal life. He wanted to know if I went to church. I told him that I did. And then we had a discussion about the state's new tax program. Having worked closely with the General Assembly as Director of the General Assembly's Bipartisan Commission on State Tax and Financing Policy, I knew a good deal about the state's tax structure. I came armed with all kinds of data about the tax rates of each county's various governmental units and the probable impact of the newly enacted state tax program on local property tax rates. I knew that the state program would keep the rates from going up as rapidly in Greene County as in the recent past since it increased the amount of money available for local schools. In some of the more rural townships, the distribution of increased revenues derived from the new state taxes would cause a substantial reduction in local property tax rates. We discussed state and local financial matters in general and reviewed some of the basic principles of public finance. Kenny Wellborn didn't agree with me on everything, but he indicated very clearly that he respected me for speaking frankly and for giving some evidence that I knew what I was talking about. He told me to come back the following day to meet a group of influential men he promised to call together. The interview was a success.

When I finished talking to Mr. Wellborn I went to see one of the gentlemen that the Lt. Governor told me to be sure to see. This man's office was difficult for a stranger to locate because it is above a store. When I finally found the entrance to the building, I climbed three flights of rickety wooden stairs up a narrow, dimly lit stairwell to the law office which also served as a residence for Parker Vosloh. Parker was a Wabash College schoolmate of the Lt. Governor. He was a life-long resident of Greene County, a former Republican Greene County chairman and an avid sports fan. To Parker, politics is a sport. He always likes to have a horse in the race. We shared one thing in common—our respect for the Lt. Governor.

After sizing me up for a while, Parker finally decided we could get along well together. He drew himself back in his chair, cleared his throat, smiled, and said, "Well, we've got to get you elected." Then he said, "Tell you what I'll do. Here's a piece of paper. Now, I'm going to give you names of some people you ought to go see. You want to tell some of them that I sent you. To others, you don't want to mention my name. We play some rough politics over here and we don't always get along. We vote the same way usually on election day, but you gotta be careful." Parker rattled off a number of names. I took them all down. He told me to see Kenny Wellborn, but not to mention his name. I told him that I had already seen Kenny and that he was going to invite several precinct committeemen in to meet me. Parker nodded his head and said, "That's fine."

About this time, a young fellow came in and Parker introduced me. "This is Jim Blackmore." Jim apparently worked with Parker on a number of business deals. Later, Jim became a valuable guide through the intricate maze of Greene County politics. He and Parker emphasized that I should see a man named Lavon Yoho. Mr. Yoho was the township trustee of Beach Creek (pronounced "crick") township. Lavon apparently had a lot of influence in the eastern section of the county—especially the northeastern part. Parker told me to see him on my way home.

I turned off the road at Greene County's Eastern Consolidated School, drove down a winding highway into the Nineteenth Century! Solsberry, Greene County, Indiana, consists of about a dozen buildings, including a filling station and a store, a cafe, a garage, and a barber shop. I went into the store looking for Lavon. When I got inside, there was a little old-fashioned pot-bellied stove. Four or five farmers sat on an ancient wooden bench. A cracker barrel and a pickle barrel stood nearby. When I walked in, these farmers, dressed in their bib overalls, looked up, sort of grunted, and went on talking. This was a picture from Norman Rockwell's drawing board. I introduced myself, passed out candidate cards, and announced that I was a candidate for the State Senate. They asked me what party—I told them Republican. They said, "Right party." Comments like that always made me feel good.

Lavon wasn't there, but his father, Dwight was. I introduced myself to Dwight. Lavon came in a few minutes later, offered me a Nehi pop and we talked politics. At the end of the conversation, he said, "Well, you'uns is the first to ask. Give us one of your posters." Evidently, we struck it off all right. In the primary I received fifty-two votes in Lavon's precinct, to two for my opponent, Star Brown. When I thanked Lavon for his support, he said, "Well, that was a pretty good vote, but we're still wonderin' who them two was."

On the way back to Bloomington, I noticed something about the names on the country mailboxes. I saw Hudson, Hudson, Hendrix, Hendrix, Hudson, Abrams, Hendrix, Abrams, Hudson all the way down the road to Ellettsville, which is just over the line in Monroe County. This gave me some insight into one aspect of Greene County politics. Families are large and interrelated. Maybe there were a few key people to see in each family. I soon found out that this is the case. Two days later I came back down the road looking for the heads of families. I was looking in particular for Wayne Abrams at Hendrixville. I found Wayne in back of his house. He and several other farmers were in the process of moving a privy. When I walked up they were too busy to bother with introductions. Instead, they yelled for me to give them a hand, which I did. After we set the privy in place, they asked me who I was. I told them my name and that I was a Republican candidate for the State Senate. They grinned and said, "Well, we'll give you a few votes around here. Give us some posters and cards." These are very genuine people. I liked them instinctively.

Once I was listed officially as a candidate, I began to receive invitations from the county chairmen and the program chairmen of the Republican women's organizations in three counties. The first rally was a new experience for me. It was held in the gym of a large country school house. Several hundred people attended. I was one of the first to arrive. When I walked in, I introduced myself to the women taking the tickets. They nodded shyly. The first man who came in wasn't very talkative. The crowd began to grow. All the farm women sat down on benches at one end of the gym. Most of them appeared to be quite retiring. The men all stood up and congregated on the other side of the room, talking politics. I moved around introducing myself to everybody. Some people were polite and talkative; others were non-committal, but they were all curious. The women brought their little children with them. They also brought beans, corn bread, fifteen or twenty kinds of pie, chicken, beef, and all sorts of vegetables, salads, and desserts. I now began to see why so many politicians have very heavy paunches in Indiana. Candidates are expected to eat lots of food. A smart candidate will sample something of everything, because the women are very proud of their contributions and are very interested to see who eats what. The women are unhappy if anything is left-over.

Russell Bontrager, candidate for United States Senator was the main speaker. The County Chairman made a long speech. Most speeches made by county chairmen are long, because protocol demands that they introduce almost everybody in the place. All we were allowed to say was, "I'm Jim Kessler, or I'm Star Brown, candidate for the State Senate."

Star's wife, who later became a good friend of mine along with her husband, was an able and effective campaigner. She quickly concluded that country people probably wouldn't have much use for college professors—so she called me "Perfesser" in a loud and clear voice at each one of these meetings. At first I thought her strategy would be devastating. After the meeting, a young man from Jasonville came over to see me and he said, "I'm glad you are running; I'm for you." I found that he was the only Republican to serve on that town's city council since 1930. His comment made me feel better.

There were many affairs of this kind during the primary campaign. The format was always the same: extended introductions, a drawing for door prizes, entertainment with local talent, and speeches by candidates for the principal state offices. Candidates for lesser office had no opportunity to air their views.

During the next few weeks I traveled most of Greene County's fourteen hundred miles of county-maintained roads. I spent more time in the Republican section of the county because this is where the relevant votes are in the primary. The people were friendly, but suspicious at first of persons not born in the county. They are intensely interested in politics.

On one of these forays, I drove to the small town of Jasonville over a long narrow road filled with chuckholes. This road winds its way over steep grades and around sharp, blind curves. No wonder the town of Jasonville is well on its way to becoming a ghost town.

These trips taught me something about the economy of Greene County. Its population is disappearing slowly but surely as the young people seek employment elsewhere. Its coal mines are being automated. Technological unemployment has created chronic poverty among former coal miners. Large numbers of people are on poor relief. There are complaints that poor relief is politically manipulated by home township trustees. The only way to eradicate such poverty is to provide economic and educational opportunities. It's clear to me that no industry would consider this town as a suitable place to establish a plant, if only because narrow bridges and roads are effective barriers to the mainstream of commerce. I resolved to make the improvement of the road connecting Jasonville and the town of Linton a major campaign issue.

CAMPAIGNING IN MONROE COUNTY

In between the frequent trips to Greene County, I attended dozens of bean dinners in Monroe and Brown Counties. I had no way of knowing in advance how my candidacy would be received in the rural sections of these counties. In fact, my opponent, Star Brown, openly predicted that I would be licked outside the city of Bloomington and probably would run behind him on the west side of the city. This latter area is more inhabited by native Monroe Countians than other sections of Bloomington.

There are two bean dinners that I remember most distinctly. One was given by "Honey" Jones, a Republican county commissioner and the owner of a trading post on Knightridge Road many miles into the country. The other was given in the poorest section of Bloomington in a public park. Hundreds of people attended both of these affairs. Both were free to all comers—Democrats as well as Republicans.

"Honey" Jones, the host at the first affair, is a legend in Monroe County politics. He got his name from his habit of calling all his acquaintances "Honey" to conceal the fact that he doesn't always remember their names. "Honey" is a self-made man. He buys pottery 'seconds' and sells them at substantial profits to tourists and others. His rambling country store has a filling station and a grocery department. "Honey" built this store with his own hands from odds and ends he acquired at auctions and from salvage operations. His store serves also as a kind of country town hall. Every Saturday night is square dance night. The country folk come down out of the hills and put on a real swinging show with guitars and hillbilly music. "Honey" is a power in Monroe County to be reckoned with. His rough exterior and speech conceal a good mind. He is politically shrewd. He is fully capable of rewarding friends and punishing enemies. If "Honey" likes you the results are easily discernible in election returns from his township.

There is a deep cultural cleavage between many of the people who live in the city and many of the people who live in the country in Monroe County. The country people are plain. They are deeply religious. They are disdainful of anyone who is not "genuine." There was a real question in the minds of some whether a college professor could communicate with these people. There was no question in my mind; I liked them instinctively and they responded to my respect for them in kind. It was in the country that old Fritz Ryan, the former county chairman, could 'do me in' if I wasn't extremely careful.

One complicating factor in this election was that Monroe County voters, for the first time, would use voting machines. There was a feeling that the old people, especially those in rural townships, might not vote because they were afraid of the voting machines—afraid that they might not use them correctly—afraid that the machines might not be honest—afraid to ask questions about their use. The county clerk, aided and abetted by the League of Women's Voters and other similar organizations, put on a campaign to explain the use of the machines. The voting machines were put on trucks and transported to each precinct in the county to be demonstrated on certain nights. This was an excellent opportunity for the candidates to meet the people.

There are twenty-six precincts in Monroe County. All the candidates were expected to be at each one of these precincts on each demonstration night. We were absent at our peril. We went. We passed out cards. We got acquainted with one another. In between bean dinners and voting machine demonstrations, we shook hands everywhere we could. We called on precinct committeemen and vice-committeemen. We called on businessmen. We talked to ministers. We went to see labor leaders. We knocked on hundreds of doors.

During the campaign I was careful to call often on elected Republican officials in the Monroe County courthouse. When I went to Greene County, I always stopped at the county courthouse in Bloomfield. Failure to call on local officials who are members of your own party may be considered a serious breach of protocol. I felt pretty certain that most of the people in the courthouse were on my side in the campaign, but you never know. Besides, there was now positive evidence that Mr. Ryan, the former Monroe County Chairman, was working actively against me, and Mr. Ryan still had some influence with courthouse officials.

While all these activities were going on, a number of young people expressed interest in my campaign. Many of these young people were associated with my university. A few were former students of mine. Some were high school students in Greene County. These young people took it upon themselves to perform a number of vitally necessary chores. They organized election day activities. They took part in parades. They talked to their parents and their parent's friends. They even organized two high school booster clubs. They also transported people to the polls. They were efficient, energetic, and dependable. I remember with great pleasure their association with the campaign.

Somtimes things run smoothly in a campaign and all is sweetness and light. Other times, candidates need very thick skins. Once when I came out of the courthouse, a precinct committeewoman from Monroe County accosted me in a very unfriendly manner and said, "Mr. Kessler, I can't support you. I don't think university people have any business being involved in Monroe County politics and I am going to work for your opponent, Mr. Brown. If you win, I will support you as the Republican nominee, but I would be less than honest if I told you that I wanted you to win." I thanked her for her frankness and told her that I didn't think a person's occupation, unless it is immoral or anti-social, should necessarily influence a person's choice of candidates, but that she was entitled to her opinion and I didn't intend to attempt to change it. This woman and another one who was also a precinct committeewoman were very closely identified with extreme right wing groups in the county. Their disdain for persons associated with the University community was evident during the rest of the primary and throughout the balance of the campaign.

CAMPAIGNING IN BROWN COUNTY

Brown County is one of the most beautiful and picturesque counties in the Midwest. It is sparsely populated and its people for the most part live in modest circumstances. The county is famous for its scenery, its art colony and its homespun environment. I have never met a more interesting and loyal bunch of people than the ones I met here.

The Democrats usually carry Brown County in a general election by 300 to 1200 votes. In past elections for the state senate, Republicans usually carried Monroe by a slight margin, lost in Greene County by a similar margin, and Brown County tipped the scales in favor of the Democrats.

Since my primary opponent owned property in Brown County and knew everyone there, I thought I probably didn't have much of a chance to carry the county. Brown Countians are very proud and are very suspicious of outsiders. The party was split by factional feuding as it was in Monroe and to a lesser extent in Greene.

The first time I went to a meeting over there, it was one called by Doris Fleetwood, the Brown County chairman. The scene was the quaint and ancient courthouse. All the precinct committeemen were present. Most of them were dressed in rough hunting clothes or in bib overalls. Each candidate was introduced and given an opportunity to speak for five minutes. Star Brown was one of the first ones there and he knew everyone by his first name.

Brown County shared a House seat with a county in another senatorial district. One of the candidates for this seat made an excellent impression on me. We became friends and coordinated our primary campaigns in Brown County. We entered into the spirit of the county's annual festival and were roundly applauded for doing so. I put on a fake beard, dressed in a Lincoln suit, wore a replica of an authentic Lincoln campaign button, and passed out cards to everyone in the parade. Almost everyone in the county was in the parade. I entered the beard growing contest, but got thrown out when the judges discovered that my beard was false. The local police placed me in the stockade on the courthouse lawn. The newspaper, the Brown County *Democrat*, took pictures of Star Brown bailing me out. I used this picture in my local advertising. People all over the county wondered who I was. It was an excellent publicity stunt.

I put a new ribbon in my typewriter, typed a letter to Brown countians, multilithed it. My campaign workers, using typewriters with type to match that used in the multilithed letter, inserted personal salutations and addresses. I signed each letter. They were sent by first class mail to every Republican in Brown County. According to the precinct committeemen, these letters made a favorable impression because they indicated that Brown County votes really meant something to me and because they were accepted as evidence that I would pay some attention to Brown County's small Republican minority if I should be elected. I didn't send letters to the other counties because I didn't have the resources to complete such an ambitious task.

ACTIVITIES ON PRIMARY ELECTION DAY

When all is said and done, there is only so much a candidate can do. He can build a precinct organization to see people for him, to write and mail campaign literature for him, and to perform numerous related tasks. He can shake hands, he can see all the people, he can collect all the necessary money, he can ring thousands of door bells, he can work around the clock, and he can spend all his own money, but finally the time comes to cast the ballots and to count the votes. Time passes very rapidly in a campaign. About five o'clock in the morning on election day, my young helpers picked up posters and cards and distributed them to supporters stationed at each of the precincts in Monroe County. My friends in Greene County did the same thing. The county chairman in Brown County took my posters around to each of the precincts in his county. Every precinct had one of my signs posted in front.

Election day was full of frenzied activity. I went from precinct to precinct, passing out cards, checking with supporters to see how heavy the vote was. It was an exciting and exhausting experience.

In Ellettsville, I found Fritz Ryan passing out my opponent's cards at one of the precincts. I really couldn't complain since Star is a native of Ellettsville. When the polls closed, I bought hot dogs, french fries, cokes, etc., for the kids who had done such a magnificent job. Dozens of them came to my house to wait for election returns. Early in the evening the returns began to come in from the Monroe County machines. First I was ahead, then behind, then ahead. It was a horse race. I watched each precinct carefully. I was running behind my estimates. About eight o'clock the Monroe County vote was complete but unofficial. My lead was a mere 185 votes. The election was not over by any means. At this time, my opponent announced that he expected to carry Greene and Brown Counties; and well he might. It was going to be a long night, since Greene and Brown County voters voted on paper ballots which had to be counted by hand. Long after midnight, some of my friends called from Bloomfield to tell me that I was winning in almost every Greene County precinct. By this time, all my young supporters were gone. My long-suffering wife and I celebrated.

AS MY PARTY'S NOMINEE

It was a great relief to know that all the effort had produced some tangible results. I was now the party's official nominee. This fact should make some difference. Once you are the nominee, all Republicans are supposed to be your friends. It should be easier to raise funds and the party organization should do much of the precinct work for you. These were pleasant thoughts indeed.

The next morning I lost no time getting over to Ellettsville to see my defeated opponent. Star took his defeat like a gentleman even though it meant the end of a colorful political career spanning more than a quarter of a century. This man clearly knew the game and played it according to the rules. During the next few months we became close allies and good personal friends.

Now that the primary was over, I looked forward eagerly to attending my party's state convention. As the nominee I might have some ability to promote the fortunes of my good friend, the Lt. Governor in his bid for the gubernatorial nomination. I knew that if he won in the convention he would campaign hard for me in Monroe County where he was very popular. In the event of his election I would have an open door to the Governor's office. In my opinion, my chances for success in the general election were closely linked to the success of the Lt. Governor in securing the nomination.

The Lt. Governor, as the highest elected Republican official, was the titular head of the Party; ordinarily, he would have had no difficulty securing the nomination. Things were different on this occasion because of the unique role forced on him by circumstances in the previous session of the General Assembly. This role and my relationship to it is described in some detail below because it became the dominant state issue. It is essential to understand the events which created that issue because it apparently had a substantial impact on the campaign of many candidates for the General Assembly.

As former Director of the General Assembly's Commission on State Tax and Financing Policy, I worked hard with members of both parties in the legislative session which ended just a few months before the primary. My commission consisted of a Republican and a Democratic Senator, a Republican and a Democratic member of the House of Representatives, two Republican and two Democratic laymen. Officials of the State's principal lobbying or interest groups were consultants to the commission. The purpose of the commission was to provide the General Assembly with information concerning the probable impact and economic effect of any tax alternatives it might consider.

Members of the General Assembly knew two years earlier, in 1961, that the 1963 session would have to raise taxes at the state level to defray the cost of educating an additional 64,000 school children entering the Indiana educational system during the biennium. If taxes were not raised, local property taxes would be increased to meet costs, or the quality of the school system would suffer. Most groups and newspapers in Indiana accepted the responsibility imposed by the facts; however, the largest metropolitan newspaper rejected this interpretation. Requiring legislators to make such decisions imposes a cruel choice on them:

Once the decision to raise taxes is made they must decide how to distribute the tax burden among their reluctant constituents. Naturally, many interest groups wanted to be exempt from any increase. This same legislature was faced with the problems of redistributing congressional and state legislative boundaries and of meeting the Governor's demand to provide funds for the construction of a port for Indiana on Lake Michigan.

The House was controlled by Republicans. The Republicans, because of the post-election death of a colleague, were deprived of a constitutional majority in the Senate (26). The Governor was a Democrat. The Indiana Constitution requires certain types of bills to be passed by a constituional majority—that is, a majority of all members and not merely a majority of those present. In the event of a tie, the Lt. Governor may cast a ballot, but his tie-breaking vote is effective in securing the enactment of legislation which requires a constitutional majority only if his vote is needed to adopt a conference committee report reconciling differences between the two Houses. The adoption of such reports is by simple and not by constitutional majorities.

Since the Legislature was unable to resolve its conflicts during the sixty-one calendar days of its regular session, the Governor called a special session. The legislature was under constant fire in newspaper, radio and television editorials for its failure to solve the problems facing it within the sixty-one day limit of its regular biennial session. The three issues mentioned above were interdependent. Each time it appeared that it was possible to reach a compromise solution to the vexing tax problems, a few legislators made their support of tax legislation contingent on having their way in redistricting or on port legislation and the majority for the tax compromise vanished. The deadlock was finally broken on the fortieth and final day of the special session. There was a tie in the State Senate on the question of whether to adopt a conference committee report resolving differences between House and Senate versions of tax legislation. The Lt. Governor broke the tie. At the time he did this, he told me that his vote probably would end his political career. He broke the tie because, in his opinion, the State needed the money to maintain the quality of its educational program; and he thought that a second special session composed of the same members, would acquire no new competence to meet problems. The continuing deadlock would damage the reputation of Indiana's representative institutions irreparably. Lt. Governor Ristine thus put his personal career in jeopardy in order to serve what he considered to be the best interests of the state. This is one of many reason why I thought he would make an excellent governor. Another reason was that he is a thoroughly honest man.

There were four other serious contenders for the Republican nomination for governor. These four candidates claimed that Ristine could not be elected because his vote passed the tax program in the State Senate. They ignored the fact that a Democratic governor had to sign the bill, and that a majority of Democrats voted for it in the Senate.

All five candidates campaigned relentlessly for delegates throughout the State.

Simultaneously, the contest for delegates to the Republican National Convention was being waged. Both campaigns were heated and conducted along ideological lines. As the 1964 elections demonstrated so clearly, these ideological conflicts and the controversy over the tax program split the Republican party wide open. This split had a profound impact on the campaigning of many Republican candidates for the Legislature.

A portent to come was clearly manifest in the vote cast for Harold Stassen in the presidential preference primary. Stassen received approximately 25 per cent of the Republican vote cast in Indiana. This vote was roughly the size of President Johnson's margin of victory in the '64 elections. The Republican State Convention, after a vicious and divisive fight, nominated the Lt. Governor on the third ballot. Subsequently, the Indianapolis Star, the largest newspaper in the State, referred to the nominee consistently as Lt. Governor Ristine, the man who broke the tie establishing the Indiana sales tax. In my own mind, the Lt. Governor's nomination was public vindication of his vote on the tax program and proof that integrity is recognized and respected by leaders in my party. I thought the nominee was the most qualified man ever to be nominated for Governor of Indiana. I was proud to be on the same ticket with him.

Shortly after the state convention, I made plans to go to the Republican National Convention. Mr. Robert Nixon Stuart, the Republican State Chairman, secured a paying position for me as a doorkeeper. The money was not important to me, but the doorkeeper's badge was. It was impossible to obtain such a credential without the approval of the State Chairman. This badge got me into every session of the National Convention and made it possible for me to go many places inside the convention hall which were barred to me otherwise. In San Francisco I saw the Lt. Governor and many people from the Indiana delegation. On one enjoyable occasion, I took the Greene County Chairman and his wife to dinner at a fine Fisherman's Wharf restaurant. With trepidation I witnessed the terribly divisive fight on the floor of my party's national convention. The refusal of the various elements in the party even to be gracious to one another signaled to me that the Republican party was clearly headed for disaster. This schism created all kinds of problems. Of course nominees for lesser offices in a presidential year make their contracts with their party to support the whole ticket before they know who will be nominated by the national convention. The national campaign absolutely overpowers their own campaigns. It is very difficult in the presence of all the background noise of a presidential campaign and the principal state campaigns to attract any attention to the issues in the contests for lesser offices.

The Goldwater nomination divided the Republican party so drastically, that it created difficult problems for all Republican candidates.

I lived in a university community. Mr. Goldwater was anathema to many inhabitants of that community. If I wished to be elected it would be necessary for me to concentrate on state issues and to avoid all vestiges of the ideological conflict raging all about me. Under the circumstances, the 1964 campaign was a strange, unnatural experience. Everybody was suspicious of everyone else. To radicals on the right and the left, all candidates not sufficiently vociferous in their support of the relevant ideology were marked for extinction. This was undoubtedly one of the most difficult years for a Republican who wanted to win to run for office.

Once the candidates were selected, the character of the campaign changed completely. In the primary, the principal focus of attention was on personalities and qualifications of rivals. In the campaign preceeding the general election, the emphasis shifted to issues. The bean dinners continued. We went to county fairs, we shook hands by the thousands on the streets and at factory gates. We took part in parades, rallies, and country square dances. I remember one parade in Bloomfield. It was an extremely hot day in the middle of summer. The Democrats rode in an air-conditioned car and the Republican candidates walked and sweltered with the masses of people. We hoped the voters took note.

ISSUES IN THE GENERAL ELECTION

I searched for some salient issues relevant to needs of the people of Greene County. The deplorable road from Linton to Jasonville seemed to provide an issue. For years Democratic politicians promised the people in Wright township to fix this road. Although these promises were always repeated just before elections, nothing was ever done.

In Monroe County, there were a number of minor public services which had been neglected. I decided to find one in each of Bloomington's principal sections on the theory that promises to correct these would have a personal appeal to the residents of that section. My newspaper advertising was designed to chide my opponent for his inattention to the needs of his constituents and to urge immediate and specific action. Two dangerous intersections of city streets and state highways were without stoplights. State action and State funds were necessary to solve these problems. My argument was that my opponent's party was in power; he was the incumbent senator; he had no excuse for failing to act. I noticed at one of these intersections that cars frequently were backed up for four or five blocks waiting to enter the main thoroughfare. Another public irritant received my attention. The State was about to complete a large new reservoir, the largest man-made lake in the State, seven miles from Bloomington. This lake had been in the planning and construction stages for years. The road between Bloomington and Indianapolis is very narrow. The traffic count has warranted dual-laning for a long time. Many people are killed on this overcrowded road each year. Now that the lake was about to open, the Governor, a member of the opposite party, boasted that some two million tourists would visit Monroe Reservoir annually. I charged my opponent with failing in his eight years in office to demand that plans be made to cope with this traffic problem. Simultaneously, at my suggestion, the gubernatorial candidate of my party promised to dual-lane the main highway from Bloomington to Indianapolis and to provide adequate access roads to Monroe Reservoir.

As an official nominee of the Republican party, I now received mail from many organized interest groups asking me to take specific stands on issues. One of these groups was the Mental Health Association. Candidates were invited to visit Muscatatuck, the State Hospital for retarded children. This is an experience I'll never forget. During our inspection of the facilities, we saw for ourselves the overcrowded nature of the facilities and that the hospital was woefully understaffed. Our guide took us through a new building that was not yet occupied. He told us that the contractors had not installed adequate heating and ventilating systems and that red tape was preventing the immediate correction of the defects. On the grounds outside, we saw unfinished street lamps. These street lamps had been in this condition for months. At lunch, we went through the regular line. The food was perfectly terrible. In fact, it was almost nauseating. I decided that public attention should be called to this state of affairs. Some friends at Bloomington's largest newspaper came back to Muscatatuck with me and made a thorough inspection of the facility. They took pictures of the empty building, the overcrowded conditions, and the unfinished street lamps. A series of articles about these and similar shortcomings of the state administration appeared in the local newspapers. My opponent was concerned by these tactics. He chided me for being irresponsible and claimed that my activities would simply make it more difficult for him to secure the cooperation of state agencies in finding solutions to the problems of the counties in the Senate District. Thus the issues developed: Roads were needed to handle the enormous traffic expected at Monroe Reservoir; roads were needed for the development of underdeveloped sections of the district; more attention should be given to the construction of adequate mental health facilities. My opponent's wife was heard to remark to some people that her husband had never been in a campaign like this.

In retrospect, I think my opponent, who is a personal friend of mine, conducted a clever campaign. He rarely went to Greene County. His theory was that he didn't need to campaign because the Republicans were tearing one another to shreds nationally and he would be the beneficiary locally.

And so the campaign dragged on. The Republican organization which I thought would be so helpful paid for institutional ads only. Such ads supported all Republicans without singling out any particular candidate. Party workers concentrated on the Governor's race, the race for U.S. Senator, and, of course, the greatest emphasis was placed on the presidential campaign.

One or two ugly incidents occurred. The woman who had stopped me in front of the courthouse during the primary to tell me she wouldn't support a university professor came up to me at one of the rallies and said that she understood my wife was opposed to the Republican presidential nominee. I told her to ask my wife about her views instead of listening to rumors. In any event, my campaign and the campaigns of all candidates were inextricably tied in with the presidential campaign.

ELECTION DAY

Once again I developed my own organization for election day, and arranged to have the polls manned as they were in the primary. Once again I touched base with all my friends in Greene and Brown Counties to pick up whatever information I could and to encourage them. And, once again, the time came when there was nothing left to do but to wait for election returns. I went to the home of a friend who is a member of the University faculty. Several acquaintances were there. We turned on the television set. The extent of the Johnson landslide was quickly established. Very early in the evening, computers conceded the gubernatorial campaign to the Democrats. The Republican nominee was losing even in Allen County (Fort Wayne), a notorious Republican stronghold in Indiana. I was so disturbed by this unexpected turn of events that I left my friends and went to the *Herald Telephone* to examine precinct returns as they came in. While I was leading in Monroe County, and running ahead of the national ticket precinct by precinct, the lead wasn't big enough. It would take an eighteen hundred vote plurality in Monroe County for me to carry the district. It was now clear, in view of the Democratic landslide in the national and state races that only a miracle could save me.

Meanwhile, the Monroe County radio reported me as the winner. The Indianapolis Star, in its morning edition, listed me as the winner. I received congratulations from people by phone and by telegraph. I knew my counties well enough to realize that I was going to be snowed under unless the last minute campaign on radio had succeeded in focusing the attention of the people in Jasonville on the adverse conditions of their roads and in fixing the blame for the inadequacies of these roads on the Democrats. The Greene County Democratic chairman and the Democratic candidate for Congress were so unnerved by this tactic that they countered it in the last days of the campaign by spending a lot of money on the Linton radio station to tell people that contracts had already been let to repair this road. Late in the evening, my opponent, agitated by the accounts of the race on the Monroe County radio, came down to the newspaper. By that time people were congratulating me and I was telling them that congratulations were not in order. I was certain that the Greene County vote would confirm my conviction that the race was lost. I didn't have to wait long for the bad news. My opponent called Greene County Democratic headquarters. They told him he was receiving the usual Democratic majorities in the western end of the county. It was all over. I congratulated the winner and went home. This was the end of nine hard months of labor.

EPILOGUE

You put all your personality into a campaign. You give it your time, your effort, your money, your heart, and your soul. It's hard to lose, but that is the way the system works. It works because there are hundreds of thousand of people each year who are willing to spend the time, the money, the effort, and the energy necessary to campaign for public office. Sometimes candidates are defeated because of the mistakes they make themselves. Sometimes they are caught in a whirlpool and are defeated by forces over which they have no control. No matter how you lose, the pain of losing is there. In order to play the electoral game, we must play by the rules. The rules say that we must be willing to accept defeat gracefully. My friends who were defeated with me knew the rules and played the game and had no regrets. Would we do it again? If we had the time and if we had the money we would.

CONRAD F. JOYNER

Conrad F. Joyner studied at Earlham College (A.B. 1953), University of Florida (M.A., 1954), University of Sydney, as a Fulbright scholar (1955–56), and University of Florida (Ph.D. 1957). He has taught at West Virginia University (1956–57), University of Southwestern Louisiana (1957–61), University of Arizona (1961–   ).

Joyner was a consultant, Louisiana Intracoastal Seaway Association; was on the staff of Governor Mark Hatfield (1960–61, 1964); of Congressman Ogden Reid (1965); Campaign Manager, Richard Burke for Congress; campaign co-manager, Lew Davis for Mayor (Tucson); Chairman, Arts and Sciences Division, Arizona State Republican Central Committee (1963–   ). In the Fall of 1967 he was elected to the Tucson City Council for a four year term.

Joyner co-authored *The Louisiana Intracoastal Seaway* (1959), *Holman vs. Hughes* (1961), *The Commonwealth and Monopolies* (1963), *The Republican Dilemma: Conservatism or Progressivism* (1963); and has contributed to numerous professional journals in the United States and abroad.

CONRAD F. JOYNER

7. Running A Congressional Campaign

PROLOGUE

On a warm pleasant Sunday afternoon in May 1962, I was invited for a swim and a "good political discussion" at the home of the Pima County, Arizona Republican Chairman. Aside from the host, the "swimmers" included the majority leader of the Arizona House of Representatives, a former Arizona Supreme Court Justice, a young advertising executive, a former county chairman, and an attorney who had taught Government at the University of Arizona prior to entering private law practice. Since the professor-turned-attorney was being mentioned as a candidate for Congress and since I had talked with him about this possibility on several occasions, it appeared that the conversation would center on his intended race. I had no notion how much this discussion would affect my life.

At first our conversation was informal. We took turns speculating on the likelihood of defeating the incumbent, prospects of the former professor making the race, need for money and organization, people who would help if the former professor ran, affect of a U. S. senatorial primary on the congressional race, Democratic registration advantage, ways in which our prospective candidate could support his family, and points on which the incumbent was vulnerable.

It became apparent that each of the individuals was asking me questions. At first, I thought it was because I had worked for Governor Mark Hatfield of Oregon and taught American politics, but these were not the real reasons. Through a simple question, "Who is going to manage the campaign?", I discovered their interest in me. Instead of an indication that one of them or some other person would do the job, the county chairman said: "We have been giving the matter some thought and wonder if you might be interested."

143

I neither accepted nor rejected but quickly began to catalog my deficiencies and reservations—only a year in Arizona, unfamiliarity with the local Republican organization and workers, general knowledge of campaigning but no substantial top level experience, lack of time due to teaching responsibilities, obligations to family, and moderate Republican in a conservative state. It appeared that they were ready for my objections, because each one was met with a seemingly plausible answer. Finally, I agreed to help subject to their acceptance of my limitations and the problems they might pose. I declined the title "manager" and asked for time to think about the proposition and to talk it over with my wife.

My wife and I talked about the situation in light of my limitations. The Head of the Politics Department, an active Democrat, gave his approval subject to meeting my University commitments. Within three days I was involved in the first of many campaign activities.

The above indicates some problems and prospects encountered in assuming an active political role. What follows is a combination of political knowledge gained through study and practical experience.

There are many ways to treat political activity. Two which have received little attention are campaign organization and management. Yet, they are at the heart of the process through which a representative democracy is maintained. To understand campaign organization and management requires more than knowledge of committees, raising money, strategy, and tactics; although they are important. We first need information about the office being sought, why candidates run, why people manage and work at other campaign jobs.

THE CONGRESSIONAL JOB

Article I of the U. S. Constitution sketches in fairly broad strokes the qualifications, powers, and duties of national legislators. Representatives have a two-year term, are subject to popular election, must be 25 years old, and live in the state from which they are chosen. Senators and representatives are free from arrest while going to or from or attending sessions of Congress, except in cases involving treason, felony, or breaches of the peace. They also are exempt from legal action for anything they might say on the floor of Congress. The Constitution authorizes them to set their own salary by law. Every ten years the House seats, which are not fixed by total number, are to be apportioned among the states on the basis of census figures. The Speaker is the only officer of the House mentioned, although "other officers" are authorized. Section 8 lists a number of positive legislative powers and contains the "necessary and proper" or elastic clause, and Section 9 places a number of direct restrictions on Congress. The first Article further provides for the executive veto and the procedure necessary to override it.

These bare bones have been filled out so that the House of Representatives has the most elaborate organization and procedures of any legislative assembly in the world. The character of the House and the individual congressman's role in it have been shaped through nearly two centuries of actual operation.

The late Congressman Clem Miller in a collection of his letters to a constituent spells out the realities of congressional life. Most of the contemporary congressman's work cannot be found in the Constitution. To be sure, there is debate on the great issues, but the vast majority of the congressman's time is spent off the floor of the House.

His time evaporates in committee and sub-committee meetings and hearings; reading and answering mail; fulfilling requests for everything from information about a bill to a special White House tour; seeing folks from back home; talking with lobbyists; reading and skimming reports, newspapers, magazines, and books; and planning for his next campaign, which is never too far away. During his first years in Congress he works with an inadequate and overworked staff in attempting to master this complex and bewildering system. His congressional salary will not permit him to balance his personal budget. The newcomer finds little opportunity to achieve an influential position. Seniority is the key to power for it provides rewards based on continuous service in the House.

Business Week magazine paints a fairly grim picture of a typical congressman's life. "He thinks of himself as overworked, struggling to keep up with a flood of mail from back home and with his committee responsibilities. If he is going to be a good House member, he soon thinks of himself as a small cog in a machine that will carry him upwards if he minds his manners, holds his liquor, and does not cross his party leaders." Clem Miller does not disagree with these observations, but he is not so gloomy: "This is a busy day, six days a week, I present it to you neither for commiseration nor vain-glory. I like it. It is very lively, and may someday be rewarding."

WHY THEY MANAGE?

Because motivations, resources, and opportunities in running for different offices vary so much, there are different types of candidates, managers, and campaign organizations. First, some candidates just want to win or retain a particular office. Not all congressmen fall into this category, but the fact that well over 50 per cent of the congressional districts are represented by the same man for five consecutive terms would seem to suggest that many congressmen have *static* office seeking ambitions.

Second, some people become office seekers for reasons other than victory. Young professional people—particularly attorneys, realtors,

and insurance men—find campaigning a cheap but ethical way to
advertise. Some people may run in order to strengthen the party
ticket or in the hope of establishing name familiarity for future
political races. Candidates who run without the expectation of victory
have *discrete* ambitions.

Third, there are many office seekers who view their quest for
particular offices as steps toward higher goals. Mark Hatfield made
his way up the ladder from the State House of Representatives, to
the State Senate, to the Secretaryship of State, to the Governor's
office, and to the U. S. Senate. The late President Kennedy's trail led
from the U. S. House of Representatives, to the U. S. Senate, and to
the White House. The "Hatfields" and "Kennedys" in the political
world have *progressive* ambitions.

I have a strong feeling that most candidates and their workers
believe they can win. In most real life campaigns the outlook and
desire for victory is present regardless of how unrealistic it may seem.
This is an important factor and colors my judgments about campaigning. In fact, I do not think that the value of campaigns to
representative democracy can be adequately appraised without account-
ing for this positive attitude on the part of campaigners.

Whatever their particular ambitions, candidates for Congress
generally have managers and campaign organizations. The exceptions
are long-time incumbents, mainly southerners, who have neither
primary nor general election opponents. Their Washington and district staffs serve as their continuing "campaign" group. Other incumbent congressmen who occasionally face primary opposition and who
generally are confronted with opponents in the general election frequently use one of their official staff members as a campaign manager.
The more scrupulous congressmen temporarily take staff members off
the government payroll and transfer them to the campaign payroll.
Regardless of who pays their salary, the fact that incumbents can use
their regular staff members in this capacity is one of the many advantages they possess.

Although these managers are not full-time campaigners in the
strictest sense, they are among the growing number of professional
campaign workers. Included in the professional managerial group are
those who are salaried and work full-time or most of the time for a
political party or office seeker. The young advertising executive who
participated in our 1962 campaign as a volunteer worker became
executive director of the Arizona Republican State Central Committee in 1963. He shifted to the staff of a Republican gubernatorial
candidate in 1966.

Another paid professional campaign managerial type is the advertising firm. For a number of years one of the most successful firms
has been Whitaker and Baxter who operates in California. Stanley
Kelley, Jr. provides a succinct description of their activities:

Whitaker and Baxter are systematic in their approach to the problems of political public relations. According to their own description, their first move, once they have accepted responsibility for a campaign, is to blueprint it. Issues are developed, the time sequence of action is plotted, and the media are selected. Then a plan for the campaign is written for the opposition and Whitaker and Baxter's own procedures are adjusted to meet it. Finally, the campaign is budgeted.

Although most candidates in competitive districts use public relations firms, it would be in error to assume that these professionals have taken over the job of directing campaigns. Most campaigns, and I suspect this applies to many congressional campaigns, are still managed by friends, party officials, and/or aspiring young politicians.

Friends of candidates with spare time on their hands, particularly retired or semi-retired people, who have organizational experience, are often found managing campaigns. The young professional person who wants to advertise or learn something about politics for his own future campaigns is also a familiar figure in the upper echelons of campaign organizations. These amateur managers can draw on the experience of party officials and the campaign guides published by the Republican and Democratic national committees and political practitioners.

Finally, there are a few instances in which a pressure group, e.g., business association, labor organization, or farm group, will "loan" one of its staff members to a candidate. This type of arrangement is open to question because it implies return favors in the form of voting the right way on issues which concern the pressure group and preferential treatment from the candidate if he is successful. In the absence of other sources of top campaign assistance, this may be a tempting arrangement for the candidate who thinks he can win if he gets manpower from a pressure group who shares his sentiments on issues.

Mixed with this description of types of managers are some of the reasons why people undertake top level campaign jobs. For many it is probably a one- or two-time affair like running for office is for many political candidates. For instance, it has been estimated that of approximately 7800 members of state legislatures more than one-half must be replaced every two years. There are no comparable figures for campaign managers of state legislative candidates, but on the basis of personal observation I estimate the turnover for managers at this level would be equally high. However, there is a growing group of semi-professional and professional managers for higher office seekers, e.g., governors, U.S. representatives and U.S. senators. In part, this trend reflects the changing requirements for campaign management. The public relations skills vital in campaigns which are conducted in cities and suburban areas have been responsible for an increase in the use of public relations firms. Some of these firms like Whitaker and

Baxter literally take over campaigns while others have an important role but do not have full responsibility.

THE CAMPAIGN ENVIRONMENT

In campaigns there are certain factors over which candidates and their organizations have very little control. They make up the general and specific environment in which candidates seek offices. Political strategists attempt to evaluate the potential impact of these environmental factors and form their strategy and tactics in light of them. The factors which are important in virtually every campaign include: the advantages of incumbency; the political demography of the constituency (the political behavior of individuals and groups which comprise the voting population); the geographical setting (urban or rural or both); and the temper of the time. In addition to these factors, candidates for Congress must take into account the unique organizational position of the congressional district in the structure of American government, relationship of congressional races to other contests for office, and the time of congressional elections.

One of the sturdiest realities of American politics is that incumbents and candidates with registration advantages generally win. Congressional challengers, i.e., those running against incumbents or candidates with a registration advantage, face such overwhelming odds that undoubtedly many potential candidates are discouraged. About 400 of the 435 sitting congressmen are renominated and seek re-election. Of these 400, more than 360 generally win re-election. Thus, on a nationwide basis the chance of beating an incumbent are less than one in ten. The less than 40 victorious challengers are joined by approximately 35 congressmen who win races in which incumbents were not running. Many of these 35 are members of the same party as the previous incumbent. Charles O. Jones points to an even more dismal statistic for challengers—70–80 per cent of all congressional districts will be represented either by the same man or the same party for five consecutive terms.

These figures indicate that incumbents will have an easier task than their challengers. Nonetheless, incumbents do not always win or even seek re-election. About 35, either because of retirement, death, defeat in the primary or decision to run for another office, do not seek another term. About 40 are defeated by challengers. This means that about 75 new congressmen are elected every two years.

The odds against unseating incumbents are weighted heavily against challengers but this has to be considered in light of other circumstances which may offer additional discouragement or rays of hope for challengers. One of the most significant factors, aside from incumbency, in determining the outcome of elections is the party affiliation of the voters. Although there is some variation from office-to-office and election-to-election, about 75 per cent of the voters cast their ballots along party lines. If challengers run against incumbents with heavy registration advantages—60 per cent incumbent vs. 40 per cent challenger—the challengers' changes are greatly reduced. However, if registration figures are more favorable to the challengers, their prospects for victory can be improved.

Some candidates win and are re-elected in districts in which they are at a registration disadvantage. Thus, in addition to registration figures, candidates should carefully review the voting history of their districts in an effort to determine any deviations from the expected voting pattern, i.e., elections in which candidates with registration disadvantages secure a large percentage of opposition party votes. If deviant results are discovered, a number of avenues can be explored in the hope of discovering lessons for other campaigns. Some of these can be formulated into questions: Were there special circumstances, e.g., charges of corruption or a statewide sweep? What kinds of campaigns were waged? What were the personalities of the candidates? Not only will challengers ask these questions, but also incumbents and those of the same party who want to replace incumbents will be asking them.

Aside from looking at these aspects of individual voting behavior, those who plan campaigns need to know about the major social, economic, religious, ethnic, racial, and other groups in their districts. This knowledge is essential for groups other than political parties and important in providing voters with attitudes about candidates and issues. For example, labor union members and Negroes tend to vote Democratic; older people and those with higher incomes tend to vote Republican. Groups also engage in political activity. Labor unions register voters and help get them to the polls. The American Medical Association through its various political action committees makes contributions to candidates.

The geography of the district is another important consideration. Rural and urban districts or combinations thereof present different campaign situations. Candidates in rural areas may find it extremely difficult because of distance and time to organize door-to-door solicitations and may rely instead on the media of communication—billboards, radio and TV spots, newspaper advertisements, and direct mailings. Candidates in large metropolitan areas like New York, Chicago, or Los Angeles quickly discover that the costs of most mass media are prohibitive. Congressional candidates in the urban areas discover that radio and TV appeals are lost among other competing advertisements. Further, these appeals reach many more voters who do not live in their districts than do. Hence, candidates in large urban centers use other devices for reaching voters—door-to-door and telephone solicitations, direct mailings, coffees, teas and cocktail parties, and street corner rallies.

Superimposed on these considerations is the temper of the times. Candidates whether they are weak challengers or prestigious incumbents have virtually no control over the condition of the economy, the state of world affairs, and natural disasters. Yet, these make up part of the campaign environment and can be important in determining the outcome of elections.

One incumbent with a harbor in his district felt the weight of a severe tide which did damage to the port and brought the wrath of the voters down on him. His opponent kept asking what the incumbent had done to get federal assistance to repair the damage. Unfortunately, the federal government's response was slow through no fault of the congressman. Yet, the voters of the port city reversed their previous strong support for the incumbent and gave the challenger a majority which was sufficient to carry the election for him.

Not all occurences are as dramatic as this, but at times external factors change votes and at other times solidify votes. The political ramifications of domestic and foreign events are difficult to measure. When economic conditions are good, no recession or inflation, and there are no major international crises, incumbents generally benefit. On the other hand, the 1932 elections went to Democrats because the depression had begun under Republican Herbert Hoover. Republicans also suffered election setbacks in 1958 when the economy suffered a recession. During the Cuban crisis of 1962 incumbent Democrats who supported President Kennedy seemed to benefit. However, the Korean crisis probably helped General Eisenhower and Republican congressional candidates who were critical of President Truman's policies.

Some of the uniqueness of congressional campaigns is related to the nature of the constituency. As a rule, the congressional district constituency is not shared by other office seekers. U.S. senatorial candidates and those who seek statewide office, e.g., governor and attorney general, share the entire state as their constituency. Candidates for countywide or citywide offices appeal to either county or city voters. The practical results of this are that state party organizations are geared to statewide campaigns while city and county organizations strive for offices within their domains. State organizations are generally combinations of local party units. This leaves congressional candidates who have several counties or part of a city or county as their constituencies without permanent party organizational bases.

There have been some attempts to offset this problem by building statewide organizations on hierarchical bases with congressional district organizations as intermediate levels between the local and state organizations. My observation of Indiana which uses such a pattern indicates that this does little to provide the congressional candidates with a party organizational base. Frequently, county chairmen serve as district chairmen. As district chairmen they are entitled to a place on the state central committee. Hence, the district chairmen are more concerned with their position on the state committee and with their county organizations. People seek district chairmenships because they carry with them seats on the state committee and not because they want to aid congressional candidates.

Senator Joseph Clark explores the affects of this organizational pattern and concludes that: "In this structure, the congressional election becomes more of a by-product than an end product of the party process." The stepchild nature of congressional candidates is augmented by the fact that the local, statewide and national candidates may have different policy interests. Also, congressional elections since they occur every two years do not always take place in conjunction with presidential elections. Senator Clark sums up these and other problems of congressional candidates very succinctly:

> Concern for the Presidency in national elections and concern with state and local offices, particularly executive offices with their attendant patronage and fund raising prerequisites, come close to exhausting the attention of the regular party organization. The Representatives and Senators are secondary considerations. In most cases they have too little patronage to build a party organization of their own, and they are too far away from the local scene to exercise control of the party machinery. The exceptions are those few Congressmen who are also party bosses in their own districts.

Based on his experience Senator Clark confirms and elaborates on the effects of the rather unusual position of a congressional candidate in relation to his party. He is on his own as far as the national party is concerned. In presidential elections he is important according to the assistance or harm he can be to the national ticket. But as Senator Clark contends:

> At the same time the regular party organization is not necessarily disposed to consider the race for Congress of weighty importance in a Presidential year. In the odd-numbered years of purely county and city elections the Congressman is often ignored.

These factors are partially offset by the growing federal involvement in both local and state affairs, but representatives generally play second fiddle to the state's U.S. senators, particularly if one or both of the senators and the congressmen are of the same party as the President. There are those rare instances (California after the 1964 election) where both senators were Republican and the President a Democrat. Certain key Democratic representatives were very influential with their national party.

Although the time of congressional elections, the unusual organizational structure of American parties, and the ambiguous relations of congressional candidates with other local and national candidates create serious problems, they offer a great challenge and an opportunity to candidates for the U.S. House, their managers and co-workers. Out of necessity they must build an organization of their own. To be sure, congressional candidates do receive some help from the local, state, and national party organizations and other candidates of their party, but to a large extent the congressional campaign is an independent operation.

The general and specific factors which make up the campaign environment should determine in large measure the kind of campaign waged. A failure properly to appraise them can doom potentially successful challengers or incumbents to defeat. On the other hand, a correct estimate of them will not necessarily result in victory. In subsequent sections of this essay these factors will be considered in light of campaign organizations, strategy, and tactics. Before this discussion it is helpful to explore some of the relationships which a campaign manager has with various groups and why people become involved in congressional campaigns. An understanding of these two points will also shed light on the impact of the political environment on campaigns.

THE MANAGER'S JOB

Campaign managers are probably not very well known by either the public or scholars. A few skilled managers like Bob Price of Mayor John Lindsay's various campaigns and James A. Farley of the Franklin Roosevelt era receive attention by both scholars and journalists, but they are the exceptions. The "Prices" and "Farleys" are noticed because of their abilities to organize and carry forward successful campaigns. Little is heard of their daily activities, and only occasionally do we learn of the various aspects of their work. In view of this and because of the importance of campaign managers, I propose to take a more general view of campaign management and to attempt to identify those relationships which congressional campaign managers have with candidates and their families, local, state and national party organizations and candidates, the public and other campaign workers.

Some campaign managers are not only loyal working associates of congressional candidates, but also frequently are close personal friends with the candidates. If managers and candidates are successful, they make "one perfect politician" as a historian pictured the relationship between President McKinley and his manager Mark Hanna. Implicit in the observation about the McKinley-Hanna relationship is that manager and candidate have different functions and generally different personalities and ambitions.

The manager is the operating head of the organization. He provides advice, guidance and, perhaps even order to the candidate and other campaign workers. The candidate does not have time for campaign details and lodges most of the daily responsibility with the manager. In successful manager-candidate relations, there is a tacit agreement that the final responsibility rests with the candidate, although he rarely exercises his authority. If he does, others associated with the campaign generally are unaware of it for the manager must be able to speak and act with authority.

Managers frequently and freely give candidates advice, because the strengths and weaknesses of the candidate and the campaign must be identified. Candidates are generally so close to events that they do not get the whole picture. They are too sensitive to minor setbacks and triumphs, and their views of the campaign often become distorted. Managers must help candidates keep their perspective by reminding them that unfavorable editorials in small newspapers do not lose elections or that standing rounds of applause at meetings of supporters do not win elections. Managers protect candidates from the petty but potentially upsetting events by taking the blame for a missed engagement or a late press release.

Frequently managers have a more difficult relationship with candidates' wives and families than with candidates. Tension can result from mutual misunderstandings of their different roles. Wives may want their husbands to win, but they also want them to be physically healthy and mentally happy and to spend time with their families. Managers have the same concerns, but their notions of how candidates can achieve these may be different.

The wives of some candidates are deeply involved in their husbands' careers. Sometimes they have strong ideas about campaigns which are at odds with the managers'. On occasions they appeal directly to their candidate-husbands. Difficult problems can result, but managers have the responsibility to put this situation into the broader campaign perspective. Happy candidates do not always win, but constant friction destroys morale and impedes campaigns. Successful managers are guided by this realization and attempt to reduce friction in any phase of the campaign.

Difficult and imprecise as the managers' relations to candidates and their families can be, they may be even more ambiguous when it comes to the party organization and the public. A few congressional campaigns are tied to the party organization while most others are independent operations. There are a number of factors which affect the relationship between congressional campaigns, the regular party, and other candidates. Relations with state and local party organizations are conditioned by the unusual position of the congressional campaign. The stepchild nature of the congressional office—and hence campaigns for it—is difficult to overcome even when there is a genuine desire on the part of all concerned.

The main question in this relationship is whether public cooperation will be beneficial for their candidates. Obviously, this question cuts several ways. Party leaders and other office seekers will ask it in relation to congressional candidates. If the answer is a strong affirmative by all hands, public cooperation ranging from united and integrated campaigns to sharing workers and joint appearances generally will result. In most instances all candidates will not perceive the same benefits and costs from public cooperation—how much certain activities will help or hurt their campaigns. In these cases a rather complex set of calculations comes into play resulting in cooperation which is a hit or miss affair.

Managers can be embarrassed when other candidates who are thought to be liabilities show up at coffees, teas, and other public affairs which have been arranged for their candidates. Zealous party leaders who want to advance the interest of the party can also present problems for managers who feel that they must disassociate the candidates from their party if they are to attract some independents and other party members. There are no easy ways in which to handle such problems. The best approach is usually a candid personal discussion with candidates and party leaders whom managers regard as hurting their campaigns. If the managers have clearly thought out their strategies and tactics, the "offenders" will at least understand even if they do not agree.

Money is usually one type of assistance managers are quite willing to accept unless it implies campaigning with other party office seekers. If this string is attached, managers must calculate both the need and the costs of financial assistance from the party.

Relationships between certain congressional candidates and the national congressional campaign committees can be vital to election victories. The Republican Congressional Campaign Committee (RCCC) based on my experiences and observations of their operations offers general assistance in the form of campaign literature, organizational guides, issues analyses, speech material, and press releases. For seasoned incumbent campaigners this material may not be of too much benefit, but for newcomers it provides helpful guides which can be adapted to particular campaigns. The ease with which this material is obtained—all Republican congressional candidates are on the RCCC mailing list—may cause some office seekers to become over reliant upon it and fail to exploit local peculiarities and opportunities.

For those congressional campaigns in which Republicans win by less than 55 per cent or lose by less than 45 per cent, i.e., marginal districts, the RCCC assists with money and personnel. Money is apportioned on the basis of the need to help marginal incumbents and the opportunity to pick up marginal seats held by the Democrats. Candidates in either of these categories can expect from $1000 to $5000. Some non-marginal candidates under special circumstances, i.e., incumbents with tough opponents and challengers with good prospects of victory, receive financial assistance. The RCCC also helps marginal candidates and others through a staff of field workers who spend a few days in districts reviewing campaign problems and offering suggestions. These men are of necessity generalists, but they have encountered most campaign problems and have observed techniques which can be successfully transferred from one district to another.

It is apparent that congressional campaign managers will gladly accept money and workers without strings. Regardless of source, if aid is conditioned on joint campaigning, careful calculations of costs and benefits must be made On some occasions managers visualize benefits which cause them to actively seek cooperation with their party and other candidates. In such situations a case for the mutual benefits which will result from cooperation must be made.

In all of their activities managers are supposed to be motivated by a desire to help their candidates. For this reason their relations with the public become very important. A manager once told me that "anonymity is the keynote to success." He said that this rule could be broken if something had to be said which the candidate or someone else in the organization should not say. He justified the anonymity rule by contending that it is the candidate and not the manager who must be elected. He feels that any publicity which the manager receives is that much less for the candidate. Also, if the manager consistently receives attention, he may let his own latent ambitions for office take over which will result in a less effective job for his candidate.

Although anonymity should be the goal, there are times when it must be broken to protect the candidate, to answer the opposition, and/or to attack the opposition. In one campaign a candidate accused his opponent of advocating sterilization of unwed mothers. This was an incorrect charge which had serious implications among certain religious groups. The attacked candidate and his manager felt that the issue was highly emotional and could not be explained in a complex way. It was further decided that the candidate should not dignify the charge with an answer. The solution was for the manager to make an equally emotional one-time answer—"He's a liar." The opposition dropped the charge, but not until the press had scolded it for being irresponsible.

In order to protect the dignity of the candidate, a particularly unsavory but important revelation about the opposition is sometimes handled by the manager. I remember one race in which a candidate for attorney general had been arrested for drunken driving on several occasions immediately prior to the campaign. The opposition manager pointed this out and raised questions about the qualities necessary in the state's chief law enforcement officer. Several newspapers were conducting a campaign for safe driving and quickly joined in asking whether a record of drunken driving arrests was compatible with service as an elected official.

Managers' relations with the public, the party, other candidates, and with their own candidates do not occupy the major portion of the working day. Most of their time is spent with other campaign workers. In their relations with fellow workers, managers' abilities are constantly tested. This is particularly the case with congressional campaign managers. They must assist in building and operating a campaign organization geared to a single office which is devoid of major patronage and economic rewards both from the standpoint of payment for campaign work and securing governmental favors for campaign workers. Those in positions of campaign responsibility must rely on tenuous incentives in order to get and keep workers.

It is vital for managers to understand the reasons why people volunteer to help in congressional campaigns. As in the case with most phases of office seeking, incumbents have the advantage in getting and keeping workers. (1) People with political ambitions may be attracted to political winners for experience and the hope that their careers will be advanced. (2) Some people who like to associate with important public officials will volunteer. (3) Incumbents will draw some workers because of their stand on issues and the feeling that helping in campaigns will aid their causes. For example, older citizens who want medicare extended may work for incumbents with similar views. (4) People committed to ideological positions and hopes of advancing them through particular candidates will assist. (5) Friends and neighbors of candidates will be found in the ranks of campaign volunteers.

Although challengers may not be able to recruit workers as easily as incumbents may, their workers are attracted for the same inducements. Whether they work because of ideological concern, desire to further their own careers or some other reason, they possess different talents and require different rewards. Some little old ladies will address envelopes day-after-day if the candidate drinks a cup of coffee with them once a week and expresses sincere appreciation for their efforts. Managers should make room for such coffee breaks in the candidate's schedule. Likewise, managers should see that the hard working attorney who wants to learn more about politics has an opportunity to accompany candidates and perhaps even represent them at some public affairs.

Managers must also recognize that there are certain basic intellectual, physical, emotional, and fiscal needs in campaigning. Although the demands for these are unlimited, they are limited in both total amount and individual amounts. Only X amount of money can be raised, X amount of enthusiasm generated, X amount of envelopes addressed and doorbells rung, and X amount of ideas written into speeches, brochures, and campaign advertisements. Unfortunately, most managers do not know how much X is available either in total or individual amounts. They find out the hard way when someone stops ringing doorbells, raising money, or making telephone calls.

One very successful campaign organization had two managers. One constantly made plans, gave orders, and asked the volunteers to work harder. Every afternoon the other one bought cokes and ice cream, passed out words of encouragement, and pats on the back, while the first fumed and bemoaned the loss of valuable time. The first one had no time for complaints, gossip, or internal rivalries. The other one kept his door open and patiently listened to all problems.

He also recognized the near genius of his partner, and gently but firmly reminded all he could reach of this and the goal of the campaign—a victory for their candidate.

Most campaigns are not fortunate enough to have either a political genius or his empathetic associate, but managers need a measure of both political genius and empathy, plus many hard working associates, to keep a campaign going.

WHO WORKS AT WHAT JOBS?

Campaign organization takes a variety of forms. Some notion of the range of campaign groups has already been presented. Campaign groups vary from the congressional staffs of incumbents from safe districts to professional public relations firms. Although the former are probably on the decline and the latter on the increase, the typical congressional campaign organizations fall in between the two extremes. The campaign organization described is primarily the one we used in 1962, although aspects of others will be mentioned.

Frequently, as has been implied, top campaign management is shared among three or four people who direct major activities—publicity, volunteer workers, finance, scheduling and research. When responsibility is shared, the manager coordinates the various activities. Regardless of whether the manager serves as a coordinator or attempts to direct all phases of the campaign, there is usually a campaign advisory committee.

The advisory committee is generally composed of former candidates for major offices, important party officials, and community leaders. Their primary function is to review strategy and provide advice. They are good sounding boards for the top level campaigners to test their ideas.

During the 1962 campaign we had an advisory committee, and I have served on such committees for candidates in elections since then. In all cases, the campaign manager reported on various aspects of the campaign, particularly the candidate's schedule, while committee members raised questions or offered suggestions. Usually one or two items were given special attention. In each campaign fund-raising was discussed at several sessions while at other meetings the public relations people reviewed the content of advertisements including the overall timing for their use.

In my experience the advisory committee is not particularly valuable for the advice it renders. Rather, through such a committee important community and political leaders are involved in the campaign. As members of the team, it is possible to call on them individually for specific assistance not the least of which is money. Through their contacts they can involve their associates in the campaign. Moreover, advisory committee members are frequently vocal as well as active participants in community and political affairs. They are apt to have opinions on a wide variety of topics including the way in which campaigns are run. Giving them an opportunity to participate in campaign planning reduces potentially harmful criticism and dissension from them. Further, they can help curb harmful criticism from their associates outside the campaign organizations.

The honorary campaign committee is even less active than the advisory committee. It is a paper list of people who do not or cannot play active roles in the campaign. When contacted for assistance they usually respond: "You can use my name, and I'll give you a check. I simply can't do anything more." Like the advisory committee the honorary campaign group is composed of prominent people in the community. Their names mean something either to the public or a particular group. Retired or current political office holders, prominent medical doctors, university professors, teachers, and community leaders are found on the rosters of honorary campaign committees. To make use of the committee, their names are announced to the news media, listed on campaign stationery, printed in some newspaper advertisements, and contained in some campaign literature.

In addition to the honorary campaign committee, there may be other relatively inactive committees—"Members of the Opposition Party for Smith," "Veterans for Smith," "Teachers for Smith," "Housewives for Smith," etc. Sometimes a few members of these committees will do a small amount of work. In our campaign we had a committee composed of Democrats for our candidate. A few of them raised some money and sponsored several newspaper advertisements.

The day-to-day work of campaigning is carried on by committees and groups other than the ones discussed to this point. The most important group in our 1962 campaign was the headquarters staff which included a few full-time volunteers and one paid secretary. This staff saw that the work got done. The secretary handled the candidate's and my personal correspondence, wrote thank you letters to large contributors, and served as bookkeeper. One volunteer worker was in charge of office supplies, campaign materials, kept the headquarters in some semblance of order and assisted the secretary with the bookkeeping. Another volunteer scheduled people who had agreed to do part-time work answering the phone, addressing and stuffing envelopes, and conducting a telephone canvass.

The part-time volunteers were recruited by two volunteers who arranged coffees and teas and accompanied the candidate to these affairs. They were responsible for keeping the candidate on schedule, supplying literature to the hostesses, taking the names and addresses of those in attendance at the coffees and teas, and talking with prospective volunteer campaign workers. In addition to these responsibilities, these two women saw to it that the hostesses received a personalized thank you letter from the candidate and that all guests received a short individually typed note indicating the candidate's pleasure in meeting them.

The women in charge of office management, volunteers, coffees and teas had part-time committee members who assisted them and were responsible to them. Because of changing needs during the campaign, the committee chairwomen and their principal assistants moved between jobs. For instance, during August and September we sent a mailing to Republicans in the district, nearly 50,000, soliciting small contributions. This was a tremendous undertaking for volunteer workers, so those who were full-time and regular part-time workers helped the chairwoman of the volunteers organize and supervise the project. In some campaigns a job like this is handled by professionals. In an effort to save money and involve people in our campaign, we turned the job over to volunteers.

Among our more than 250 volunteers was a group of college and high school students who were particularly adept at envelope addressing and stuffing. (In soliciting funds by mail we also enclosed a block of stamps with the candidate's picture on them, a campaign brochure, and a window sticker for automobiles.) At times our young volunteers created problems, because they liked to listen to popular music as they worked. Their output appeared to be directly related to the volume of the radio—the louder it was the more they produced. I dubbed them the "rock 'n roll" committee. Since they were good workers, I urged the chairwoman of the volunteers to arrange their schedule so they were not working alongside some of our less understanding older volunteers.

In addition to the major working committees which operated out of the headquarters, our campaign organization consisted of several other committees—public appearances (other than teas and coffees), research, speaker's bureau, public relations, and finance. The public appearances committee contacted the program chairmen of the major organizations in the district and indicated that our candidate was available as a speaker. The chairman of this committee in conjunction with the coffees and teas chairwomen and I coordinated the candidate's schedule. The research group prepared speech material, made an analysis of the incumbent's voting record, and kept a current file of campaign clippings. Several young attorneys arranged for speakers whenever there were conflicts with the candidate's schedule.

The public relations committee consisted of a young advertising executive and a few of his associates. In conjunction with an advertising agency, this volunteer group planned the uses of the media and actually produced billboards, T.V. and radio spots, newspaper advertisements, and the campaign brochures. News releases which are an important part of public relations were written by a newspaper man on a fee basis. The candidate or I would inform him of the subject matter and the candidate's views. He would write a release, clear it with me, and distribute it to the news media. Although our public relations work was handled through both volunteer and professionals, no major conflicts developed. Through this approach we reduced costs and involved more people in the campaign.

Money is the life blood of campaigns. We were able to secure a prominent medical doctor as finance chairman. Through him, the young advertising executive, and the candidate, we enlisted about 15 men and women with experience in raising money for political, civic, and/or charitable causes. This committee experimented with a number of devices to raise money, but four approaches seem to have worked best.

First, letters were sent to past congressional campaign contributors followed by personal telephone calls and visits from committee members. Second, special solicitation letters went to particular groups, e.g., doctors and dentists, followed by personal requests. Third, several fund raising luncheons and cocktail parties were held. And, fourth, the mailing to all Republicans was sent. In all cases, except the latter, finance committee members tried to write or call on people they knew. For instance, a realtor on the committee wrote letters and personally called on professional colleagues.

There were not many active finance committee members, but each one worked hard at getting both small and large contributions. In some instances they did not receive cash, but were given such items as a campaign automobile, lumber for small signs, paint, typewriters, postage stamps, etc. Through the committee's efforts we raised approximately $25,000 in cash or kind from about 4000 individual contributors, including about 3000 contributions from the general mailing. We received additional sums of $2000 from the RCCC and $10,000 from the Republican State Central Committee making our total income approximately $37,000.

Since the bulk of the money was raised as the campaign progressed, some problems in planning for media expenditures developed. However, this procedure had advantages in terms of attracting volunteers. We were not running a "poor man's" campaign, but we felt we could only afford one paid worker, the secretary. The absence of a large quantity of money at the start of the campaign and a paid staff helped to recruit volunteers and to give them the feeling that they were making an indispensable contribution to the campaign.

The groups, committees, and individuals discussed thus far worked out of the central campaign headquarters, a storefront on a busy street in the district's largest city which was located in a county with approximately 60 per cent of the district's total population. In addition to the central organization, committees were formed in the district's four other counties. These committees were composed of active civic, political, and agricultural leaders of their areas.

The county committees' most important contributions were the links they provided to local people and the word-of-mouth publicity in the smaller communities. The chairmen of the committees were responsible for scheduling the candidate in their counties on the days allocated to them. Whenever there was a big affair in one of the counties, e.g., a county fair, we tried to arrange the candidate's schedule to incorporate it. Fortunately, we knew about most of these before the campaign began, so we had to do very little shifting after the overall schedule was established.

The discussion of campaign organization and personnel would be incomplete without elaborating on the efforts of the high school and college students and women volunteers. One task, the mailing to Republicans, could not have been completed without the students' assistance, but they also worked at dozens of other jobs. They placed small signs on vacant lots, distributed literature at rallies, placed bumper strips on cars, ran errands, answered the phone, drove the candidate's car, and cleaned the headquarters. Their unending energy and enthusiasm was a great delight and inspiration to our older volunteers. No task seemed to be too large or too small for our young workers.

The largest group of volunteers was housewives. They ranged in age from their early twenties to their late seventies, some had small children and some had adult grandchildren. At almost any time of the day, there were ten or more of these women in the headquarters addressing envelopes, typing letters to contributors and those who attended teas and coffees, answering the phone, and welcoming visitors. Those connected with our campaign think of these women as a very special group. Without them we could not have run the kind of campaign we did. However, I am inclined to believe that wherever there is an active campaign, there will be a corps of hard working housewives who are just as special as those who worked in our campaign.

The campaign organization we developed was in response to both general and particular circumstances including the geography of the district, availability of campaign funds, quantity and quality of volunteers, party registration and past voting history of the district, and certain strategic and tactical considerations. Other districts with different circumstances require different campaign organizations. Nonetheless, assuming the absence of the extremes—no organization or turning the campaign over to a public relations firm—many of the features of our organization will be found in the groups supporting congressional candidates throughout the country.

HOW THEY RUN

In every campaign a particular pattern develops. In some campaigns, activities are undertaken without any apparent logic. They are carried along by whatever momentum the separate and unrelated activities produce. Decisions are made by default or in response to situations as they arise. No one, least of all the candidate and his organization, knows why actions are taken or which ones are important. Such campaigns are generally doomed to defeat from the outset.

Most campaigns for major office do not drift along. They run the scale of those which have a general plan and vague tactics to those which have a well thought out strategy and specific tactics. Regardless of the type of campaign, there are still many mysteries in the art and science of campaigning. There are no exact formulae of strategies and tactics which will produce victory. Campaigning for different offices is different. Strategies and tactics are formulated to win particular offices at particular times.

I remember one successful candidate who asked a knowledgeable political observer what he thought about his campaign. The candidate kept pressing the observer to tell him which strategies and tactics had been most beneficial or harmful. Finally, the observer said: "Look! Now that you've won it appears that almost everything you did was right. If you'd lost, people would have said you were a fool for doing what you did the way you did it."

It is hard to argue with this logic, but it misses the fact that there are general strategic and tactical guidelines which candidates should not lightly ignore. In discussing the campaign environment a number of factors which condition congressional campaigns were described— unique organizational problems created by congressional districting, advantages which incumbents have, partisan breakdown of voters, group affiliations, temper of the time, time of the election, and population distribution (urban or rural or a combination). These factors are not difficult to discover, but their potential impact is not easy to evaluate. Yet, good campaigns require planning and activities which are geared to the political environment.

Because of my experience working for a defeated congressional candidate, my inclination is to ask what strategies and tactics can be used to make the seemingly runaway election a close contest or possibly an upset. I do not intend a post mortem, but out of our experience I feel that I discovered some activities which were more effective than others. Further, there are hard ways to campaign and easier ways.

A general strategic point is to fish where the fish are. Of equal importance is its corollary that there are different fish and they can't all be caught with the same bait. It is easier to convince party supporters to vote for candidates than it is to convince latent supporters, neutrals, or opposition party supporters. If they get to the polls, those who share the party label of candidates and are moderately to actively interested in politics will generally vote for them. These are the people the candidate should go after first. This holds true for both incumbents and challengers.

Challengers can improve their prospects if they surpass the incumbent and/or majority party candidate in percentage voter turnout. The point can be illustrated in a district with 200,000 registered voters.

Registration	Normal Turnout	Challenger Increases His Party Turnout
120,000 Democrats	60,000 (50%)	60,000 (50%)
80,000 Republicans	48,000 (60%)	64,000 (80%)

There is no assurance that challengers will win if they are able to increase their party's turnout. However, 75 per cent of the voters cast their ballots along party lines. Thus, challengers' chances will almost automatically improve if they can induce a higher percentage of their party members to go to the polls than can their opponents. Incumbents with a slight registration advantage or with a registration disadvantage are very vulnerable to challengers whose strategy is to increase the turnout of their party supporters.

Since majority and minority party candidates want to activate the people who are most likely to vote for them, i.e., their own party supporters, appropriate appeals have to be used. Lewis Froman and others conclude that appeals which stress party symbols, images, and heroes serve to identify candidates with their party and will be most effective in activating party supporters. For example: "I ask you to vote for me as one who stands in the tradition of Teddy Roosevelt and Dwight Eisenhower. I promise to carry on the Republican tradition of a sound money policy at home and a vigorous foreign policy abroad."

Although elections can be won by activating party supporters, campaigns are directed to other elements in the electorate. A straight out party appeal is mixed with other appeals—there are different fish and you can't catch them all with the same bait. Latent party supporters and neutrals are very difficult to reach. They are generally not interested in politics and have a low degree of political awareness and involvement. Among latent supporters party identification is weak while neutrals seldom identify with a party. The best approach to these groups is to arouse any sense of party identification they might have and to associate their party identification with that of the candidates.

The opposition party supporters are not difficult to reach if they are moderately to actively interested in politics. However, they tend to vote for their party's candidates at about the rate of three to one if they go to the polls. Appeals to these voters by candidates of the other party should emphasize that they are different from the ordinary candidates who run under their party's label. This can be done by indicating to the opposing party members that on certain issues the other party's candidates views are actually in keeping with theirs. This is not easy, because the prime thrust of candidates is to activate their party supporters through essentially partisan appeals. One possible tactical device in appealing to opposition party supporters is through an "Opposition Party for Jones Committee." This committee can use special media ads and mailings to their fellow party members to demonstrate that the opposition candidate is really closer to their point of view than their party's candidate.

Political parties are not alone in influencing voting decisions. They share this function with interest groups. Candidates must therefore design special appeals to interest groups which indicate that the candidate agrees with the group's positions and can help advance them if elected. Committees like "Veterans for Jones" can be helpful in indicating the candidate's sympathy with the group's goals. Convincing them the candidate can actually get something done when elected is a difficult task. This is a particularly difficult job for challengers who are running against incumbents. If the group is a significant voting bloc, incumbents have probably already demonstrated their capacity to help the group achieve some of its goals. Groups are understandably reluctant to ditch such incumbents for unknown quantities.

This can be illustrated through a Democratic representative who has labor support despite his vote against repeal of Section 14b of the Taft-Hartley law which permits states to enact right-to-work statutes. Labor leaders in this congressman's district would not support his Republican opponent even if the Republican indicated a willingness to vote for repeal of Section 14b. First, the incumbent has supported other labor positions, e.g., raising the minimum wage. Second, he has seniority and is in a position to influence legislative decisions. Union leaders acknowledge that the incumbent has demonstrated his willingness to use his influence on behalf of labor. Third, a majority of union members generally vote Democratic. Their leaders know that it would be difficult to convince the membership to vote for a Republican on the basis of one issue.

The dilemma of both incumbents and challengers in making appeals to party supporters, latent supporters, neutrals, and opposition party supporters and interest groups is further complicated because those who are the easiest to reach are the most difficult to change. Moderate to active partisans receive political messages, but are not necessarily changed by them. Latent supporters and neutrals seldom receive political messages, but can be swayed by them if they retain them. This can be explained by what Lewis Froman and others call the trilogy of selective exposure, perception, and retention. First, moderate to active party supporters are more apt to hear, see, and read items about their party and its candidates than about the opposing party and its candidates. Second, they interpret political matter in ways which fit their predispositions. Third, they retain those impressions which are congenial and congruent with their predispositions. In contrast with party supporters, latent supporters and neutrals do not pay much attention to politics and have difficulty interpreting political messages. As a consequence, they do not retain much political matter.

In addition to the trilogy of selective exposure, perception, and retention, a large percentage of voters, perhaps as high as 80 per cent, make up their voting minds as soon as nominations are made. In campaigns candidates work with a small number of voters who can actually be influenced to vote for them. Thus, one major problem of campaigning is timing—deciding when major campaign activities will be undertaken. Since the principal strategy is to activate party supporters, latent party supporters, and neutrals and to convert some of the opposition party supporters, the campaign should reach its peak on election day. The major tactical ingredients of timing a general election campaign might be scheduled as follows:

Phase One
    Choose immediate staff and headquarters site
    Review campaign environment with staff and advisors
    Establish campaign organization and begin to recruit principal
        volunteer workers
    Solicit campaign funds from most likely contributors
    Contact influential citizens, political leaders, and representatives
        of major news media
Phase Two
    Coffees, teas, and cocktail parties
    Speaking engagements by candidate
    Broaden solicitation for funds and recruitment of volunteers
    Begin general and special mailings
Phase Three
    Media advertisements—billboards and newspapers first followed
        by radio and TV
    Continue general and special mailings
    House-to-house and telephone canvasses beginning with candi-
        date's party members
Phase Four
    Get out the vote

If possible the first phase should be completed about four months prior to the election. Many second phase activities should be continued to election day with third phase activities beginning about a month before the election. There are no hard and fast lines in either the contents of these phases or the time when they take place. Some activities should be undertaken first like building a solid organizational base, and some are more effective closer to the election like media advertising. Campaigns should gradually gain momentum during the early campaign period and end with a swirl of carefully planned activities.

In timing and planning the campaign to get out the voters, challengers once again face a dilemma. By creating an awareness of the campaign, they assist incumbents. Surveys of contested congressional elections indicate that 39 per cent of the voters know the incumbents while only 20 per cent know their challengers. Because of this general tendency, challengers cannot be content with low key campaigns. Moreover, low turnouts generally favor incumbents, because they probably mean that many voters are not emotionally involved in the election. As turnout increases either as a result of the activities of challengers or of some other causes, factors other than party identification are probably at work. Since congressional incumbents usually represent districts in which their parties have registration advantages, alterations in the normal voting pattern, i.e., a minimum of 75 per cent of the voters casting ballots for candidates of their parties, favor challengers. But in attempting to alter this normal pattern, the dilemma for the challengers becomes apparent—greater awareness of the campaign generally helps incumbents.

To complete this discussion of campaign strategy and tactics it is helpful to indicate some specific techniques including the uses of candidates and workers time, campaign theme, uses of the media, treatment of the opposition, and getting out the vote on election day.

Volunteer workers are the cheapest and best resource in congressional campaigns. Volunteers talk about their work with friends and associates outside the campaign organization. They become little opinion leaders in a position to influence others around them. Those responsible for campaigns should hardly ever refuse volunteer workers and should actively encourage them. Equally important, volunteers must be given work which uses their talents. This is one of the reasons we used the general mailing and let volunteers do it.

Another inexpensive resource in terms of cash outlay is the candidate's time. He should be scheduled to meet as many people as possible. Personal contact by the candidate makes a more lasting impression than any other form of solicitation. This is why coffees, teas, and handshaking tours are important. When candidates make public speeches or attend rallies they should arrive a little early and stay a little afterwards in order to personally greet as many people as possible. This is especially the case when it comes to party supporters. If they go to the polls, they are inclined to vote for their party candidates. Only minimal efforts like personal contacts from the candidate are needed to turn them out.

A simple and short campaign theme is the best for several reasons not the least of which is the trilogy of selectivity. Voters are not attuned to complicated political messages. Moreover, if the campaign theme is to be used on billboards, brochures and other advertisements, requirements of time and space make short themes a necessity. One of the most effective themes I can recall was used by a former basketball player—"Big Man! Big Job!"

Not only should the campaign themes be brief and simple, but so should most media exposures—TV and radio spots, billboard and newspaper advertisements, bumper strips and brochures. A number of 30 to 60 second radio and TV spots are less costly than a few 15 to 30 minute programs in comparable time periods. Ten half-hour TV programs before 5:00 p.m. on a local TV station in one town of 350,000 costs a total of $670. For this same amount of money and during the same time period, it is possible to buy 47 one-minute spots. More important than the number of separate exposures, 47 vs. 10, is that with half-hour programs many viewers, probably all except those vitally interested in the campaign, would switch channels or leave the television viewing area. One minute spots interspersed throughout regular programs and between programs offer a better chance of keeping the regular program viewing audience.

Billboards and bumper strips should contain eye-catching, easy-to-read, and short messages, because most people only see them when moving. Brochures and newspaper advertisements should be designed with the same criteria in mind. Most people simply will not read or retain long political messages.

On occasions the rules governing the uses of certain media, brochures, newspaper, TV, and radio advertisements, can be broken to serve a very definite purpose. This purpose most frequently is to provide a more detailed campaign statement to active and interested supporters. Some supporters need fairly large doses of reassurance to keep them working. For instance, during the last ten weeks of our 1962 campaign, we purchased a regular 15 minute weekly TV program at 5:00 p.m. for a rate of $500. This program became a must for our campaign volunteers, and it appeared to give them a great psychological boost.

One problem which seems to concern every candidate is his public attitude towards his opponent—do I mention his name, share the same platform with him or engage him in debate. As a general rule candidates should steer clear of their opponents. Mentioning his name or sharing the same platform only gives the opponent free publicity. If candidates get into arguments with their opponents, their opponents might win. Like every other rule this one has its exceptions. Challengers with serious registration disadvantages might do any one of the three things mentioned in order to increase their name familiarity and identify them as candidates for a particular office.

The best strategies and tactics are useless unless people go to the polls. Activities aimed at getting out the vote have become fairly standard. Through many elections parties and candidates have discovered those techniques which work. The major ingredients in successful election day activities are good organization and an abundance of workers. Politicians' efforts are often supplemented by public service announcements in newspapers and over radio and TV urging people to vote. Groups like the Boy Scouts and Kiwanis also undertake non-partisan campaigns to get people to the polls.

These general activities do not and can not replace the specific efforts of parties and candidate organizations, mainly telephone and personal reminders and rides to the polls. Many local party organizations have workers stationed at polling places to keep records of those who vote. Typically, those who have not voted by noon are given a telephone reminder by their party or a candidate. In some instances, party members who have not voted several hours before the close of the polls receive personal visits from political workers.

Since election day work requires large numbers of people, candidates frequently release their workers to regular party organizations which direct centralized voter drives. Some candidates do not cooperate in general party appeals and establish their own election day organization. They do this because the regular party cannot do an adequate job, or they feel that a general party appeal would hurt their cause.

One of the biggest problems in developing an election day program is that workers are generally physically and emotionally tired when the day of decision arrives. This let down plus the magnitude of the get-out-the-vote organization makes it necessary to do a great deal of advance planning.

Regardless of whether prospects for victory are good or bad, a party for campaign workers with free refreshments and food should be scheduled on election night. Win or lose, those who have campaigned want to share their joy or sorrow with fellow workers. Candidates can also find election night parties helpful. The party is partially a means of saying thanks to their workers. Also, winners and losers can launch their next campaigns.

One final note needs to be added about thanking workers after election day. All who work in the campaign should receive a note of thanks and perhaps an inexpensive momento. For many workers the campaign is an important experience in their lives. If they found it satisfying, they will probably volunteer for other political work. In view of the need for political workers, those who do become active should be given some tangible symbol of appreciation.

This discussion of campaign strategy and tactics has attempted to be realistic. The quality of voters and the appeals which attract them to candidates have been treated candidly. To some the picture which emerges is that of a plot to fool the voters dreamed up by cunning politicians. It would be foolish to deny that this is not characteristic of some campaigns.

In view of the advances which have been made in campaign techniques, it is necessary to ask whether the essentially cynical campaign can be avoided. Aside from the strictures against the obvious forms of dishonesty, there are several principles which can illustrated in the form of questions for candidates.

Am I doing or saying things which are not in keeping with my stand on issues? Am I letting others do or say things on my behalf which distort or conceal my position?

Am I picturing myself as possessing qualities or personality traits which I do not have? Am I letting others picture me different than I am?

Am I attributing false stands, qualities, or personality traits to my opponent which are not in keeping with what is known or can be discovered about him and his workers? Am I permitting my workers to do any of these things?

Although these questions are phrased for candidates, with some slight changes campaign workers can ask themselves the same questions.

At the start of the campaign these questions seem easy to answer. As issues arise, opponents act differently than was anticipated, and more is learned about the voters' wishes through actual campaigning and perhaps public opinion polls, answers to these questions become harder and more complex. Spurred by the visions of victory and the feeling that it is vital to defeat their opponents, candidates and their workers may be tempted to reverse their first answers. In some cases, questions which once seemed vital to ask and to answer are shoved aside.

Such a process is probably natural, because the questions can never be answered in a clear-cut manner. Changing circumstances and unexpected occurrences are part of the campaign process. If candidates and their workers realize this and continue to wrestle with the questions, they can be assured that their concern aids them in meeting their moral and ethical responsibilities.

Answers should not be based on unrealistic moral or ethical codes. Campaigning requires candidates and workers who provide value frameworks in which facts are presented to the voters. I see nothing immoral or unethical about this procedure. I do feel strongly that candidates and workers who fail to recognize their values or distort them have not been honest with the voters. Those who refuse to ask the proper questions about their activities have conducted cynical campaigns.

EPILOGUE

Five months later and thirty pounds lighter, my wife and I joined about twenty other people in the county chairman's living room waiting for the first election returns. From scattered early reports it was apparent that a clear majority, 58 per cent when all votes were counted, had decided to retain the incumbent. Although my emotions had caused me to hope for a victory, my training as a political scientist had told me early in the campaign that it would take nothing short of a miracle to win.

Fortunately, I had a few minutes to myself that evening in which some of the disappointment I felt could be washed away by the hard realities we had confronted—a 3 to 2 registration disadvantage, popular incumbent with a good record of service to the district and an equally good campaign organization, a minimum budget, and the Cuban crisis of October 1962, which knowledgeable commentators agreed had helped the Democrats throughout the country. As my disappointment subsided and private post mortems with friends and public statements for the press, TV, and radio were taking place, I began to feel a sense of personal and civic satisfaction. Somehow nomination petitions had been filed, schedules met, mailings of literature sent, volunteers secured, money raised, thank you notes sent, TV and radio spots made, press releases issued, candidate and coordinator (I never used the title manager) remained good friends.

But more than this I had taken part in the continuing election dialogue between citizen and government. Through our candidate we met an official of the government in campaign combat and raised issues which caused the incumbent to explain more fully—in some instances for the first time—his position to the voters. We had made some of the people in our district aware that there was a different personality with a different stand on issues ready to assume part of the official governing responsibility. Through contributions of money and time we involved many people in politics for the first time. Through a straightforward and hard working campaign we had encouraged others to assume the responsibility of running for office in the future. In sum, we had given an affirmative answer to one of the questions which the critics of representative democracy raise: Can it work?

TYPICAL CONGRESSIONAL CAMPAIGN ORGANIZATION

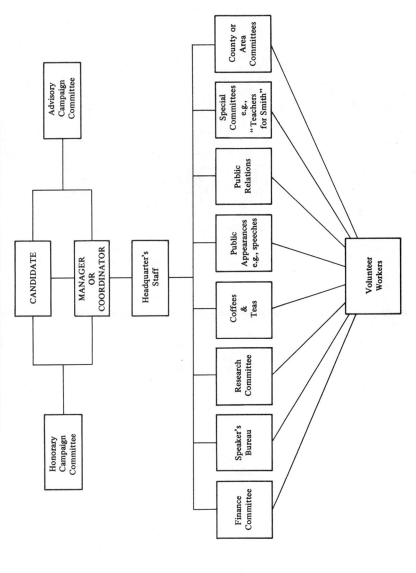

ROBERT J. HUCKSHORN

Robert J. Huckshorn studied at Southwest Missouri State College (B.S. 1950), University of Missouri (1951), State University of Iowa (M.A. 1954, Ph.D. 1956). He has taught at University of California at Los Angeles (1956–57), University of Idaho (1957–62), and presently at Florida Atlantic University. He was associate director, Bureau of Public Affairs Research at University of Idaho (1958–62).

Huckshorn was a National Committee Faculty Fellow from NCEP, Republican National Committee (1962–63); associate director of National Center for Education in Politics (1963–64); chairman, Advisory Policy Committee to the Republican Governors' Association (1965–   ); and, member of the Republican Co-ordinating Committees' Task Force on Federal-State-Local Relations (1965–   ).

Huckshorn is the author of *The Idaho Legislature* (1960), co-author of *The American Government Annual 1964–65*, co-editor, *Republican Politics: The 1964 Campaign and Its Aftermath* (1968), and has contributed to numerous other books and professional journals.

Robert J. Huckshorn

8. Political Defeat

INTRODUCTION

The wreckage was complete! The candidate leaned against the back wall and surveyed his headquarters. The limp decorations, the littered floor, and the urn of unwanted cold coffee stared back at him. A slightly disheveled lady sat to one side wiping an occasional tear away. With false enthusiasm the candidate moved to her side to comfort her. He was dreadfully tired himself and his disappointment was manifest. For scattered among the headquarters rubble of the campaign were his hopes and aspirations. A solid year of nerve-wracking work based on many years of community effort and solid personal accomplishment had been rewarded by a devastating defeat. He had bettered his party's record of two years before but had fallen several thousand votes short of unseating the incumbent congressman. It was only 9:30 on election night and it was all over. Concession made, he forced a smile, thanked a few loyal stragglers and moved to his car for a long drive home.

This scene is repeated with some variations in towns and cities throughout the nation every election night. From city councilman to president, the elements and manifestations of defeat are the same, except that the higher the office the greater the stakes and the greater the impact of the loss. For every victor there must be a loser. Yet, we concentrate our attention on the winners and we tend to ignore the losers. Studies in political science and the writings of journalists are devoted to the reasons for victory. Few spend much time or space on the lessons of defeat.

Americans think of politics in highly competitive terms. There is always a winner and a loser and the "best" man usually wins. We give awards to the best team, the best movie, the best book, and the best

173

student. In truth, none of these prizes is based solely on merit, just as the voters do not always select the most demonstrably worthy candidate for public office. Extraneous factors are woven into the fabric of any victory. A clearly outstanding man with bountiful financial resources, a well-disciplined organization, and clear understanding of the issues is, at times, an ignominious loser.

This chapter reviews the campaign problems which haunt those who are defeated. It is based upon questions put to all losing non-incumbent candidates for Congress (Republicans and Democrats) in 1962, and the responses given by the 65 per cent who returned the questionnaire. The Republican questionnaires were distributed by the author, who was then attached to the Republican National Committee; those going to the Democrats were handled by Robert C. Spencer, then Research Director of the Democratic National Committee.

Non-incumbent congressional candidates are well suited to illustrate the problems which attend upon or to which political defeat are attributed. Their reflections upon their campaigns are particularly significant in a political system in which we set the goal of fielding opposing candidates for each of the 435 House seats every two years, attempting to accomplish this opportunity for voter choice in a context in which experience tells us that the vast majority of House seats are not competitive—i.e., are safe for their incumbents. The non-incumbent's problems begin with the nonincumbent status of the candidate, and go on to methods of recruitment, campaign organization and management, fund-raising and finance, issues, and the effect of national trends on congressional elections. Each has a bearing on the reasons for defeat and is representative, to a degree, of experience at other levels of electoral activity. Collectively they represent a catalog of areas to which the citizen can most effectively apply himself with some expectation that his talents will receive maximum exploitation.

THE PROBLEM OF NON-INCUMBENCY

Sometimes an election is decided before the campaign ever begins. A large majority of the seats in the House of Representatives are "safe" for one party or the other. Of the 435 seats in the House only about 125 are actually competitive in the average congressional election year. Once entrenched in one of these "safe" seats, an incumbent's longevity is virtually assured. The non-incumbent challenger begins each campaign at a decided disadvantage—one over which he has little control. From 1952 to 1962 only 22 per cent of the congressional districts in the United States switched political parties. Over half of the total number of districts were held for the entire decade by members of a single party. In essence most members of the House are removable only by voluntary retirement or death.

One scholar has pointed out that this element of non-competition, if it continues, will support a prediction that the incumbent will win five consecutive elections in from 70 to 80 per cent of all congressional districts. Obviously, the odds on a non-incumbent defeating a congressman are not very great.

The high percentage of non-competitive districts is not an accident. Election districts are drawn by state legislatures, many of which have traditionally been dominated by rural legislators, and most of which have had at least one house controlled by a single party for long spans of time. State legislators, quite naturally, carve out congressional districts which will protect the interests of the majority party in the legislature. Incumbent congressmen, also quite naturally, bring as much pressure as possible to bear on the legislatures in their home states to see that district realignments protect their seats. As a result of these political machinations, incumbents remain entrenched; districts remain in the control of one party for inordinately long periods of time. Reapportionment (and subsequent re-districting), resulting from the recent rulings of the Supreme Court, will almost certainly cause some redress, but these changes had not been felt at all in 1962.

A congressional candidate runs in a *local* election to fill a *national* post. Congressional candidates do not fall under the aegis of the national party committees which are primarily oriented toward presidential politics. The committees are active in off-year congressional campaigns but most of the effort is in research, preparation of speech materials on national and international issues, and other general assistance.

Congressional campaign committees were created to assist candidates for the House and they are far more active in off-year election campaigns than are any other party units. Nevertheless, even they do not always occupy an important place in the planning and activities of the non-incumbent candidate. They are composed of incumbent congressmen and much of their campaign activity is directed toward the re-election of incumbents.

The state central committees are far more interested in electing statewide offices than they are in trying to assist congressional candidates. They devote their time, money, and energies to the election of governors, state constitutional officers, judges, and U.S. Senators and leave the congressional candidates to fend for themselves.

Local party officers emphasize control of city hall and the county courthouse rather than congressional politics. Most of their patronage is local and they often represent but a small part of a congressional district. In fact, the average local party has all it can do to stimulate interest in local races without dissipating its energies on larger contests.

The incumbent can live with this situation. He is known within the district and has been through earlier campaigns. He probably has developed his own personal organization. He has developed his own sources of campaign funds which are usually distinct from those of the party. He is the principal beneficiary of the largess of the congressional campaign committees and he is in a better position to make use of their services. His position has allowed him to build a reservoir of good will with the constituents through personal favors and governmental projects. Members of the House agree that as incumbents they possess extraordinary advantages over their non-incumbent opponents. Many argue that, except for isloated contests, there is little excuse for an incumbent's defeat. There is considerable substance to that argument. There are a number of advantages of officeholding that can be exploited to the fullest at campaign time as well as between elections. The congressman has an opportunity to correspond directly with constituents. He can put his ideas in writing and distribute them on House letterhead directly to the voter. His possession of the franking privilege relieves him of a considerable financial burden entailed in mass mailings. And, the existence of his personal office staff to handle correspondence and to distribute materials cannot be over-estimated. Many members maintain district offices and others assign part of their regular office force to work in the district at campaign time.

Here, then, is the dilemma facing the non-incumbent candidate. More often than not he is running in a district which is "safe" for the opposition and against an incumbent who, with a minimum of effort, can parlay the office he holds into an advantage that can only rarely be overcome. The non-incumbent congressional challenger is the have-not of American politics. He does not have a tested organization; a staff; the franking privilege. He is not assured capable research assistance; established connections with financial angels; or sufficient volunteers and experienced workers.

Despite these disadvantages there is seldom a shortage of non-incumbent candidates to make a race. Most of them, in fact, must undergo a dogged fight with other prospective losers just to get their party's nomination. What motivates them to engage in a time-consuming and costly effort to get elected when the odds are so greatly against them?

WHY DO THEY RUN?

Most non-incumbent candidates say they run because they just cannot resist the challenge. Most candidates fit within one or more of three motivation groups: (1) those who take part in politics for the sheer love of the game; (2) those who run as a sacrificial candidate in order to enhance the prestige of a political party or a particular ideological conviction; and, (3) those who run for reasons of personal prestige or personal gain.

Some men are of a competitive spirit and run for political office for sheer self-gratification. Political campaigns offer channels through which an individual's natural gregariousness can manifest itself. Some men like to talk and to be listened to and there is no better forum than the political stump. A 1962 loser summed it up this way:

I have loved politics since I was old enough to know what it was. My father was in politics in a minor way and I worked in elections all through high school and college. I love it because the people I meet give me pleasure. I knew it would take a miracle for me to win this election but I worked for a miracle. I guess I'm just naturally competitive. I'll try again.

The second group of candidates, and the largest, was composed of those who ran to enhance the prestige and the competitive position of a party or of an ideology. Many expressed altruistic motives for their decision to run. They often expressed the hope that they could prevent the minority party from defaulting upon its responsibilities to the two party system and, ultimately, to the voters who "must be given a choice." They usually had little to gain politically and most did not hope to benefit from personal gain. They were convinced that the party owed it to the people to present a full ticket. The party must appear as a viable force even though it might be moribund. Some candidates contended every citizen owed it to his party to be a sacrificial candidate if called upon. One stated, "I consider it to be a citizen's duty like jury service. Someone has to do it in a two party system."

Shortly after the 1962 election, a defeated Republican candidate for Congress from Alabama circulated a two page letter explaining his view of the GOP defeat in that state and his reasons for running in the first place. He said:

> Everyone in the Republican Party of Alabama has made serious mistakes and miscalculations. Some of us have made minor mistakes only because we held decision-making positions of minor influence. The converse of this premise is also true. In overall terms, however, we should not despair over that which has not yet been accomplished, but should be proud of what has, and use that pride to build up our party further, well remembering the Alabama lesson of the 1962 election—no matter how well our ward and precinct organization plays the cards, they cannot win against a deck stacked by our political naivete. . . .

Another effort to enhance party prestige, this time with a particular voter group, was described by a young Negro Republican candidate in a major midwestern city. In a letter to the author he said:

> I do feel that my candidacy did make a positive contribution to the party. However, I would limit the value of that contribution to my district. . . . In the beginning I figured my relatively young age would be a negative factor. However, I felt that if I could show the Negro community that a young law student could climb into the political arena with a seasoned incumbent and hold his own, this would be an 'eye-opener' to the Negroes and start them to thinking about sending a Negro to Congress [from this district]. For although the Negro community has for over thirty years voted consistently Democratic, they have not gotten the political return due

them because local Democrats know that the Negro vote is in their hip pocket.

Some discussed their candidacy in ideological terms. A Republican cryptically notes, "Incumbent Congressman had extreme 'liberal' voting record. I felt the 1962 elections were last chance to preserve two party system and protect private enterprise from 'democratic socialism.' " And, a Democratic loser stated, "My opponent was not a Birchite but he was in agreement with most of what one believes. I didn't think the people of my district would want to send such a man to Congress. I was wrong."

Among those who might be classed as ideologically-oriented candidates were several who expressed the need for political education as their prime motivation for running. One defeated candidate said:

> This district has, since its present formation, polled about 3 to 1 Democrat. Republican party locally beset with apathy and factionalism. Somebody had to do it. Last time (1960) nobody filed for the primary, and the write-in candidate made no campaign. The opportunity to do some basic political education should not be missed.

Various studies of political socialization and career development have demonstrated the existence of a sizeable group of candidates who run for some element of personal gain. The 1962 defeated congressional candidates were no exception. Some of these men viewed the campaign as a means of improving personal or social positions within the community. There is some modicum of honor attached to a candidacy for Congress even though it may not be taken seriously by the voters. This view was expressed by one candidate as follows: "I ran because it was an honor. I have found in the weeks since the election that people I barely know come up and tell me that they respect my interest in serving." Another reported: "My father ran for Congress in 1936 and, although he lost, his high-level campaign brought honor and respect to him that lasted until he died."

Probably the most familiar group of candidates seeking personal career enhancement is the young attorneys who hope to enlarge their practices. One such candidate noted that he inserted the name of his law firm in every document distributed during the election campaign. Another reported that his partnership suffered from too close affiliation with the opposition party and he ran to offset some of the effects of the liaison. There is nothing sinister about this behavior. Attorneys are not permitted to advertise and a political campaign, even a hopeless one, can bring a vast amount of publicity to the candidate and his profession.

At times an overriding issue may attract members of some particular profession into politics on a self-protective basis. The Medicare issue in 1962 and 1964 brought the latent political interest of many doctors to the surface. Some were moved to run for office. Businessmen often cite a particular governmental regulation affecting their business as a reason for entering politics. The level of political involvement by farmers is often a barometer of the extent of agrarian problems or crop reversals caused by adverse weather conditions.

In summary, thousands of new-born politicians enter the political arena every election year. Even though there may be no hope of victory, they enlist because they love the game or want to take part in the drama; they seek to build their party or sell their ideology; or, they strive to enhance personal prestige or professional careers in their local communities. Many are running because they sense a compulsion to. They feel that people must volunteer to run in hopeless races because the two-party system demands that the voters be offered a choice. They run because this is what makes the system work. They may admit to personal motives but most of them must be credited with idealism and conviction to do their part. There is the possibly apocryphal story of Goodwin Knight who was running for U.S. Senator from California in 1958. Supposedly he learned in mid-campaign that the respected California Poll showed him trailing his opponent. In a moment of desperation he asked, "Why should I try?" He needed no answer. He had to try because trying is what makes the system work. To fail to try would let down his party, his state, his supporters, the system, and himself.

THE PROBLEM OF RECRUITMENT

Most textbooks flatly state that recruitment of candidates is one of the prime responsibilities of political parties. It has been said that the political party that cannot attract and nominate candidates for office surrenders its reason for existence. If in the U.S. parties have not assumed responsibility for supervising congressional elections, however, we can hardly expect to find them undertaking the recruitment of candidates. The fault cannot be laid entirely at the doorstep of the parties although they must share it. The fact is that the advent of the direct primary method of selecting candidates seriously modified the role of political parties in recruitment and nomination at all levels.

For the most part the idea of party membership and party loyalty is not highly regarded by the American people. Even though most of them are committed to a party and would not consider changing affiliations they take their responsibilities in the primary rather lightly. The typical voter does not understand the theory of the primary as a method through which party members choose party candidates.

Candidates, too, have been affected by the primary. Formerly, party leaders used the convention system to choose candidates. No one could honestly argue that conventions uniformly resulted in the selection of first-rate men. Some leaders used their power to select henchmen who would do their bidding. It was upon this ground that some of the more virulent machines were built. The advent of the primary has encouraged prospective candidates to place themselves before the voters, in many instances, without so much as clearing their intentions with the party leadership. These men are willing to take a chance with the voters and they are prepared to undertake a campaign with no guarantee of party support.

Obviously there are as many ways of becoming a candidate as there are candidates. Every candidate makes his own decision which may be the result of motivations and sets of personal relationships impossible to predict. Even so, there are two major paths to congressional candidacy. Where local and state party organizations are controlled by knowledgeable and energetic leaders, the recruitment of candidates may be an accepted responsibility. These organizations assume their proper role in recruitment.

When the party leadership is inactive or non-existent, however, a vacuum exists and the field is left open to anyone who wishes to pre-empt the party's nomination. Self-starters, sometimes with little to recommend them but ambition or exhibitionism, move into the vacuum and file nomination papers. Some will subsequently seek out party leaders in an effort to build support. Others will operate throughout the campaign as though the party does not exist. In either case the party has forfeited, or by law has been deprived of, an elemental responsibility—that of recruitment. Nonetheless, officials at different levels of the party hierarchy may concern themselves with finding candidates for Congress. In 1962, two-thirds of the losing candidates reported some contact by a party official prior to the announcement of candidacy. Recruiters ranged all the way from state chairmen and governors to ward leaders and precinct captains. Candidates reported being approached by several different officials, sometimes independent of each other's knowledge.

According to the candidates, the motives of the recruiters were mixed. Some wanted to put together a ticket that would be attractive to voters. Others hoped to fill the ticket so as to avoid criticism from cohorts within the party. These leaders were notably sensitive to criticism over vacancies on the party ticket. A few undertook recruitment responsibilities to avoid an intra-party primary fight. They hoped to bestow the party's blessings on a selected candidate, thus foreclosing the nomination of an undesirable one.

The nomination once received, however, the candidate was cloaked in the mantle of the party and was its standard-bearer. But *his* was the responsibility to organize the campaign, establish whatever working arrangements he could with the party, and try to persuade a majority of the voters to select him over his opponent. Although he might have gained the nomination almost single-handed, to wage an effective campaign in the general election he would need to depend upon many people. These people would form the core of his personal campaign organization. The management of this organization would be a major responsibility and the chances for success might, in large part, depend on the effectiveness of its operations.

THE PROBLEM OF CAMPAIGN ORGANIZATION
AND MANAGEMENT

With the certificate of nomination in hand, the candidate is faced with the responsibility of organizing his campaign. The differences between the campaigns of an incumbent and a non-incumbent are most apparent at the organizational level. Incumbents, once elected, transform the organization that elected them into a permanent, personal vehicle devoted to maintaining them in office. Even in those districts where the party is active and assumes a responsible role, the congressman will attempt to mold it to his own needs. The party may then become his permanent campaign tool.

The non-incumbent faces a very different range of organizational problems. He may begin the campaign with no organization at all. The state and local party people are concerned with other more immediate contests. National leaders are willing to assist but cannot personalize their assistance in a way that makes it meaningful to individual candidates. The non-incumbent candidate, newly nominated and ordinarily new to national politics, does not have a large, district-wide personal following from which to construct an organization. The foundation may be there, but the completion of the super-structure is up to him and must be his first order of business. These differences between incumbent and non-incumbent organizations are important and, as much as anything else, affect the outcome of the election.

We might also note the differences in campaign style developed by urban as opposed to rural candidates. These differences are apparent regardless of whether the candidate is an incumbent or not. Districts differ in social, political, economic, geographic, racial, and ethnic characteristics. An organization must exploit natural advantages in the constituency and these are key factors in the development of a campaign establishment. The organization, in short, must complement the constituency and the district.

Urban candidates have more concentrated population patterns within their districts while the rural district may be distributed over a large geographic area. Furthermore, district populations vary greatly across the nation as well as within a single state. In 1962, for instance, the largest district in Texas (and the nation) contained 951,527 people while the smallest district in the same state had only 216,371. The former was the city of Dallas and the latter was composed of a string of small rural counties. The candidates in these two districts would not attempt to campaign in a like manner. The organizational structure of the campaign is necessarily different from one district to the next.

The urban candidate will not need to devote much time to travel arrangements. He must organize a saturation campaign. He may not want to devote time and money to television and radio since those media may extend well beyond the reach of the district to voters who cannot cast votes in his race.

The rural candidate, on the other hand, must devote more time to travel and to scheduling arrangements. Since he must cover a large geographic area, he must arrange to arrive at various locations at the proper time. He can expect the electronic media to reach most of the people in the district with little wastage. He may have fewer distinct ethnic, racial, or religious minorities with which to deal.

In a rural district the candidate may choose to "play it by ear" and rely on his own intuition. He may carry his organization around in his head and conduct a highly personal campaign. The cost of his rural campaign may be 15 to 20 times less than that of his urban counterpart. Fund-raising, under those circumstances, need not always be as professionalized in an urban district. An urban campaign may need a far more detailed plan of assault. The candidate cannot rely on intuition in a constituency which is in a constant state of flux. He attempts to get the votes of those who do not know or feel any sense of loyalty to him. The same pattern of campaign organization will not fit both kinds of district.

An election campaign presents formidable administrative problems for those responsible for its management. The recognized canons of public and business administration do not apply to the management of political campaigns. Confusion sometimes reigns. Money is spent before it is raised; there are few orderly procedures of budgetary control; planning is necessarily short range and must be highly flexible; personnel are not selected but, hopefully, volunteer; and, in short, any semblance of scientific management is rare. It is no wonder that most candidates believe that only an experienced manager can possibly understand and organize a political campaign. Those who are intimately involved will insist that a "good" organization under a "good" manager is one of the keys to victory.

Disputes over the "best" type of campaign organization are exercises in futility. Even so, professionals have created organizational models which they recommend to each new crop of congressional candidates. These represent distillations of the varied experiences of the professional organizers as well as experts in political finance and public relations. Models are seldom ever followed to the letter by candidates but they do serve as organizational blueprints. They are especially valuable to the non-incumbent inexperienced candidate who has never before undertaken a campaign.

The famous *O'Brien Manual,* re-written for the Democratic congressional campaign in 1962, described in simple but effective terms the model for that party's candidates. Lawrence F. O'Brien, a key figure in President Kennedy's 1960 presidential campaign, prepared the handbook originally as the organizational base for that Democratic effort. The first part described the organizational procedures recommended for district and county party groups and contained detailed descriptions of various campaign techniques. If properly followed, the document asserted, the manual "would provide a solid and powerful campaign organization."

The *O'Brien Manual* (and it differed but little from similar GOP publications) recommended the appointment of certain chief officers for the campaign. Among these principals were the district chairman and the executive secretary.

The district chairman in this model had the major responsibility for the proper functioning of the campaign committee. He should undertake to establish a program for the district headquarters by renting space, maintaining campaign supplies (brochures, bumper stickers, buttons), preparing mass mailings, recruiting volunteers, and appointing community and other local campaign leaders. He was responsible for organizing the candidate's public appearances in the district and making travel arrangements.

The executive secretary, on the other hand, provided liaison with the national and state party headquarters and organized and supported activities in the field. He was responsible for developing campaign itineraries in local areas such as counties and other geographic areas. Liaison with county committees is one of his important duties. The distinction drawn by this manual between the duties of the district chairman and the executive secretary are highly ambiguous. There is no clear-cut line of demarcation between the two.

Most candidates in 1962 were unable to recruit more than one chief campaign officer. The duties outlined in the *O'Brien Manual* were combined by most in the post of campaign manager. Some candidates did appoint a campaign chairman in addition to a manager. The chairman usually was a distinguished citizen in the community who lent his name and prestige (and maybe his money) to the candidate. He had few campaign responsibilities but usually was as active as his time would allow. He was by no means a campaign aide in the same sense as the manager.

In practice it is very difficult to locate an experienced manager; many of the candidates studied in 1962 were unable to find a qualified one with whom they could work. One said:

Let me say here that I found it extremely difficult to locate anyone who could give time out of his regular employment for this very temporary assignment covering only three or four months of activity. We tried but we never came up with anyone.

One of the problems in finding a manager is the span of time needed to develop a campaign. Most managers can arrange for a leave of absence during the campaign but the necessities of economic survival require them to begin their campaign activity too late and end it too soon. In a close district it may be necessary to devote over one year to the campaign effort. The job of manager, like that of the candidate, should not begin with the nomination and end on election day. Before the primary or the convention the manager should be working for the nomination and preparing for the general campaign. After the election he must pay the bills, close the headquarters, and wind up the general affairs of the campaign. These are time-consuming activities. It is not so much that good men are not available—rather than knowledgeable ones rarely are able to break away from their regular employment.

Candidates respond to the problem of manager-selection in different ways. Sixty per cent of the 1962 losers relied on a trusted friend or associate to serve as manager while 22 per cent either served in the role themselves or selected a relative. Although the political party organization should be a source of management skills, only 14 per cent of the 1962 respondents used party people as managers, and only 4 per cent buttressed their campaigns with full-time paid professional managers. This represents a luxury beyond the means of most candidates. Many of the defeated candidates, in retrospect, rated a professional political manager as their foremost campaign need.

On any table of priorities, headquarters staffing occupies a high position. A campaign headquarters cannot operate without people to answer the telephone, prepare mass mailings, clip newspapers, do research, and distribute materials. Even an expert full-time manager and an experienced candidate cannot organize a campaign without volunteer workers. The routine operations of a campaign headquarters are burdensome and time-consuming. Workers are essential if these tasks are to be performed. As noted by the *Democratic Campaign Manual 1962*:

> Volunteer workers are the backbone of every political organization. It would be difficult and impractical—if not impossible—to conduct a successful campaign without adequate numbers of dedicated volunteer workers.

And, the *Republican Manual* agreed:

> Plan ahead on use of volunteers and try to schedule their services at times they'll find convenient. Keep a record of the special abilities of volunteers—not just on clerical and secretarial prowess, but for purposes of training and education programs, absentee ballot programs, public speaking, research work, etc.

Some candidates did not have happy experiences with volunteers. They needed much advance planning and considerable supervision to guarantee that their time would not be wasted. Problems of this type were vividly illustrated by the comment of one candidate from a midwestern state:

> The volunteers didn't show up or showed up late. All of them wanted to be policy makers but none of them wanted to answer the phone or paste stamps. My manager almost quit at one point and it took all my powers of persuasion to get him to stay. He was seriously dissatisfied with the volunteers most of whom were middle-

aged housewives. I think the principal problem for the non-incumbent is finding people to do the work.

There are three distinct sources of volunteer workers in congressional campaigns. Most are drawn from auxiliary non-party organizations set up especially to attract them to the cause of the candidate. These are *ad hoc* groups which rise out of the campaign and fall with the ballot count. A second major source of volunteers is the non-group affiliated individual who wishes to assist from some personal motivation —a love of politics, a hope for aggrandizement, loyalty to the candidate, or for some other personal reason. Finally, a major source of volunteers is the established non-party group which, through joint group-action, undertakes to inject itself into a particular campaign. Two of these— labor unions and medical societies—were prominent sources of campaign workers in 1962.

The popularity of the non-party group in 1962 was illustrated by the fact that 73 per cent of the candidates relied on them as an adjunct to their campaigns. Some of these, it should be noted, were in one-party districts where the minority candidate attempted to use self-generated auxiliary groups as bases upon which to build his campaign in lieu of a party organization. One southern Republican noted that "there was absolutely no party structure in my district and consequently no campaign structure. I built my entire campaign organization around local groups called '_____ for Congress Clubs.'" Most of the "members" of his "clubs" were disaffected Democrats and transplanted northern laboring people who found the blatant racism of the Democratic candidate unpalatable and unacceptable. The groups not only served as an organization for the Republican but helped him play down his party affiliation which was very much an albatross in this district of the old Confederacy.

A second large group of volunteer workers simply report to the candidate's headquarters and offer to help. These individuals are primarily housewives and students. Women, especially those with no small children, are a bulwark of many campaigns. They have the time and the interest to involve themselves in politics and usually the patience to undertake the mundane everyday office jobs that must be accomplished.

Students are more often used in field work. They are young and enthusiastic and, above all, energetic. Some simply report to headquarters and offer to help. Others get involved through their membership in the Young Democrats or Young Republicans. Most candidates in 1962 agreed with the statement of the Democratic National Committee in one of its publications:

> College and high school students are particularly good for leg work —house-to-house distribution, errands, taking material to the post office—and, the girls, especially, for mailing, addressing, and telephone campaigns.

In 1962 over 15,000 volunteers were active in the campaigns of non-incumbent congressional candidates. Eight per cent of the candidates reported some volunteer workers. These ranged from as few as two to as many as 1000 in a single campaign. Republicans were more successful in recruiting volunteers, averaging over 99 per candidate to an average of 49 for the Democrats. This is not a representative figure, however, since a few candidates with hundreds of volunteers caused the average to be much greater than was actually the case in most races. The difference between the two parties might be explained by the serious efforts of the GOP to cut into the overwhelming House margins of the Democrats and the greater response to the GOP by suburbanites who tend to be better paid, better educated, and to have more leisure time that can be devoted to political activities.

Finally, organized non-party private groups served as a major source of campaign workers. Chief among these groups were labor unions and local medical societies, both of which were very active in the 1962 campaign because of the prominence of the Medicare issue. Unions, in recent years, have funneled more and more resources into congressional election campaigns. Although ostensibly non-partisan, most of this assistance has been channeled to Democratic candidates. Labor's contributions have been both in finances and manpower.

Medical societies were active in the campaigns of many GOP candidates. Since doctors ordinarily have little time to take an active part in a campaign, the contributions of these groups were, for the most part, financial. Some, however, benefited from organized groups of doctors' wives which were directed by the American Medical Political Action Committee (AMPAC), a group organized by the medical profession especially to fight Medicare. Few respondents actually mentioned these groups but other reports suggest that they were quite active in many campaigns.

The separation of the non-incumbent candidate from his party organization can be demonstrated in any number of ways. He is forced to set up his own personal organization, locate a manager, raise his own money, and recruit his own volunteers. This proved to be a revelation, if not a traumatic experience, for many candidates. To some it didn't matter. They did not need to rely on an established organization anyway. Others, however, were at a loss as to how to proceed and use valuable days and weeks attempting to pull together the elements necessary for a good working campaign unit. Most did not succeed and all were defeated on election day.

THE PROBLEMS OF FINANCING THE CAMPAIGN

Defeated candidates might well echo the late Will Rogers who once said, "Politics has got so expensive that it takes a lot of money to get beat with." The role of money in American politics is a difficult subject to explain because of the problems of getting information. Federal law requires candidates for the House of Representatives to file with the Clerk of the House personal financial statements of receipts and expenditures, but it does not require reports on those of a campaign committee if the committee does not extend across state lines but merely works within the congressional district. Furthermore, a candidate must report only those expenditures which were handled by him personally or by a colleague if the candidate had personal knowledge of the transaction. These loopholes leave the candidate relatively free to raise and spend money as he wishes.

Contributions to congressional campaigns come from many sources. Tapping these sources is one of the major problems of the finance chairman. The finance chairman must strive to make the campaign financially self-sufficient, oversee compliance with state finance and filing laws, raise and distribute funds, and pay the bills. The job is one of utmost importance in any campaign. The man who holds the position should be a prominent person in the district with wide acquaintance and important contacts with people able to make significant contributions. Those who contribute usually represent a number of different groups who are involved at the congressional campaign level.

The 1962 non-incumbents depended upon friends and associates, personal and family resources, interest groups, and contributions from political party units. Many contributors will not open their pocketbooks for a non-incumbent. They hope to back a winner and are well aware of the slim odds on a challenger candidate. This forces the non-incumbent to rely heavily on funds from family, friends, and associates.

The largest number of candidates in 1962 reported contributions from friends and associates. Over 84 per cent received money from this source and well over one-third financed from 50 to 100 per cent of their campaigns in this way. It is difficult to determine what a "friend" or an "associate" really is. To a desperate candidate anyone who makes a contribution may become a "friend" at first meeting. In most cases, however, candidate comments suggested that these contributions came from people with whom the candidate had been associated for a long period of time. Associates usually turned out to be individuals with whom the candidate was connected occupationally or had met through political party activities.

The following is representative of many candidates' comments:

> I guess my biggest problem in the campaign was raising enough money to keep going from week to week. There were some periods when we didn't know whether we would be able to go on or not. Most of the money in the campaign came from personal acquaintances. My fellow members of the bar helped a great deal as did some of the doctors. I made up much of the difference by loans from my wife's relatives. I owe about $3000 to them right now.

Fifty-nine per cent of the non-incumbents reported some personal contribution to their own campaigns. Almost half of these indicated that personal contributions accounted for less than 10 per cent of the total monies spent; but 20 per cent of them exceeded 50 per cent of the total costs of the campaign. Five individuals reported 100 per cent personal financing of their campaigns.

Pressure groups have an obvious interest in the election of particular individuals. One way to express the interest, and at the same time make sure the elected incumbent remembers it, is to contribute to his campaign. Thirty-six per cent of the non-incumbent respondents reported receiving contributions from such groups. Slightly over half were supported by contributions from business groups and the remainder by medical and labor groups. Business and medical association input into campaign coffers was principally beneficial to Republican candidates. That of labor was predominantly channeled to Democrats. Some Democrats received labor money even though labor did not represent an important interest in their districts. These contributions, in most cases, were to incumbents who had demonstrated friendship for labor through their voting performance. In some cases the same group contributed to opposing candidates. As noted by one Republican, "A number of groups make contributions to both sides. This assures them a hearing regardless of who is elected."

Funds from the national Democratic party are channeled through both the national committee and the Congressional Campaign Committee. In 1962 the former distributed only $31,500 directly to candidates while the latter divided up $161,450 among 129 candidates. The largest of these contributions was $3000 and the smallest was $100. The median amount given to Democratic candidates by the Congressional Campaign Committee was $1000 while the mean was slightly more at $1250. The Democratic National Committee contributed fewer but larger amounts, with one candidate receiving $5500 while two others got only $500 each.

The total Republican expenditures, made entirely through the National Republican Congressional Committee, amounted to $229,593. The median was $1000 while the mean was slightly more at $1100. The largest single contribution to any candidate was $6593 while the smallest was $100.

The Congressional campaign committees decide to whom they will give money. They have limited resources and many campaigns which need support. Both with incumbents and non-incumbents the committees attempt to parcel out the available money in a manner that will do the most good. They must rely on judgments, based on whatever evidence is available, as to the chances for victory in any given race. Neither the candidate who clearly will win nor the one who has no chance will ordinarily be given financial assistance. If, however, the district is marginal (i.e., was won or lost in the last election by 5 per cent or less of the votes) both parties will classify it as a target and will channel resources into it. Fifty-four per cent of the non-incumbent candidates received some financial assistance from party sources in 1962. These funds came from national, state, and local party groups as well as from individual party officers.

Figures representing total campaign receipts and expenditures are unavailable. The records of the Clerk of the House contain those personal and committee reports that candidates wish to file, but the law is replete with exemptions and loopholes and the figures are not accurate. Several candidates, representing both parties, reported expenditures of $50,000 or more, even though such spending would appear technically to violate the law. In this survey the highest estimated cost of a campaign was $55,000 for a Republican who was in a tight race against an incumbent. Most campaigns, according to the personal estimates of the candidates, cost from $10,000 to $25,000.

The candidates surveyed were asked to estimate what it would have cost to mount the kind of campaign which might have carried them to victory. A few bluntly stated that no amount of money could have resulted in their election. Most, however, felt that money was about all that stood between them and a seat in Congress. Although their answers were equivocal and hedged with qualifications, those who ventured a guess usually claimed that an additional $15,000 to $25,000 would have been necessary.

There is nothing very scientific about campaign finance. Most non-incumbent congressional candidates take what they can get and seldom do they believe that it is enough. It is very easy for a defeated candidate to rationalize his defeat entirely in terms of money. He does not wish to admit that he did not project well, or that his stand on the issues was unpopular. Therefore, he blames his failure on the problems of campaign finance. Even so, it is difficult to argue with the point. There can be no doubt that, all things being equal, the more money that is available the more effectively the campaign can be carried out. Even unpopular issues or colorless candidates can be sold to some voters if the money is available to bring off the sale.

THE PROBLEM OF ISSUES

Among all the other problems generated by the orphan's role played by non-incumbent candidates for the House is that of finding issues. His campaign is local and is often based on local issues, but the office he is seeking is national and is concerned with national and international problems. The candidate's overriding goal must necessarily be to get elected or re-elected. Most congressional aspirants will not let the issues stand in their way. The attitude often expressed by them is, "I've got to get elected first—then I will consider the issues." Analysis of the responses of the 1962 candidates to questions concerning issue orientation in the campaign suggested that most of them had concluded that: (1) the interests of the district or other locality must be emphasized in the campaign; (2) the sentiment of the constituents must be honored if they are known irrespective of the candidate's personal beliefs; and, (3) the issues are relatively unimportant when compared to the base of support which can be built through personal favors or promises of assistance. This does not mean, however, that the candidate reacts in the same way the congressman does. Once elected he may view the matter in a considerably different light. But our concern here is with the man as a candidate and with his views toward the uses of issues in the campaign.

The non-incumbent has no reputation outside the district nor does he have a voting record to defend. He can base his campaign on any issues in which he may arouse voter interest. He usually has no record of performance and cannot point with pride to political prizes he has won from the Federal Government for the district. Consequently, he must rely on promises to the constituents while at the same time assuming postures on national and international matters which he thinks will be attractive to the voters.

The 1962 congressional non-incumbents believed themselves well-equipped to discuss issues. Each candidate was asked to evaluate his defeat according to a given set of criteria including his knowledge of the issues. An astounding 98 per cent of the Democrats and 90 per cent of the Republicans stated that inadequate knowledge of issues was of little or no importance as a cause of their loss. This does not necessarily mean that they believed themselves adequately prepared to discuss the issues but many of them volunteered comments indicating that this was, in fact, the case. In some campaigns issues were of little importance. In others the opposing candidates were not in basic disagreement on the issues. And, in still others, there was little evidence that issues had any impact at all, even when hotly contested.

The 1962 defeated candidates were categorized according to four distinct types of issue orientation. All of the campaigns embraced more than one of the types. No one based his campaign on a single type of issue. The four issue categories were ideological, policy, personal, and service.

Candidates who hang their campaigns on an ideological framework are normally attempting to associate themselves with a chosen point on the liberal-conservative continuum. They may attempt to capitalize on what appears to them to be a popular philosophy. In a district thought to be conservative the candidate would tailor his treatment of issues toward the purported conservatism of the electorate. A number of Republican candidates, particularly in the South and in southern California, sought to capitalize on what they viewed as a "Goldwater tide." One, for example, said:

The only reason the Republican party has not been able to win this seat has been that we have always run me-too candidates. This is a conservative district and I was certain that a conservative candidate could win it. The fact that I didn't win doesn't mean the district is not conservative. I am sure it is.

Others, including many of the "peace" candidates, flaunted deeply-felt personal views in the faces of the electorate even though there was little evidence of support for their beliefs. Some of them were quick to admit the hopelessness of their campaigns but saw the election as an opportunity to purposefully exploit unpopular ideological issues.

Most of the ideologically-oriented candidates (about 10 per cent) spoke to their audiences in terms of "liberalism," "conservatism," or "right-wing" and "left-wing." They seldom discussed specific issues or personalities choosing instead to concentrate on the over-riding ideology. There were fewer of them than in any of the other four issue groups.

Policy-oriented campaigns are those in which the candidates offer different approaches to the solution of major problems or criticize each other on attitudes toward particular issues. These may be local, national, or international and many campaigns are based on all three. Some discuss a wide range of issues and policy alternatives while others concentrate their fire on a single overriding one. In this categorization the degree of specificity with which issues were discussed was important to their classification. Thus, a candidate who suggested that "Medicare" was evidence of "creeping socialism" was classed as ideological whereas one who discussed the issue of medical care as a problem in itself was clearly policy-oriented. This is a rather narrow interpretation but one that was not required often since most campaign issues were clearly in one category or another.

Policy issues were clearly dominant in 1962, with 37 per cent of the candidates in both parties concentrating their efforts on them. As is usually the case, the issues were both of a domestic and foreign policy nature. Republicans concentrated on the increasing size of the national government, federal aid to education, and high taxes. Some GOP candidates based much of their campaign discussion on the issue of medical care to the aged. In the field of foreign affairs most Republican fire was directed at the "inadequate response of the Administration to the Cuban menace." This issue was somewhat blunted in mid-October but was a staple of many campaigns before that time.

Democrats, in general, had little choice but to defend and support President Kennedy's domestic programs. These were somewhat overshadowed by the overriding interest in the Cuban situation both before and after the fourteen-day crisis. Prior to mid-October many Democratic candidates were on the defensive regarding the Administration's alleged weak handling of the problem and much pressure was applied to the White House to attempt to counteract Republican thrusts. After the missile crisis, the candidates in the President's party were able to point to the successful culmination of the affair and many reported upturns in public support.

Political attacks on an opponent's qualifications or personal attributes have been a part of American campaigns from the genesis of the party system. At times, these attacks have played so dominant a role that they must be considered as political issues in themselves. About 12 per cent of the candidates, equally divided between the parties, engaged in discussions of personal issues of this kind in 1962. Some of them allowed such matters to overshadow authentic policy or ideological issues which might reflect adversely upon them. And, in a few cases defeated candidates suggested that personality attacks were used as a means of papering over the lack of basic issue differences between the candidates. At times they were discussed openly—at others they took the form of whispering campaigns. Their substance ranged from attacks upon an opponent's age (either too young or too old) to marital infidelity and religious backsliding. One of the commonest forms of personal attack was that embodied in unsigned throw-sheets distributed too late in the campaign to be answered. Most issues of a personal nature, as suggested by these examples, were derogatory in nature.

Finally, about 21 per cent of the candidates discussed issues which might be classed as of a "service" nature. The candidate who campaigned on the assertion that "in twenty years in Congress _____ has never done a single constructive thing for his district or got a single important bill passed," represented an example of a "service" type of issue campaign. These questions usually centered on the incumbent's inadequate service to his constituents, lack of respect among fellow members of the House, failure to receive committee assignments of benefit to the constituency, and legislative unproductivity. Incumbents based similar charges on their opponents' service in state legislatures or city governments.

Both the candidates who developed "service" issues and those who engaged in "personal" attacks were, in effect, creating do-it-yourself campaign strategies. Ordinarily the national party committees do not personalize the materials furnished the candidates in a way which makes them useful in these two types of issue campaigns. Both national parties furnish non-incumbent candidates with the voting records of their opponents but these are then left to the individual to do with as he pleases. Other materials from national party organizations are predominantly ideological and policy-oriented. Many candidates simply parrot the national party line on these matters while devoting their personal ingenuity to developing attacks upon the incumbent's personal and service record.

If one assumes that issue-understanding is relevant to voter choice it is difficult not to agree with an incumbent who stated, "The member has everything going for him on issues. If he tends to his knitting he can usually talk circles around an outsider." He was referring to the vast amounts of issue information available to the congressman and the research facilities of the national party which are put at his command. The non-incumbent simply cannot match these resources.

NATIONAL TRENDS AND LOCAL ELECTIONS

In presidential election years the composition of the House of Representatives often reflects the "coattail" influence. There are exceptions to the rule but a successful presidential candidate can usually add votes to the congressional tickets simply by his position at its head. He attracts attention to the entire ticket. There have been two recent exceptions to the rule. In 1956, President Eisenhower was unable to transfer his personal magnetism to lesser Republican candidates and the Democrats maintained strong majorities in both houses of Congress. In 1960, for a variety of reasons, House candidates on the Democratic ticket out-polled their presidential candidate, John F. Kennedy, even though he was elected. Most of the time, however, the coattail effect is clearly evident. In 1964, President Johnson carried scores of Democratic congressional and state legislative candidates into office on a surge of voter reaction against Barry Goldwater.

In off-year congressional elections the results are often reversed. Without a presidential campaign to attract the voters' attention, candidates for the House must rely solely on their own initiative or, at the very least, have strong candidates at the top of the state ticket. Because of the lack of a presidential contest fewer voters go to the polls to vote and those who do are most strongly committed to the party. In the presidential year of 1964, 65.7 million votes were cast for candidates for the House of Representatives while in the off-year elections of 1962 only 51.1 million voted in House elections. It is almost a truism in politics that the out-party gains strength in off-year elections. In every off-year since the Civil War, with the exception of 1934, the President's party has lost seats in the House. The year 1962 was almost an exception when President Kennedy's popularity combined with the mid-campaign Cuban crisis tended to offset expected gains by the Republicans. The GOP only gained a net of two seats in that year.

The importance of the absence of the coattail phenomenon to non-incumbent House candidates in an off-year cannot be exaggerated. Furthermore, in 1962 the impact of Kennedy was unknown and caused some consternation among Democrats and Republicans alike. Democratic House candidates were not sure that the incumbent President would be a favorable factor in the congressional elections. He ran behind the cumulative total of House Democrats in 1960 and some expressed serious reservations about his influence on their particular races in 1962. One said, "I didn't feel that I could rely on the support of Kennedy in this election since I ran over 8000 votes ahead of him two years ago." He noted that he had refused to accept the help of all national Democratic leaders since personal efforts had been successful in the past and he did not wish to risk a change in style.

Although difficult to project, each candidate must consider the effects of national trends on his own race. Some non-incumbents in the opposition party campaign more actively against the President than they do against their own opponent. Others try to localize the contest in order to minimize the effects of public support for or resentment against the national leadership. They want to control their own campaigns and they hope to win on the basis of their own efforts. Occasionally, however, a momentous event, such as the Cuban crisis, will completely re-direct the campaign and overshadow almost every other issue. Non-incumbents fear the injection of these issues into the campaign since they are unable to maintain control over them.

THE EFFECTS OF DEFEAT

As he drove home the candidate thought back over the long campaign. The hours at the factory gate at 6:00 a.m.; the seemingly endless luncheons with Kiwanians, Rotarians, Elks, and union leaders; the television session with the ladies of the League of Women Voters; the constant search for precinct workers and the pleas for contributions; the hand-shaking tours; the county fairs and supermarkets; and, above all, the unpaid bills. The memories flooded back and just thinking of them tired him. In the final analysis, though, he had learned from his defeat. He would know how to go about it next time. Maybe it wouldn't be so bad to try again. If he could get his debts paid and maintain some semblance of an organizational entity he might just do it. He would have two years to campaign and the Congressman would have two more years of mistakes to live down. He definitely would think it over during the coming weeks. But, right now his only interest was sleep.

Defeated candidates react to defeat in as many different ways as there are districts. Some are bitter: "I would not run for office again if they gave me a million dollars. I've had it in politics." Some are realistic: "This district could be won by the Republican party but it would take a better candidate than I to win it. I didn't seem to project well." Some were hopeful: "I'm going to run again. I will begin my campaign as soon as I get my debts paid and the party has already told me it will support me because of my good showing this time." Some are evangelical: "It doesn't really matter who the candidate is. He must sell the conservative philosophy of government. When we have finally educated the voters they will support our candidate." Some were evaluative: "I know now what my problems were. I needed many more volunteers and precinct workers. My organization stank."

Even among those who, in the first flush of defeat, believed they would try again, few actually followed through when the time came.

During the first month after the 1962 election each of the defeated candidates was asked whether or not he intended to run for national office again. Thirty-five per cent of the Republicans and 41 per cent of the Democrats replied affirmatively. Of that group 82 per cent specified that it was their intention to again seek a House seat in 1964. When the 1962 candidate lists were compared to those of the 1964, however, it was apparent that their initial ardor had substantially cooled by the time the 1964 campaign got underway. Forty-five candidates in each party signified their intention of running again, but only 15 in each party actually did. A few made the attempt but did not survive the primaries. Most simply changed their minds. Of the 30 who ran again, only 8 were elected in 1964—7 Democrats and 1 Republican.

In retrospect, what appeared to be wrong with the campaign strategy and/or organization of the defeated candidates? What would they do differently another time around? What did they view as the major problems of their campaigns? Answers to these questions represent the type of retrospective analysis candidates put themselves through after an unsuccessful campaign. They also serve as road maps for future campaigns.

For the citizen and voter, answers to these questions point up those areas which are most susceptible to volunteer political action. Above all they emphasize the need in most campaigns for every sort of volunteer participation and support. Such support may not bring victory but it will not allow defeat to be laid at the door of default.

One of the most vital of all political assets is the active participation of volunteer workers. The very fractionalization and decentralization of American politics offers unlimited pathways for political entrepreneurs. Most people become party workers or officers— few actually plunge into active candidacy. Political campaigns offer channels for gregariousness and forums for oratory. They provide a form of psychological fulfillment to those willing to take part. Politics is a many splendored thing and it provides an especially attractive outlet for youthful enthusiasms. The satisfactions of winning a hard-fought campaign cannot be measured. They are only slightly greater than those of losing a campaign that has been well-fought.

This evaluation of one congressional campaign emphasized the importance of solving problems of recruitment, organization and management, the relationship of party units to each other and to the candidate, the inadequacy of existing fund-raising methods, and the need to improve public relations and political research methods. Proper application of the solutions to these problems would go far to redress the imbalance between the two types of candidates—incumbents and non-incumbents.

The parties can do more to assert leadership over congressional and other campaigns. The power of recruitment is theirs and, even though they have performed reasonably well in that role, there is room for considerable improvement. If the party has recruited the candidate it might feel more responsible for helping to elect him. It might lend a hand to him in setting up his personal organization, locating a campaign manager or finance chairman, and in furnishing public relations and research assistance. Selected state committees already do these things and do them well.

A viable two-party system can grow only if party members strive to cultivate it. In politics a key element of such cultivation is to run even though defeat seems inevitable. Years may go by before a competitive party system emerges, but the effort must be made because the system demands it. There is bountiful evidence that hard work does pay. For the first time in decades, Vermont has a Democratic governor and the traditionally Republican states of Iowa and Nebraska have also elected Democrats in recent years. The Democratic states of Oklahoma and Rhode Island, on the other hand, have elected Republican governors. Many congressional districts in the Republican midwest and the Democratic south have changed party hands in recent years. Admittedly, these changes in fortune have not happened merely because a few dedicated stalwarts kept the spark of life alive in the minority party. National and regional trends and issues have affected the growth of the minority parties in these formerly one-party regions. Nevertheless, a two-party system is emerging and it has been nourished by the many men who have run for office when the chances of victory were slight. They have been the necessary stimulant to the volunteer workers needed to build a strong party apparatus.

The role of the citizen in this party-building exercise was well-stated in July 1920, when Elihu Root, the American statesman, was invited to present a statue of Abraham Lincoln to the British people. He took the occasion to expound his views on the role of politics in life. He said:

> Politics is the practical exercise of the art of self-government, and somebody must attend to it if we are to have self-government; somebody must study it, and learn the art, and exercise patience and sympathy and skill to bring the multitude of opinions and wishes of self-governing people into such order that some prevailing opinion may be expressed and peaceably accepted. Otherwise, confusion will result either in dictatorship or anarchy. The principal ground of reproach against any American citizen should be that he is not a politician. Everyone ought to be.

part
four

PRESIDENTIAL POLITICS

AMERICAN POLITICS *comes to a quadrennial pinnacle of feverish activity with the presidential campaigns. The ritual of selecting party candidates is elaborate, and begins with delegate selection for the national conventions. This is followed by the semi-tragic, semi-comic, always intensely purposeful national conventions, nationally televised, and disruptive of the public business for the better part of two weeks in the summer of election years. Finally there is the campaign, and, of increasing interest to voters and politicians, its cost. These are the concerns of the three chapters in Part Four.*

DONALD BRUCE JOHNSON

Donald Bruce Johnson studied at the University of Minnesota (A.B., 1943; A.M., 1948) and at the University of Illinois (Ph.D., 1952). He has taught at the Duluth Junior College (1946–48), the University of Illinois (1948–51) and the University of Iowa (1951–   ). He has been a visiting professor at Emory University (1955) San Francisco State College (1962), and the University of Maine (1966).

Johnson was Associate Director, Citizenship Clearing House (1959–60) and has been active in civil rights groups at national, state, and local levels. He is a Consultant-Examiner for the North Central Association of Colleges and Secondary Schools.

Johnson is the author of *The Republican Party and Wendell Willkie* (1960), *The Impact of Grants in Aid on the Structure of State and Local Government in Iowa* (1954), co-editor of *National Party Platforms, 1840–1964* (1956, 1961, 1966), co-author, *The Dynamics of the American Presidency* (1964) and has contributed to numerous other books and periodicals.

DONALD BRUCE JOHNSON

9. Delegate Selection For National Conventions

The quadrennial process of narrowing the number of prospective candidates for President from a score or more to two begins to take on a formal aspect a year before the national nominating convention when each national committee determines the size of its delegation and selects the convention city in which the convention will be held. The process of delegate selection, the convention spectacles, the nominations and campaign, concluding with the inauguration may well be to most people the most fascinating drama of American politics. This is also the part of American politics that involves more people—both as workers and as voters—than any other. It is in the electoral process that the citizen can play his most active role. A democracy exists if the people have choices among leaders. In the United States today, citizens can participate in the recruitment, evaluation, and selection of those leaders. That is what this chapter is about.

NOMINATING METHODS

Presidential candidates have not always been nominated as they are today. In the first two elections, no nominations were necessary. George Washington was chosen by the members of the electoral college—acting independently as the men who wrote the Constitution expected they would. But immediately thereafter, political parties became better established, men began pursuing goals which were more clearly in conflict, and competing tickets were chosen in advance by men with common political, social, and economic interests.

This slatemaking was achieved at gatherings called caucuses, which were meetings of influential persons—often elected legislators—at which group endorsements were given to certain candidates before the elections were held. At first, these caucuses were used primarily at the local level, but they were soon institutionalized, and within a few years after the Constitution was written, nominations by caucuses reflected a relatively firm two-party division at all levels of government. As more and more offices were created and increasing numbers of people went to the polls, a narrowing of the choices had to be made by some representative body; the legislative caucus decisions were accepted as legitimate by most party leaders for several decades. John Adams, in 1796, was nominated by a congressional caucus—as were his successors Thomas Jefferson, James Madison, and James Monroe.

As early as 1804, however, opposition to the caucuses began to develop. Many persons felt that the selection of presidential candidates by a caucus of Congressional leaders violated the spirit of the Constitution and its provision for a separation of powers. Other political officials complained that it was basically undemocratic in that states and districts that had no representatives of a given party in the Congress had no voice in the selection of that party's nominees for President and Vice-President. Moreover, the caucus system imposed a national control over what many citizens believed to be a local matter—nominations. Finally, some aspiring politicians felt that a historic Virginia dynasty was being established by the use of the caucus.

This turmoil came to a head in 1824, when five of the six leading aspirants to the presidency found that the caucus worked against their best interest. Consequently they first attacked the institution and later their followers boycotted the caucus and ignored its decision. William Crawford was nominated by the caucus, but Andrew Jackson, DeWitt Clinton, John Quincy Adams, Henry Clay, and John Calhoun were nominated by state legislatures and state conventions. All over the nation, mass meetings in 1824 and 1828 revolted and endorsed various candidates; this was the end of king caucus. State conventions and legislatures became widely regarded as legitimate nominating bodies, but because state meetings were likely to make too many disparate choices, some coordination was essential. Parties seeking to be nationally strong, of necessity, had to rally behind a single leader. The national nominating convention was the result.

The anti-Masonic party held the first national convention in Philadelphia in September 1830 and another in 1831. The National Republicans convened in a similar convention in December 1831; the Democrats met in their first convention in 1832. The Whigs used the convention for the first time in 1836. Theoretically, the conventions were more representative than the caucus. Citizens, other than Congressmen, could have a role in the selection of party candidates; the candidates selected would be free of subservience to Congress, and the diverse interests of the new American nation could be reflected in the unity of one single nominating body. During the Whig-Democrat period of our national history (roughly 1832–1854) the convention system became firmly established. The mechanics of the convention—some of which exist to this very day—became firmly rooted in tradition. The unit rule, which was not abandoned until 1968, and the two-thirds rule, which lasted for an entire century in the Democratic party, were instituted.

Although no drastic changes took place during the following half century, conventions developed some shenanigans over the years. At the state level, party bosses in certain states used devious maneuvers to control the selection of delegates and to insure that their adherents would be in positions of power. Conventions were held before the hour scheduled; they were held in saloons; notices of their meetings were torn down so only insiders would know of their existence. Delegations of handpicked supporters were manipulated with ease, and outsiders were systematically excluded from participation in the convention process. Obviously this did not happen everywhere but where political stakes are high, men will scheme for them with ingenuity and shrewdness. Consequently, conventions were the center of serious external and behind-the-scenes attempts at persuasion, argument, pressure, and manipulation. By 1900, machine control of many delegates was an accepted fact, and in certain areas the rank and file of the parties had virtually nothing to say about the delegations.

ORIGINS OF THE PRESIDENTIAL PRIMARIES

Among the progressives and reformers of the day, the cure for such an ailment was an extension of direct democracy by law. It was widely suggested that the nomination process would be improved if voters selected the delegates to the convention and also expressed their choices for party nominees at pre-November elections. Primary elections for the selection of state officers were popular, and it seemed logical that the same system could be used for presidential nominations. In effect, this was an effort to transform the convention from a representative decision-making body into a recording device merely to approve action taken by voters in the states.

Florida, in 1904, enacted the first statute providing for the election of delegates to the national conventions in a primary. It was an optional law that allowed any party recognized by law to elect its convention delegates in this way. No direct preference poll was provided. Florida Democrats have used the primary fairly frequently. In 1906, Pennsylvania adopted a similar law for district delegates but it was not used for half a dozen years. Wisconsin, in 1905, enacted the first law specifically designed to provide for the election of slates of pledged delegates, and the statute was used by the supporters of Robert LaFollette to elect a progressive delegation in 1908. In 1910, the legislature in Oregon passed a law providing for both a preferential poll for a Presidential candidate and direct elections of all district delegates. The movement began rolling and by 1912, fourteen states had adopted some form of Presidential

primary. By 1916, the number had risen to twenty-two, but then it
began to decline. Many states have since authorized primaries and
repealed them shortly after when they failed to serve the purposes of
the strongest elements of the state's politics.

Today, presidential primaries are of two basic types, the presidential
preference poll and a primary election for the selection of convention
delegates. Both methods will be examined in more detail shortly. First,
however, something should be said about how the number of delegates
who attend the convention and the number of delegates to be chosen
from any particular state are determined.

THE APPORTIONMENT OF CONVENTION DELEGATIONS

When the convention system was first instituted, apportionment of
delegates was erratic and unequal. Some states had larger delegations
than others solely because they were physically closer to the convention
city. This, however, was soon changed. The Democrats in 1852 and the
Republicans in 1860 decided to allot the states twice the number of
delegates to national conventions as they were entitled to electors in the
Electoral College. In other words, the convention delegations would be
double the states' delegations in Congress. Since the House was, at least
in theory, equitably apportioned on the basis of population, and the
Senate evenly represented each state, the values of state sovereignty and
population were balanced in the nominating convention.

This ratio, which remained unchanged for more than half a century,
produced some grave sectional inequities for the Republican party.
Southern states, unlikely to contribute electoral votes to Republican
candidates, were greatly overrepresented at GOP conventions. Alabama
had more delegates than Kansas; Texas was as influential as Illinois.
During the nineteenth century most southern states had only skeleton
Republican organizations that were used to distribute patronage and to
serve the wishes of the President. Both Theodore Roosevelt and William
Howard Taft exploited southern delegations to control nominations.
But the deep cleavage in the party after Taft utilized the South to
secure the nomination from Roosevelt in 1912 led to some reflection
about the reapportionment of delegates. The result was a series of
changes in the formula aimed at giving more influence in conventions
to the states in which Republicans were likely to win.

Since that date, the apportionment has been changed several times.
The present formula, refined over a period of fifty years and last used
in 1964, is as follows:

Four delegates-at-large for each state
Two delegates-at-large for each Representative-at-large
Six additional delegates-at-large for each state that voted for the
Republican candidate for president in the preceding election or
elected a U.S. Senator or Governor later

> One district delegate for each Congressional district which cast
> 2,000 or more votes for the Republican presidential candidate or
> for Republican House candidates in the last election
> One additional district delegate for each Congressional district
> which cast 10,000 or more votes for the Republican presidential
> candidate or Republican House candidates
> Special allotments: District of Columbia, nine; Puerto Rico, five;
> Virgin Islands, three

When the original variation of this plan was instituted in 1916, the
southern states lost seventy-eight delegates. But even then, the allocation still overrepresented the GOP vote in the southern states. From
1916 to 1948, the South—so unlikely to go Republican during that
period—consistently had about fifteen per cent of the delegates and
much more convention influence than many traditionally Republican
states the party was more likely to carry. Nevertheless, the formula was
a more accurate reflection of party strength. In 1964, only one Mississippi congressional district did not qualify for two votes. Due to Goldwater's victories in the South in 1964 and the strengthened Republican
organizations throughout the area, there is an increasing likelihood of
two party systems in all of the southern states. If the present trend
continues, the South could be more influential as it sends larger delegations to future Republican conventions.[1]

The Democratic party, less bothered by sectionalism, retained the
same basic ratio of delegates to electoral vote for practically ninety years.
During this time, as a consequence of the two-thirds rule, the southern
delegates felt that they had a partial veto over Democratic nominations
so they made no move to increase the delegate strength of their one
consistently Democratic area. After the two-thirds rule was repealed
in 1936, however, southern leaders demanded that their loyalty be
rewarded. Therefore, the 1936 convention instructed the national committee to develop a formula that would provide bonuses for states that
went Democratic. The committee in 1940 provided two additional delegates for each such state in 1944; but the South was still dissatisfied,
and so two additional bonus votes were again added in 1948. In 1956,
another bonus rule was adopted. But in 1960, all this was abandoned
when the committee returned to an allocation of two-and-a-half convention votes for each member of Congress. This was designed to end some
discrepancies that had arisen because of reapportionment and bonuses
during the 1950's. Although no state was to have fewer votes than at
the previous convention, midwestern and northwestern areas profited
slightly more than the South under the formula. But this lasted for only
one convention. In a drastic shift in philosophy, on January 11, 1964,
the Democratic National Committee adopted an apportionment plan

---

[1] For an interesting analysis of this problem, see "On the Possibility of Major
Political Realignment in the South," by Philip E. Converse, in *Elections and the
Political Order*, by Campbell, Converse, Miller, and Stokes. New York: John Wiley
& Sons, 1966, pp. 212–242.

based almost exclusively on party voting strength. It recognizes the Democratic strength in the large urban areas and greatly augments the influence of the states that cast their electoral votes for Kennedy in his narrow victory over Nixon in 1960. The plan provides rewards for Democratic voter turnout, and even larger rewards for Democratic victories at the state level. It also substantially increases the size of the conventions. The formula:

Three convention votes for each electoral vote

One vote for every 100,000 popular votes or major fraction thereof cast for the Democratic nominee in the preceding presidential election

A bonus of ten votes if the state cast its electoral votes for the national Democratic nominee

One vote each to be cast by the National Committeeman and Committeewoman

Additional allocations are made for the Canal Zone, Puerto Rico, the Virgin Islands, and Guam. The allocation for the District of Columbia was determined at the average of the other three-electoral vote states under the new plan: sixteen votes

Democrats allow the casting of half votes, but National Committee members have no alternates. Therefore, in 1968, the formula allowed 2622 votes to a maximum of 2989 delegates and 2512 alternates. Legally, 5611 Democrats were authorized to attend the 1968 convention!

SELECTION OF DELEGATES BY PRIMARY ELECTION

Once the national committees have decided the number of delegates who may attend the national conventions, the *method* of selection is determined by the States—either by the state legislature or by the party acting under some kind of state authorization or without a statute. The delegates are selected in one of three different ways:

1. by appointment by a state party committee
2. by selection at state conventions
3. by election in presidential preference primaries

All states have variations of one or more of these methods and there are many minor legal differences within state plans. Some states even have the two parties use different methods of selection but the general pattern follows one of these three methods.[2]

_____

[2] Four states, Arkansas, Georgia, Louisiana and Rhode Island authorize state executive or state central committees to select the delegates to the National Conventions. Actually, in Georgia and Rhode Island this system is used only by the Democrats; Republicans use the state convention. Also, in New York and Pennsylvania, the delegates-at-large may be chosen by committees. When delegates are chosen in this manner, party autonomy is greatest and ordinarily the rank and file citizen has virtually nothing to say about the selection of delegates. In order to influence such a selection, one usually must become a part of the ruling hierarchy within

In the light of previous discussion of conventions and caucuses as modes of selecting candidates and delegates this section will focus upon delegate selection by primary election.

Today, about forty per cent of the delegates can be chosen in primaries in seventeen states and the District of Columbia. The statement is conditional because not all states hold primaries even though authorized by statute. There is much variation among the primaries and each year new developments take place. In 1964, for example, largely through the efforts of supporters of Barry Goldwater, Republicans in Texas held a preference poll for the first time. And in 1966 and 1967, several distinctive amendments were made to existing primary election statutes; legislatures in at least four states, Colorado, Michigan, New Mexico, and Washington, seriously considered adopting presidential primaries but failed to pass the necessary legislation. Although the array of primaries seems confusing, it can be clarified by carefully examining the basic categories in Table 2.

In most states the primary election enables the voters to select the actual *delegates* for the national conventions. But in some states, candidate preference *polls* are held either separately or as part of the delegate selection process. The most widely reported primaries are those in which major contenders campaign against each other. The New Hampshire primary, for example, held early in March as the first primary of the presidential election year, contains both a poll and direct election of delegates. Consequently, it invariably produces an interesting contest and inordinate amounts of publicity for the state. In contrast, New York and Alabama voters elect unpledged delegates and rarely if ever have an opportunity to express a preference among candidates.

Sixteen states have closed primaries; Wisconsin's is open. A closed primary limits voting to registered or declared party members. An open primary allows the voters in the secrecy of the polling booths to decide in which party they intend to vote. They need tell no one they are Democrats or Republicans and they can change their affiliation from election to election. This system supposedly facilitates "raiding"—the

---

the state through hard work over long years. Although this may seem to be an overwhelming task, energetic and ambitious newcomers have proved in recent years that it can be achieved. The Republican organizations in the four states that use this method recently have been penetrated, developed and strengthened by workers anxious to enjoy the power and experiences of political life.

More than half the delegates, from twenty-nine states, are selected in state or district conventions of various kinds. These delegates are chosen at-large or by areas. It is not uncommon to have the important political figures of a state—senators, governors, state chairmen, or national committeemen and women—designated delegates at-large by a state convention after district delegates have been chosen at district conventions or caucuses held shortly before state conventions. As Calhoun remarked, these state conventions contain delegates who were selected at county conventions which in turn were made up of people chosen at precinct caucuses—several steps removed from the voters!

Selection of Delegates to National Conventions[1]

State	1. Delegates selected at State or district conventions or by State executive committee	2. Delegates elected at primary with no presidential candidate involved	3. Delegates elected at preferential presidential primary where choice for President is expressed by voters			4. Delegates elected at State convention but separate preferential presidential primary where choice for President is expressed by voters at Presidential candidate's request with vote binding on delegates.
			(a) Yes or no	(b) Is vote binding on delegates, viz, are delegates pledged?	(c) Is consent of presidential candidate required?	
Alabama	Democrats at primary. Republicans at State and district conventions.	Democrats only, and only in event of a contest among delegates.	No			
Alaska	State convention		No			
Arizona	State convention		No			
Arkansas	State committee		Optional. (A preferential primary must be held by a presidential candidate's party if such candidate so petitions the State committee 6 months prior to the national convention.) Yes	Yes [2]	Yes [3]	
California			Yes			
Colorado	State convention		No			

State	Method of selecting delegates					
Connecticut	Democrats at State convention; Republicans at State and district conventions.	. . . . .	No	. . . . .	. . . . .	. . . . .
Delaware	State convention	Yes	No	. . . . .	. . . . .	. . . . .
District of Columbia	. . . . .	. . . . .	No	No	Yes [3]	. . . . .
Florida	. . . . .	. . . . .	Yes	. . . . .	. . . . .	. . . . .
Georgia	Republicans at State and district conventions; Democrats by State committee.	. . . . .	No	. . . . .	. . . . .	. . . . .
Hawaii	State convention	. . . . .	No	. . . . .	. . . . .	. . . . .
Idaho	State convention [4]	. . . . .	No	No	. . . . .	. . . . .
Illinois	State convention selects delegates-at-large only.	. . . . .	Yes; district delegates only.	No	No; that candidate's name must go on ballot if he so files with secretary of state.	Yes.
Indiana	Democrats at State convention; Republicans at State and district conventions.	. . . . .	No	. . . . .	. . . . .	. . . . .
Iowa	State conventions	. . . . .	No	. . . . .	. . . . .	. . . . .
Kansas	Delegates-at-large by State conventions; district delegates by district conventions.	. . . . .	No	. . . . .	. . . . .	. . . . .

See footnotes at end of table.

SELECTION OF DELEGATES TO NATIONAL CONVENTIONS[1] (Continued)

State					
Kentucky	Delegates-at-large by State conventions; district delegates by district conventions.		No		
Louisiana	Democrats by State committee; Republicans by State and district conventions.		No		
Maine	Republicans at district conventions so authorized by State convention; Democrats at State convention.		No		
Maryland	State convention		No		
Massachusetts			Yes	Yes [5]	Consent not required but must be filed if delegate's statement of preference for him is to appear on ballot; presidential candidates nominated by State committees

			and by petition.
Michigan	Delegates-at-large by State conventions; district delegates by district conventions.	No	
Minnesota	Democrats at State convention; Republicans at State and district conventions.	No	
Mississippi	State convention	No	
Missouri	Democrats at State and district conventions; Republicans at State and district conventions.	No	
Montana	State convention	No	
Nebraska		Yes	Only if he signs a pledge.	Yes, if petition is filed; candidate's names may also be placed on ballot at discretion of secretary of state.
Nevada	State convention	No	
New Hampshire		Yes	Only if he signs a pledge.	No; [3a] candidate's name goes on

See footnotes at end of table.

State	Method of selection				Remarks
New Jersey			Yes	No	ballot by petition and will be withdrawn at his request. Yes; 3 candidate's name goes on ballot by petition and will be withdrawn if he declines.
New Mexico	State convention		No		
New York	Delegates-at-large chosen at State conventions or by State committee; other delegates elected at primary. See col. 2.	District delegates elected at primary	No		
North Carolina	Republicans at district and State conventions; Democrats at State convention.		No		
North Dakota	State convention (delegates sign a pledge of loyalty to their party).		No		

Ohio	. . . . .	. . . . .	Yes	Only if he signs a pledge to vote at the convention for candidate winning presidential primary.	Yes . . . . .
Oklahoma	. . . . .	Delegates-at-large by State conventions; district delegates by district conventions.	No		
Oregon	. . . . .	. . . . .	Yes	Yes; for winner of presidential primary.	No; the candidate's name is printed on the ballot at the discretion of the secretary of state, or by petition.
Pennsylvania	. . . . .	Delegates-at-large chosen by State committees; other delegates elected at primary. See col. 3.	Yes	Only if he signs a pledge to vote at the convention for candidate winning presidential primary.	No; the candidate's name is printed on the ballot upon petition of voters.

See footnotes at end of table.

State					
Rhode Island	Democrats by State committee; Republicans by State convention.		No		
South Carolina	State convention		No		
South Dakota			Yes	No; unless nominating petition states a preference.	No
Tennessee	State and/or district conventions.		No		
Texas	State convention		No		
Utah	State convention		No		
Vermont	State convention		No		
Virginia	Democrats at State convention; Republicans at State and district conventions.		No		
Washington	State convention		No		
West Virginia			Yes	No	Yes; and must pay filing fee.
Wisconsin			No; may be named by candidate filing for presidential primary,	Yes; if selected by presidential candidate.	Yes

		and, if not, by State and district committees.		
Wyoming	State convention	No		
Canal Zone	Democrats by territorial convention.	No		
Puerto Rico	Commonwealth convention.	No		
Virgin Islands	Democrats by territorial convention; Republicans by territorial committee.	No		

[1] Replies were not received from all State and/or territorial party committees.

[2] Unpledged slate may be elected at primary.

[3] If slate of candidates for delegate, pledged to presidential candidate, files.

[3a] But presidential candidate must file written consent if delegate-candidate is to be designated as "pledged" on primary ballot.

[4] Statute requires that at least one-third of the delegates be elected from each congressional district of the State and the remainder from the State at large.

[5] Delegates elected shall vote on 1st ballot at convention for presidential primary winner regardless of preference, unless released.

Information in this table is from *Nomination and Election of the President and Vice President of the United States*, compiled under the direction of Francis R. Valeo by Richard Hupman and Robert Tienken. U.S. Govt. Printing Office, Washington: 1968, pp. 60–63.

voting in the primary of one party by voters of the other party. For example, it was widely thought by members of Minnesota's Democratic-Farmer-Labor Party that more than 100,000 Republicans crossed over to the D.F.L. side of the ballot in the 1956 presidential primary in order to vote for Kefauver instead of Stevenson who had been endorsed by the party's state convention. This belief led the Minnesota legislature to repeal its elaborate primary in 1959 after it had been used only once.

Defenders of the open primary believe that raiding is infrequent, that this type of election protects privacy and that it enables ordinary citizens to be more influential in the vitally important nominating stage of selecting public officials. Whether or not an open primary is considered desirable depends on one's conception of the political process and party regularity. If Republican and Democratic nominations should be solely the province of party adherents—and this is what most party leaders desire—then cross-overs in the primary should be made difficult. If nominations, on the other hand, are viewed as wide open attempts by all voters simply to get "the best man" or even a distinctive opponent for an incumbent leader, then a more open primary may be preferable.

The impact of the primary vote on the delegates also varies throughout the nation. Local customs and traditions govern the strength of the legally "binding" commitment of elected delegates to a presidential contender. The mandatory preference polls usually bind a delegate for one ballot or until his candidate's cause is hopeless; in others, the delegates may abandon a candidate when a majority of the delegates decide this is desirable. These polls are disliked by many delegates because they reduce their bargaining maneuverability, take away their decision-making power, and occasionally produce some problems of timing a shift—so much so, that some delegates make no pretense at being bound by the laws. But the polls which are merely advisory can be even more confusing—particularly when a state's voters express a preference for one candidate while a state's delegation favors another. In the most famous case of this kind on record, in the 1920 Republican Primary in Illinois, the statewide preference poll was won by Frank Lowden although at least one district was pledged to Hiram Johnson and the district preference vote went to General Leonard Wood. The implication is clear; a poll assures no convention votes. Unless a mandate is expressed so unequivocally as to represent extraordinary majority sentiment, advisory polls are interesting but not always valuable either in determining popular will or in controlling the delegates.

Mandatory preference polls are less likely to be ignored by the delegates but, in times of convention crisis, they may be. Such polls also run the risk of giving endorsements to slates of delegates supporting candidates who are no longer in the running by Convention time. Such a situation arose in 1964. Delegates who were pledged to Henry Cabot Lodge and Nelson Rockefeller early in the year found that their commitments were out of date when the GOP convention was held. In 1968, delegates pledged to Robert Kennedy were in the same situation.

SELECTION OF DELEGATES BY
PREFERENCE PRIMARY EVALUATED

If it is assumed that the purpose of primaries is to provide a popular mandate for delegates to follow in voting for a nominee or to allow a majority of the voters to indicate their preference for the nomination, the record has been mixed—more impressive some years than others and subject to varied interpretations. The winners at conventions often have not been successful in a majority of the primaries. For example, Warren Harding ran fourth in the primaries the year he was nominated. Wendell Willkie, in 1940, did not win a single primary. Adlai Stevenson was not much of a primary participant in 1952, and even in 1956 he did not win all the primaries. Harold Stassen won more primaries than Thomas E. Dewey in 1948 but did not win the nomination, and Estes Kefauver was a strong primary contender who did not get the convention nod. This encouraged the late liberal Tennessee Senator to announce "Kefauver's Law: Winning a primary can't get you nominated but losing one can be sudden death." In 1968, Vice President Hubert Humphrey was chosen by the Democratic Convention although he had won no primary victory.

Other indictments could also be leveled at the presidential primary system:

1. The primaries begin too early in the year and span too long a time. Often candidates have not decided to run in March and April and their campaigns develop after the primaries. An excellent illustration occurred in 1964. Governor Scranton, who had not been an active candidate in a single seriously contested primary, decided to be a contender for the nomination after the primaries had been concluded. Nelson Rockefeller, and Henry Cabot Lodge, who won primaries, were no longer being discussed as logical nominees.

2. If primaries worked as some reformers originally planned, they would interfere with nominations rather than facilitate them. Bound and pledged delegates would be unable to maneuver and unable to reach a decision.

3. The various primaries do not in every case attract all the candidates. Candidates run in primaries they expect to win and avoid those they expect to lose. Historically, in any election year, only a third to a half of the states having primary elections have had contests of even regional or provincial significance. Therefore, the voter who supports a candidate who is not running in the primary cannot express his preference and may end up aiding an opponent. If he stays away from the polls, he, in effect, gives a psychological boost to the other party.

Several recent changes in presidential primary laws have sought to remedy this situation. A 1965 amendment to the Nebraska law grants the Secretary of State "sole discretion" in placing names of potential nominees on Nebraska's presidential primary election tickets. Once the Secretary of State acts for an election scheduled on the second Tuesday in May, the only way a man can remove his name from the ballot is to supply "an affidavit . . . stating without qualification that he is not now and does not intend to become a candidate for the office of the President of the United States at the forthcoming Presidential election." Thus, the Nebraska primary could involve all of the well known contenders in any year unless some alleged candidates are willing to flatly disclaim any interest in running for President. Such a law could be used to force an incumbent President into a primary or to reserve the Nebraska primary for a favorite son.

The Wisconsin legislature in 1967 also passed an elaborate statute designed to give the voters a more comprehensive slate of candidates. An eleven-man bipartisan committee determines who will be on the ballot although any candidate named may withdraw by filing an affidavit similar to that used in Nebraska. But the ballot also provides for write-in votes as well as a space designated "None of the names shown." Each candidate may choose a slate of convention delegates. If the candidate who wins the primary has not done this, a state committee will select a list to be approved by the winner. The state will send an uninstructed delegation if "no" votes are in the majority. Moreover, district delegates are legally bound by their district votes and delegates-at-large are bound by the statewide vote for one convention ballot, or until the candidate receives less than one-third of the convention votes cast, or until the candidate releases them. Thus, laws in both states could enable voters to choose among all recognized presidential aspirants. Massachusetts and Oregon have similar laws; the Oregon affidavit disclaimer for a man to get off the ballot even forces a candidate to state that he is not interested in becoming a candidate for Vice-President!

4. This leads to a related conclusion: primaries are beneficial primarily to underdogs, long shots, or persons who have to prove they can win. A favorite has much to lose and little to gain in primaries. A Kennedy in 1960 or Goldwater in 1964 enters primaries to show that he can attract votes. An incumbent or proven leader does not go where he will risk his status against an ambitious opponent.

5. Favorite sons, who are not serious party contenders, often run in primaries to control or unite an undecided delegation. Given the rationale of a delegate election statute, this violates the purpose of the primary and frequently eliminates a contest. It is an unwritten rule of American politics that an aspirant to the presidential nomination does not invade the province of a favorite son. Therefore, when a favorite son decides, for one political reason or another, to enter the state's presidential primary, he reduces the impact of the primary system on the nomination. When a favorite son is a stand-in for the President or some other candidate, this rule does not apply.

6. Primaries are not decisive because less than half of the delegates are chosen in primaries. Therefore, many shrewd candidates stress negotiation for state convention votes rather than risk a primary. If they privately obtain commitments for specific votes, all well and good; if not, they have not lost face with the delegates and voters. Moreover,

the convention-selected delegates are regular party leaders who, to be sure, want a winner most of all, but who also appreciate a proven fellow party leader who understands the organization man.

7. Primaries are isolated geographically and are not exceedingly representative. It gives us only a hint of total public sentiment to know that New Hampshire voters prefer Cabot Lodge, that Oregon voters favor Rockefeller or Gene McCarthy, or that California voters (particularly those around Los Angeles) like Goldwater or Robert Kennedy. The mass media, in reporting these elections as effectively as possible, inflate their significance out of proportion to their national comparative strength. Primary results do not give a balanced picture. Often a single primary (Oregon in 1948, West Virginia in 1960, and California in 1964) seems to be given inordinate importance—an unfortunate phenomenon. Or the voters in one state, in torpedoing a candidate, too often may be taken to be representative of voters in all states in a region.

8. Primaries are exceedingly expensive. For example, in 1964 Governor Nelson Rockefeller reportedly spent nearly a half million dollars on the Oregon Primary and over two million dollars in California. Such campaigns tax the candidate who is not wealthy almost beyond his ability to bear it, and certainly force him to restrict his activities.

9. Primaries are also expensive for the state to hold—particularly if there is no significant race. A presidential preference primary .nay cost the taxpayers hundreds of thousands of dollars and not produce a contest.

10. In addition, with reference to voting behavior, primaries do not attract voters in many cases. Frequently only thirty-five or forty per cent (or less) of the electorate bothers to vote. Many persons stay home or, in other cases, voters cross party lines and distort the results.

11. Finally, and most importantly, professional party people believe primaries tend to divide the party rather than unite it. Delegates to a convention prefer a candidate who will solidify the party to one who has been ripping his fellow partisans to shreds in primaries. And yet, this intra-party competition is an integral part of the primary system. In 1964 the *New York Times* of June 12 quoted Governor Rockefeller as asserting that the positions taken by Barry Goldwater could spell disaster for the Republican party and the country. In the same issue the paper quoted Mr. Goldwater as having referred to Richard Nixon as a man who talked himself out of contention for the nomination. He added that Nixon was "sounding more like Harold Stassen." In 1968, the attacks by Gene McCarthy on the Johnson foreign policy was similarly harsh. These statements illustrate the point that the primary system is inevitably, by its nature, divisive in character and therefore can never be an adequate nominating device by itself.

What, then, can be said for the primaries as a desirable institution? Do they have any attributes? Certainly.

First, primaries have served to indicate to candidates that they had little chance for victory. Willkie in Wisconsin in 1944; Stassen in Oregon in 1948; Bob Kerr of Oklahoma in Nebraska; Hubert Humphrey in

Wisconsin and West Virginia in 1960, Margaret Chase Smith, and scores of other candidates have learned in primaries that they would do well to save their money, energy, and time because the race was fruitless.

Secondly, the primaries do create some interest—albeit distorted in certain cases—in the quadrennial election. Even if only thirty-five per cent of the voters turn out, they serve to alert the public to certain candidates. They indicated Eisenhower's tremendous popularity in 1952; and in 1960, early in the year commentators were saying that John Kennedy was not available, that he could not win, and that he was at best a dark horse candidate. By winning seven consecutive primaries, John Kennedy virtually clinched the nomination at Los Angeles. Although the primaries were not necessarily representative, he proved that he could win in the East, Midwest and West—in Catholic and Protestant states. And in the process, he forged a competent organization that persuaded a majority of the delegates at the Convention that he would be a winner.

Finally and most importantly, presidential primaries keep the channels open for a talented maverick popular with the people although unpopular with the party power elite. Although the primary is not and cannot be an adequate substitute for the convention system, coupled with it, it is a desirable combination of party control and popular expression. When the whole system is considered, it can stand non-participation and weaknesses. In spite of all of the primaries' ills—and they are very real—these elections nevertheless provide several of the hurdles that serve a screening function for some candidates if they desire to make the try.

A NATIONAL PRIMARY?

One additional facet of presidential primaries deserves a brief discussion. Public opinion polls often indicate that the general public would favor a national presidential primary election, or the selection of delegates through such a nationwide primary. Such an attitude was particularly prevalent after the 1968 conventions. At various times over the years, several congressmen and senators have introduced measures that would provide for some kind of national system. The most persistent supporters of some form of national primary have been the late Senator Estes Kefauver of Tennessee and Senators Paul Douglas of Illinois, Margaret Chase Smith of Maine, and George Smathers of Florida. Scores of other Senators and House members also have submitted variations of these plans during the past few years.[4] The bills usually have

---

[4] Kefauver may have favored primaries not only because he believed in extending the influence of the people but also because he was frequently ignored by Convention leaders after proving his popularity in polls and in elections. Cabell Phillips, in his book, *The Truman Presidency*, (New York, the Macmillan Company, 1966, p. 33) points out that Kefauver "almost certainly did himself out of the

included a change in the method of choosing the President through the electoral college, but that is a topic beyond the scope of this essay. The national primary proposals usually have taken one of several forms:

(1) A law to select all the delegates to the national convention in uniform state primaries to be held on the same day in August throughout the country. Delegates would be pledged either in proportion to the votes received in their states or as part of the slate pledged to specific candidates. Grants-in-aid (20¢ per vote) would be appropriated to states that conduct primaries under a national program.

(2) A constitutional amendment providing for one national primary similar to a national general election among candidates who filed petitions bearing the names of one per cent of the voters in the United States;

(3) A law giving Congress a vague authorization to do what the members think best about a primary;

(4) A constitutional amendment authorizing Congress to legislate for state primaries to be held on the same day throughout the country;

(5) A law providing for national primary held after the conventions to choose between the top two choices of the convention delegates.

None of these proposals has ever passed either house of Congress for various reasons:

(1) They would make campaigning even more expensive than it is today. Not many candidates could carry on a nationwide-campaign in every state.

(2) A national primary might open the election to many spurious or extremist candidates who would merely want publicity.[5]

(3) Certain plans could result in an exceedingly minority candidate or else another run-off primary would be necessary.

(4) Similar to our present system, primaries in every state would tear the party to shreds as candidates endeavored to eliminate their competitors.

(5) If one party won too frequently only the totally committed would remain in the minority party. If only bitter-enders were nomi-

---

Democratic Presidential nomination in 1952 because his Senate crime investigation splashed suspicion on a number of important party functionaries in cities like Jersey City, Chicago, and Los Angeles. The massive grass-roots support he piled up in the primaries was set at naught at the convention because the big city bosses (and President Truman as well) wanted nothing to do with him."

[5] Senator Kefauver, at frequent intervals, described modifications of plans to meet some of these objections and to take care of such possibilities as no-decision conventions, boss control, deadlocks, and minor procedural problems. He also urged that a nationwide primary was feasible because television makes it possible to campaign in every state without visiting each one. Strangely, because he was never a candidate with an excessively large campaign chest, Kefauver also asserted that the race in a primary would not necessarily be won by the candidate with the biggest organization and the most money. If networks made free television time available to all serious candidates, this might be correct, but if they did not—or if they extended time only infrequently—national primaries would be exceedingly expensive if not prohibitive to say the least.

nated, they might never win and the party system might disintegrate.

(6) Such plans would produce almost insurmountable problems dealing with the distribution of votes either under some weighted electoral system or a straight one-man one-vote formula. This is an important question in certain states; states' rights advocates fear a nationalization of elections, and are wary of such plans. In any event, given the fact that some of these proposals might necessitate a constitutional amendment to change the state's election provisions, and considering that such amendments require approval by two-thirds of both houses of Congress and approval in three-fourths of the states, all of the propositions for a national primary have been politically nonfeasible.

The 1968 conventions bred serious demands for change in the system. But reformers should remember that our national conventions, coupled with our fractionated primaries, generally make a satisfactory system by which to select our party leaders. The record of the convention is good, almost excellent in choosing popular candidates for approval or disapproval by the voters.

CONTESTED DELEGATIONS

In many years, from various states, sets of competing delegates arrive at national conventions, each claiming to be the legitimate delegates from their respective states. We have a long history of such competition dating back to the first conventions in the 1830's. Abraham Lincoln, David Wilmot, Stephen A. Douglas, James G. Blaine, Mark Hanna, Rutherford B. Hayes, and William McKinley were involved in such disputes during the nineteenth century.

These conflicts arise because of manipulations of delegate-selection conventions, resultant competing conventions, manipulations of rules, and factional contests for control of state parties. They invariably involve delegates chosen at conventions; not since 1912 has a slate of delegates chosen at a primary election been seriously contested at the national level.[6]

At Republican conventions, most of the disputed contests have involved the South; for Democrats, until very recently, the contests have generally originated outside the South in one-party dominant states. For example, in the GOP the two most memorable conflicts embraced Southern delegations attached to President William Howard Taft or Theodore Roosevelt in 1912 and to Robert Taft or Dwight Eisenhower in 1952. In both cases regular party members were challenged by old and new members who wanted to alter the delegations. But these are only the most prominent instances. Between 1916 and 1952, some southern delegations were involved in disputes at nearly every Republican convention.

---

[6] An excellent examination of this problem is contained in David, Goldman, and Bain, *The Politics of National Party Conventions* (Washington, The Brookings Institution, 1956) pp. 258–267.

On the Democratic side, the civil rights issue recently has caused serious dissension in the conventions. Threatened bolts have been common during the past twenty years, and in 1964, Negroes from Mississippi, rebelling against the failure of the Mississippi party to give them a representative share of the delegation, sent their own "Freedom Party" delegation (which was not seated) to the Convention in Atlantic City. But in 1968 a bi-racial Mississippi delegation was seated in place of the regular delegation.

Early in their history, the parties established procedures to deal with disputed delegations. The National Committees set up Credentials Committees to rule on the validity of claims by delegates. But these committees themselves were sometimes the product of decisions by the National Committees involving which delegates would be placed on the temporary roll. In any event, after the Credentials Committee had ruled on delegates, appeals could be made to the entire Convention. Any final decision rested among the delegates on the floor. In the past, national conventions have sometimes supported and other times overruled decisions made in the Credentials Committee. Votes of this kind are, of course, highly indicative of which faction in the party has the power to control the nomination. In a dramatic floor vote, the 1968 Democratic Convention confirmed a Credentials Committee decision to seat both the regular Georgia delegation and a more fully integrated, challenging group.

Conflicting delegations usually are attached either to candidates or to efforts by state or local politicians to obtain control of the party. If a faction vindicates its legitimacy in a convention fight and supports the victorious candidate, it usually gets control of the state's patronage and the state's access to the national party. Thus the stakes are high and we are likely to continue to have competing delegations. National party leaders, however, realizing that such contests divide the party and debilitate its effectiveness at the local level, have tried to adopt rules that penalize bolting or failure to support the convention nominees and that also encourage the settlement of such disputes at home. Strong state parties would be at least a part of the answer to the problem.

CHARACTERISTICS OF DELEGATES

Writing around 1905, M. Ostrogorski asserted that a considerable proportion of convention delegations consisted of astute "wire-pullers, office-seekers or office-holders, . . . and, in general, of mercenary politicians." He described other delegates as "small folk full of petty vanity" and also "persons of higher rank who court homage" and another "category of obscure, humble, delegates who are sincerely desirous of discharging their task for the public good."[7]

But this is subjective judgment by one man, and must be evaluated as such. Every four years, newspapers contain similar sweeping judg-

[7] M. Ostrogorski, *Democracy and the Party System in the United States* (New York: The Macmillan Company, 1905), pp. 120–121.

ments. Recently, however, a few more systematic surveys that give us better evidence have been made.[8] And although these surveys apply only to specific conventions, they indicate general demographic characteristics of the people who nominally choose our presidential candidates. They also disclose that many delegates to our conventions have very impressive credentials.

Age.   Most delegates are in their late forties or early fifties although they range from representatives of the Young Democrats and Young Republicans to senior citizens.

Sex.   Seventy to ninety per cent of the delegates are men; women are underrepresented. David, Goldman, and Bain found that states with tightly-knit party organizations had more male delegates than states with loosely organized parties. Women were more frequently chosen in the far West than in the South and Northeast. States with more conservative social structures were less likely to have women delegates.

Race.   Negroes are also underrepresented in ratio to the population. A generation ago, many of the Republican southern delegations contained a remarkable number of Negroes, but newsmen reported that only fourteen Negroes were delegates to the 1964 Republican convention but this situation was improved somewhat in 1968. Most Negro delegates in both parties now are from northern districts and states with large Negro populations. Both parties have minorities divisions to encourage Negro support, and as more Negroes vote each year, they will undoubtedly become an increasingly important factor in party politics. Actually, a strong case can be made for an argument that they have been a crucial minority in several recent presidential elections.

Religion.   Protestants, particularly Episcopalians, Methodists, and Presbyterians, are found in greater percentages in the Republican delegations than among the Democratic delegates. In 1968, eighty-two per cent were Protestant. Consequently, in the conventions studied, Catholic delegates were represented in the Democratic party about four times as frequently as in the GOP Jewish delegates are also more prevalent among the Democrats. While Anglo-Saxon Protestants now make up less than one-third of the American population, but they still tend to be overrepresented in conventions. A substantial majority of the delegates in both parties subscribe to Protestant faiths.

Education.   The delegates have completed more years of school than their constituents. About four-fifths of them have attended college,

<hr />

[8] Again, the best data are collected in Chapter 14 of *The Politics of National Party Conventions, op. cit.* This volume also contains references to studies made during the Truman-Eisenhower years by Daniel Tuttle, Jr., Charles L. Braucher, and Paul Meadows which provided the information on which these generalizations are made.

and over one-third have completed college and have had some post graduate education. Many of them, as noted below, are lawyers, and younger delegates generally have had more years of formal education than the older delegates. There is little apparent difference between the parties on this factor.

Income. In the conventions studied, delegates in both parties represented the upper-middle and upper income brackets. In 1948, for example, four per cent of the Democrats and nearly ten per cent of the Republicans had reported annual incomes of more than $50,000. About half of all the delegates received more than $10,000 a year. The figures indicated that the delegates made well above the average income throughout the nation at that time; they were not at all financially representative of the general run of voters. In view of the occupational characteristics of the delegates and the high costs of attending a convention these figures are not too surprising.

Occupations and relations with Pressure Groups. According to the data available, lawyers made up more than forty per cent of the delegations to the combined conventions. About a quarter of the delegates were businessmen, one-eighth were professional people (educators, physicians, engineers, etc.); homemakers constituted about five per cent of the delegates. Although many persons associate the Democratic party with organized labor, only two per cent of the delegates from the party were union officials in 1948; but in 1948, 1952, and 1964, about ten per cent were members of unions. About sixty per cent of the delegations had labor union officials or members on them. Only one delegate in fifteen in 1948 and one in twenty in 1952 called himself a farmer, although sixteen per cent belonged to the Farm Bureau. Professor Dan Tuttle found that about half of the delegates belonged to the Chamber of Commerce.

Public and Party Office. Confirming part of Ostrogorski's turn-of-the-century observations, the data reveal that public and party officials continue today to attend national conventions. Distinguished public officials make up from twelve to eighteen per cent of the delegations. In 1952, thirty-two governors were members of delegations and many of them were delegation chairmen. In 1956, the number was thirty-four. Also in 1956, nearly two-thirds of the United States Senators were delegates. In 1968, at the GOP Convention, forty-two per cent of the delegates had held public office.

Many categories of party officers are also present. State Committee chairmen almost always attend, and district committee people frequently make the trip. In 1960, the important New York Democratic delegation provided a splendid example. Over eighty-five per cent of the delegates held government jobs or were active in the party. More than twenty-five per cent were civil servants or appointees to boards or commissions. A sixth of the delegates were county chairmen or vice-chairmen. More than half of the state's sixty-three county chairmen went to the Democratic National Convention—primarily as delegates rather than as alternates. Nearly a third of the delegates were lawyers and another quarter were businessmen. The role of women was very limited; only one-eighth of the delegates were female and three-fourths of them were alternates.[9]

The Chairmanship of a delegation regularly goes to an experienced party member with some public or party title. In a 1956 survey made on recent conventions, about forty per cent of the delegates had attended previous conventions at least once. About thirty per cent had attended two consecutive conventions, ten to twelve per cent had attended three; thereafter the number drops off rapidly. Distinguished delegates—persons whose names are in *Who's Who in America*—are more likely to attend consecutive conventions than less prominant delegates. David, Goldman, and Bain found that the hundred key persons who are the convention decision-makers almost invariably have long convention records.[10] Delegates with specific assignments (perhaps a quarter or third of those present) usually have had some prior experience. The newcomers make up the remainder of the delegations. Except in extraordinary conventions, they do not have much to do, although they, of course, vote, speak, and may be influential within their state delegations.

William Baum and his colleagues found that in recent Republican conventions, turnover has been relatively high! From two-thirds to three-fourths of the GOP delegates did not return four years later. Only 27.3 per cent of those (including alternates) who attended the 1960 GOP Convention were present in San Francisco in 1964, and only thirty-one per cent of all the 1968 delegates had attended the 1964 convention. Between 1956 and 1964, eleven states had complete turnovers in delegations and thirteen had only one holdover delegate during this period. "Between 1956 and 1964, almost half of the Republican state delegations had a turnover which was total or within one delegate of being so. This high level of turnover in state party delegations takes place at all levels and affects both leadership and the rang-and-file levels to a substantial degree."[11] The opportunities for newcomers interested in politics are obvious.

---

[9] See "The Presidential Convention as a Stage in the Struggle for Political Leadership: The New York Democratic Delegation," by Bert Swanson, in *Inside Politics: The National Conventions, 1960,* Paul Tillett, Editor. (Dobbs Ferry, New York: Oceana Publications, 1962), p. 199.

[10] *Op. Cit.,* p. 351.

[11] States with complete turnover in delegations, 1956–64: Arizona, Delaware, Kansas, Missouri, Montana, Nevada, New Hampshire, Oklahoma, Vermont, Washington, Wyoming.

States with only one delegate carry-over in delegations, 1956–64: Alaska, Arkansas, Georgia, Hawaii, Idaho, Kentucky, Maine, Mississippi, Rhode Island, South Carolina, South Dakota, Utah, Virginia.

States with High Delegate Continuity—three or more delegates attended conventions held 1956–64: California, Connecticut, Florida, Indiana, Illinois, Iowa,

Attitudes. Herbert McClosky, a political scientist now at the University of California in Berkeley, conducted another extensive study of the opinions and attitudes of approximately 3000 delegates attending the 1956 convention. When he compared their reactions to those of nearly 1500 adults from the general population surveyed by the Gallup Poll, he found that the party leaders of the two major parties diverge more strongly in their feelings towards issues than do their followers who differ only moderately. The delegates were more willing to see the parties divide sharply into liberal and conservative groups, and they were more likely than their followers to take stands on issues, choose reference groups, and express preferences on people and issues. For many people among the rank-and-file, political apathy seemed to be a more "natural" state. Many voters feel "remote from the centers of political decisions and experience an acute sense of political futility." In contrast, the delegates are "sensitive to political ideas" and they unite more firmly (though imperfectly) behind the "values of the American tradition."[12] Moreover, on the twenty-four major issues polled, Republican "followers" disagreed markedly with Republican leaders. GOP delegates were so much more conservative than rank-and-file Republicans that these members of the public were actually closer to the Democratic leaders on issue preferences. Leaders of Democrats and their followers also disagreed on some issues but with much less frequency. McClosky found that in general, Republican delegates are united on issues that grow out of the party's association with business; Democratic delegates achieve homogeneity on issues involving lower income groups.

DELEGATE IMPACT

The delegate's freedom and sense of significance are dependent, at least in part, on (a) how he was chosen; (b) the instructions given to him when he was chosen and whether or not he feels an obligation to honor the commitment; (c) the party system in the state; (d) the leadership of the delegation; (e) the interests he represents; and (f) the stage of the convention at which he is balloting. If the delegate was chosen in a binding primary, he may feel compelled, sometimes unhappily, to remain with the candidate who won the election in his state—at least for one ballot. If he was chosen by an instructing convention, he might feel equally committed. A majority of the delegates, on the other hand, usually are not bound by such formal requirements; consequently, their

---

Michigan, Nebraska, Ohio, Texas, Pennsylvania, New Jersey, New York, Massachusetts, Wisconsin. See William Baum, Rene Beauchesne, and Anne Bryant, "The Myth of the Republican 'Establishment' and the Goldwater Nomination in 1964," *The Dalhousie Review*, Volume 45, no. 4. p. 482.

[12] Herbert McClosky, "Consensus and Ideology in American Politics," *American Political Science Review* (June, 1964), pp. 361–379 and "Issue Conflict and Consensus Among Party Leaders and Followers," by Herbert McClosky, Paul Hoffmann, and Rosemary O'Hara, in the same *Review* (June 1960), pp. 406–427.

freedom fluctuates with their commitments to principle, party leaders, or their own desires to act in such a way as to enhance their own political reputations with those who ultimately will hold power.

The party system is also influential. Observers at conventions have noted distinctions in the amount of "control" by leaders over delegates in strong, unified delegations such as those from Illinois, Indiana, and Pennsylvania in contrast to those in loosely organized states such as California.[13]

Similarly, delegates representing unions, management, or certain government groups may feel that they have obligations to follow private instructions.

Finally, the freedom and influence of the individual delegate increases if the outcome of the contest is unclear after several ballots. We have already noted the decreasing frequency of this situation, but when it exists, floor leaders must court specific persons or approach leaders in the hope of getting "x" number of votes from certain wavering delegations. At this stage the delegate can be more independent, more influential, and indeed, can feel that his presence at the convention is meaningful.

Patterns are difficult to predict in this area because the factors of influence change so much from convention to convention. Delegates may go along with leaders under certain circumstances for many reasons in any one election year and revolt in another, but it seems to be generally the case that delegates chosen by conventions are more committed to leaders and more conscious of the necessity for organizational unity than those who are elected at primaries.

But regardless of how delegates are chosen, most of the bargaining is within delegations rather than among delegates primarily because delegates do follow the leader. The reasons for this are also complex and elusive, but they are undoubtedly related to the delegate's conception of his functions and role in the party. James MacGregor Burns, biographer of Franklin Roosevelt and John Kennedy, believes that candidates, leaders, and delegates are united by *expectation, access, and recognition. Expectation* of reward and the recognition of obligations are important parts of political (and one might add, human) currency for many persons. If a man backs a winner, the argument runs, some kind of psychological or political payoff is regarded as legitimate.

---

[13] James Robinson, noting that the Illinois delegation at the 1960 Democratic Convention willingly went along with Mayor Daley of Chicago, stated "It would be easy to interpret the lack of participation, listlessness, and sheeplike behavior of the Illinois delegates as a failure of representative democracy. That sort of criticism should not be drawn. . . . The unity of the Illinois delegation was, of course, a function of the strength and capacity of its professional party organization. The success of a president in carrying out his and the party's program depends upon his capacity to marshal the kind of political support which Kennedy was able to obtain from Daley and the Illinois delegation." See "Rationality and Decision-Making: The Illinois Democratic Delegation," in *Inside Politics: The National Conventions, 1960, op. cit.*, p. 25.

Access is similar and it means that in return for loyalty the supporter will be able to contact, and get recognition from, the leader over and above that which the average party member would obtain. And *recognition*, of course, is simply deference, significance, or status emanating *from* the supported person. To many people in politics, recognition is more desirable than reward. Acknowledgment when the leader comes to town or consultation when patronage is to be distributed are reasons enough to follow the leader and the rules of the game.[14] We might add two more elements that inspire intradelegation cooperation—*principle* and *personal loyalty* to some candidate. Followers have often been completely devoted to a symbol representing some social, economic, or political values—even when they are unpopular and even when there is no prospect of a payoff. Although major party conventions are not usually devoid of some kind of recognition as a reward, there are nevertheless delegates so dedicated to principle that they need little more than the acknowledgment of the principle.

And as we all know, devotion to some charismatic *candidate* may *well* be a catalyst in a delegation without any personal *quid pro quo*. For example, the wearing of a button that declared "I like Ike," and the fealty that went with it may well have been no more than a deep-seated hope on the part of the wearer that Ike liked him or her—and this was sufficient in itself.

But delegates do not want to be taken for granted. Karl O'Lessker found that although the hierarchy of influence and power in a delegation undoubtedly exists, many delegates insist that they are free—that they follow the leader only because they choose to do so.[15] They deny that they are bossed by any leader, and assert their duty and obligation to make up their own minds. Delegates interviewed by O'Lessker felt strongly that they must remain free to choose the candidate they thought best or the one they believed the people back home would want, or one favored by the delegation leader. This seemed to be a psychological necessity to be one's own man rather than just to be part of a group. O'Lessker also found a smaller group who believed that solidarity was the very purpose of an organization and that it was more important than independence.

Most delegates regard themselves as part of a group that is most effective when unified. But each participant must strive for his own significance. He finds he has a role to play and, in some conventions, an objective to fulfill. Delegates try to act in such a way as to increase respect others have for them and to expand their political influence. Observing the exercise of influence at conventions, shrewd delegates assess the outcome of various courses of action and generally find it profitable to try to obtain their goals as their knowledge dictates. This

---

[14] "Inside View of the Big Powwow," James MacGregor Burns, *New York Times Magazine* (July 10, 1960), p. 7 ff.

[15] See Karl O'Lessker, "State Delegations, Leaders and Followers," in *Inside Politics, op. cit.,* p. 175.

may mean solidifying a state position by remaining as part of a unified group or it might mean bolting to another candidate as soon as it is politically feasible. But it is more likely that if the latter candidate is an apparent winner, the two options will blend. The whole delegation will declare for the nominee and the dilemma will not be present. Again, the hierarchical controls that exist within a party at the state and local level assert themselves in the national convention.

In summary, the effectiveness of the delegates—and of delegation leadership—are dependent upon many different factors at each convention. The unique characteristics of individual conventions, the factional patterns within the delegations, the expectations and commitments of the delegates, the cohesion of the state party, and such institutional factors as the laws of the state governing the selection of the slate all affect the delegation's activity. But eventually a state joins others in support of the nominee.

Only in the broadest sense—and in increasingly rare instances—is the convention a deliberating and decision-making body. It ratifies, or it may refine, and it legitimizes, but the crucial decisions are with increasing frequency made before the convention takes place. Consequently, the average delegate, semi-committed before he arrives in the convention city, votes as he is expected to. He may know little more about what is really going on than the person watching the show on television back home. But he is concerned about his state party in which he is a cog—or even a wheel—and he is interested in fostering state harmony and cooperation with leaders who can influence his future and so he follows the rules of the game. It all becomes part of achieving a mandate for what he hopes will be a winning team in the November election.

SELECTION OF DELEGATES TO THE 1964 REPUBLICAN CONVENTION

Throughout this chapter, occasional references have been made to the fact that the selection of delegates to the Republican convention in 1964 was somewhat distinctive. This was due to the many people who had been outside the decision-making process for years who were suddenly more influential in 1964 than ever before. Mr. Goldwater's nomination was an unexpected phenomenon that revised some of the existing criteria for availability. The margin of his defeat was also extraordinary. The activities and fate of the Republican party in 1964 have been examined and well documented in other sources; they undoubtedly will be discussed, analyzed, and evaluated for many years to come.[16] They are relevant because the 1964 GOP delegate selection

[16] Among the most fascinating examinations of the topic are Theodore H. White, *The Making of the President, 1964* (New York, Atheneum Publishers, 1965), particularly chapters 3, 4, 5, and 7; William Baum, Rene Beauchesne, and

process provides a case study of the state of our parties in many locations, the condition of the Republican party that year, and the possibilities that exist for dedicated partisans to become active and influential in political parties at the grass roots. By comparison, the selection processes in 1968 were much more customary.

The Republican party had a strange history of nomination politics from 1960 to 1964. In 1961, most leaders were quite optimistic because they had lost the presidency by only a narrow margin in 1960. Early in 1962, however, the polls began to indicate that President Kennedy was becoming increasingly popular, and that the Republican party could count on a base of no more than forty per cent of the national vote. In the off-year election of 1962, the party held its own, but did not gain as expected. The titular head of the party, Richard Nixon, was defeated for the governorship of California and he promptly retired—at least temporarily—from politics. But Republicans were gratified that three heavily populated industrial states with seventy-six electoral votes changed from Democratic to Republican control, while Nelson Rockefeller retained his governorship in New York. George Romney won in Michigan, William Scranton became governor of Pennsylvania, and James A. Rhodes won in Ohio. In addition, Republicans also took over Oklahoma, Colorado, and Wyoming. The total population of states in which Republicans replaced Democrats exceeded thirty-three million persons. On the other hand, Hawaii, Iowa, Massachusetts, New Hampshire, New Mexico, and Vermont exchanged Republicans for Democratic governors. The population of these six states that shifted to the Democrats was only ten and one-half million.

Rockefeller became generally acknowledged as the leading candidate for the 1964 presidential nomination. Romney also looked exceedingly attractive; both men were available in terms of experience, characteristics, and membership in the liberal wing of the party. Governors William Scranton and Mark Hatfield of Oregon were considered as dark horses for the nomination. The possibility, in 1962, of a presidential nomination for Senator Barry Goldwater, the Chairman of the Republican Senatorial Campaign Committee who was then touring the country in behalf of his Senate colleagues, seemed unlikely but not out of the question. At that time, it was widely recognized that conservative groups were increasing in numbers, and there was no rush by many liberal Republicans to oppose John Kennedy. There was the outside chance that the Arizona Senator would be allowed to have the nomination by default. As one observer wrote in April of 1962:

Anne Bryant, *loc. cit.*; Richard Rovere, *The Goldwater Caper* (New York, Harcourt, Brace, and World, Inc., 1965); Frank Munger and James Blackhurst, "Factionalism in the National Convention, 1940–1960: An Analysis of Ideological Consistency in State Delegation Voting," in the *Journal of Politics*, vol. 27, no. 2 (May 1965), pp. 375–455; Ultraconservatism in the 1964 Presidential Election, Reprinted from the St. Louis *Post-Dispatch*; Aaron Wildavsky, "The Goldwater Phenomenon: Purists, Politicians, and the Two-Party System," in *The Review of Politics*, vol. 27, no. 3 (July 1965), pp. 386–413.

The Old Guard has never been given its reward for footing the bills and holding the Republican Party together for thirty years. The debt could be finally paid by giving it a candidate of its own. Such an eventuality would at least reveal just what percentage of the popular vote a conservative nominee can obtain in mid-1960 America.[17]

While this type of speculation was taking place, a small band of non-official, dedicated conservatives, under the leadership of F. Clifton White of New York, was holding meetings and formulating plans to make the nomination of Mr. Goldwater more than a remote possibility. In October of 1961, White met with twenty-two close confidants in a Chicago motel to form a committee to try to "seize the Republican party for the Conservative cause. . . ."[18] In December of the same year, at a similar meeting with twenty-seven persons present, a decision was made to divide the nation into nine regions in order to better mobilize conservatives and to raise $60,000 to help the cause. Soon a New York headquarters was established, and in April of 1962, a larger group was assembled; in December, the group met again to lay further plans. Goldwater knew of the group's activities, but neither assisted White nor even encouraged him at this time. In February 1963, the executive committee decided to publicize the movement and to seek national support from conservatives everywhere. Officers were chosen and a national Draft Goldwater rally was planned for July Fourth. The response to these plans was immediate and enthusiastic. More than seven thousand people—many of them traveling by bus and train—showed up in Washington for the July Fourth meeting, and all over the country, other conservatives began to contribute money and time to the endeavor. The Goldwater movement was underway!

The fortunes of the planners were given a boost when Rockefeller began to decline in popularity after his divorce and remarriage. Romney decided early that 1964 was not the most auspicious time for him to run for the presidency; Nixon assumed a posture of neutrality; Eisenhower was indecisive. Scranton also did not want to make the fight in 1963 or early in 1964; when he was finally angered and inspired, it was too late. Thus, during this interim period between two elections, there was no strong opponent of Goldwater—no genuine mass movement for any charismatic favorite, and no champion, other than the fading Rockefeller, who wanted to take on the Democratic President.

Moreover, because of the unstructured situation in the GOP and a lack of hard data, the Goldwater supporters could make a strong case. Goldwater, they believed, could unify more of the party at the time than any of his opponents. Republicans in the South and portions of the West and Southwest were anxious to join the operation and were

---

[17] See article by the author in *The Nation*, May 12, 1962, pp. 413–416.

[18] I have relied on T.H. White, *The Making of the President, 1964*, p. 90 *ff.* for information about these organizational meetings.

confident that Goldwater could carry their states. No one was certain just how strongly he might run in other regions; for years, certain political columnists had been lamenting a lack of choice between the parties and the plethora of "me too" Republican aspirants for the presidency. It was possible Goldwater might hit an extraordinarily responsive chord among the people. In any event, his supporters saw him as a symbol of a cause—the cause of conservatism, more local control, smaller government, fewer programs—and they set out to work with ardor and intensity.

In August 1963, when White established an office in Washington, other previous Goldwater associates accepted regular positions in the organization. Regional volunteer organizations already had been established by zealots in thirty-two states; in several the delegate selection was completely assured for Goldwater. By November 1963, Goldwater had decided to make the race against John Kennedy. After the assassination of the President, however, the whole political situation had to be reassessed. By mid-December, after much consultation with and urging by his supporters, Goldwater again decided to run because of the "principles" in which he believed.

This historical vignette is relevant here because the conservative political organization developed by the Goldwater advocates throughout the country had a significant impact on our political parties and the nominating process. For an entire generation, the Republican party selected moderate presidential candidates in an effort to attract independent as well as conservative voters. In order to court more liberal and undecided citizens who live in urban centers where large numbers of electoral votes are up for contest, candidates such as Willkie, Dewey, Eisenhower, and Nixon—middle of the road Republicans—were allegedly chosen by an "Eastern Establishment" that purportedly dictated the choice of the GOP standard bearer.

Popular and political literature is full of statements asserting this widespread belief that conservatives have not been influential in presidential nominations. James MacGregor Burns in *The Deadlock of Democracy* described the presidential and congressional wings of each party, and called the national convention "the bulwark of the presidential parties."[19] An editor of *Newsweek* wrote in the July 20, 1964 issue that the Goldwater victory was a "revolt against the 'me too' remedies that the Eastern moderates seemed always to offer against the Democrats." On another page, a reporter characterized the Goldwater people as "middle class, middle brow, faintly smug, [who] want to take the party back from the Eastern liberals." *United States News and World Report*, on July 27, 1964, pictured the 1964 convention as a gathering in which the "western amateurs were spurned by the 'pros' from the East." This source quoted a Midwestern leader as explaining:

[19] James MacGregor Burns, *The Deadlock of Democracy* (Englewood Cliffs, New Jersey: Prentice-Hall, 1963), pp. 195–203.

Conservative Republicans just got tired of having the Eastern King-makers snatch the presidential nomination away from them at the last minute and bestow it on a candidate with a liberal image. Ever since 1940, when, in the end, Robert Taft was pushed aside in favor of Wendell Willkie, the conservatives have been whipsawed by the Eastern liberals. This year, finally, they got tired of it. This was a deep and fundamental revolt within our party.

The Goldwater victory indicated that in any one convention, the concept of an Eastern establishment can be absurd. Unless a great effort is made by many persons from eastern population centers, they will forfeit control of the nomination. The revolt of 1964 was made possi-ble, not only because of the default mentioned previously, but also because many Republicans were genuinely upset by what they felt was an inexorable trend towards a larger and larger federal government, and a decline of what they called individualism. They responded to organ-ized recruitment of conservatives in great numbers, and they illustrated how easily and effectively a party can be captured.[20] Typical of such action is that described by Theodore White in which a young business-man organized a new Republican party in the state of Washington. When he began his task in the state, only 2500 of the 5500 precincts were organized; of the 1800 precincts in Seattle, only 300 to 400 had precinct leaders. Goldwater workers simply were recruited to fill the vacancies. When the state delegates nominating convention was held, seventy per cent of the delegates were controlled by Goldwater lieutenants.

In Texas, a young man named Peter O'Donnell revolutionized Republican politics. He sent out husband and wife teams to canvass Dallas, he hired field workers to solicit funds, visit voters, and recruit conservatives in other communities. He and his cohorts soon had the whole state organization united for Goldwater. In other states the story was much the same. In Alabama, John Grenier was chairman of a small Young Republicans Club in 1960. By 1964, after traveling thousands of miles within Alabama for four years, he became the state Republican Chairman with thirty thousand volunteers organized for Goldwater in sixty-four counties. In Georgia, according to Richard Freeman, Fifth District Chairman, the Goldwater groups:

---

[20] F. Clinton White, on March 19, 1965, told a group of political scientists, ". . . it was clear that the nominee who was going to win the nominating conven-tion was going to have to get a large percentage of his votes from the convention states. . . .

Obviously, if you have the delegates to the state convention elected upon the basis of a predisposition toward your candidate, then the delegates that are going to be elected from that state convention to the national convention are going to share your predisposition, *and much of the fanfare and publicity that goes with a convention selection of delegates for a national nominating convention is occurring after the fact, at a time when the complexion of that state convention will already have been predetermined.*" [emphasis mine] took over the Republican party in this state by design and plan. They were ruthless in doing it and in kicking out everybody who had worked long and hard for years. I saw people in our county convention I had never seen before.

Similar patterns appeared all over the South; in most places it was easy to move in on nearly non-existent organizations. By May 1964, of the 655 votes Goldwater needed, three hundred Southern delegates were firmly committed to him. At the convention several months later, ten of the nineteen states in which Goldwater had consolidated first ballot support were from the South.

But it was not only in the South that these newcomers were effective. The Rocky Mountain area was easily brought into control. Similarly in Missouri, one reporter described a St. Louis County town meeting held to select delegates to the state convention as follows:

Hundreds of Goldwater supporters packed many of these meetings. They overwhelmed the regular party organizations by sheer weight of numbers, or held rump meetings and named rival slates to support Goldwater.

The Goldwater backers had done their homework well. They were effectively organized and fully prepared to meet any contingencies that might have cast a legal doubt on their efforts. In townships where a fight was anticipated, Goldwater supporters showed up with notaries public to take affidavits of persons attesting that they were Republicans. They had shorthand reporters to record the proceedings of any rump sessions that were necessary.[21]

At the state convention in June, the Goldwater supporters took control. They defeated regular delegations in disputes and finally selected their own national convention delegates who voted 23-1 for Goldwater on the first ballot.

Richard Rovere, the well known political analyst, summarized the basic reasons why Goldwater backers were so successful. He pointed out that they had both energy and zeal and that they used them for their candidate's cause:

. . . One of the prices we Americans pay for our unideological parties is a shortage of these two qualities, particularly the latter. Generally speaking, anyone who is willing to give a few hours a month to party work will be rewarded with some measure of authority. . . . [if a person] attends all the meetings, puts stamps on envelopes, and uncomplainingly empties the ashtrays—he will soon enough find himself drafting the resolutions, chairing the meetings, and being given his choice of committee assignments. The Goldwater people were the sort to arrive early at meetings, endure the tedium, and stay on, bright-eyed, after adjournment, to

21 This description is from an excellent series of articles by Richard Dudman, William K. Wyant, Herbert A. Trask, and Robert Collins which appeared in the *St. Louis Post-Dispatch* (December 6–12, 1964). Cited in Baum, *op. cit.*, p. 486.

fold the chairs and put the coffee cups away. Great stores of sub-
versive power are to be found in these useful traits. In time, the
chairfolders are writing platforms, conducting purges, and threaten-
ing to wreck the organization if their rule is challenged.[22]

"Goldwater workers," added another newsmagazine, "were a well
trained, well-led army, quick to receive commands and quick to obey,"[23]
and they carried their states in spite of the columnists, polls, and many
Republican voters who opposed their candidate.

After Goldwater defeated Rockefeller in California's primary election by 68,000 votes (or 51.6 per cent) other states rapidly jumped on
the bandwagon. By the middle of June, the Arizona Senator had 580
delegates. He told a *New York Times* reporter that he had expected to
face more tribulations and tougher competition than he did.

No condemnation or commendation of Goldwater's nomination or
his campaign is implied here. His later strategy, which failed miserably,
is beyond the scope of this monograph. This summary of the 1964
GOP activities is presented to illustrate that prior to and at the convention Goldwater's supporters clearly demonstrated that people who
are willing to learn the minutiae of precinct politics and work with petitions, meetings, rules, and manipulation, can be effective—particularly
in the party out of power.

The "in" party, on the other hand, is less likely to be invaded by
new forces any one year. The party in power has members who are performing official as well as party functions and they are more resilient to
invasion at the precinct level because the *quid pro quos*, rewards, hierarchical powers, and expectations generally are different; the locations
of influence are more protected. But the evidence is clear that a devoted
and determined party worker who has a reasonable disposition and
some intelligence can be influential in party activities. The extent of
that influence is the product of so many variables that it has not been
adequately measured. James Farley, the famous chairman of the Democratic National Committee under President Franklin Roosevelt, once
declared, "The essence of winning a nomination is simply mastery of
detail." That may be an understatement, but it is a foundation on which
one with political ambitions might well build.

What we can learn from recent history is just how malleable our
nominating system is when a power vacuum exists and a group ardently
seeks to fill it. When many new delegates can be chosen, it is possible
to exploit the turnover. This is what happened at the Convention that
nominated Barry Goldwater in 1964. On the other hand, in any one
year, the ruling oligarchy at a national convention may be constituted
of essentially the same leaders who controlled the previous convention.
Yet, because they are sensitive to popular pressures and political rewards,
they may be persuaded to nominate an entirely different candidate

---

[22] Rovere, *op. cit.* (Fn. 16) pp. 113–114.
[23] *United States News and World Report* (July 27, 1964), p. 42.

than the one they supported four years earlier. This is what happened at the Convention that nominated John F. Kennedy in 1960. The point is that decisions at national nominating conventions are often the result of the long process by which American citizens *nominate and select delegates.*

CURRENT EVALUATIONS AND CRITICISM

In the early pages of this essay corruption of the convention system was cited as a reason why reformers demanded that delegates be selected by popular vote. As we have seen, the primary is not without its own difficulties. It did not fit ideally into the American nominating process, and it has not been developed in all states. Thus we still have conventions in conjunction with primaries. But in recent years, many politicians and newspaper men again have criticized the national conventions —and in some cases justifiably. It has been charged that the conventions are not representative—that is, they do not reflect the number of party *voters* in the various states. This is true, of course, but the new formulae used by the parties help remedy this, and other attempts to change the selection of delegates would be jealously opposed by states with low turnouts at the polls.

Secondly, many people think the conventions are just vehicles for the maneuvers of the party bosses rather than expression of the wishes of the party voters. This opinion was frequently heard after the 1968 conventions, and it is probably an accurate evaluation in some states, but as long as party leaders are willing to devote time, energy, and talent to becoming party bosses, and the people remain politically acquiescent, this will be true. Nevertheless, a substantial body of political experts believes we should have more delegates selected by the voters and fewer advisory polls.

A third charge is that conventions are undignified—full of parades, demonstrations, and nonsense—and that they present an atmosphere of confusion to the entire nation. The fact is, however, that Americans like a certain amount of noise and nonsense at their conventions—as any examination of the conventions of other groups will attest. What we must remember is that the decisions and work at the national conventions do not take place on the convention floor. Agreements are reached before the convention takes place or in delegation caucus rooms and in private negotiations among the aspirants and delegation leaders. In spite of all this the amount of secret activity probably has been reduced in the past few years as the arena of conflict has been expanded all over the country. The convention system provides several weeks for the examination of prospective candidates and an opportunity to try to reach some kind of consensus on them. When coupled with the primaries, the conventions pose a test of mastery of political techniques by the candidates—a test forcing them to show their political acumen, their ability to negotiate, their talent for maneuver in a political situation, their political skill, and also their success with the voters. They must deal with constituents, other politicians, the press, state and local leaders, competitors and leaders of interest groups. This is a good preparation for a future President.

Finally, it is often charged that the vice-presidential nominees are almost invariably hand-picked and hastily chosen for reasons of political expediency rather than for qualifications as future presidents. It is true that vice-presidential candidates frequently are chosen by the presidential nominee from the other faction of the party and from a different geographical location—to balance the ticket. But, given the size of our country and the divisions in our parties, this seems to be inevitable— even desirable. Moreover, it would seem that recent choices for second place on the tickets, on the whole, have been rather good. The increase in vice-presidential function—fostered by Mr. Truman and developed even more by Mr. Eisenhower—together with the assassination of President Kennedy, certainly must have made the leaders of the nation more aware of the need for first-rate people in the Vice-Presidency.

Conventions provide a focal point for fostering party unity—and the unity of the country as a whole. Our federal system, the checks and balances, the federal nature of our parties, sectional ideological beliefs, state and local jealousies, interest groups, race and religious differences, and many other forces tend to drive the parts of our nation asunder; in the national convention we have a compensatory institution that provides a modicum of unity among the local leaders. Negotiations are often bargaining sessions of states and regions, sections, socioeconomic blends, interest groups, and organizations. It may be that the promotion of such intra-party unity—particularly among those in the majority—is a national good in itself.

The present system is recognized as legitimate. The nominees are accepted. We rarely stop to wonder about this, but it is surprising that there have not been more bolts (such as in 1860 or 1912) at our conventions. It is remarkable that people will fight so hard for so long for a candidate who loses the party nomination and then turn around and immediately accept his successful competitor as the man with the party mandate, transferring loyalty and effort to him during the campaign.

Perhaps the conventions would be improved if nominating speeches and demonstrations were restricted to the major candidates, if the delegations were made smaller, if their size and selection were based strictly on votes cast, if the primaries were closed and were for delegate selection only. But these are minor mechanical changes; we must realize that given our federalized, fractionated, parties (and, paradoxically, a trend towards the nationalization of our politics and an increasing development of the President as the national party leader because of our mass media and the mobility of our citizenry) the conventions as we know them today are an integral and desirable part of the system.

If our local governments are autonomous, the conventions are meetings of autonomous leaders who convene to coalesce behind a candidate they believe can win. It may be that in 1968 the delegates did not select the most popular candidates, but we have no way to prove this. The leaders at conventions inspire enthusiasm for a party ticket; they often heal wounds, make concessions, and solidify support. There is no proof that a higher quality of individual would be obtained by another method. Conventions neither preclude nor insure the most intelligent candidates, but they produce the politically talented. The conventions train men to bargain, analyze, and make decisions—abilities they will need as Presidents. They usually, but not always, sift out the extremists. They select men with mass and personal appeal. Their record is commendable and as long as politics in America remains the domain of the few who are willing to work at it, the most appropriate system for selecting our candidates seems to be the present system with possibly a few minor reforms. But we should not tamper unnecessarily with our Presidential recruitment procedures. They achieve their basic purposes.

KARL O'LESSKER

Karl O'Lessker studied at University of Pennsylvania (A.B. 1954), Northwestern University (M.A. 1956), Indiana University (Ph.D. 1959). He has taught at Indiana University (1957–58), Chatham College (1958–59), Wabash College (1959–66), Georgia State College (1966–67), the University of Illinois in 1967–68, prior to going to Hollins College in 1968.

O'Lessker was a NCEP Democratic National Convention Fellow (1960), participated in the 1956 national conventions, legislative assistant to former Indiana Governor Matthew Welsh (1962–63), Democratic candidate for Congress (1964).

O'Lessker is co-author of a book on Indiana government and politics (with Philip Wilder), and contributed to *Inside Politics: The National Conventions, 1960* (1962).

KARL O'LESSKER

10. The National Nominating Conventions

ORIGINS OF THE NATIONAL CONVENTION

Except when they are imposed upon a people by force of arms, political institutions arise and flourish in response to a society's needs— which is perhaps an unnecessarily solemn way of saying that our political doings are almost never pointless or arbitrary.

National nominating conventions are an excellent case in point. It is unlikely that anyone would have sat down and designed them as they are today out of whole cloth. But given the historical context in which they first appeared some 135 years ago, it is not at all surprising that they took shape as they did and evolved as they have.

Consider the circumstances: a Constitutionally prescribed method of selecting the President and Vice-President involving an Electoral College based on the states; the electors chosen by popular vote in every state but one (South Carolina); the voters casting a party ballot for slates of electors pledged to one candidate or another; the parties themselves having no national organization in an era of unimaginably poor communications; a number of presidential and vice-presidential hopefuls each having a fairly strong local base of support; and the inexorable requirement that one candidate receive an absolute majority of the Electoral College vote (or, failing that, of the House of Representatives) in order to be elected President.

The crucial problem of political engineering, then, was to devise a method by which each party could effectively agree on a candidate and a program so as to present a solid front to the voters and thus enhance its chances of winning the necessary 50 per cent plus-one of the Electoral College ballots. No one of that day, of course, confronted it as a generalized "problem of political engineering"; instead, candidates and their supporters wrestled with the far more practical problem of winning the exclusive nomination of a united party.

The situation in 1824 illustrates nicely the difficulties involved.

As President Monroe's second term drew to a close, no fewer than five major contenders prepared to make a bid for the Democratic presidential nomination; no other national party then existed. But no one was at all clear as to what agency or institution had the authority to designate *the* candidate. To be sure, from 1796 through 1816 the Democrats (then called Republicans) had largely relied upon their members in Congress to meet in caucus and nominate candidates for President and Vice-President. But the other major party, the Federalists, had not used the caucus since 1804 and even the Democrats in 1820 held only a poorly attended, inconclusive Congressional caucus that adjourned without nominating anyone. In this sort of institutional vacuum, then, the Tennessee legislature "nominated" Andrew Jackson and at the same time declared the congressional caucus "unconstitutional," while the Georgia legislature, favoring William H. Crawford, resolved that *only* the congressional caucus could legitimately make nominations.

In the event, a minority of Democratic members of Congress held a caucus and nominated Crawford. The three other contenders—Henry Clay, John C. Calhoun, and John Quincy Adams—received the nomination of state legislatures or conventions. Adams ran second to Jackson in the Electoral College balloting for President, no candidate receiving the requisite majority, and Calhoun won a clear majority for Vice-President. For the second, and last, time in our history the presidential election was thrown into the House of Representatives, with Adams emerging as victor—quite in accordance with the Constitution but widely condemned by public opinion on the grounds that Jackson had won a substantial plurality in both the Electoral College and the total popular vote.

This brief account of the election of 1824 takes us back to the central problem facing presidential aspirants of that era: how to win the exclusive nomination of a united party. "King Caucus" was now thoroughly discredited—as much for its ineffectiveness as for its inappropriateness to the American constitutional system. Nomination by individual state legislatures must have appeared even more anachronistic despite the personal popularity of Andrew Jackson. And a no-nomination system promised to throw nearly every presidential election into the House of Representatives—a prospect abhorrent to informed opinion of every shade. The solution ultimately arrived at seems so obvious to us today—135 years after the fact—that we may find it hard to believe that when it was first propounded few people gave it serious consideration.

The idea of a national nominating convention was by no means brand-new when Senator Martin Van Buren proposed it in 1827. A Federalist convention, with delegates from eight of the 17 states, had in fact been held as early as 1808 and had nominated Charles C. Pinckney for President and Rufus King for Vice-President. Four years

later, a second Federalist convention met to nominate De Witt
Clinton. Both conventions however, were held in closed session with
the general public unaware of their existence and many states not
even represented. Of greater practical significance, surely, is the fact
that party conventions had been held for many years at the county
and even state level in many areas. Hence, "The practiced ease with
which American politicians organized national nominating conventions
during the age of Jackson was made possible by long experience with
low-level conventions during the Jeffersonian era."[1]

Van Buren's proposal of 1827 met with no response; but three
years later a short-lived and otherwise eminently forgettable splinter
party, the Anti-masons, held what can truly be called the first national
party convention, an organizational conclave which met in Philadelphia
on September 11, 1830. And one year later, this same party held the
first national *nominating* convention, composed of 116 delegates from
13 states; it nominated William Wirt for President and Amos Ellmaker
for Vice-President and established two other historic precedents, a
party platform (called an "address to the people") and a national
committee to manage the party's affairs till the next convention (which
it did not survive long enough to hold).

Next to adopt the convention system was the so-called National
Republican party of Henry Clay. Though Clay had already been
nominated by several state conventions, party leaders evidently concluded that they "needed some device to give them a semblance of
nationwide representation for the coming election"[2] and seized upon
the Anti-masons' idea of a national convention. Accordingly, 168 delegates variously chosen from 18 states and the District of Columbia
met in Baltimore in December 1831, nominated Clay and John
Sergeant of Pennsylvania unanimously, and composed an address to
the people attacking President Jackson's policies.

The still dominant Democratic-Republican party added its own
organizational imprimatur to the new system in May 1832, with a
Baltimore convention composed of delegates from all states but Missouri. Jackson, like Clay, had already been renominated by a number
of state legislatures. But influential men agreed that a national convention would emphasize Jackson's great popular strength and, moreover, serve the very useful purpose of choosing a Vice-Presidential
nominee in the face of fierce intraparty strife raging among the
supporters of incumbent Vice-President Calhoun and Secretary of State
Van Buren. With Jackson's firm endorsement, the latter was nominated
on a first-ballot vote of 208 to 75.

---

[1] David H. Fischer, *The Revolution of American Conservatism* (New York:
Harper & Row, 1965), p. 81. Reprinted by permission.

[2] Paul T. David, Ralph M. Goldman, Richard C. Bain, *The Politics of National
Party Conventions*, rev. ed. (Washington, Brookings Institution, 1964), p. 54. Reprinted by permission.

Though perhaps no one would have wagered his fortune on it at the time, the national convention had come to stay: from that day until this every major party has used the convention device for nominating its two principal candidates. And within the astonishingly short space of a decade, national conventions developed virtually every organizational feature we now associate with them. The reasons for this rapid and decisive success of an institution for which we can find little or no historic precedent have been summarized by Roseboom:

> The national convention . . . made its appearance in the 1830's to fulfill a need that the old Congressional caucus and the state legislative or state convention nominations of Presidential candidates could not supply. It was representative in character; it divorced nominations from Congressional control and added to the independence of the executive; it permitted an authoritative formulation of a party program; and it concentrated the party's strength behind a single ticket, the product of a compromise of personal rivalries and group or sectional interests.[3]

How national conventions operate today and how well they continue to serve the purposes for which they came into existence are the subjects we shall be dealing with in the remainder of this chapter.

ORGANIZING THE CONVENTION

The color and drama of a national convention begin several days before its formal opening. Hordes of delegates, alternates, newsmen, and convention-watchers of every description, official and unofficial, begin to flock into the chosen city during the week preceding the call to order; candidate headquarters are established and their level of activity quickly escalates to seeming chaos; the candidates themselves arrive a day or two in advance to be met by hopefully tumultuous welcomes at airport or train station; and by the weekend prior to the first session, the lobbies of the convention's headquarters hotel are jam-packed from early morning till late at night. (The late Adlai Stevenson made one of his memorable quips in 1960 when he told a roaring convention, "After getting in and out of the Biltmore Hotel . . . I decided that I know who you are going to nominate: it will be the last survivor.")[4] Party festivities of one sort or another—receptions, dinners, rallies—enliven the final pre-convention hours and set the emotional stage for this unrivalled political show.

The general order of business does not differ very greatly from one convention to the next. Usually it goes like this: High points of the first day's activities include welcoming addresses, installation of

---

[3] Eugene H. Roseboom, A *History of Presidential Elections*, 2nd ed. (New York: Macmillan, 1964), p. 106. Reprinted by permission of publisher.
[4] Democratic National Convention, *Proceedings*, 1960, p. 61.

temporary officers, appointment of committees, and the keynote address. Committee reports, sometimes contested, are the main business of the second day. The climactic event of the whole convention comes the third day with the nominations for and selection of the presidential candidate. On the fourth day a vice-presidential candidate is designated, and the two candidates make their formal acceptance speeches amidst congratulatory and commendatory resolutions and addresses.

Let us see how these events function within the context of the intra-party and inter-party struggles.

Installation of Temporary Officers and Keynote Address. Some months prior to the opening of the convention, the National Committee selects a slate of temporary and permanent officers, including the chairman and co-chairman of each major committee, to recommend to the convention for its approval. The convention itself, however, is the supreme governing body of the national party and is legally competent to reject any or all of these selections. But this hardly ever occurs, and a floor fight challenging National Committee recommendations can usually be taken as the sign of a badly split party.

This is particularly true of the designation of a temporary chairman, whose duties involve presiding for the first one or two half-day sessions during which little business of consequence is conducted. A challenge to the proposed temporary chairman, therefore, can have as its only object an all-out effort to discredit the National Committee —a step not lightly taken by even the most inflamed party dissidents. We have, in fact, to go back to the conventions of 1912 to find a floor fight on the temporary chairmanship; and in that year intra-party cleavage ran so deep that the Republicans at least were split into two warring camps during the election.

The temporary chairman's most important job, traditionally, has been to give the keynote address, a relentlessly partisan speech designed to infuse party activists and supporters with an unconquerable will to victory in November. It may also aim at rallying uncommitted voters in the radio and television audience; but given the usual extravagance of its rhetoric, this would seem to be a rather idle hope. (Republicans departed from customary practice in 1952 by separating the jobs of temporary chairman and keynoter, giving the latter to General Douglas MacArthur; and for reasons not entirely clear they have continued the disjunction in subsequent conventions.) Other functions of the temporary chairman include recognizing speakers, entertaining motions, and maintaining a minimal degree of order until the permanent chairman is installed the following day.

On rare occasions factional strife may erupt during the opening hours and the temporary chairman may be called upon to wield a more than ceremonial gavel. Some recent examples occurred at the Republican conventions of 1952 and 1964, the former involving temporary rules, the latter the seating of certain delegates. But in neither case can it be said that the factional loyalties of the two temporary chairmen had any discernible effect on the outcome of those fights.

Permanent Organization and Committee Reports. With the temporary chairman still presiding, the Committee on Permanent Organization brings in the first of four sets of recommendations to come from four major committees. The others are Rules, Credentials, and Resolutions. The job of the first, Permanent Organization, is to present a slate of permanent officers for the convention, and in practically all cases the delegates duly endorse the committee's nominees. In fact, of course, the selection has been made some weeks or months in advance by the National Committee; a floor fight challenging the proposed permanent chairman is, therefore, evidence of a factional attack on the dominant forces within the National Committee. Unlike selection of a temporary chairman, however, that of permanent chairman can have significant consequences for the entire nominating struggle; so the normal inhibitions against exposing the party's "dirty linen" do not operate nearly as strongly as in the case of the former officer.

Nevertheless, one has to go back more than a generation, to the Democratic convention of 1932, to find this kind of assault on the National Committee. In that year the spearhead of the attack was the Committee on Permanent Organization itself, which brought in a report reflecting the wishes of Franklin Roosevelt's supporters and ignoring the recommendation of the National Committee. Forces opposed to Roosevelt's nomination, therefore, offered a substitute motion calling for the selection as permanent chairman of one Jouett Shouse (the National Committee's choice) as against Senator Thomas J. Walsh, nominee of the Committee on Permanent Organization. The substitute motion was defeated by a vote of 626 to 528—a result which correlates almost perfectly (.90) with the vote Roosevelt received on the first ballot.[5]

The permanent chairman presides over the most eventful days of the convention: battles may erupt over subsequent committee reports, demonstrations on behalf of candidates may threaten to get out of control, recognition of one delegation leader rather than another during the balloting may have enormous effect on the final outcome. In any of these eventualities the character and personal preferences of the presiding officer can have profound influence; hence the close scrutiny that is always, and necessarily, given to his selection. Polsby and Wildavsky make the point nicely:

---

[5] James A. Farley's account of the fight over the permanent chairmanship is invaluable. *Behind the Ballots* (New York: Harcourt, Brace, 1938), pp. 102–107 and 126–127. For a briefer account and statistical analysis see Richard C. Bain, *Convention Decisions and Voting Records* (Washington: Brookings Institution, 1960), pp. 240–241. All other statistical material and voting records in this chapter have been drawn from this same essential source.

The importance of being chairman was demonstrated at the 1920 Republican Convention when Senator Henry Cabot Lodge wanted to permit the party leaders to find a way out of the [balloting] impasse that had developed. Shortly after the fourth ballot, Senator Reed Smoot of Utah moved to adjourn the proceedings. A resounding "no" echoed throughout the auditorium as Lodge put the motion to a vote and immediately declared the convention adjourned. Twenty years later, at another Republican Convention, Senator Bricker of Ohio asked Chairman Joseph Martin for a recess before the sixth ballot. This would have given the Taft and Dewey forces time to make a deal. Partial to the Willkie cause, however, Martin refused the request and the balloting continued, to be ended by victory for Willkie.[6]

There are, to be sure, many times when the designation of a permanent chairman is virtually automatic no matter how unhappy a particular faction within the party may be about it. Men who hold the office of Speaker of the House of Representatives will normally be selected for the post unless they themselves wish otherwise—as did the late Sam Rayburn in 1960 when he preferred instead to devote his full energies to the candidacy of Senator Lyndon Johnson. But it seems reasonable to assume that, had Rayburn chosen otherwise and despite his obvious strong preference for Johnson, not even the aggressive forces of Senator John Kennedy would have attempted to prevent the Speaker from assuming the post he had so often held in previous Democratic conventions.

Following installation of the permanent chairman the three other major committees make their reports. That of the Committee on Rules and Order of Business ordinarily provokes little if any controversy; but the 1932 Democratic convention narrowly escaped a major battle when Roosevelt forces backed away from an effort to eliminate the two-thirds rule, and the Republicans in 1952 "avoided" an explosive Taft-Eisenhower confrontation on the permanent rules only because it had already taken place on an earlier (usually routine) motion to adopt the temporary rules.*

The report of the Committee on Credentials has often provided matter for factional battles of the bloodiest sort. There are three reasons for this. First of all, there are states in this nation in which the term "political party" has almost no legal or even practical referent. "Party officials" are self-appointed, "party meetings" are little more than informal gatherings of interested persons, "party decisions" have no force

---

[6] Nelson W. Polsby and Aaron B. Wildavsky, *Presidential Elections* (New York: Charles Scribner's Sons, 1964), p. 84. Reprinted by permission of publisher.

* At issue at the 1968 Democratic convention was the so-called "unit rule." After a short, sharp debate and a dramatic roll-call vote, the unit rule was declared illegal not only at the 1968 and subsequent national conventions but at all other party functions.

of law. In these circumstances it is easy to see how more than one group of "party" activists can decide to send themselves to the national convention claiming to speak for the entire state "party." It then becomes the job of, first, the National Committee and then the convention's Committee on Credentials to decide which of the competing groups ought to be awarded that state's seats and votes in the convention.

The second reason for the frequency and ferocity of credentials fights is a consequence of the first. Competing factions from a state with no real party organization are almost always associated with—and indeed created by—factions within the national party. Thus one group fighting for that state's credentials will be pledged to support of Candidate X, the other group to Candidate Y. The convention's decision on credentials will therefore very likely presage which candidate will emerge as presidential nominee by providing him not only with additional votes but with great psychological impetus for a "bandwagon" strategy.[7]

Owing, no doubt, to the peculiar nature of the Republican party in the South until very recent years, GOP conventions have provided the most dramatic examples of credentials fights crucial to the outcome of the entire nominating process. In 1912, Theodore Roosevelt's managers forced contests for 72 seats on the floor of the Taft-dominated convention, losing all of them by a margin of about 60 votes; contested delegates were permitted to vote on all other contests save their own, and in so doing provided the margin of victory for the Taft delegates and, ultimately, for President Taft's renomination.

Forty years later, a hauntingly similar battle took place between the son of the former President and General Dwight Eisenhower. Once again rival delegations from Southern states were seeking credentials; once again the key issue was whether contested delegates would be permitted to take part in the voting on the report of the Credentials Committee. Taft forces argued for continuing the precedent of 96 years standing; Eisenhower's managers demanded the kind of change in rules that Theodore Roosevelt's people had unsuccessfully fought for in 1912, that is, contested delegations would not be permitted to vote on the question whether or not to seat other such delegates. The change was adopted by a margin of 110 votes, the bulk of the Eisenhower delegates won their contests, and the General went on to be nominated. Whether a different outcome to the rules and credentials fights would have resulted in different nominees emerging from the two conventions is, of course, a moot question. But the extraordinary degree of bitterness engendered by the contests is testimony to the importance of the stakes which each side perceived to be at issue.*

---

[7] See p. 257, for a discussion of bandwagon strategies.

The Committee on Resolutions and Platform presents the report that has customarily been most productive of conflict at conventions. On the surface, at least, this is a political paradox of the highest order, for the conventional wisdom of American politics holds that party platforms are largely irrelevant to subsequent governmental policy-making. Gerald Pomper has summarized the charges in this way:

> (1.) Platform statements are essentially unimportant, ambiguous, and often contradictory. . .
> (2.) No differences exist between the platforms of the major parties. They are therefore of no value to the voter in making his choice of party.
> (3.) The party principles are not binding on party candidates. "The principal object of the platform is, in the present day, as formerly, to catch votes by trading on the credulity of the electors. . ."

Pomper then goes on to note that these charges "are not entirely valid." He amasses significant evidence to show that "Platform provisions often have been meaningful, distinct from the opposition and fulfilled upon the party's election."[8] And although substantial portions of major party platforms over the years have indeed been irrelevant as charged, an attentive reader would have no difficulty in discerning in them long-term policy differences that accurately reflect real distinctions that have existed between Democrats and Republicans on a wide range of issues.

It is nevertheless true that U.S. Presidents have not often felt themselves to be bound by specific platform provisions when it seemed to them unwise or even inconvenient to attempt to implement those pledges. So one might well ask: if the party's nominees can in effect "unwrite" the platforms on which they were assumed to have run, why do national conventions make such a fuss over their specific provisions? Why, indeed, have platforms at all? Why not simply let the two presidential candidates spell out their own positions in the course of the campaign? Or, finally, why not *first* nominate the party's standard-bearer and *then* have him compile a platform to submit to the convention for ratification?

A partial but important answer to all these questions has to do with the internal dynamics of American parties. No party is ever completely united on all major policy issues. More to the point, enduring factions of conservatives and liberals within each party wrestle with each other untiringly for control. And, as at least one perceptive student of American politics has argued, our most significant political

---

[8] Gerald Pomper, *Nominating the President* (Evanston: Northwestern University Press, 1963), p. 68.

* A third cause of credentials fights in recent years has come about as an offshoot of the Civil Rights Movement. First in 1964 and then more fully and fiercely in 1968, Democratic conventions have had to grapple with the tortuous problem of whether to seat certain Southern delegations which had been challenged on the

battles customarily take place not *between* the parties but *within* the majority party of any given era.[9]

It is in this connection that convention battles over the content of the party platform take on their greatest consequence. What goes into the platform, with or without a floor fight, reveals a good deal about the existing balance of factional forces within the party (at least at the national committee and presidential level; the congressional party might well exhibit a strikingly different balance of factional forces). Let us therefore see how the platform is put together and dealt with in the convention.

In recent years the national committees of both parties have appointed "temporary" chairmen and co-chairmen of platform committees some months in advance of the meeting of the convention and have directed each state party organization to designate one man and one woman as members of the committee as soon as possible after the delegates have been elected. The newly constituted platform committee can then set about the job of holding public hearings, mostly for the benefit of representatives of large and small interest groups, usually one week before the opening of the full convention. Important preliminary drafting may actually have begun months earlier under the supervision of the committee chairman and his staff, gathering material through regional hearings and consultations with party leaders. Formal hearings before the full committee tend therefore to be more in the nature of ritual than information-gathering sessions. By the end of the pre-convention week the committee's leadership group hammers out the final wording to be presented to the convention, and other members may if they wish prepare minority reports on especially controversial planks.

Usually on the second, sometimes the third, day of convention, the chairman of the Committee on Resolutions and Platform ascends the podium, reads the proposed platform in its entirety, and moves for its adoption. More often than not, the motion will be approved there and then without further discussion. But if a minority report has been prepared, it will be offered at that point by a member of the committee, debated perhaps at great length, and duly voted upon. Other amendments, too, may be offered from the floor, consistent with

---

grounds that the party in those states systematically discriminated against Negroes in the selection of delegates. A rule was adopted in 1964 prohibiting such discrimination in the future. In 1968 challenges were formally presented both to the Credentials Committee and to the full convention, alleging violations of the 1964 rule. These resulted in a refusal to seat the "regular" Mississippi delegation, replacing it with integrated group from that state; in the seating of two opposed delegations from Georgia and dividing the state's votes between them; and in hard-fought but narrowly unsuccessful efforts to replace Alabama and Texas delegations with their challengers.

[9] See Samuel Lubell, *The Future of American Politics*, 3rd ed. (New York: Harper, 1965), Ch. 10.

normal parliamentary procedure, and must be voted upon before the entire platform can be adopted.

So much for the formalities. It should be clear from this brief review of the "bare bones" of platform-making that initial advantage lies with whichever faction of the party is dominant in its National Committee. The great majority of the 100-plus members of the platform committee enter the process at a rather late stage and have little opportunity (should they wish it) to mount a serious attack on the chairman and his close associates. But the balance of forces on the National Committee may by no means accurately reflect factional strength in the party as a whole. It is this possible incongruence between balance of forces in the two major institutions of each national party that opens the door to successful floor fights on the platform. (We should note, however, that a minority faction in the National Committee, the platform committee, or the party as a whole can also provoke a floor fight; but it is very unlikely to be successful.)

Three conventions during the past two decades produced especially dramatic illustrations of the way platform-making can throw a spotlight on intraparty power struggles.

Fireworks began early in the 1948 Democratic convention when a move to deny credentials to Mississippi's delegates narrowly failed— and failed only because a bloc of Northern liberals chose not to aggravate obvious party disharmony. A rules fight followed, again pitting North against South, with the former winning on a voice vote. Then the Resolutions Committee submitted the proposed platform, containing a middle-of-the-road civil rights plank which, in Richard C. Bain's judgment, "undoubtedly represented the limit of compromise to which a majority of the northerners were willing to go. . . ." Southerners, however, submitted three "states rights" amendments which in turn provoked much stronger pro-civil rights amendments offered by Northern liberals. After an unusually passionate debate the principal Southern amendment was defeated by 925 to 309 and the Northern liberal amendment was carried 651½ to 582½.[10] Humiliated in the platform fight and having no hope of blocking President Truman's nomination, a number of Southerners bolted to form a States Rights party, which in November won five states and 39 electoral votes.

An altogether different sort of platform fight took place at the Republican convention of 1960; but the issues were fought out within the platform committee itself and never actually reached the floor.[11] The immediate problem was the precise wording of the civil rights plank. A deeper question was whether the party's sure nominee, Vice-President Richard Nixon, was entitled to "dicate" to the platform

---

[10] Bain, *op. cit.*, p. 275.

[11] This discussion of the 1960 Republican platform imbroglio leans heavily on Karl Lamb's fine essay, "Civil Rights and the Republican Platform: Nixon Achieves Control," in Paul Tillett (ed.) *Inside Politics: The National Conventions, 1960* (Dobbs Ferry: Oceana, 1962), pp. 55–84.

committee. But the deepest question of all was whether conservatives or moderates would dominate the Republican party and set the tone for its 1960 campaign.

When the platform committee had almost completed its pre-convention draft, Mr. Nixon and New York Governor Rockefeller held a private meeting in the early hours of Saturday morning preceding the convention's Monday opening. The outcome of that meeting was a Rockefeller press-release outlining policy statements that were to be incorporated in the platform. And although on a number of points Rockefeller did no more than give his assent to language which had already been worked out by the various subcommittees, the press-release made it appear that the Governor had virtually imposed a whole new platform upon a compliant Vice-President, leaving the Platform Committee itself unconsulted and voiceless.

Conservatives, led by Senator Goldwater of Arizona, exploded. Goldwater called the Nixon-Rockefeller meeting a "Republican Munich." He accused Nixon of sacrificing principle for expediency and deliberately insulting the members of the platform committee. Resentment within the committee itself mounted quickly. Three days of almost round-the-clock meetings ensued until at last the Nixon-Rockefeller views won final acceptance by the committee, though with certain concessions on wording granted to the conservative bloc. The convention accepted the entire platform without dissent, and the only evidence of lingering factional bitterness showed up in an enormously enthusiastic demonstration on behalf of Senator Goldwater, when his name was unexpectedly placed in nomination. Refusing the honor, Goldwater made an impressive appeal for party unity and Nixon was nominated by a vote of 1321 to 10.

Four years later still another kind of platform fight injected high drama into a Republican Convention. Following a climactic primary election victory in California, Senator Goldwater entered the San Francisco convention an odds-on favorite for the nomination. His supporters were firmly in control of the platform committee (and indeed of every aspect of convention organization) and had drafted the kind of platform for which conservative Republicans had yearned for a generation. Much too late, as it turned out, liberal and moderate Republicans closed ranks around Governor William Scranton of Pennsylvania; now, as the convention opened, they realized that their only hope of stopping Goldwater lay in a frontal assault on his alleged "extremism"—manifested, in their view, in the proposed platform.

Key issues were civil rights, extremist political groups, and civilian control of the military. When the platform was presented for adoption, a succession of eminent moderates moved amendments from the floor calling for, among other things, explicit approval of the recently passed Civil Rights Act of 1964 (which Goldwater had voted against) and equally explicit condemnation of the Ku Klux Klan and the John Birch Society (whose support Goldwater had refused to

disavow). The moment of greatest drama came when Governor Rockefeller took the podium to argue on behalf of one of the proposed
amendments. Delegates and spectators jamming the Cow Palace
erupted in a frenzy of boos, jeers, and shouted obscenities, so tumultuous and persistent that for long periods the New Yorker was unable
to speak. Only the most strenuous efforts of Chairman Thruston
Morton succeeded in restoring the minimal order necessary for Rockefeller to make his statement. In the end, all amendments were voted
down overwhelmingly and the Goldwater platform and candidacy
went on to massive defeat in November.[12]

These illustrations* should suffice to show that party platforms are by no means as devoid of meaning as critics allege. Despite
their admitted shortcomings—as compared, say, to British party programs—it seems reasonable to assume that political parties are hardly
likely to risk tearing themselves apart over a set of policy declarations
that their leaders are cynically prepared to disregard. Platforms can
never be taken as *totally* reliable guides to future governmental action; nevertheless they speak importantly to the question of what we
can generally expect in the way of executive leadership from the men
who emerge from each convention as candidates for the office of
President of the United States.

Following adoption of the platform the convention is ready to
turn to its principal business, the nominating of candidates for President and Vice-President. The strategies and procedures leading directly to those decisions form the subject of the next section. It would
be well to conclude the present discussion, as a lead-in to the next,
by indicating the ways in which pre-nominating convention actions
may impinge upon the nominating process itself.

We might note first that a number of decisions taken prior to the
nomination have little or no relevance to the nomination itself. Even
in conventions where two major contenders are ready to go at each
other with club and hatchet, the choice of officers, of rules, and even
of the platform may often be taken by consent of both sides. In
other cases, controversy may erupt on some matter not strictly related
to the nomination. In still others, a candidate may choose to make a
fight, or to refuse a compromise, on an item of business that appears
on the surface at least to be of little consequence to his chances for

---

[12] The story is well told in Theodore White, *The Making of the President
1964* (New York: Atheneum, 1965), pp. 200–202.

* A contest of extraordinary interest and importance took place at the Democratic convention of 1968 over the issue of Viet Nam policy. The majority on the
Platform Committee wrote a plank generally approving President Johnson's conduct
of the war and particularly his refusal to order a total bombing halt over North
Viet Nam. A minority report, however, called for an immediate cessation of the
bombing and early de-escalation of American military efforts. Debate lasting some
two hours and featuring many of the party's most distinguished leaders culminated
in a roll-call vote rejecting the minority report. The approximately 60/40 split on
that vote clearly presaged Vice-President Humphrey's nomination the following
evening; but it testified as well to the depth of division within the party.

victory. In this latter kind of situation we have what Pomper calls the "test of strength," which he describes as "an excellent means by which a faction can demonstrate latent, but as yet undeclared, support."[13]

The test of strength can come on any issue which any candidate chooses to make a fight about. In 1932, Franklin Roosevelt's forces decided to contest the National Committee's candidate for permanent chairman, Jouett Shouse. They had what James Farley describes as "adequate reasons" for opposing Shouse; but it is not at all clear that that gentleman would actually have abused his convention office in attempting to prevent Roosevelt's nomination. It seems more likely that FDR's managers wanted a chance to demonstrate that they had unbreachable majority support in the most difficult of situations (and in a convention that still required a two-thirds vote for nomination); and conversely, they might well have feared that to accept as permanent chairman a man who had worked actively against Roosevelt would seem to many wavering delegates an admission of weakness. The result, as we have seen, was a Roosevelt victory that virtually ensured his subsequent nomination.

More recently, at the Republican convention of 1952, the Eisenhower-inspired rules fight was in one respect an almost pure example of the test of strength. Though the proposed rules change itself would clearly have been to the General's advantage, Taft forces had already agreed to it and had asked that an exception be made only in the case of seven Louisiana delegates whose credentials, they felt, ought never to have been contested. Eisenhower's managers could have accepted this proferred compromise and still have won an important victory; they chose instead to bring the matter to a roll call vote, which they then won handily with the help of votes from delegations that were still holding aloof from both major contenders. This then was a clear test of strength and it demonstrated for all to see precisely what the Eisenhower forces had hoped it would show: that when the more important "favorite-son" candidates dropped out, their support would shift overwhelmingly to Eisenhower rather than to Taft. It seems fair to say that the former's nomination was never in doubt following the vote on the rules change.

Tests of strength can be confident and aggressive gestures on the part of those who instigate them; they can also be acts of desperation. We have seen how, at the 1964 Republican convention, forces opposed to Senator Goldwater's nomination tried unsuccessfully to change the platform in such a way as to embarrass the Senator and bring about a last-minute repudiation of his candidacy. Earlier in the convention they had attempted a desperation test of strength in a move to block the seating of delegates from states which excluded Negroes from participating in the selection of those delegates. Had they succeeded, it seems obvious that Goldwater's prospects would have dimmed con-

---

[13] Pomper, *op. cit.*, p. 147.

siderably; for everyone recognized that the vote was designed precisely to disclose previously unrevealed weaknesses in the Senator's assumed strength. The failure of that anti-Goldwater move served instead only to confirm the futility of the opposition's position.

In sum, given the prevailing condition of imperfect information among delegates and candidates alike as to who has how much latent as well as manifest support, the test of strength can provide one candidate or another—depending on its outcome—with an important, perhaps indispensable, boost to victory. Even so, it constitutes only one item in the total strategic package which each contender puts together in his bid to woo a majority of delegates to his support. Let us now look closer at the nominating process itself.

NOMINATION STRATEGIES AND PROCEDURE

By the time the candidates for a presidential nomination arrive at the convention city, a day or two before the start of formal proceedings, most of the work of lining up delegate support is over: the primaries have been fought, the state conventions met, the understandings (or lack of them) with party leaders arrived at. But it is here at the convention, and only here, that the prize can be finally won or lost; and so not even the most confident of contenders can afford to rest quietly in the glow of pre-convention success.

What each candidate will do in these few critical days before someone receives an official majority of delegate votes depends very largely on what he believes his situation to be vis-à-vis that of the opposition. To be sure, certain kinds of activities are common to all declared contenders. But the underdog or dark-horse hopeful must pursue a strategy markedly different from that of the frontrunner, and the frontrunner in a two-man race faces certain problems quite unlike those of the frontrunner in a multi-man contest.

In any convention the most significant question is whether anyone appears to have, or is close to getting, a majority of delegates committed to him on an early ballot. And one of the striking characteristics of presidential nominating politics in our own times is that the likelihood of an early-ballot victory has become the rule rather than the exception. Since the end of World War II there have been 12 major party conventions; in only two has it taken more than a single ballot to reach a nomination. By contrast, in the 12 conventions prior to Franklin D. Roosevelt's long incumbency—that is, in the period 1912 to 1932—six conventions had to go beyond the first ballot to choose a presidential candidate. And when we eliminate those conventions in which an incumbent President sought renomination without challenge, we find that of nine contested nominations during 1948–1968 only two required more than one ballot; whereas in the earlier period, five of the nine contested nominations involved multiple ballots. Finally, we might note that there has not been more than one ballot in any convention since

1952, despite the fact that seven conventions from 1956 through 1968 had non-incumbents seeking the nomination.[14]

The upshot of all this is that, for whatever reasons, much of the uncertainty as to who is going to win the nomination has effectively ended by the time the opening gavel falls.[15] And more to the present point, candidates today have substantially less room for maneuver during the convention itself than they had in those earlier years when virtually no strategic options were foreclosed until the last hours before the last ballot was to be taken. This is not to say that *every* convention henceforth will open with a kind of predetermined winner waiting to receive the garland. But it seems very improbable that many future conventions will be such "wide-open" affairs as those of, say, 1920, when the Republicans took 10 ballots to nominate Warren G. Harding and the Democrats 44 ballots to pick James M. Cox.[16]

It would be hard to overestimate the impact of these trends on convention strategies. Put briefly, the job of the frontrunner has become substantially easier, the job of the underdog incomparably harder. For both of them the critical fact is that the convention's choice will be made swiftly—which lends superb urgency to the frontrunner's traditional call to "get aboard the bandwagon while there's still time" and makes almost a mockery of the underdog's traditional plea to "just hold the line for a few ballots while we see what happens." Since delegates seem increasingly prone to feel that they simply do not have time to wait to see what happens, the underdog must attempt to devise some dramatic and massive assault capable of decimating the frontrunner's strength before it manifests itself all too clearly in the balloting.

The near-impossibility of bringing off any such *coup* is a consequence of the fact that there are rarely any surprises left by the time the convention convenes. It comes, after all, as the climax of a long season of pre-convention campaigning, during which time (if not long before) any personal or political vulnerability in the leading candidates is sure to have been discovered. So that when, for example, Senator Goldwater's opponents in 1964 attempted to smash his convention support by attacking him for his conservative policy positions, whatever else they may have accomplished they assuredly did not reveal anything about Goldwater that everybody did not already know.

---

[14] For details on balloting at every major party nominating convention from 1832 through 1956, see the invaluable compendium and analysis by Richard C. Bain, *Convention Decisions and Voting Records* (Washington: Brookings Institution, 1960). Copyright by and used with permission of the Brookings Institution.

[15] Paul David *et al.* suggest that the great improvement in polling techniques and the much wider currency given to poll results are the main reasons for this development. *The Politics of National Party Conventions* (Washington: Brookings Institution, 1960), pp. 432–433.

[16] A large part of the Democrats' problems was caused by the requirement of a two-thirds majority for nomination, in force till 1936. In 1924 they exhausted themselves—and the public—by taking 103 ballots to nominate John W. Davis.

We come back, then, to what we earlier identified as the most significant question for convention strategy: as the time for balloting draws near, how close is anyone to having a majority of delegates committed to him? And in the event that no majority is in prospect for the first ballot, the critical question becomes: how firm is each candidate's existing strength? To be at all effective, the strategies of frontrunners and underdogs alike must be geared to what they believe to be the correct answers to these two questions.

For the frontrunner the job is to convince as many delegates as possible that his nomination is inevitable. The candidate whose victory *looks* like a sure thing is virtually unstoppable, because many delegates who might really prefer other contenders will vote for the presumed winner so as to be able to share more fully in the fruits of his triumph. Politics holds little comfort for the also-ran; those who stick with a loser till the bitter end may receive much consolation for the spirit but little nourishment for the body. Hence the strong desire of delegates, and especially delegation leaders, to make a timely appearance on the winning team.

The job of all other candidates, accordingly, is to convince as many delegates as possible that the frontrunner simply does not have enough support to put him over the top, that prudence dictates a firm holding action on everybody's part until the convention's will becomes clearer. At the same time, each underdog will attempt to develop positive support for himself; but whether he will aim for first-choice or second-choice support (or both) will depend on how he views his position in the total field of challengers. A candidate running a close second to the leader must be able to manifest strong additional support as soon as the frontrunner shows signs of faltering; and this requires that he have in reserve a bloc of delegates willing to move to him as soon as the occasion demands. Challengers farther back in the field, by contrast, try to establish themselves as second-choice or compromise candidates in the event that something like a deadlock develops in the balloting.

The 1960 Democratic convention affords convenient illustrations of how these strategies may be implemented in practice. Senator Lyndon Johnson of Texas recognized that he was running a rather poor second to John F. Kennedy, but second nevertheless. This meant that he had to contrive to stop Kennedy on the first ballot and then be able to make an impressive move forward on immediately subsequent ballots. His multi-pronged efforts to this end included: aid and comfort to another man's candidacy; a frontal attack on Kennedy himself; an argument that a first-ballot nomination was beyond Kennedy's grasp and that massive defections were bound to occur on the second and third ballots; a further claim that he himself would be the principal gainer from these defections, thereby making his own nomination "inevitable"; and a demonstration that, if nominated, he would be a sure winner in November.

Senator Stuart Symington of Missouri, on the other hand, un-deviatingly pursued a pure second-choice strategy, appealing to Kennedy and Johnson supporters alike to turn to him if their man could not make it. On occasion he made oblique references to "bossism" and "steamroller tactics" in an effort to detach a few delegates from their Kennedy-pledged leaders. But this line was always muted, for Syming-ton realized that to offend Kennedy supporters would not move him materially closer to the presidential nomination but might instead take him out of the running for a vice-presidential nomination. His one chance lay in a deadlocked convention—but he himself had almost no leverage with which to help produce a deadlock. He could only try to make himself appear the most attractive compromise candidate and hope against hope that first Kennedy, then Johnson could be stopped.

Efforts of a rather more Byzantine nature showed up in connec-tion with former nominee Adlai Stevenson's "non-candidacy," which appears to have drawn strong undercover encouragement from the Johnson and Symington camps; theirs being a well-merited conviction that Stevenson could do what neither of them could, namely, take votes away from Kennedy on the all-important first ballot. But, despite intense pressure on every side, Stevenson refused to make any gesture on his own behalf until the very day of the nomination—and without his leadership the last best hope of the stop-Kennedy forces evaporated.[17]

Conventions in which no candidate appears to be close to an early-ballot nomination offer strategic opportunities and problems of a very different sort. Being the "leader"—in the sense of having more pledged votes than anyone else—is almost as much a liability as a virtue, for it encourages "stop-the-leader" movements that are only too likely to succeed in the absence of any significant potential for the bandwagon. And the contender who is well back in the field in terms of pledged votes operates at almost no comparative disadvantage in the crucial business of putting together a winning combination on the scene; for he can properly claim that no one has yet demonstrated enough strength to deserve the nomination.

It is virtually impossible to summarize the variety of strategies and tactics that go into putting together a winning combination in conventions of this sort. One candidate must somehow persuade one or more other candidates to throw their support to him at some critical point in the balloting period. But the techniques by which this is accomplished are as varied as the personalities of the principals themselves. To be sure, bargaining is the very essence of the matter: so long as the outcome is indeterminate, no one is likely to resign

---

[17] In *The Making of the President 1960*, Theodore White devotes what seems to me excessive attention to the Stevenson candidacy and too little to Johnson's. He does not mention Johnson's covert encouragement of Stevenson. Many of us who attended the convention, however, were led by reliable sources to believe that it occurred.

his own chances for the nomination except in return for value given. But while nothing less than the vice-presidential nomination may seem adequate value to one man, another may deem it a fair bargain if he receives only policy commitments on matters he deems vital to the nation, the party, or himself. More often than not, a complex of considerations will enter into a candidate's (or delegation leader's) decision to throw his support to another candidate; as for example in 1932, when John Nance Garner of Texas requested that delegates pledged to his own candidacy give their votes to Franklin Roosevelt: the vice-presidential nomination had certainly been offered to him, but he seems to have been at least as strongly motivated by a desire to avoid the kind of 103-ballot fiasco that had torn the party apart in 1924.[18]

Once a candidate has received significant new support in the balloting, he is in a fair position to attempt to start a bandwagon rolling. Virtually all students of national conventions agree that lack of reliable information is a prime characteristic of the institution. Delegates therefore tend to seize upon all manner of omens, portents, and rumors for voting cues. Hence the actual switch of a major delegation from Candidate X to Candidate Y lends itself admirably to the proposition that "Y is the man—the bandwagon's rolling." Whereupon almost invariably, it does.

The most recent example we have, by way of illustration, of a convention in which the eventual nominee did not have a commanding lead on the first ballot was the Democratic assemblage of 1952. The reluctant Adlai Stevenson of Illinois, with only 22 per cent of the first-ballot vote, finally gave his assent to being nominated after it became clear that no one else could as effectively unite the party. On the second ballot he still trailed Senator Estes Kefauver of Tennessee. But on the third ballot the bulk of the Massachusetts delegation switched from a favorite son to Stevenson and the entire Michigan delegation switched from Kefauver to the Illinois governor. The rush then was on, and Stevenson gained an additional 80 votes in New York and 30 in Pennsylvania, among others, to bring him to a majority.

It is perfectly true, of course, that bandwagons do not just happen. More to the point, the catalytic switch of a major delegation from one candidate to another can hardly come about except as the result of a newly reached agreement between the fortunate candidate and the delegation's leader(s). And agreements of this sort inevitably give rise to all manner of speculation about unsavory "deals" consummated in "smoke-filled rooms."

The indignation that tends to well up in us as we contemplate such behavior is almost certainly misplaced. For the national conven-

[18] See James A. Farley, *Behind the Ballots* (New York: Harcourt, Brace, 1938), pp. 132–153; also Arthur M. Schlesinger, Jr., *The Crisis of the Old Order* (Boston: Houghton Mifflin, 1957), pp. 296–311.

tion is the arena, and delegates the agents, we rely upon in our political system for bargaining, negotiating, and engaging in all other such activity as may be required to provide us with one presidential candidate from each party every four years. We have, in fact, no alternative to *some* form of deal-making (i.e., bargaining) within the context of presidential nominating politics; and if an insufficient number of primaries have been won or deals consummated prior to the opening of a convention—if, that is, no one man has managed to gain the support of a large enough number of state party leaders during the preceding year—the convention itself necessarily becomes the final ground of decision. This being the case, there can hardly be any cause for surprise or alarm when candidates and state leaders attempt to hammer out deals or agreements in the quiet of a hotel room (no matter how smoky) rather than on the tumultuous floor of the convention.

It is also important to point out in this connection that many more deals are offered than are made, and not just because the *quid pro quo* is inadequate. For despite politicians' fervent desire to be on the winning side and to receive the rewards and perquisites that victory in politics has to offer, significant numbers of delegates in contested conventions do manage to resist both the deal and the bandwagon to stay with their favored candidate. As Munger and Blackhurst have shown in a recent article,[19] ideological factions in each party persist from convention to convention—conservative Republicans stick with Robert Taft in 1952 in the face of an Eisenhower bandwagon, progressive Republicans stick with William Scranton in 1964 in the face of a Goldwater bandwagon. And the indifference of Southern Democrats to Northern-led bandwagons since World War II is only the most notable example of Democratic factionalism.

The upshot of all this is that tactics such as the deal and bandwagon can be used effectively only within certain rather narrowly drawn limits. No amount of dealing can make a presidential candidate out of a man not widely regarded as being of presidential stature (the unfortunate example of Warren G. Harding may be taken as the exception that proves the rule); nor can bandwagons be set rolling on behalf of contenders who have not already gained the kind of widespread support that only a handful of men each four years can ever hope to attain.

So far we have been discussing broadside strategies and tactics designed to influence delegates en masse, either directly or through their leaders. Other fairly routine efforts of this kind include receptions to which all delegates, alternates, and friends are invited; establishment and staffing of candidate headquarters which delegates may visit to obtain souvenirs and campaign literature and receive individual pep-talks from knowledgeable staff members; and all the varieties of demonstrations both inside and outside the convention hall that contribute so much of the color and noise to a national convention. Few campaign managers, however, regard these activities as anything but expensive nuisances which are required because of tradition and because "the-other-fellow-is-doing-it-and-if-we-don't-we'll-look-bad." They change no votes; at best, they serve as reinforcement for one's own delegates who, in their absence, might be lured to support some other candidate.

A very different—and relatively new—type of activity takes the individual delegate as an object of attention. The staffs of major contenders now make an effort to accumulate information on every single delegate: whom he favors for the nomination, how strong is his attachments to the candidate, personal and party background, and anything else it might be useful to know should the need arise for pressure or appeal.

The idea of accumulating a fund of information about each individual delegate, which probably originated with James A. Farley, served as a point of departure for the much more elaborate operation put together by Senator John F. Kennedy's staff, beginning at least a year before the 1960 convention opened. Kennedy's system, however, represented an important advance over earlier efforts of its kind on the elaborateness of arrangements for conveying information from individual delegation to campaign headquarters back to delegation. By such arrangements, the Kennedy staff was able to enjoy an unparalleled degree of flexibility and control for dealing with all sorts of previously unmanageable problems—bolstering sagging support in one delegation, exploiting a potential opening in another, and at all times having a near-perfect idea of how many nominating votes were available from hour to hour. One additional feature of this communications network was the setting up of six telephone stations at strategic spots on the convention floor itself (underneath the seats of pro-Kennedy delegation chairmen), for use in dealing with whatever problems might arise during convention sessions. Perhaps the best testimony to the effectiveness of this kind of operation is the fact that Senator Goldwater's very able campaign staff copied the system in 1964 and derived the same advantages from it. It seems highly improbable that any serious contender in the future will go into convention week without having set up a very similar system for his own use.[20]

Balloting: The Moment of Truth. The climactic event to which all strategies and tactics are directed is, of course, the nomination itself. The formal process begins with an alphabetical roll call of the states and territories for the purpose of placing names in nomination. As the

---

[20] A detailed and instructive account of the Kennedy communications system can be found in Fred Burke's "Senator Kennedy's Convention Organization," in Paul Tillett (ed.), *Inside Politics: The National Conventions*, 1960 (Dobbs Ferry: Oceana, 1962). See also White, *op. cit.*, pp. 187–189.

state is called its delegation chairman can either pass, yield to another state farther down the list, or have one of the members of the delegation take the podium for a nominating speech. Who nominates which candidate has all been worked out very carefully in advance; no surprises are in order at this point. The invariable object on the part of the candidate is to have his nomination effected as early as possible so that the accompanying "demonstration" (also carefully planned) can take place before everybody is sick and tired of the long round of speeches and parades. Accordingly, a candidate from, say, New York will arrange for a friendly delegation early in the alphabetical list to yield its turn—no very difficult matter for a serious contender with fairly broad national support.

The nominating speakers will be chosen with some care. Major party figures are very much in demand for this sort of work (for example, 1964 when Goldwater's managers chose the not-very-Goldwaterite Senate Minority Leader Everett Dirksen) as a means of indicating the candidate's supposed strength. But lesser candidates usually have to make do with prominent persons from their own state or region. The speeches themselves are rarely distinguishable one from the other, but tend instead to follow an almost ritual pattern. The personality and style of the orator, however, may do much to generate real, instead of merely obligatory, enthusiasm among the packed delegates and viewers.

Following each main nominating speech comes a well-planned "spontaneous demonstration," designed to look like hundreds upon hundreds of delegates swept to their feet in a frenzy of enthusiasm, marching, cheering, singing, waving signs and banners. In fact, of course, though large numbers of delegates do participate more or less voluntarily, principal candidates will normally have at least a hundred paid musicians and sign-carriers from outside the convention hall participating noisily in the demonstration; by prearrangement with convention authorities they march in, around, then out—often to take part in the next candidate's display. Prior to the advent of television, demonstrations would sometimes last as long as an hour or more. Now, however, officials attempt to limit them to about 20 minutes so as to keep the nationwide audience from becoming too bored with the whole affair.

But what may well prove to be a change of lasting effect took place at the 1968 Democratic convention. A week or so in advance of its opening, officials announced that demonstrations were to be prohibited altogether, with delegates restricted to waving banners and cheering for a few minutes when their man's name had been placed in nomination. Impetus for the change had been largely provided by the Republicans at Miami three weeks earlier: so many demonstrations for so many "favorite-son" candidates had consumed so much time that network TV commentators were moved to frequent expressions of annoyance and even contempt. So with no discernible unhappiness, Democratic convention managers seized the opportunity provided by apparent public disgust and issued their anti-demonstrations edict. It now seems a fair bet that the Republicans too in 1972 will follow the welcome precedent, thus putting an end, once and for all, to a feature of convention activity that appears to have long since outlived its usefulness.

After the main nominating speech and the demonstration come the seconding speeches on behalf of the candidate. These, usually four in number, are limited to five minutes each in length. Seconders may be selected with attention to dramatizing the breadth of a candidate's support throughout the country. In 1960, for example, then-Senator Lyndon Johnson could show impressive strength outside his native South in the form of seconding speeches by Governor Hickey of Wyoming, Senator Dodd of Connecticut, and Representative Inouye of Hawaii. But for favorite-son and dark-horse candidacies, seconding speeches serve only the negative function of preventing the nomination from appearing even more bootless than it actually is—no easy task.

When the roll call of the states for nominations has been completed, the convention is at last ready to perform its principal task, the choosing of a presidential candidate. Once again the states are called in alphabetical order. Each delegation chairman arises to announce, as dramatically as possible, how his state casts its allotted number of votes. For reasons we shall examine more carefully in the next chapter, a delegation's total vote may not be a very accurate reflection of the real state of opinion within its ranks: most notably, the so-called unit rule when used by a state requires that the delegations' *entire* vote be cast for that candidate whom only a majority of delegates prefer. In any event, each chairman's announcement customarily produces an outburst of cheers and groans throughout the hall—the larger the state, the more vocal the reaction.

As any one candidate's total vote begins to approach the "magic number" needed for victory, activity within and around delegations yet to be called may become quite frenzied. Partisans of the leading candidate will urge delegates to climb aboard the bandwagon while there is still time; partisans of other candidates fight just as hard to keep their lines intact, to prevent the bandwagon psychology from taking hold and becoming irresistible; delegates wishing to change the way they had previously intended to vote plead for their chairman's attention; news and cameramen close in upon the delegation that might cast the clinching vote. At last it comes:

> "Mr. Chairman—Mr. Chairman, Wyoming's vote will make a majority for Senator Kennedy. Mr. Chairman—Mr. Chairman . . . Wyoming votes—we have 15 votes. There are 15 votes from Wyoming for Kennedy."[21]

When a candidate finally receives the necessary majority of votes for nomination, it is, or has been, customary for one of the defeated contenders to move that the vote be recorded as unanimous. The pre-

---

[21] Democratic National Convention, *Proceedings*, 1960, p. 167.

siding officer would invariably entertain such a motion, call for the ayes and nays, hear none of the latter, and declare the victor to have been nominated "by acclamation." And with this ritual gesture the convention celebrated its own most important reason for being: to bestow upon one man the exclusive nomination of a united party. The fact that no such gesture was even attempted at the 1968 Democratic convention suggests, again, the amount of bitterness and disunity that characterized the entire proceedings.

Choosing the Running-Mate. One principal task remains to be performed before the convention can adjourn. It must choose—almost always at the behest of its newly selected presidential nominee—a candidate for the Vice-Presidency. At issue here is the problem of finding a running-mate who can add some measure of strength to the party during the coming campaign. This he can do as a consequence of either his own broad popular appeal or his standing with a particular geographical or ideological wing of the party. In 1960, Richard Nixon chose Henry Cabot Lodge because of his presumed strong appeal throughout the country generally and among moderate Republicans and Independents in particular. In the same year, John Kennedy selected Lyndon Johnson to be his running-mate because of the strength he believed Johnson would add to the ticket in the South and Midwest.

We have already noted that Roosevelt's selection of Garner in 1932 was almost certainly the result of a "deal," as was Dewey's choice of Warren in 1948. But we should recognize, too, that both Garner and Warren were men of considerable political stature on their own, both enjoyed important support for the presidential nomination, and both added a desirable element of geographical balance to their tickets. Put another way, in the absence of any "deal" at all it is not unlikely that these men would have been selected anyway for reasons most observers would regard as eminently proper.

Two of the most dramatic vice-presidential nominations in our history occurred in 1944 and 1956, both at Democratic conventions. On the earlier occasion Henry A. Wallace of Iowa was the incumbent Vice-President, and Franklin Roosevelt quite probably wanted him renominated. But Wallace, long a controversial figure and closely identified with the most liberal elements in the party, was cordially disliked by a number of important Democratic leaders. They were able to prevail upon the ailing and war-distracted President to accept the dumping of Wallace if it could be accomplished in the convention. Roosevelt, therefore, instead of insisting upon Wallace's renomination (as he had done in 1940) merely issued a statement saying that if *he* were a convention delegate he would vote for the incumbent, but behind the scenes prepared a list of four men who would be acceptable to him as running-mates and gave this list to National Chairman Robert Hannegan. Hannegan and David Lawrence of Pennsylvania, among others, then determined that, of the four, Senator Harry Truman of Missouri would be the strongest foil to Wallace in the convention. Twelve names in all were placed in nomination. On the first ballot Wallace led Truman, 429½ to 319½, with 589 needed for nomination; on the second, Truman overtook Wallace slightly, but a rash of vote-switching at the end gave the nomination to the Missourian—with consequences for the nation and the world that remain today literally incalculable.

Very different considerations were operative in 1956 when the newly renominated Adlai Stevenson told an astonished convention, "I have concluded to depart from the precedents of the past. I have decided that the selection of the Vice Presidential nominee should be made through the free processes of the Convention . . . so that the Democratic Party's candidate for this office may join me before the Nation not as one man's selection but as one chosen by our Party even as I have been chosen."[22]

At the time, three men had taken the trouble to establish convention headquarters of a sort for the sake of impressing delegates with their "availability" for the vice-presidential nomination: Senators Hubert Humphrey of Minnesota, Estes Kefauver of Tennessee, and John Kennedy of Massachusetts; but none had actually thought that the convention would be allowed a free choice among them. Following Stevenson's surprise announcement, the candidates rallied their supporters and began a frantic 12-hour buttonholing of delegates and leaders in an effort to secure what votes they could. Kefauver led on the first ballot, Kennedy overtook him on the second and at one point came within 39 votes of a majority. But in the turmoil of vote-switching that ensued, Kefauver received significant new support and went on to win the nomination. A perplexed and disappointed John Kennedy moved that it be made unanimous.

No one has yet explained why Stevenson took so unprecedented a step, but two main reasons seem to have been compelling. First, the Democratic nominee probably hoped to offer a refreshing contrast to what he assumed (correctly) would be the Republican procedure of the following week, namely, President Eisenhower's insisting upon the renomination of Richard Nixon, to whom there was a certain amount of objection within the party. Second, and doubtless more important, Stevenson faced in effect an embarrassment of riches in the three candidates already mentioned, plus Senator Gore of Tennessee and Mayor Wagner of New York, all of whom he regarded as well qualified, politically and personally, for the job. In the event, he appears to have decided that he had nothing to lose and quite possibly a good bit to gain by letting the convention do the choosing for him.

The 1944 and 1956 exceptions aside, however, standard practice continues to be that a presidential nominee can—and is expected to—select his own running-mate, in consultation with whomever he pleases and for whatever reasons seem to him appropriate. We might only

---

[22] Democratic National Convention, *Proceedings*, 1956, p. 420.

note, in conclusion, that an increasing number of observers have begun to insist that factors more weighty than geographical balance ought to be uppermost in the minds of presidential candidates when selecting their running-mates. With the grim examples so close to us of President Eisenhower's illnesses and President Kennedy's assassination, occurring as they did in times of almost constant national peril, most of us would probably agree that Vice-Presidents can hardly afford to be men of substantially lesser stature than those whom they might have to succeed in the White House. But, in all fairness, that consideration has almost certainly not been lost upon most of our presidential nominees in the past couple of decades.

DELEGATIONS, DELEGATES AND LEADERS

As the authors of the most comprehensive study of national conventions have remarked, "For many purposes, the working unit at a national convention is the state delegation rather than the individual delegate."[23] In this section we shall first examine the way this basic working unit operates, then move on to consider the part that its leaders and rank-and-file members play during convention week.

Organizing the Delegation. Each delegation will normally organize itself shortly after its members have been selected, or at the latest two weeks prior to the opening of the convention. The size of the delegation will have been partially determined some months earlier by action of the National Committee, which is empowered to declare to how many *votes* each state will be entitled. But it is then up to the individual state parties to decide how the delegates are to be selected and whether each will be granted full votes or half-votes.[24] Until recent years some states even used one-third and one-quarter votes so as to make it possible for more members to attend conventions as participants; but both national parties have now decreed that half-votes will be the smallest permissible quotient. So, for example, a state which is entitled to 34 total votes is likely to have 64 delegates with one half-vote apiece plus one full vote each for its national committeeman and national committeewoman.

Once the delegates have been selected, by whatever means, they must meet as a body to elect the delegation chairman and other officers and choose two members for each of the major convention committees. The delegation will usually not then meet again until the

---

[23] Paul T. David, Ralph M. Goldman, Richard C. Bain, *The Politics of National Party Conventions* (Washington: Brookings Institution, 1960), p. 355. Much of the material of this section, relies heavily on the pioneering work of these authors.
[24] See *ibid.*, Ch. 8, for a detailed discussion of apportionment procedures. Delegate selection is treated comprehensively in Chs. 10 and 11. See also Donald B. Johnson's Chapter in the present book.

day before the convention opens. At that time it will necessarily take up such "housekeeping" details as distribution of credentials (the badges and tickets which entitle delegates and alternates to get to their respective places in the convention hall), allotment of guest tickets, and the time and place of future meetings. If especially difficult or contentious matters are in prospect for the early hours of the convention, the delegation may also have to discuss these substantive matters and decide how it wishes to deal with them. At the 1952 Republican convention, for example, all delegation leaders (if not all delegates) were aware that the Eisenhower forces intended to wage a fight on the normally non-controversial question of adoption of temporary rules; hence it was necessary for each delegation to figure out at least tentatively how its vote was to be cast on the issue.

The frequency of subsequent meetings will largely depend on the progress of the convention itself, though as a rule most delegations seem to hold one meeting a day even when no important decisions need to be made. When events demand, however, they can meet as often as it is physically possible to get most members together—on the floor of the convention if need be.

Selecting the Leaders. Party rules as well as practical necessity require every delegation to have a chairman: the party demands it so that one and only one person will be able to speak for the delegation during formal proceedings (such as announcing the results of roll call votes) and receive official communications regarding procedural matters; and someone, after all, needs to preside over meetings and attempt to maintain at least a minimal degree of order.

Chairmen tend to be drawn overwhelmingly from the ranks of public and party office-holders within the delegations, with governors much the most likely to be chosen for the post when they are present as delegates. Though the chairman may not be the delegation's effective leader (if there is one), he nevertheless

> occupies a strategic position. The *ad hoc* nature of most convention arrangements, the short time span, and the characteristic confusion, all tend to place responsibility on him, and presumably give him a considerable measure of power . . . In a cohesive and disciplined delegation, his powers may approach those of the traditional political boss; in a splintered delegation, he is at least an important communication center.[25]

In practicaly every case where a delegation does have one effective leader, that person will take the chairmanship himself. Where real leadership exists but is shared out among two or three strong men, the tendency is to designate as chairman someone who is acceptable

---

[25] David *et al.*, revised edition (New York: Random House, 1964), p. 251. Reprinted by permission.

to all. But where factionalism is unusually intense, the dominant group may attempt to impose their own man on the minority and not bother with the niceties of compromise and consensus.

The problem of identifying the real leader(s) of a delegation is not as difficult as analogous problems in other political situations, largely because the national convention must do its job within a very short period of time and because its decisions are irrevocable, public, and of immediate consequence. This means simply that the men in whose hands decision-making power lies must make their wishes known in direct and unambiguous fashion and through the final medium of a delegation's roll call vote. And even if it were not possible (as it almost always is) to infer from the latter who wants what from whom, the ubiquity of the news media and the notorious looseness of politicians' tongues make secrecy a practical impossibility. In fact, however, political leaders in America are not generally disposed to hide their lights under a basket. Power is where power is believed to be. The real leaders of delegations need to be known as such, else they are not likely to be able to accomplish what they wish.

It is not always easy to tell whether strong leadership is present in a delegation. Even when a delegation is split right down the middle on a crucial roll call vote, the possibility exists that there are two rival leaders each with his own dedicated band of followers. Conversely, when a delegation votes with near-unanimity on every issue, this may well be a consequence of perceived identity of interests among the delegates rather than of a strong hand pulling the strings. The only fairly reliable information we can have as to whether a delegation is or is not strongly led is of an informal, journalistic sort—prior information about the nature of the party organization in a particular state and conversations or interviews with individual delegates on the scene.

In general, it seems fair to say that completely leaderless delegations are a rarity, and delegations under the thumb of one all-powerful "boss" have been almost equally rare in recent years. The conclusion that Paul David and his associates reached on the basis of the 1952 and 1956 conventions was born out by studies made in 1960: "Most commonly . . . delegations seem to contain some sort of an inner circle that supplements the leadership of a strong chairman or takes the initiative in mobilizing when the chairman is weak."[26]

Delegation Leaders and Followers. No matter how strongly led a delegation is, no matter how firmly committed to a particular candidate and program, the pervasive confusion, misinformation, and disorder attendant upon a contested convention require a kind of continuing reassesssment by the delegation of its objectives and positions. In politics as in war, nothing guarantees disaster as surely as inflexibility. And while a delegation may be quite willing to go down to defeat

---

[26] *Ibid.*, pp. 251–252. Reprinted by permission.

with its candidate, hardly anyone in politics is prepared to accept defeat-without-compromise in preference to victory-with-compromise.

It is this continuing need for reassessment—with all that it implies in the way of readiness to shift positions when necessary—that places the highest demands upon the skills of the leaders and the loyalty of their followers. (This would not be true, of course, of those rare delegations, if any, which conform to the classic image of the "bossed.") From the point of view of the leaders the problem is twofold: first, what decision *ought* to be made, and second, how can it be presented most effectively to the rank-and-file so as to insure their continued cooperation? From the point of view of the ordinary delegate the salient questions are: is the leader's recommendation a sound one? Does it advance *my* interests and the party's as well as his? If I disagree with the recommendation, how can I balance the claims of loyalty and/or self-interest against the mandate of my own judgment?

No one who has ever found himself in an even roughly comparable situation is likely to suppose that such questions lend themselves to facile answers. The difficulties are somewhat alleviated, however, by the mutual recognition among leaders and followers that the former have attained and held on to their position because of personal qualities that are intrinsically necessary to sound decision-making: good judgment and superior information resources. To the leader, this means that, on balance, he is likely to be given the benefit of the doubt; to the rank-and-file it means that he is *entitled* to the benefit of the doubt. One other vital factor is the desire among most members of any political organization to manifest as high a degree of unity as possible in conflict-situations—of which a contested convention is pre-eminently one.

These general reflections are supported by what (relatively little) hard evidence we have. Put simply, it has been found that voting divisions in a convention occur more often "*between* delegations than *within* them—in other words, that each delegation tended to take on an identity as an organized group, and even when its vote was split, a more lopsided majority was usually given one candidate or the other than was the case in the convention as a whole."[27] David and associates go on to note that there has been a long-term decline (1896–1956) in this "average index of candidate agreement"; but when we apply the same measure to the 1960 Democratic and 1964 Republican conventions, we find a reversal of the long-term trend.

Evidence with respect to non-nominating convention decisions is at best fragmentary and impressionistic. But the sense one gets from reading contemporary newspaper accounts or a book of essays like that on the 1960 conventions[28] tends also to support the view that delega-

---

[27] David *et al.*, *op. cit.*, p. 253n. Reprinted by permission.

[28] Tillett (ed.), *op. cit.*, contains a number of unusually insightful essays by political scientists attached as observers to various delegations in the conventions of 1960.

tion leaders succeed far more often than not in carrying a majority of
their delegates with them on changes in tactics and positions. Recent
dramatic examples include the Republican platform fight in 1960,
when a lack of leadership within the delegations might have led to
severe embarrassment for Vice-President Nixon, and the Democrats'
near-explosion in 1964 over credentials for the Mississippi delegation,
which could have given a splitting headache to President Johnson
had Northern liberal delegations not been strongly led. To be sure,
neither instance seriously involved the question of who would be the
party's presidential nominee. But the very absence of a nominating
contest should only have increased the difficulties that delegation
leaders must have had in keeping their troops in order.

For leaders and followers alike, the principal objective of the
delegation will be to render as timely and effective assistance as possible
to their favored candidate. By so doing they may reasonably expect due
consideration from their man, if he is elected President, on matters
like patronage, pork-barrel, help in state and local elections, and the
very general but to politicians deeply important commodity called
"recognition." These are the lifeblood of organization politics, and
even delegations whose commitment to a particular candidate is largely
ideological, or policy-oriented, are not likely to lose sight of them
altogether in their convention decision-making.

This is a fact that has tended to become obscured in recent years
with the increasing frequency, noted in the preceding chapter, of one-
ballot nominations. Delegations have shifted the bulk of their vote
from one candidate to another far less often since World War II than
previously—but, then, there have been only two conventions during
the whole period when they would have had a chance to do so. Voting
strategies may therefore appear rather more inflexible than they could
be under circumstances allowing more room for maneuver. In any
event, the result has been to place delegations, and especially their
leaders, under very intense pressure to make a nominating decision
that they must regard as irreversible once the balloting has started.

For this reason, too, divisions within a delegation become more
significant than formerly as each faction recognizes that there will be
no chance for restored unity on later ballots. (To what extent factionalism in the delegation is a reflection of factionalism in the entire
state party is a question that can be answered only by reference to
the politics of each individual state. But conflicts that are exacerbated
at the national convention will not be any easier to resolve when the
delegation returns home.) Rival leaders must therefore try to reach
some accommodation *before* the balloting starts—if indeed there is any
real desire for unity; quite often there is not.

There is another side to the factional coin, however. Rival leaders
may sometimes be in support of the same candidate—New York
and Ohio Democrats in 1960 are good examples—and confine their
factional struggles at the convention to matters not related to the

nomination. In these cases, one-ballot conventions have the virtue of papering over a good deal of inherent stress and strain; the factional disputes that may erupt if the balloting wears on too long remain dormant, and the delegation can go home no less unified than when it arrived.

One other point to be made in this connection concerns the so-called unit rule according to which a delegation's entire vote must be cast in accordance with the wishes of the majority. The Republican party now prohibits its use at national conventions (though the Idaho state party continues to instruct its delegation to vote as a unit), with the increasing frequency, noted in the preceeding section of one-while in the Democratic party its use, once widespread, was abandoned in 1968.[29]

Conclusions. The delegation is the basic working unit of a national convention not only because convention procedures require it but, more importantly, because the men and women who are formally involved perceive themselves as members of delegations far more than as "conventioneers." And the decision-making they engage in is largely conditioned by this perception. They represent states—frequently, state party organizations; more often than not they share common views as to what candidate and what policies will be most congenial to the voters of their state.

Predominantly organization-minded as they are, they understand and accept the need for leadership. They are willing, within all reasonable limits, to defer to the judgment of their leaders. Indeed, in view of the chaos of rumors, alarms, and conflicting information so characteristic of a contested convention, they are only too likely to *want* some leadership to which they can defer. But leadership, too, is located almost exclusively in delegations; and the leaders themselves tend to be the most organization-minded of any participants at a convention.

The great bulk of decision-making, therefore, must take place within the context of a delegation, whether by an inner circle of leaders or by the rank-and-file delegates after open debate. Given the decentralized, state-oriented nature of our American party system, it could hardly be otherwise.

NATIONAL CONVENTIONS IN PERSPECTIVE

There appears to be general agreement today among students of American politics that, in the late V.O. Key's words, "The national convention represents the solution by American parties of the problem of uniting scattered points of political leadership in support of candi-

---

[29] See David *et al.*, *op. cit.*, pp. 183–186.

dates for the Presidency and Vice Presidency."[30] To do this, the convention must perform two essential functions: most obviously, it must select the candidates; but it must also induce divergent elements of the party to close ranks behind the newly anointed leaders, at least to the extent of refraining from actively opposing these leaders.

Conventions have always, with the single ominous exception of that of 1860, succeeded in performing the first function (though there must have been moments during the Democrats' epic 103-ballot struggle of 1924 when it looked as if everyone should have just gone home). And if the *quality* of the candidate is taken into consideration, one can make a rather strong case in support of the view that conventions have worked about as well as any alternative selection-mechanism in Western representative democracies.[31] But they have failed at least twice in this century to perform their second main function: in 1912 supporters of Theodore Roosevelt split the Republican party in half when they refused to concede the propriety of convention mechanisms that led to the renomination of President Taft; and in 1948 a number of Southern Democrats found themselves unwilling to accept a racially liberal platform and the renomination of President Truman. On both occasions the dissenters formed new parties, the earlier of which ensured Taft's crushing defeat, the latter of which hurt Truman only marginally.

Those, however, are only the most dramatic examples of convention failures to rally all elements of the party around its nominees. In every election since 1948 significant segments of one or the other party have repudiated the convention's choice: Adlai Stevenson had Southern party leaders working openly against him in 1952 and 1956, and John Kennedy in 1960 and Lyndon Johnson in 1964 faced similar, if less flagrant, revolts in the South, and in 1964 also Barry Goldwater found his candidacy condemned by important Republican leaders in the East and Midwest.

The difficult and significant question raised by these events is this. Does the convention system itself contain certain basic defects that account for this string of failures adequately to perform its second most important function? Let us be clear as to what the question involves: We are not assuming that adequate performance requires that all elements of the party be enthusiastic in their acceptance of convention decisions, but only that they refrain from actively opposing their party's nominees during the ensuing election campaign.

Even with the question hedged about in this fashion, a reasonable answer would seem to be that a convention can perform its unifying function only so long as victory for the national party takes precedence

[30] V.O. Key, Jr., *Politics, Parties, and Pressure Groups,* 5th ed. (New York: Crowell, 1964), p. 399.
[31] See Gerald Pomper, *Nominating the President* (Evanston: Northwestern University Press, 1963), pp. 9–10.

over other values likely to be held by political leaders—victory in their home states, for example, or dedication to some particular social order. Gerald Pomper has said of his own excellent work on presidential nominations, "One fundamental axiom underlies this study: American national parties are chiefly interested in winning the Presidency."[32] But American national parties scarcely exist as such. It is a commonplace of our politics that the two great parties are each coalitions of fifty state parties. So when state party leaders regard the decisions of a national convention as injurious to the success of their own organizations, they are only too likely to take steps to disassociate themselves from those decisions—that is, from the convention's nominees and platform.

Conventions are not now able—nor have they ever been—to paper over cracks as wide as those that have separated the Northern and Southern wings of the Democratic party during the past two decades—a fact not unconnected with the rise of the Republican party in the South. Nor is it conceivable that any other nominating mechanism would do any better. It would appear, therefore, that the present convention system cannot fairly be said to contain "certain basic defects" which prevent its successfully performing the unifying function. We should have to say, instead, that the internal convulsions of American parties may sometimes impose the kind of strain that *no* party institution could tolerate.

In this connection, finally, we should note that conventions often succeed in forging a greater degree of unity in our highly factionalized parties than anyone has a right to expect. In 1956, for example, Northern Democratic liberals were persuaded in the interests of party unity to accept a weaker civil rights plank than they had wanted, with the result that far fewer Southern leaders campaigned against Stevenson than otherwise would have done. And in 1960, Senator Goldwater successfully convinced a number of disgruntled conservatives that they ought to give full support to Richard Nixon despite his alleged "sellout" to Rockefeller on the platform—a move on Nixon's part, in turn, to head off the incipient disaffection of liberal Republicans. In fact, it is precisely this ability of conventions to create at least the appearance of party unity that gives rise to the oft-heard charge that American parties are "unprincipled."

In pursuance of the two great objectives of selecting candidates and uniting the party behind them, conventions have come to exercise a third notable function, that of serving as a gigantic campaign rally.

As any convention-watcher can testify, substantially more time is spent on rallying than on decision-making during formal proceedings: orator follows orator in stupefying succession to "point with pride" at his own party's achievements and "view with alarm" the ineptitudes of the opposition. Delegates cheer, more or less enthusiastically, for the

---

[32] *Ibid.*, p. 4.

keynoter and one or two grand old men of the party; most of the other pre-nominating speeches they simply ignore. Television viewers and radio listeners are relieved to have newsmen corner important people for interviews while the speeches drone on. The entire business looks to be in imminent danger of turning into an ordeal.

But the convention as campaign rally is not unique in this respect: with rare exceptions, most political rallies do drag on too long, most speeches are boring and repetitive from the spectators' point of view. Still, party notables have to be "recognized" somehow, and free television coverage poses an almost irresistible temptation to convention managers who wish to give maximum exposure to senatorial and gubernatorial candidates facing tough opposition in the fall.

Pomper suggests that the convention functions effectively as a campaign rally. Indeed, he remarks, "it may serve too well. There is a danger that the decision-making purposes of a convention will be subordinated to the demands of party managers and television directors for a 'good show.' "[33] Other observers, however, raise serious questions as to whether the manager and directors are not defeating their own purposes in the attempt to subordinate decision-making to spectacle. For it is a fair presumption that the home audience is far less interested in campaign oratory than it is in the conflict inherent in the convention's decision-making.

In any case, whether effective or not, the convention as campaign rally is directed to two very different audiences: the party faithful, either present or watching at home, and the mass electorate. Party faithful are quite used to the ordeal aspects of a rally and they almost certainly come away from the convention with their fighting spirits raised and their loins girded. But the effects of a campaign rally on the general public are simply unknown, and it seems premature to suppose that convention oratory does actively serve "to reinforce a partisan commitment, or to activate a predisposition to one party."[34]

The question of the convention's function as campaign rally raises related questions about other influences of the mass media upon convention participants and practices.

As we have already noted, a pervasive problem at conventions is the lack of reliable information as to who intends to do what on crucial issues—most notably, the balloting for the presidential nomination. Given the widespread (though not universal) desire of delegates and their leaders to support the winner, that candidate who appears to be close to victory has an immeasurable advantage over his opponents. Delegate polls therefore take on very great significance to all those at the convention who are not irrevocably committed to a par-

---

[33] *Ibid.*, p. 85.

[34] Pomper rightly reports these as the effects of the total election campaign, of which the convention is only one aspect. My own reservations have to do with how much, if any, the convention contributes to the achievement of these effects.

ticular contender. But not all delegate polls will be regarded as reliable, for it has always been the custom for leading candidates to issue optimistic estimates of their strength. When, however, one of the wire services or TV networks reveals its own poll the day of the balloting which shows one candidate clearly ahead of the field, most delegates are likely to accept it as authoritative and act accordingly.

> In 1956 both the AP and UP began rechecking their polls of the Democratic delegates at intervals of a few hours just before the convention and during the opening days, maintaining a running tally that was continuously available . . . both press polls showed Stevenson steadily gaining during Monday and Tuesday; the majority point was reached and passed in the early hours of Wednesday morning. A bandwagon shift then occurred, and Stevenson polled 66 per cent on the first nominating ballot on Thursday.
>
> At Los Angeles in 1960, the developments were not as striking but followed some of the same pattern. . . .[35]

A different but almost equally important news media influence was operative at the 1952 Republican convention. Reporting of an apparent nationwide public consensus in support of Eisenhower over Taft seems to have had a significant impact on numbers of delegates whose personal preferences were clearly for the man they had come to acknowledge as "Mr. Republican" over against the glamorous General of uncertain political views. But in the face of what appeared overwhelming evidence—as reported by the news media—that Eisenhower would be a sure winner in November and Taft a doubtful prospect at best, most delegates not firmly committed to the Senator determined to back Eisenhower—thereby giving him the first-ballot victory that had seemed unattainable only a few days earlier.*

One other related effect of the mass media is the focusing of public attention upon the pre-convention nominating process in a way that lends much greater weight to popular opinion than the actual number of primary election votes would seem to warrant. Television networks especially have contributed to this effect by their dramatic reporting of some of the more important primary contests—Kennedy's 1960 victory in West Virginia, for example, or Goldwater's

---

* Network TV polls appear to have had an even more marked effect on both conventions in 1968. Several days before each opened, delegate polls conducted by the individual networks showed the frontrunner as having gained a majority of pledged votes; and the TV commentators duly reported the nomination as being ("barring some miracle") all wrapped up. Other contenders were thus faced with the practically hopeless task of persuading uncommitted or wavering delegates that there was reason for *not* getting on the frontrunner's bandwagon—when the most respected personalities in network news were telling them nightly that the bandwagon was unstoppable.

[35] Paul T. David, Ralph M. Goldman, Richard C. Bain, *The Politics of National Party Conventions*, revised edition (New York: Random House, 1964), pp. 34–35. Reprinted by permission.

1964 success in California. With the public having been told repeatedly by the media that these were the "decisive" contests of the whole nominating campaign, it would have been at least embarrassing to convention delegates to have turned their backs on the winners in the absence of considerations that the news media would have been willing to convey back to the public with equally dramatic emphasis.

Summarizing, the principal effects of the mass media in connection with national conventions are these four: (1) they greatly magnify the campaign rally potential of national conventions, which in turn appear to be modifying some of their practices to meet the presumed tastes of the television audience; (2) they sharply increase the amount of information available to convention participants as to the relative standing of the candidates, thereby lending important impetus to potential bandwagons; (3) they similarly provide participants with significant information about popular preferences in regard to rival candidates; and (4) they help to create the very preferences they report by focusing public attention on certain pre-convention events and making it appear that one candidate or another is "entitled" to the nomination.

These effects, plus the growing importance of presidential primaries, have led some observers to the view that conventions are becoming obsolescent as decision-making agencies, that their primary purpose even now is to ratify decisions that have effectively been made elsewhere. Certainly there is strong evidence to support this view—especially the increasing frequency of one-ballot nominations. And as Professor Derge has noted, the very need for the convention to serve as a mechanism for party deliberation has decreased with the remarkable advances in our own era in telecommunications and high-speed travel.

> The necessary elements of deliberation have been decentralized and extended over a longer period of time, producing party decisions with more popular control and sober judgment than the convention can hope to provide. In this sense the "open" convention marked by uncertainty, confusion, and hasty decisions is pathological rather than normal. It manifests a breakdown or stalemate in the longer and less spectacular process of reaching consensus within the party through decentralized deliberation. . . .[36]

Yet we should not overlook the fact that "breakdown or stalemate" continues to remain a possibility in the present state of American parties, and that conventions will almost certainly be called on again from time to time to resume their primal task of identifying presidential nominees acceptable to most elements of the party. No other agency, surely, is an even remotely satisfactory substitute for

---

[36] David R. Derge, "Hoosier Republicans in Chicago," in Paul Tillett (ed.), *Inside Politics: The National Conventions, 1960* (Dobbs Ferry: Oceana, 1962), pp. 131–132. Reprinted by permission.

decision-making in a situation in which no one man has been able to demonstrate sufficient popular support or political acumen to have earned immediate "nomination by ratification."

And the other functions of conventions will continue to be vital to our total political system. Party workers must be rallied, public attention must be focussed—in a way the long campaign itself can hardly do—on the momentous electoral choice to be made, the diverse elements of each party must be brought together as effectively as possible in support of their nominees. To these purposes the national convention is admirably suited; these purposes alone would seem to justify its continued existence, while always retaining its capacity to act as an effective decision-making organ when need be.

Changes there will surely be. More equitable apportionment of delegates, more tightly organized procedures, more reliable and effective communications within and between delegations—these are only a few of the more salient reforms that appear to be winning support among party officials as well as non-party observers.[37]

The changes will come as circumstances require, and the convention will adapt itself to whatever needs the party system confronts it with. This is the way of political institutions, those that survive. National conventions look a good bet to survive.

---

[37] Both Pomper and David, in the works cited, have good discussions of possible reforms in the convention system, Chapter 9 and Chapter 16 respectively.

Herbert E. Alexander

11. The Cost of Presidential Elections

DIMENSIONS OF THE PROBLEM

The problems of financing political campaigns are widespread; and few candidates or political committees have found satisfactory ways of meeting the necessary expenses inevitable in competing in a system of free elections.

The implications of the ways in which we finance our politics are many. Affected are: candidates and parties at all levels, from the White House to the courthouse, in both the nominating and electing phases of the electoral process; the two-party system and the structure of each party; candidate recruitment; the decision-making process and public policy at all levels; campaign practices and techniques (which are in turn affected by problems of political finance).

Scores of millions of dollars are needed—and spent—to elect our public officials at all levels of government. Consider the following:

... In 1952, about $140 million was spent on politics at all levels of government. In 1956, the amount rose to perhaps $155 million. In 1960, about $175 million was spent, while in 1964, at least $200 million was expended.

... Over 500,000 public offices, from President to the proverbial dogcatcher, are filled by election, yet Federal and state constitutions contain no provision for the necessary—and costly— campaigns. (And the number of campaigns is even greater considering the large number of primary elections at which candidates are selected to run for office.) So the money must be raised from private sources.

... In some states a campaign for U.S. Senator may cost over 100 times the salary paid during the term of office.

...The annual budgets of the major national party committees, such as the Republican National Committee or the Democratic National Committee, run several million dollars even in non-election years.

...Our electorate is rapidly expanding while the development of the means of communications makes it easier—but also more costly—to carry on political campaigns.

These items add up to an important fact: Money—lots of it—is essential to the smooth conduct of our system of free elections. If one considers how much is spent in this country each year on chewing gum or cosmetics, $200 million is not a lot. It is not a lot if considered as the cost of tuition for the education of the American people on the issues confronting them. True, political campaigns are not always edifying, but they nevertheless contribute mightily to the public dialogue in a democracy.

The items noted above do raise several crucial questions for citizens in a democracy:

...What effect has money on the ideal of equality of opportunity to serve in public office?

...Is the man of little or no wealth disadvantaged in entering public life?

...Can the ill-financed candidate win nomination or election?

...Is the voice of the political contributor—particularly the big contributor—more influential than the voice of the average citizen?

...Can political costs be reduced without damage to our democratic system?

A healthy political system is one which permits the electorate a sufficient opportunity to judge the attitudes, characteristics, opinions, and qualifications of all political candidates. Once elected, public officials should be responsive to the public interest as well as to the interests of constituents.

What happens to these objectives if some qualified persons do not become candidates for lack of sufficient financial support? Or if the public is not given the chance adequately to hear all candidates because the costs of presenting their views are prohibitive for some candidates? Or if a candidate, because of desperate need for campaign funds, becomes beholden to large contributors or special interests?

Focus on the financing of presidential elections—about which most is known—will permit us to point up the many problems of political finance. But it should be remembered these problems are as urgently felt by candidates for public office at other levels as well, though on a smaller scale. But the lesser the office, and the lesser the public interest in it, the lesser the visibility of the candidate on the ballot, the greater is the problem of raising even a few dollars for campaign necessities. Or the money may be easily raised—but from those who seek favors and preferment.

FINANCING PRESIDENTIAL ELECTIONS

A modern presidential campaign is a vast and complex operation, cost-ing many millions of dollars, and is in sharp contrast to the notion of John Quincy Adams that ". . . the Presidency of the United States was an office neither to be sought or declined. To pay money for securing it directly or indirectly, was in my opinion incorrect in principle." In American history, more often the man has sought the office than the office sought the man. Whether campaigning was for nomination or for election, somebody had to pay. Whether campaigning was by torch-light and cider or TV and jet, somebody had to pay.

Today, scores of millions of dollars are needed—and spent—to elect a President of the United States. Consider the following:

... In 1964, the Democratic and Republican parties together spent about $29.2 million for the national campaigns of Lyndon B. Johnson and Barry Goldwater.

... No one knows how much more was spent on behalf of the Johnson-Humphrey and Goldwater-Miller tickets by individuals and committees at the state and local levels.

... The combined national total of almost $30 million reported spent in 1964 for the two major parties presidential campaigns compared with:

$20 million reported spent in 1960
$12 million reported spent in 1956
$11 million reported spent in 1952
$ 7 million reported spent in 1940

Major party national campaign costs in 1964 were 41 cents per voter for the two parties combined for the 70,642,496 votes cast in the presidential election. This compares with roughly 32 cents per vote cast in the 1960 presidential election. A study comparing costs in presidential years 1912–1928 showed that though direct expenditures of the two national committees rose from $2.9 million in 1912 to $7.2 million in 1928, the cost per presidential vote cast remained between 19 and 20 cents—at the same time that the price level rose 40 per cent. Costs in 1952 were 18 cents per presidential vote cast, and in 1956, 19 cents.

Yet historic trends may deceive. Over $15 million was reported spent in the Republican campaign of 1936 when the electorate was much smaller and the dollar was worth much more. The election of 1936 was probably the costliest presidential election before 1964.

The expansion of the electorate and the popularizing of the Presi-dency have greatly increased the costs of campaigning for it, and fund-raising has not often kept pace. The general price level rise accounts only partially for the rise in costs. Clearly, the introduction of new cam-paign techniques, the vastness of the presidential constituency, the increase in our population, and the high stakes involved in success give assurance that costs will continue to be high.

CURRENT SOURCES

In 1964, the Republicans at the national level raised $18.5 million, over $7 million more than was raised in 1960; the Democrats reported receipts totaling over $11 million, or $4 million more than in 1960. Major sources of Republicans funds in 1964 are shown in Table 3:

TABLE 3. REPUBLICAN NATIONAL AND CAMPAIGN INCOME SOURCES OF FUNDS, 1964
(Rounded to Nearest Hundred)

Source	Amount	%
Direct Mail	$ 5,815,100	32.4
State Payments	2,710,100	15.1
Dinners	2,476,800	13.8
Associates ($1,000 or more contributors)	2,171,700	12.1
TV Appeals	2,458,900	13.7
Special Events	1,058,900	5.9
Miscellaneous	807,700	4.5
Raised by Congressional Committee	448,700	2.5
Total	$17,948,000	100%

The financial base of Democratic support in 1964 differed from that of the Republicans. No comparable table of Democratic source is available for 1964, but their base was comprised mostly of a wide geographic and occupational diversity of large contributors. About 69 per cent of the dollar value of total individual contributions came in sums of $500 and over. Compared with the Republican financial base, which included unparalleled numbers of small contributors, the Democratic base was narrow indeed and can be considered broad only in relation to times past when there were only a handful of very large contributors who financed campaigns; and only in relation to the Republicans' smaller number of large contributors.

Despite the seeming Republican advantage in raising money (and in spending it in 1964), the Democrats have never in recent times conducted such a well-financed national campaign. Spurred by the President's Club, which throughout the country had about 4000 members contributing at least $1000 each, they raised more money than ever before, reporting receipts totaling over $11 million, or $4 million more than in 1960. While the Republicans had a surplus, the Democrats stated there was a deficit of $1 million or more at the national level, a figure that compares favorably with the larger $3.8 million deficit incurred in 1960.

National income for both parties has traditionally been heavily dependent upon large contributions. The percentage of major party campaign funds at the national level contributed by individuals in sums of $500 or more from 1948 to 1964 has varied between 74 and 28 per cent and is more often closer to the higher percentage. In 1948, while Democrats were in power, of total amounts contributed by individuals to selected national-level committees, 69 per cent of dollar value was contributed in sums of $500 or more; in 1956, while Republicans were in power, their proportion was 74 per cent; the Democrats in 1964 were at 69 per cent. The Republican decrease to 28 per cent in 1964 is the lowest percentage yet reached; it is remarkable so much big money in small sums was raised, which must be considered a tribute to their recent quest for small contributors.

Most striking is the long-term growth in Democratic financial support from low points in the presidential elections in 1948 and 1956. From 1960 to 1964 the dollar value of contributions received in sums of $500 increased more than two and one-half times, while total receipts from all sources more than doubled from 1956 to 1964. Significant are the changing bases of Democratic financial support, accentuated in 1964 by the easy willingness of certain businessmen and nominal Republicans to join the President's Club or otherwise contribute to Democratic committees. Of equal importance is the decrease in emphasis on small contributors, on the Democratic National Committee Sustaining Fund and on the national Dollars for Democrats program, subjects to be covered in detail shortly.

By most indices, Republican contributions in sums of $500 and over have notably decreased at the national level since 1956—from contributors of $10,000 or more, from members of 12 prominent families, from leaders of 13 selected groups. This partly results from candidate attraction. Any given candidate attracts certain big donors, for example, as Dwight D. Eisenhower did. But later candidates of the same party do not necessarily attract the same or as many donors. Though the identity of large donors will vary from election to election, there still remains a solid core of large contributors who give to the party regardless of who the presidential candidate may be.

Democrats attract money also because they control the federal government. As will be noted, money tends to go with success at the polls, though 1964 was some exception.

In 1964, data limited largely to the federal level indicate about 10,000 persons made contributions in sums of $500 or more; innumerable others made contributions in these sums at the state and local levels. But of the 10,000, at least 130 made reported gifts aggregating $10,000 or more; 11 individuals (including some husband and wife combinations) each contributed in the aggregate more than $30,000.

One husband and wife combination contributed $61,300 in 1964. Of the 130 persons on the 1964 list, it was found that:

>   ...a hard core of 17 had given an aggregate of $10,000 or more in 1952, 1956, and 1960.
>   ...35 gave $10,000 or more in 1960.
>   ...35 gave $10,000 or more in 1956.
>   ...25 gave $10,000 or more in 1952.

Of the hard core of large contributors who gave $10,000 or more in 1952, 1956, 1960, and 1964, 12 were Republicans, 4 were Democrats, and one switched from Republican to Democrat in 1964. Since 49 of the 130 contributors had given as much previously, about two-thirds of the 1964 list consists of new names in the elite class of political financiers as revealed in Citizens' Research Foundation files. If more state and local data could be obtained for 1964, probably many more than the 130 would have been found to have contributed $10,000 or more, and some of those listed might be shown to have contributed more than indicated.

It was found that in 1964, members of 12 selected families of wealth contributed a total of $603,000, of which $445,000 had been contributed to Republican committees and candidates. The total amounts contributed by members of these families in 1960 and 1964 was only about half as much as they had given in 1956; and increasingly in 1960 and 1964, more money had been given to Democratic committees and candidates from these sources.

In 13 selected professional, business, and other special interest groups, such as the American Bar Association and the United States Chamber of Commerce, officers or directors in 1964 contributed a total of $468,000. Of this amount, $226,000 went to the Democrats, which is a large increase from amounts contributed to them from these same sources in 1956 and 1960. Some individuals in these groups have been found to contribute to both Republicans and Democrats in a single year.

One measure of increasing business attraction to the Democratic party is the case of the Business Council, an elite group of American businessmen and financiers. In 1956, 68 members were found to have contributed a total of $268,000 to Republican candidates and committees, while only four members contributed a total of $4000 to the Democrats. The Democrats did better in 1960, but in 1964 received even more than the Republicans: 33 members contributed $135,000 to Democrats while 36 members contributed only $87,000 to Republicans.

Another measure of business attraction plus the personal factor is the case of the American Petroleum Institute. As a Senator from Texas, Lyndon B. Johnson had many friends in the oil business. In 1956, the Republicans attracted $172,000 from 37 officers and directors of the API, while the Democrats reported none. While the Democrats fared a little better in 1960, in 1964 they prospered as never before: 24 API officials were recorded as making gifts to politics in amounts of $500 or more, with the Republicans getting $48,000 and the Democrats $24,000.

Since the 1930's, both major parties have relied heavily upon expensive fund-raising dinners. Republican net proceeds at the national level for two events, Dinner with Ike and the 1960 Campaign Dinner—both $100-a-plate dinners held simultaneously in numerous cities linked by closed-circuit TV—were slightly over $3 million. From the time President Kennedy took office in January 1961, until his assassination in November 1963, he attended party fund-raising events at which over $11 million gross was raised, mostly in the sale of $100 tickets. During 1964–65, President Johnson attended fund-raising events at which $9.7 million was raised. Some of the large contributions accounted for above were raised at fund-raising dinners or such events as President's Club receptions or dances.

Both major parties also rely upon state party payments; the Republicans have a quota system in which shares are assigned to each state for the financial support of the national party.

Attempts in recent years to broaden the financial base have been stimulated by national party initiative in establishing a Dollars for Democrats program and a Republican Neighbor to Neighbor drive. Local efforts in recruiting sufficient numbers of volunteers to solicit others for money have not been uniformly successful. Where good management and great effort go into them, the programs can be successful. But sometimes the amounts collected at the local level are witheld for use by the local party, and are not shared with state and national committees. Because of only spotty success in collecting and sharing, the amounts reaching the national party for the presidential campaigns have been insufficient. Hence, there is great need for money to be contributed directly to the national presidential campaign.

The Democratic National Committee has had for about a decade a Sustaining Fund program, designed to attract small sums from many individuals to help finance annual operations. Annual dues of $10 entitle a citizen to party membership, to party publications, and such. The program grossed more than $600,000 in 1960, its highest level of income. Thereafter, until 1966, it was permitted to languish and less income has come from this source.

The Republican National Committee in 1962 undertook a similar Sustaining Fund, consisting also of $10-a-year memberships. The program has been pursued with vigor, time, effort, and money, and has been very successful, providing substantial proportions of Republican funds at the national level. The Sustaining Fund grew and developed until in 1964 more than $2.3 million was raised by this means. Sustaining funds are solicited by mail, and in 1964, Republican mailings for the Sustaining Fund and other campaign appeals totaled more than 15 million pieces of literature.

These mailings in all brought in about $5.8 million, accounting in a large part for the remarkable Republican fund-raising success of 1964.

In that year, the Republicans at the national level were able to maintain support from some but not all of their usual sources, but they broadened their appeal dramatically through massive direct mail drives and effective television appeals for funds. Neither method had heretofore been very successful in national fund-raising, but in 1964 the Republicans received an unprecedented 32 per cent of total income from direct mail and almost 14 per cent from TV appeals. Most of these funds came from an outpouring of about 650,000 contributions of less than $100.

The Republican financial achievements of 1964 resulted in part from Goldwater's attraction to certain elements of the population, but also from the Republican mail efforts already described. It was remarkable indeed that so much was raised from so many in view of the widespread belief that Senator Goldwater would not win the election—a condition that usually hinders fund-raising appeals. In addition, some normally Republican sources were closed to Goldwater, and some actually aided the Johnson campaign. The Republicans were the "out" party, usually considered a disadvantage, especially in seeking contributions from special interests. All these detriments suggest that raising big money in small sums for political purposes can be achieved even in adverse circumstances.

The Democrats in 1964 probably spent about half as much as the Republicans on presidential pre- and post-nomination costs. But given their control of the Presidency, the advantages of controlling government forums (such as the White House) that attract media attention, and their favorable poll results, they did not need to spend more. Yet with their national dominance in the Executive and Legislative branches, and other favorable factors, they attracted funds in 1964 far in excess of the Truman, Stevenson, and Kennedy candidacies.

Both parties have been aided in recent years by a nonpartisan American Heritage Foundation—Advertising Council campaign of advertisements and spot announcements urging Americans "to contribute to the party or candidate of your choice." This program, which operated in 1958, 1960, and 1962 was designed to help create a favorable climate for widespread political giving, but solicitation remained a purely partisan matter. The parties have also been aided by labor and business, which have increasingly made possible the collection of political funds at places of work where large numbers of persons can be solicited efficiently.

Labor unions, like corporations, are prohibited by Federal law from using union dues for partisan political purposes. Such funds can be used, and are used, for bipartisan registration and citizenship programs. Many unions also have emphasized voluntary political contributing by rank-and-file members, with funds used directly for partisan political purposes on behalf of candidates whom labor unions endorse.

Corporations are prohibited from contributing for partisan activities, but some corporations have undertaken bipartisan "register, vote, and contribute" drives. The corporate fund-raising drives have usually been conducted with the cooperation of labor unions. A partial list of corporations with bipartisan political contributing programs illustrates the wide variety of companies so far enlisted: Aerojet-General Corporation; American Telephone and Telegraph Company; The Boeing Company; Chase Manhattan Bank; Ford Motor Company; General Electric Company; Hughes Aircraft; Inland Steel Company; Minnesota Mining and Manufacturing Company; Thompson Ramo Woolridge Inc.; Tidewater Oil Company; Union Carbide Corporation; Weyerhauser Company; and Whirlpool Corporation.

The most successful of the corporate bipartisan programs has been that of Aerojet-General Corporation. Since its beginning in 1958, it has grown and developed to the point where as many as 80 per cent of its employees contribute; in 1962, about $97,000 was contributed by about 25,000 employees, for an average of almost $4 per contributor. In 1964, about $136,000 was contributed by about 20,000 employees. Aerojet withholds donated funds from employees' paychecks, if requested, and permits earmarking of funds for campaigns at any level. However successful, this sort of program does not begin to meet the needs for campaigns even in the states in which corporate facilities are located.

HOW MANY GIVE?

About 12 million individuals gave money to some party or candidate at some level in 1964. This represents a remarkable increase from the 3 million contributors in 1952; it is an amazing increase from the handful of contributors at the turn of the century.

Yet these figures are only small percentages of the numbers of actual voters or eligible voters in those years. In 1964, there were over 70 million voters in the presidential election, yet only a fraction of the voters in that year gave to the presidential campaigns. We know that more persons contribute in presidential election years than in other years, but we do not know how many contributions are specifically directed to presidential campaigns. The number of contributions—and the amounts—to the volunteer presidential committees can only be estimated. In 1952, there were about 16,000 Citizens for Eisenhower-Nixon clubs in operation. Some raised and spent only a few dollars, but others raised and spent substantial amounts, which added to money spent by the party committees, totals the amount noted as being needed for presidential campaigns in recent years.

Federal and state elections are held simultaneously, thus handicapping the development of independent fund-raising by the national parties for presidential campaigns. Presidential candidates must compete for political dollars with others running for elective office, usually those running on the same party tickets. The competition for funds has sometimes been brisk for the hitherto scarce political dollars.

Yet polls indicate that many millions of persons say they would contribute $5 to the party or candidate of their choice if asked. In a single year, not more than 20 per cent of the population has been asked to contribute, and not more than 12 per cent has actually contributed.

HOW DO THEY GIVE?

Apart from holding dinners, seeking large contributions and building sustaining funds through mail solicitation, the most that national and state committees can do is to initiate and guide the search for broadly-based funds by local committees. For success, they require the cooperation of local committees to do the actual work of recruiting solicitors and organizing their efforts. If the most effective form of solicitation is personal, then the largest number of personal confrontations can be had only at the local level, where millions of solicitors need to ask their friends and neighbors to contribute. Just as registration and get-out-the-vote drives are organized locally though perhaps coordinated nationally, so must fund raising campaigns. If there are difficulties at the local level in reaching or soliciting whatever potential exists, similar difficulties also militate against the filtering up of funds to the state and national committees.

To be sure, a few local committees—chiefly those with enlightened leadership or without adequate sources of funds—cooperate with national committees and agree to organize their fund-raising efforts on a wide basis, and then channel funds upward in the system. Others— chiefly those with reliable sources of funds—do not cooperate in nationally-inspired drives because local leaders fear such drives will threaten their usual sources or draw off a substantial share of the proceeds.

Many local organizations are little more than clubs for local office-holders, with few financial or policy ties to the national party. Our party system is weighted heavily toward such local party units, each with justifiable concern for immediate needs and little incentive to achieve financial margins large enough to share with higher-level committees. Local leaders are selected through local party processes, not appointed from above, so they normally feel no urgent need to look beyond their immediate constituency. Their attention or cooperation sometimes cannot be bought by either money or federal patronage—they can raise the money they need locally, and federal patronage is not as appealing as is local patronage which really counts to them. Nor do they always recognize the financial needs of higher-level committees or understand why higher-level committees—or they themselves—cannot or should not continue to rely mainly upon traditional sources and large contributions.

Those local leaders who fail to cooperate in national drives to broaden the base do so for a variety of reasons. To solicit broadly, they would need to enlist large corps of fund raisers organized on a block-to-block basis; to reach the whole constituency, they might need to enlist non-regulars, the amateurs who for reasons of party sympathy or candidate enthusiasm would agree to canvass their areas. But the politicians ask: Why take the trouble to raise excess funds for the state and national boys to spend? Can't we better spend our money electing mayors, state legislators, and other officials? Why stir the regulars who may resent the intrusion of outsiders? Why bring in people who are interested more in issues than in jobs, who think in national rather than local terms, who might challenge our control? Moreover, many local leaders are aware that if national committees have sufficient funds to provide more services and monies to senatorial and congressional candidate, the national committees might earn obligations that otherwise would rest with the state and local leaders.

A common sentiment was expressed by Ed Flynn when he wrote that political committees, like businesses, are run on margin; when the margin is large, funds collected locally may be transferred upward. But there are conditions under which local organizations—even those with the best intentioned leadership—find it extremely difficult to solicit broadly or to share funds.

LOCAL PROBLEM AREAS

First, there are one-party areas where the main election contests are between party members in primaries. Despite party dominance, organization is particularly weak because campaigns are built around candidates, each with his own following. Incumbents in such areas tend to build up personal organizations. If they face tough primary fights, they need every dollar for their own campaigns; if they do not have primary fights, there is little incentive to campaign at all—or to raise funds. Moreover, such situations tend to encourage conservative leadership which may be out of step with the state or national party policy. In such cases, dollars are not likely to be forthcoming in large quantities for state or national purposes.

Second, there are rural areas where distance counts—and counts heavily against broadly-based solicitation. Of course, many rural areas are one-party areas as well. In any case, there are not large funds available to filter up within the party structure.

Third, there are urban areas which contain low-income residents, where political dollars are scarce. Other urban areas contain patronage machines of the type described. In many of these areas, the local machines have been challenged by insurgents, as in New York, or by reform movements, as in Philadelphia. Here, primary fights may be the main election contests; both the regulars and the challengers are fighting for their political lives, and funds on both sides are used for the local fracas with little concern for national party needs. Even after one side

wins, cases like this breed bitterness, which reduces organization effectiveness and fund-raising ability.

Fourth, there are numerous hotly-contested two-party areas where
local funds need to be used locally. About 100 congressional districts
are considered marginal, and increasingly one-party domination in others
is being challenged. Where such conditions prevail, even if funds are
solicited broadly, there is not much chance that excess funds will be
available for higher-level committees.

The list of unfavorable conditions is by no means exhausted; some
local organizations may be reluctant or understaffed to take the responsibility for organizing workers and keeping proper books. Money may be
collected locally but improperly reported to state or national committees
so that greater amounts can be retained for local use. There are disputes
over proportions to be kept locally and amounts to be sent to higher-
level committees. Nationally-inspired money drives may interfere with
the dates for registration drives or primary campaigns in some states.
Sometimes the existing cooperation is a result of the lack of support in
national and other party programs and is extended to prove party
loyalty. This occurred in the case of Arkansas, when quota payments to
the Democratic National Committee were in recent years made on time,
but this does not indicate a healthy cooperation.

And a paradox exists; manpower rather than money may be a more
important factor in winning elections, but money is needed in part
because there is not enough manpower; money is needed in part to buy
services that are not volunteered. Yet to raise funds from a broad base
requires manpower not otherwise readily available. It is difficult to
recruit sufficient numbers of solicitors to reach large numbers of persons.
There are over 166,000 election districts in this country; if each party
were to recruit an average of only ten solicitors per district, 3.5 million
solicitors would be required. This number compares with the results of
polls indicating in 1962 about 4.4 million volunteer party workers; in
1964, a presidential election year when interest runs high, there were
more than 6 million volunteers. Even if some of these counted fund
raising as party work, the problem of getting enough volunteers to solicit
and also do other party work is apparent. Though other Gallup polls
have shown as many as 38.6 million adults who signify willingness to
serve as party volunteers, no-where near this number have ever actually
served the parties.

Of course, all the obstacles to mass fund-raising are not always
operative in a given situation. Federal and state elections are not always
concurrent. Nor are some of the described conditions permanent; for
example, the movement to the suburbs should reduce the importance
of unfavorable urban conditions. Local political leadership changes,
too—often for the better, with displays of greater national conscious-
ness and greater party conscientiousness as well. And even when campaign funds are spent exclusively at the local level, benefits redound

to the party at all levels. But water does not run uphill—without a pump.

Conditions of local unwillingness or inability are fairly widespread, sometimes forcing state and national committees to rely upon their limited financial constituencies. Many state committees have in the past been content to live primarily on the monies their annual fund-raising dinners provide, exacting no more from county organizations than the sales of allocated blocs of dinner tickets. Many fail to spend the time and energy needed to prod local organizations into undertaking broadly-based solicitations and providing quota support.

FINANCIAL ORGANIZATION

Fundamental reasons related to the American political system, party structure, and modes of campaigning make especially difficult either a broadening of the financial base or a wider sharing of funds collected at the local level.

America lacks a British-style, party-oriented politics. In Britain, with its centralized party structures, the important functions of fiscal coordination and distribution of money repose on national party committees. British politics is oriented toward these national parties rather than toward particular candidates.

American politics centers around candidates, not parties. Our methods of campaigning, especially since the advent of radio and television, often work to project candidate personality, not always stressing party identification. Money is often contributed to the candidate or his non-party campaign committee rather than to the party. Thus party solicitation, even when undertaken, may find competition for the available dollar.

The American political system is diffused in two ways. Vertically, the parties are composed of layer upon layer of precinct, city, county, congressional districts, and national committee, each layer tending toward autonomy and each commanding individual loyalties—and receiving individual contributions—based upon diverse personal and often parochial social, economic, and political interests. Horizontally, candidates, party and non-party committees, and labor and miscellaneous committees all campaign side by side, sometimes cooperating, sometimes not—but all competing for scarce political dollars.

The relevant problems will become apparent in the exposition of party finance structures which follows. An examination of financial organization cannot but reveal the complexities involved in establishing a dependable channel between the ultimate source of funds at the local level and the pinnacle where funds are needed for the national party.

Republican Party Financing. The Republican practice is to form separate united finance committees to conduct fund drives for the regular operating organizations. At the national level, the Republican National Finance Committee is the central fund-raising agency for the national, senatorial, and congressional committees, though each determines how it will spend or allocate its funds independently. In most states, finance committees are set up independently to supply funds to the state committees. In metropolitan areas, united finance committees have been established, sometimes, as in New York City, in lieu of a state finance committee.

Quota and allocation agreements are made under which the political organizations retain some funds—normally those derived from fund-raising dinners—but the rest are raised, channeled, and allocated through the state or metropolitan finance committees. The finance committees assume some responsibility to help with local financing and allocate funds to pay assessments to the national party.

This system is businesslike, and it helps to avoid multiple solicitation—one source of extreme irritation in political fund-raising. The system relieves politicians of onerous fund-raising tasks by utilizing volunteers headed by large contributors. Money is raised where it is available and spent where it is needed through finance committee allocations to operating party committees. Political fund-raising is rightly considered a year-round, election and non-election year activity, requiring full-time staffs and constant efforts to produce steady and reliable income. The technical skills of professional fund raisers are sometimes employed on a consulting, if not a permanent, basis.

The Republican finance committees are not organized on a neighborhood basis as regular political organizations are. The finance committees are normally divided functionally into a special gifts division to solicit contributions of $500 and over; a women's division to undertake teas, telephone campaigns, et cetera; a business and professional division to comb each industry and profession for funds, and in some areas a membership division to get sustaining funds. But often there is no small gifts division.

The Republican Neighbor-to-Neighbor Program—the small contributions drive—is in effect divorced from the finance committees at the national as well as state levels. Raising small gifts is considered basically a political rather than a finance committee function. This distinction points up the Republican doctrine of financial apartheid. For the top Republican leadership to encourage the solicitation of small gifts requires the cooperation of national and state finance committees, in their role as the sole legitimate fund-raising units, and also the politicians who are needed to help recruit and organize volunteers on the precinct level. But apparently channels of communications between the political and financial hierarchies are not always clear. Thus a successful mass solicitation based upon unified drives, but built around small rather than large contributions, would depend upon a rationalized Republican fund-raising structure more closely integrating the political and finance functions.

The Republican system already requires some degree of integration of financial units—to coordinate fund drives and to get agreements on budgets, quotas, and allocations to needy committees. The system centers responsibility within these identifiable party agencies, but it has been less than successful in cooperating with the operating political agencies.

The establishment of the Republican National Sustaining Fund in 1962 represents a departure from normal Republican practice. For the Sustaining Fund permits the Republican National Committee to develop a source of funds independent of the national quota system; though contributions to the Sustaining Fund are credited to each state's quota, the names of contributors are now being passed on for local use in unified fund-raising campaigns. And the Sustaining Fund thus means duplicate solicitation when names on the national lists are also on local lists. Since only $10 per contributor is being solicited nationally, however, the effect will probably not be great on local unified solicitation campaigns. The Republican Sustaining Fund program originally was carried on as a political function but is now handled by the finance managers.

Clearly, the Republican system requires overcoming the twin frictions that exist on the one hand between the fund raisers and the politicians at the national, state, and local levels.

In 1964, there were special frictions brought about by the nomination of Senator Barry Goldwater. Because Senator Goldwater was not considered by many to be within the mainstream of American politics; a polarization occurred within the Republican party in which Goldwater supporters tended to give directly to Goldwater committees in Washington to avoid normal Republican finance channels wherein funds would be shared with moderate Republican candidates for other offices. Nor were moderate Republicans anxious to have portions of their funds shared with the national campaign of Goldwater, so certain contributors tended to give directly to moderate candidates and not to the party committees.

Following the 1964 defeat, Republicans made new efforts to achieve some semblance of the traditional financial unity in fund raising. Certain Republican leaders openly complained that post-1964 splinter groups of a right-wing or conservative orientation were hurting the Republican party by diluting sources of its income.

Democratic Party Financing. At all levels, Democrats normally raise and disburse funds through regular party committees. Finance sub-committees, comprising party officials and volunteers with access to funds, are responsible for furnishing money, but the party officials directly control finance activities.

Democratic fund-raising has been aptly characterized as frenzied, a condition resulting in large part from the composition of most Democratic financial constituencies, and present dependence upon the sources

in those constituencies. The Democrats in the past could not systematically canvass middle- and high-level industry, business, and professional
elements as the Republicans could. At present, the Democrats solicit
systematically in the areas where Dollars for Democrats programs are
carried on and in higher money brackets where industries, such as
textiles in New York and entertainment in New York and California,
tend to be Democratic. And of course, intense solicitation occurs in
liberal and labor circles as well as in traditional categories, such as
among contractors.

During 1961–64, the Democrats emphasized the President's Club,
galas, and fund-raising events at which the President and Vice-President
spoke, as the major means of raising funds. During the 1964 campaign,
more systematic efforts were made to attract contributions from individuals in industry, business, finance, and the professions, with greater
success than ever before. It remains to be seen how much of this was
newly found Democratic support, how much the attraction of President
Johnson, and how much fear of Barry Goldwater. During 1965 and
until mid-1966, Democratic fund-raising did not keep pace with spending demands, and Democrats claimed throughout this period to have
continuing deficits at the national level. Clearly their failure to court
the small contributor has hurt them and points up the futility of even a
party as solidly in power as the Democrats of trying to depend upon
large contributions in the context of American national politics in the
1960's.

At the national level, the search for money has been especially
frantic. In the aftermath of the 1960 presidential campaign deficit, it
was decided to merge the financial operations of the DNC with the
congressional campaign committees—a practice the Republicans long
had through the RNFC. The DNC agreed to provide $350,000 to the
Democratic Senatorial Campaign Committee (DSCC) and $200,000
to the Democratic Congressional Campaign Committee (DCCC) from
March 1961, through Election Day 1962, and it met the agreement
handsomely. Though the DNC agreed to provide funds, the congressional committees remained autonomous organizations in other respects,
with each spending and allocating funds to candidates independently.
The agreement to merge financial operations represented a major change
in Democratic financing operations.

Agreement was extended through the end of 1966 but then broke
down. Under President Kennedy, separate Congressional dinners were
eliminated and national fund-raising was centralized, with the DNC
responsible for supplying funds to the Capitol Hill committees. Under
President Johnson these committees once again held their annual dinner.
But the DNC continued to supply other funds through 1966 and in
imaginative ways provided important services; for incumbent congressmen, by helping with transportation costs; during the 1964 campaign
by giving candidates for Congress time at the end of paid presidential
broadcasts; by releasing secreted funds in certain states, intended for

use in the presidential campaign; by automating broadcast relay, telephonic, computer, and other facilities for use particularly by freshmen Congressmen. Whereas in the past Senatorial and Congressional Campaign committee disbursements to candidates had been made to bolster the Democratic leadership in each House, sometimes as against a President of the same party, during and after the 1964 campaign, disbursements to candidates increasingly were made with an eye to the interests of the White House; most services were supplied through the DNC and not through the Capitol Hill campaign committees at all. By late 1965, however, there was increasing disenchantment over the arrangements whereby the DNC provided funds to these committees; and there was a dimunition of staff, computer, and other services to the Congressional candidates, caused by lack of funds at the DNC. Tensions developed as the White House sought more control over the distribution of funds to candidates for Congress; indications of a system breakdown became clear in 1966 with the announcement that each committee would raise its own funds, and in 1967 that a new Congressional Finance Committee would be established. The DNC has separately distributed to certain congressional candidates certain money when it is available.

The Democratic finance structure was supplemented by the establishment of a Democratic National Finance Committee (DNFC) early in 1960. Its purpose was to assist party financial operations by building a network of members in each state and territory to aid the efforts of the party chairman, treasurer, and national committee member—in some respects similar to the RNFC structure. Part of the original purpose was to strengthen financial bonds between the National Committee and state committees by providing a more stable party quota system. The success of the quota system, however, depends in large part on the ability and willingness of the state and local organizations to undertake more broadly-based financing, so that ample funds will be available to share with higher-level committees.

The DNFC, in effect, was not much more than a paper organization. During the 1960 campaign, its top leaders solicited actively, but relationships with state groups were loose and often in conflict with political elements. During 1964, it did not function at all. In 1966, there was talk of its revival.

Non-party Committees. Candidates normally establish their own ad hoc campaign committees to appeal independently for funds and votes. These committees are often carry-overs from the nomination campaign when the party normally does not participate. Since the candidate cannot rely upon party funds, even in the election campaign, he must raise funds personally or through his committees—unless he has financial resources of his own.

Sometimes these "temporary" candidate organizations tend to linger on or be revived, as was the case with the Citizens for Eisenhower

(CFE), which in 1954 and 1958 made a logical attempt to elect a Republican Congress to accommodate the President whom the CFE had helped to elect in 1952 and 1956. Following 1964, as noted, some Goldwater organizations sought permanent status. Sometimes such organizations compete successfully for funds and services of volunteers, putting the party units to shame. Sometimes conflict develops in the competition between the professional politicians in the regular party organization and the amateur politicians in the non-party organizations.

In addition, labor unions and management groups enter campaigns, directly or indirectly. Sometimes they campaign independently on behalf of candidates; sometimes by organizing financial support of specific candidates; sometimes in non-partisan corporation drives for funds. Corporations, business or trade associations, and labor organizations are natural financial constituencies because they command ready-made channels of communication capable of reaching large aggregates of voters. Thus they have been used to tap funds and mobilize political energy—in fact, to do the very jobs for which local party units are organized.

Such groups compete for party dollars, although the funds they collect may eventually reach parties or candidates as contributions. In many areas, political solicitation by such groups fills a void because the parties do not attempt to reach small contributors.

Additionally, there are permanent independent political groups with specialties or particular causes. For example, the National Committee for an Effective Congress, the National Committee for a Representative Congress, Americans for Democratic Action, and Americans for Constitutional Action all participate in political campaigns and compete for political dollars.

While it is true that some of these labor, business, and independent groups raise some "emotional" or other funds that otherwise would not be contributed, even if the parties solicited widely, these groups do tend to draw off an undetermined amount of political money as well as contribute to the diffusion of the overall campaign effort.

Non-party groups abound on the Democratic side, reflecting the labor and liberal composition of the party coalition. Republican unified fund drives appear to have reduced the number and effectiveness of non-party appeals, although the Eisenhower, Nixon, and Goldwater organizations raised many millions of dollars.

Party and non-party groups often achieve real cooperation. For example, unusually large expenses, such as television broadcasts, often require joint spending. Joint spending for special purposes is one reason why so many transfers of funds occur among party and non-party committees—money is sent from where it is available to where it is most urgently needed. But conflict often develops as the party and citizens groups find that they cannot work together, and the result may be a Janus-faced campaign monster.

Increasing need for professional campaign operation may eventually reduce the importance of non-party appeals directed by amateurs—although either professionals or amateurs can, if they have the money, hire campaign specialists.

The most far-reaching effect of all this upon the party system, however, is that private economic units or volunteer ad hoc committees are performing functions that rightfully belong to public political units. The parties have failed to undertake their fund-raising functions on a broad basis, which leaves a vacuum that economic interests or interested citizens naturally try to fill.

WHY DO THEY GIVE?

The basic assumption is that an individual seeks gratification of some kind when he participates in politics. Since the giving of money is a form of political participation, it is clear that a direct return, no matter how inconsequential or how unconsciously sought, is gotten from all contributions or their consequences. The gratifications can be summarized in terms of goals. First, there are goals that are extraneous to the party or organization to which the contribution is made. Among these are a belief in the two-party system, a sense of responsibility, a feeling of duty, patriotism, a desire for good government, and a desire to support a candidate out of friendship or non-political motivation. Second, there are goals that result in moving the party or candidate or some faction of the party into power. These consist of such as ideological identification with faction or party, or the belief that the party's or candidate's ascendance to power will in some way create benefits. Third, there are goals that result in moving the actor in various ways within the party. These consist of such as movement into positions of authority in party or government, or movement into contact with those in the high ranks for purposes of power, prestige, or deference. Whatever the motives, it is known that contributors sometimes expect—and sometimes get—some kind of favor or preferment, policy or appointment consideration. Professor Heard has written about the things contributors get as follows:

> . . . What contributors buy is not as tangible as is often supposed. Mostly what they buy is "access." Politicians who get the money, along with solicitors who raise it and contributors themselves, state invariably that in return for his funds a contributor can get, if he seeks it, access to the party, legislative or administrative officials concerned with a matter of interest to him. One lobbyist called it "entree" and another called it "a basis for talking." Access may not give the contributor what he wants, as the number of disgruntled (and talkative) contributors indicates. And if he is eligible for what he wants, a government contract or a job, he will often get it anyway. The main result of access, said a former national treas-

urer noted for his persuasion with the fatter cats, is to "speed things up." The number of cold bargains that are struck for campaign funds are negligible. The real influence derived from big contributions is a latent one, derived through access. This access can be obtained through any sort of political service, and many politicians argue stoutly that campaign work at the right level produces greater influence than money. But large contributors pave a sure road to the decision-making centers of government for those who want to present their case, which is often all they need, and this consequence of our way of financing elections looms as far more significant than the difference in the volume of funds available to the parties.

As another study put it, however, access can be considered to be ". . . indirect evidence of power and influence. On any given issue the gauge of an individual's influence is the extent to which he avails himself of his access to decision-makers or to publics, and on the attention his views receive from those whose opinion or behavior he seeks to change." For those who do seek influence, of course, the giving of money is not the only way to attain it. One may attain influence as a result of faithful party service, or as the result of an intimate relationship with a decision-maker, or on the basis of one's skill or knowledge. One can contribute and not seek influence or access. But money must be recognized as a factor that can act as a good-will agent or catalyst in the direction of political influence and power.

DOES THE MONEY WIN?

That the Democrats were able to win and hold the Presidency from 1932 to 1952 while spending less than the Republicans indicates that money is only one factor among many affecting the outcome of presidential elections. Influences such as the way people vote, the way they think about issues, the personalities and records of candidates, are perhaps more crucial.

Probably the more evenly divided the electorate, as in 1960, the more important money is in providing the extra marginal activity that may affect the outcome of an election. In 1960, the Republicans ended the campaign with a deficit of $700,000, but the Democrats went $3.8 million into debt. Campaign deficits are not unusual in American history—Al Smith's campaign had a $1.5 million deficit, and Wendell Willkie's $900,000. But the 1960 Democratic debt was undoubtedly the largest in history, equalling in amount the extraordinarily large campaign fund Mark Hanna raised for William McKinley in 1896. The Democrats by 1963 were able to pay off the debt, but had they lost in 1960, they would have had a troublesome problem; it took almost four years to pay off the Republican 1960 campaign deficit of $700,000, and no sooner had the deficit been erased than fund-raising began for the 1964 presidential election. In politics there is no let up, for as soon as one election is over, fund raising begins again—to pay off debts or prepare for the next election. The national committees must help finance the Congressional elections in between Presidential elections.

Generally each candidate will try to outspend the other on the assumption that the amount of spending will affect the outcome. But with politics, as with most other enterprises, there is no guarantee against waste and inefficiency. The amount spent does not necessarily have any relationship to the caliber of the campaign or to the discussion of crucial issues or to winning. Campaign spending varies according to the availability of money, the nature of the contest, and the constituency to be reached. For example, a candidate may win because he was able to spend more money, or he may have attracted more money because he is likely to win. The more popular candidate is likely to attract not only more votes but also more money because he is likely to win. The more popular candidate is apt to attract not only more votes but also more money. But there are exceptions, as in the case of Goldwater in 1964. Yet despite raising so much—and spending so much—in 1964, the Republicans lost heavily. Most observers would agree that minimal amounts must be spent in any competitive situation to give the candidate's name prominence and to ensure visibility, even to remind voters of the names of well-known incumbents. But beyond minimal spending, little is known of the marginal increment per dollar or of the differential effectiveness of various campaign techniques.

No amount of spending may overcome certain disabilities such as religion, divorce, color, or other factor—at the polls in given circumstances. On the other hand, the challenger who is running against the well-known incumbent, or the reformer running against the party organization, may not have much chance to win unless he spends heavily. This is especially evident in campaigns for nomination, as the next section indicates.

PRE-NOMINATION FINANCING

The American people seem willing to overlook the accident of birth in electing Franklin D. Roosevelt, Averell Harriman, Nelson A. Rockefeller, and John F. Kennedy. Whatever the merits of a wealthy candidate, he must expect adverse comments regarding his wealth and its impact upon events. This is especially true in pre-nomination campaigns, in which observers consider the impact of money as greater than in general elections. Alexander Heard has written: "Money probably has its greatest impact in the choice of public officials in the shadowland of our politics where it is decided who will be a candidate for a party nomination and who will not . . . the effect of money in politics is probably more certain in determining who the candidates will be than in determining the outcome of elections."

Admitted expenses of campaigns for candidates seeking the Republican presidential nomination in 1964 total $9.6 million, as follows:

Goldwater	$5,500,000
Rockefeller	$3,000,000
Scranton	$ 827,000
Lodge	$ 100,000
Nixon	$ 71,000
Stassen	$ 70,000
Total	$9,568,000

In addition, there were considerable amounts raised and spent at the state and local level in numerous states (excluding California where state and local Goldwater expenses are included in the $9.6 million total, and Oregon where $60,000 are included in the national total), particularly in behalf of Senator Goldwater. And the total does not include the Rockefeller payroll and personal expenses assumed by the candidate and his family. Moreover, the Nixon expenditures are thought to be incomplete, and the campaign of Margaret Chase Smith is not even included. Rarely totaled up are costs borne by supporters such as the 1000 or more Goldwater Gals at the Republican Convention who bought their own costumes at $12.75 each; or by the thousands from far-away states who chartered trains or planes to attend a Washington rally for Goldwater as early as July 4, 1963.

The impact of money is highlighted by comparisons between the personal resources of Senator Kennedy and Senator Humphrey in 1960, or between Governor Rockefeller in 1964 and some of the other Republican candidates for presidential nomination. In 1964, reported estimates of Rockefeller expenditures ranged from $3.5 million to $5 million and more, practically all of it coming from the Rockefeller family. According to close associates, admitted out-of-pocket Rockefeller expenditures were as follows:

New Hampshire	a little under	$ 100,000
New England	another	$ 100,000
(having a bearing on N.H. primary)		
West Virginia		$ 80,000
Oregon		$ 477,135
California	a little over	$2,000,000
New York Office		$ 100,000
(having a bearing on primary campaigns)		
Republican Convention		$ 70,000
	Total	$2,927,135

The California primary was a battle royal, with the Rockefeller and Goldwater camps each spending about $2 million in "go-for-broke" efforts. The primary campaigns in California in 1964 cost almost as much as the entire national pre-nomination campaigns of Dwight D. Eisenhower and Robert A. Taft in 1952.

Yet the 1964 pre-nomination campaign of Governor William W. Scranton of Pennsylvania is revealing because it consisted of campaign activity for only about one month before the Republican Convention, plus some preannouncement maneuvering, yet cost $827,000, divided as follows:

TV-Radio	$245,000
Candidate Travel	110,000
Convention	200,000
Printing	58,000
Polls	12,000
Fund raising	10,500
Hotels	27,000
Miscellaneous	162,425
Total	$827,025

Except in California, Goldwater supporters won by seizing state delegations, not by winning primaries. This was a significant accomplishment for the Goldwater amateurs but perhaps indicates the weakness and vulnerability of many state party organizations. The organization route Goldwater supporters followed has been thought to be cheaper than the primary (media) route, but the Goldwater costs were so high than we must conclude that in modern day campaigning even the organizational route is expensive.

WHERE THE MONEY GOES

A presidential campaign constitutes a vast and arresting spectacle and in its hectic circumstances some inefficiency must be expected. Politicians are often poor business managers. But presidential campaigns suffer from a special malady, brought on by the vastness of the electorate and the high stakes. In effect, a multi-million dollar operation is run by an amazing assemblage of amateurs and professionals, family and friends, specialists, job-seekers, old Washington hands and new faces, party bureaucrats, statesmen and hangers-on. The problem is in part the traditional one of attaching a going pre-convention apparatus to a party structure, and in part one resulting from the decentralized nature of a national campaign carried on simultaneously by party and citizens' committees in fifty states.

The costs of political campaigning fall roughly into four general categories, of which the first is general overhead, including the cost of maintaining campaign headquarters and staff; the second is field activity, which includes meetings, rallies, travel, and other expenses incurred in bringing the candidate into direct contact with the voters; the third is publicity, which means all forms of advertising, literature, and means of communication, including radio and television; and fourth, election day expenses, used mainly to pay election day workers, watchers, for cars and drivers.

The effectiveness of any single category of expenditure has not yet been effectively measured, but many campaign activities are essential. Many people think there is great inefficiency in campaign spending, with each candidate trying to outdo the other. Many people think half the campaign funds spent are wasted, but no one knows which half.

There is no uniformity in patterns of spending. Nationwide and statewide campaign committees may spend one-third or more of their funds on radio and television broadcasts, but local organizations may spend relatively little in those categories but more on newspaper ads, billboards, brochures, and bumper strips. In 1964 at the national level, Republican committees spent over $7.3 million on items identifiable as publicity, including the following: TV and radio time, $4,540,000; TV and radio production, $1,060,000; printing and reproduction, $555,000; printed advertising, $530,000; promotion and campaign supplies, $380,000; motion pictures, $125,000; and outdoor production, $100,000.

Salaries and travel expenses may account for over 20 per cent of total expenditures at the national level, but for less on the state level and even less on the local level. Republicans at the national level in 1964 paid more than $1.5 million in salaries, and spent more than $1.7 million for travel. The Democrats paid $149,000 to the United States Treasury for use of Air Force One and other presidential aircraft in connection with the 1964 campaign.

A campaign headquarters recently prepared a breakdown of what dollars will buy:

One dollar will buy 500 sheets of campaign stationery
Five dollars provides 1000 campaign folders
Ten dollars will get 250 bumper stickers or 100 large campaign buttons
$25 will pay for four days of wire news service
$50 will purchase 250 glossy photos of the candidate

These figures are most meaningful if one realizes that in a presidential campaign many millions of such items may be utilized. For example, in 1964, the Democrats reported using in the presidential campaign 7 million brochures and 4 million posters.

Of the $34.6 million spent on radio and television in 1964, combining networks and stations in primary and general election periods, $12.8 million, or about 37 per cent can be isolated as having been spent on the presidential and vice-presidential contests. A half hour of network television may cost $100,000 for air time alone. At all levels, about 60 per cent of dollars spent in the general election period went for spot announcements of one minute or less, while 40 per cent went for program time. Obviously, program time, in which issues can be spelled out in detail, is not as highly valued as spot announcements. The listener is a captive of a spot, which is over before he can switch stations or turn off the set. Spot announcements permit the candidate to gain name recognition, to identify with an issue or a party, but they do not edify or contribute much to the public dialogue; complex issues cannot be reduced to brief slogans or simple themes. Yet many candidates prefer to spend their normally scarce dollars for spots, and many stations prefer to sell them and not risk longer programs that might lose audiences.

Some radio and television stations sometimes provide limited amounts of time free to candidates and supporters, which they can do on a basis of equal time. The most memorable free time provided by broadcasters occurred in 1960 permitting the four Great Debates between John F. Kennedy and Richard M. Nixon.

There is no average total campaign cost. Rather, there are ranges of costs depending on whether the campaign is in an urban or rural area, whether the campaign is hotly contested, and so on. A campaign for U.S. Senator or Governor may range from $75,000 to more than $1 million; campaigns for the House of Representatives may range from only a few dollars to as much as $250,000; campaigns for state legislature sometimes run as high as twenty to thirty thousand dollars. And so it goes.

Some aspects of modern campaigning would be funny if they did not reveal how serious are some of the problems of surmounting them. The urgent need for money during a campaign is illustrated, for example, by the occasion in 1948 when Harry Truman's train was stranded in Oklahoma for want of funds. It would have been embarrassing for the President of the United States to have hitched his way back to Washington. Fortunately, the Governor of Oklahoma and a leading fund-raiser held a collection party in the President's private car, raising more than enough cash to finance the rest of the trip. As the reader will recall, Harry Truman won the election.

For finance managers, the urgency of needing funds is equalled only by the need for knowledge as to which large contributors to turn to next. Broadcasters and certain others who supply goods or services now demand payment before delivery. Last minute efforts to raise funds for expensive TV programs occur frequently, to the occasional chagrin of all concerned.

Modern campaigns require the skillful mobilization of men, organizations, and money—all designed to help bring the campaign to the people, to attract their attention, and to project the candidates and issues.

Some aspects of modern campaigning may be overdone, and may be thought to be an affront to the dignified and cherished electoral system, but even George Washington found it necessary to make expenditures to one "John Muir for his fiddler."

REGULATION

America is marked by considerable dissatisfaction with present practices, with some evidences of ferment and experimentation and groping for better ways of financing and regulating politics, and some searching for legal and practical remedies for long-standing deficiencies.

Existing federal and state laws relating to political finance are essentially negative in character, containing numerous prohibitions, limitations, and restrictions. Early enactments were designed to remedy or prevent flagrant abuses at a time when political costs were relatively low and funds came from the privileged few or from corporations. Efforts to prevent excessive spending usually took the form of imposing limitations on expenditures. The rationale was that limitations would prevent money from being a dominant factor in elections and would lessen undue advantages of better-financed candidates and parties. Efforts to lessen the degree of candidate dependence upon any one person or interest group usually took the form of imposing limitations on contributions, or prohibiting contributions from certain sources. Legislative enactments both on the federal level and in the states have taken five basic forms:

1. To meet the problems of some candidates having more funds than others and of rising costs, ceilings on expenditures have been imposed. The federal government and 30 states limit the amounts that candidates can spend on campaigns. But such limits are gotten around by the device of establishing independent committees to raise and expend funds on behalf of the candidate. Present federal limitation are $10,000 for a U.S. Senate candidate and $2500 for a U.S. House candidate. By federal law, political committees cannot raise or spend in excess of $3 million.

2. To meet the problems of candidates obligating themselves to certain interests, prohibitions against contributions from certain sources have been enacted, and ceilings imposed on individual contributions. For example, corporations, national banks, and labor unions are prohibited from contributing funds. Corporate executives may contribute out of their own pockets. Labor unions usually establish special committees to collect voluntary contributions from the rank-and-file members for political purposes, and for certain purposes union funds can be used despite the ban. Moreover, federal law limits individuals from contributing more than $5000 to any one federal candidate or committee supporting a federal candidate.

3. To prevent government power being used to solicit contributions, regulations protecting government employees have been legislated. All but top policy-making positions are protected, thus reducing the effects of the "spoils system" and patronage, and making illegal the assessment of government employees.

4. To provide the public, both during and after campaigns, with knowledge of monetary influences upon its elected officials, to increase financial accountability by making secret funds illegal, to increase public confidence in the electoral processes, and to help curb excesses and abuses by increasing political risk for those who would undertake sharp practices, the law has required disclosure and publicity for contributions and expenditures. Federal law, however, does not apply to campaigns for nomination.

5. To prevent domination of the airwaves for partisan purposes, federal law regulating radio and television permits stations to make available free or paid time to a candidate for public office, but other candidates for the same office must be afforded equal opportunity to receive free or buy the same amount of time. The so-called equal time provision applies to candidates of different parties for any office, federal or not, and it applies to candidates of the same party for nomination to any public office.

HISTORICAL DEVELOPMENT

Federal legislation relating to money in politics first took the form of protection against political assessment of federal employees in 1867. This provision was later extended and broadened in the Civil Service Reform Act of 1883 which forbade the solicitation of campaign funds from any federal officer or employee by a fellow officer or employee, or by any other persons on federal premises. A 1907 law prohibited political contributions by national banks and corporations in elections of federal officials. A 1910 Act of Congress, providing for publicity of election campaign receipts and expenditures, was amended in 1911 to require similar pre-election statements and to limit the amounts that could be spent by candidates for the House and Senate. These provisions extended to primary elections and conventions, but provision for this coverage was struck down by the Supreme Court in the *Newberry* decision in 1921. Subsequent court cases, mainly *U. S. vs Classic*, would permit such coverage today, yet Congress has not fully reasserted its power over the nominating phase of the electoral process, and publicity provisions still reflects the *Newberry* decision.

Relevant federal legislation was codified and revised, but not substantially changed, in the Federal Corrupt Practices Act of 1925, which still remains the basic law although amendments were made to some of its provisions in 1944, 1947, and 1948. This act regulates the reporting of receipts and expenditures of political committees that are active in two or more states.

The Hatch Act, enacted in 1939 and amended in 1940, established a $5000 limitation, backed by criminal sanctions, on the size of individual contributions made during a calendar year in connection with a campaign for federal office; the act also put a $3 million limitation on the amount that can be spent by an interstate political committee, to influence or attempt to influence the election of a candidate for federal office. And it put limitations on Senate and House candidates, as noted.

The prohibition against corporate contributions has been complemented by similar ones against contributions by labor unions in both the Smith-Connally Act of 1944 and the Taft-Hartley Act of 1947. Thus it is unlawful either for unions or corporations to make direct contributions or expenditures in any federal election, primary election, political convention, or caucus.

The "equal time" provision became law as part of the Federal Communications Act of 1934; it was suspended for the period of the 1960 presidential election, but only with respect to the presidential and vice-presidential candidates. This permitted the Great Debates between John F. Kennedy and Richard M. Nixon and other free time volunteered by the broadcasting industry to the major party presidential and vice-presidential candidates without incurring broadcasters' obligations to give "equal time" to other than major party candidates for the same offices. Suspension was not renewed in 1964.

In 1959, certain types of news programs were exempted permanently from "equal time" provision, but broadcasters were not relieved of the obligation imposed upon them under the Federal Communications Act to operate in the public interest and to afford reasonable opportunity for the discussion of conflicting views on issues of public importance. Thus appearance by a legally qualified candidate on any (1) *bona fide* newscast, (2) *bona fide* news interview, (3) *bona fide* news documentary (if his appearance is incidental to the subject covered by the news documentary), or (4) on-the-spot coverage of *bona fide* news events (including but not limited to political conventions and incidental activities), are not deemed to be uses of a broadcasting station within the meaning of this provision.

Stations are prohibited from censoring material broadcast by candidates for public office. The charges made for the use of any broadcasting station by candidates cannot exceed the charges made for comparable use of such station for other purposes.

State legislation has followed much the same pattern as the federal. The financial activities of candidates for the United States Senate and House are regulated concurrently by the federal and state governments, or by the states alone: campaign finance for all state and local candidates, parties, and committees is regulated by the states alone. Only certain committees operating in two or more states or for the election of federal officers are beyond the control of the states.

The action by New York in 1883 to prohibit the solicitation of contributions from state employees, and to prevent the levying of political assessments upon office-holders, represents the first state attempt to regulate campaign contributions. Other states followed this same procedure. In 1890, New York passed a publicity law requiring the filing of sworn financial statements by candidates, and again other states followed suit. A California statute of 1893 extended the publicity requirement to political committees, enumerated legitimate and illegitimate expenditures, and limited to a percentage of the salary of the office sought the amount which might be spent on behalf of a candidate. Strong enforcement procedures were enacted in California also in 1893, but the law was repealed and a weaker one enacted in 1907. By 1905, when the National Publicity Law Organization was formed and pressure was brought to bear for federal legislation, fourteen states had some form of campaign finance laws in operation. The demand for prohibition against contributions started about this time, but the prohibitions against labor unions' contributions were not enacted until the 1940's.

In the regulatory pattern there has been an underlying pattern of reliance upon public reporting of campaign contributions and expenditures, based upon the assumed cleansing and policing power of disclosure and publicity. Publicity was designed as a preventive rather than as a punitive measure, and as a supplement to limitations and prohibitions on certain sources of funds.

Only Alaska, Delaware, Georgia, Illinois, Louisiana, Nevada, and Rhode Island do not require public reporting of campaign funds. All other states require some degree of disclosure, as follows:

Thirty-six states require the filing of reports which detail campaign fund receipts; of these,
Thirty-four require reports for both primaries and general elections; Thirty-two require them from both candidates and committees.
Forty-three states require the filing of reports which detail campaign disbursements; of these,
Thirty-eight require reports for both primaries and general elections; Thirty-four require them from both candidates and committees.
However, only thirty-two states require statements from both candidates and committees in connection with both primaries and general elections. Of these, only fifteen states require reports both before and after elections.
Only ten states require filing of reports from both candidates and committees detailing sources of funds and types of expenditures both before and after primary and general elections.
Of eight states requiring reporting by candidates only, five require reports only for primary elections, and four of these only after the primary election has been held.
Of the seven states requiring reporting of disbursements only, three require reports only after the primary election.

Although the history of public reporting of information about campaign funds attests to American faith in the power of publicity, agencies of government receiving such reports are given little responsibility to assume even minimal administrative duties once reports are submitted. This results in an ineffective system of publicity administration.

Disclosure is only a first step; the larger purpose is to inform the public about sources of funds and categories of expenditures, ideally prior to elections so as possibly to influence the conduct of campaigns and even affect voting results.

Limitations did not, perhaps could not, control the level of campaign costs. When political costs increased, few efforts were made to relieve financial pressures in politics. Early reformist clamor led to state assumption of the costs for the conduct of elections, including party primary elections, by paying the bills for election machinery. This major reform was adopted universally by the states, but few states have gone beyond this minimal form of assistance. Of the states that did go further—usually by adopting some form of publicity or voters' pamphlets distributed at state cost to the electorate—most have now repealed such provisions. In recent years, four states have attempted to encourage broader financial support for candidates and parties by enacting tax incentives for political contributions. A few states have adopted other measures to help relieve financial pressures.

Historically, no major reform movement in America centered on problems of money in politics, and few positive statutes attempted to ease the financial plight of candidates and parties. When "macing," or the assessment of government employees, was prohibited, the gap was filled by contributions of corporations; when corporate contributions were prohibited, the gap was filled by wealthy individuals; when contributions by wealthy individuals were restricted, the gap was filled by a miscellany of measures, such as fund-raising dinners. But usually no compensatory or positive measures were adopted to fill a gap after closing off a traditional source of political money, or to replace an undesirable or outmoded practice.

Puerto Rico offers an example of a constructive effort to fill a gap left after a traditional source of political money was closed off. When Puerto Rico undertook to replace its system in which the majority party was financed largely through assessments of government workers, the reduction in revenue was made up for in part by a system of partial government financing. This positive approach in replacing an outmoded practice is not often found among the states.

Publicity has not wholly fulfilled its promise of policing politics, perhaps because disclosure does not in itself ensure publicity. Legislative enactments generally did not face up in positive fashion to the right of the electorate to know who gives, how much, to whom, and for what. Only one state—Oregon—has adopted a publicity mechanism to help the press inform voters of what the reports contain.

Penalties for violations of public reporting statutes—and of limitations and prohibitions and other corrupt practices—are provided in federal and many state laws. But frequently there is no statutory responsibility for enforcement, and procedures to be followed are either not clear or, for political among other reasons, not followed. Loopholes and ways to bypass limitations and restrictions have been found in many loosely-worded statutes.

Corruption and dishonesty have not been serious regulatory problems because bribery, fraudulent voting, personation, and other similar practices were prohibited under the common law and had been regulated at an early date.

In short, existing statutes often hinder or have the effect of inhibiting financial as well as other types of political participation, and they sometimes actually promote unnecessary costs, as in recount elections. Often the laws are unenforced or unenforceable; generally they fail to take into account high campaign costs and new campaign techniques; they have failed to relieve financial pressures on parties and candidates by providing subsidies or other ways for government to provide assistance, as in registration and get-out-the-vote drives; they have failed to provide meaningful encouragement to a broadening of the financial base.

To the extent present laws are negative, unenforced or unenforceable, they invite public cynicism and fail to promote healthy attitudes toward politics, politicians, and political money. To the degree unhealthy attitudes persist, parties and candidates have difficulty in raising necessary funds. To the extent political money is difficult to raise, regulatory problems have persisted. America has not yet demonstrated its ability to break out of this cycle.

PRESIDENTIAL CONCERN

Of our more recent Presidents, Mr. Truman, Mr. Eisenhower, Mr. Kennedy, and Mr. Johnson have publicly expressed concern about the ways money is raised to pay for political campaigns. In 1961, President Kennedy took a major initiative, moreover, by appointing a bipartisan presidential Commission on Campaign Costs; he asked it to recommend ways that the costs of runnning for the Presidency could be reduced, if possible, and ways in which candidates and parties could be helped in meeting the costs that have to be met for effective campaigning. At the time he said:

> Election of the President of the United States is the supreme test of the democratic process in this country. Because the duly nominated candidates of both our national parties must campaign throughout the country, carrying their views to all the nation's voters, there are great financial burdens in conducting Presidential campaigns. To have Presidential candidates dependent on large financial contributions of those with special interests is highly undesirable, especially in these days when the public interest requires basic decisions so essential to our national security and survival. The financial base of our Presidential campaigns must be broadened.

The Commission *Report* was submitted to the President in April 1962. The *Report* was unanimous and was endorsed by the Chairman of the Republican National Committee and the Chairman of the Democratic National Committee. It was also endorsed by former Presidents Truman and Eisenhower, and by Messrs. Nixon, Stevenson, and Dewey—all the living persons in both major parties who had run for President in the last quarter century. President Kennedy accepted the Commission's recommendations, and proposed to Congress several bills to give effect to the Commission *Report*.

The members of the Commission shared beliefs in a strongly organized and effectively functioning two-party system and in the desirability of voluntary, private action wherever such effort is sufficient to meet needs. They wanted to increase public confidence in the ways campaigns are financed, and to instill public respect for the legal system regulating political contributions and expenditures. These basic beliefs led to a series of recommendations designed to improve the climate for political giving and spending.

While major recommendations dealt with improved disclosure and publicity about sources of political money and the ways it is spent, tax credits and deductions for political contributions, political broadcasting, and other matters, it is notable that the Commission's first recommendation was that ways and means be sought to encourage individuals and private organizations to take part in and to make expenditures for voluntary bipartisan political activities, and, where subject to taxation, that the reasonable costs of such activities be declared a deductible expense for tax purposes.

Subsequently, the Internal Revenue Service ruled that business firms could deduct certain impartial or nonpartisan expenses to encourage wider and better informed participation by individuals in national, state, and local elections.

A verbatim summary of the recommendations of the President's Commission on Campaign Costs follows:

While our recommendations are directed toward problems of presidential and vice-presidential campaign finance, in accordance with our charge, our recommendations carry implications for campaigning for other offices. We are aware of the possibility of overemphasis of a presidential campaign to the detriment of congressional, state, and local races, but it is our view that the measures we propose would have a desirable effect on all political fund raising.

We recommend—

1. That individuals and private organizations—including corporations, labor unions, farm organizations, civic societies, and other appropriate groups—be encouraged to take part in and to make expenditures for voluntary bipartisan political activities, and where an individual or organization is subject to taxation, that the reasonable costs of such activities be declared a deductible expense for tax purposes.

2. That for an experimental period extending over two presidential campaigns: Political contributors be given a credit against their Federal income tax of 50 per cent of contributions, up to a maximum of $10 in credits per year;

Contributors be permitted, alternatively, to claim the full amount of their contributions as a deduction from taxable income up to a maximum of $1000 per tax return per year;

The only contributions eligible for these benefits be ones made to the national committee of a party, and to a state political committee designated by such a national committee (provided that no more than one committee per state be designated by a national committee).

3. That an effective system of public disclosure be adopted which requires that the principal sources and uses of money in presidential campaigns be reported to a Registry of Election Finance;

That toward this end periodic reports be submitted by all political parties, committees, and other campaign groups receiving or disbursing as much as $2500 per year, any part of which aided a presidential or vice-presidential candidate for nomination or election;

That such reports show total income and outgo, and itemize contributions that aggregate $250 or more from one source (including purchases of tickets to dinners or other fund-raising events), expenditures of $100 or over and transfers of funds and debts;

That candidates for nomination or election to those offices be required to submit similar reports;

That any individual or family (husband, wife, and dependent children) contributing to the above committees as much as $5000 in the aggregate in a single year, or spending and contributing a combined total of that much on behalf of such a candidate or candidates, shall also submit reports of such disbursements;

That similar reports of both direct or indirect expenditures be required of individuals and groups taking part or spending money in bipartisan political activities as urged in our first recommendation, if such expenditures total $5000 or more in a year; and

That the present meaningless ceilings on individual contributions and on total expenditures by political committees be abolished.

4. That the present equal treatment of corporations and labor unions by Section 610, Title 18, United States Code, that prohibits direct, partisan campaign contributions and expenditures, be maintained and strictly enforced.

5. That all other statutes regulating the financing of political parties and candidates be vigorously enforced.

6. That the political parties take full advantage of opportunities to modernize and increase the effectiveness of their fund-raising practices.

7. That research to increase campaign efficiency and help reduce campaign waste be encouraged among individuals and organizations, public and private.

8. That the Congress provide funds to pay the reasonable and necessary costs of preparing and installing in office new administrations during the "transition" period between the election and inauguration of a new president.

9. That a further temporary suspension of section 315 of the Federal Communications Act be enacted to permit broadcasters to make their facilities available on an equal basis to the nominees of the major political parties for President and Vice-President without the legal compulsion of doing likewise for minor party candidates for those offices.

10. That a nonpartisan White House Conference on Campaign Finance be called by the President of the United States to launch broad solicitation programs by all parties following the adoption of measures to stimulate such giving, such a conference to include representatives designated by the important political parties, as well as representatives from various sectors of political life and the communications media, and to lay the groundwork for further continuing efforts to encourage voluntary, private action in meeting campaign costs.

11. That the several states consider measures similar to those recommended in this report along with others that would help to reduce the costs of campaigning and make it easier for the parties and candidates to meet them, and that the Post Office Department make its change-of-address files available to the parties as well as to election boards as a way of assisting in local registration drives.

12. That, after a trial period with the measures here proposed, the President should provide for another nonpartisan evaluation of presidential campaign finance, and that, if the objectives sought by our proposals have not been realized, study be given to additional measures to achieve them, especially a "matching incentive" system to stimulate party solicitation.

In addition, President Kennedy proposed a registration system, under the terms of which committees undertaking activities affecting candidacies reportable under the law would be required to file official notice of intention to operate. Once registered, they would be required to report periodically. The effectiveness of a registration system would be best ensured if accompanied by the establishment of a Registry of Election Finance, which no state now has.

The Registry would distribute lists of registering committees— and later campaign fund data—to the press, to the parties and to the candidates. It would also have responsibility to receive, examine, tabulate, summarize, publish and preserve data reported under law, and disseminate it both before and after elections.

President Johnson failed to follow through on the Commission recommendations for two years, until he stated his intention in his State of the Union address in January 1966, to make his own proposals to Congress. Meanwhile Congress had passed only item number 8, providing for federal assumption of transition costs from Election Day until Inauguration Day.

In May 1966, President Johnson submitted to the Congress specific proposals, in some ways stronger, in other ways weaker, than those proposed by President Kennedy, as based on the Commission recommendations. The Johnson proposals were broader in scope than the Kennedy ones, for they applied to all federal offices (including campaigns for U.S. Senate and House of Representatives) whereas the President's Commission was limited in jurisdiction to presidential and vice-presidential elections; and at some points they applied broadly to primary elections and to state and local elections. But they failed to require a central depository to receive and audit the reports.

While the Johnson proposals were not faultless, they did lead off a series of legislative events in which the Congress began to bestir itself into adopting statutes to remedy and improve the ways we finance our politics.

First, after years of dormancy, the House Subcommittee on Elections undertook to report out a meaningful bill, in many ways improved from the Johnson proposals, particularly by the provision for a bipartisan Federal Elections Commission with strong powers to receive, audit, and publicize campaign fund reports; at first a similar Senate Subcommittee balked at moving ahead. Then, the following year, President Johnson made new proposals that curiously were weaker than the ones the House Subcommittee proposed, because the reports would be filed as at present with the Clerk of the House and the Secretary of the Senate, and without strong powers of administration. This time the tables were reversed: The Senate passed the weaker bill, without the Federal Elections Commission, though it was nevertheless an improvement over existing law; but the Committee on House Administration then balked at reporting out the strong Subcommittee bill. These efforts came to naught in 1968.

Meanwhile, the Congress took two other significant actions, both on its own initiative and without White House prodding. In March 1966, both Houses passed as an amendment to a tax bill a provision that unequivocally and completely outlawed tax deductions for corporate advertisements in program books sponsored by political committees; despite the federal prohibition of contributions to political activities by corporations, the practice had developed under which corporations bought advertising space in political program books designed mainly for the purpose of selling such advertising at expensive rates to corporations, and using the "profit" for political purposes, while the corporations were allowed to claim the cost of the ads as regular tax-deductible business expenses.

Then in late 1966, the Congress unexpectedly passed, also as an amendment to another bill, a tax check-off subsidy plan applicable to general election campaigns for President. Despite mounting public,

Presidential and Congressional support for tax incentives for political contributions, their adoption at the federal level had continually met resistance. To everyone's surprise, without any visible support of the public, the press, or opinion leaders, the subsidy amendment passed on the last day of the Second Session of the 89th Congress. The surprise was the greater because subsidies had often been proposed in this country as a means of easing financial pressures in politics, but had not received very widespread support.

The act provided for the creation of a Presidential Election Campaign Fund from which federal payments would be made directly to political parties, under differing formulas for major and minor parties, for reimbursement of their Presidential campaign expenditures. Every taxpayer who filed a federal income tax return which showed the imposition of $1 or more of income tax for the year, could designate that $1 of tax liability be paid into the fund. Married individuals filing joint returns would both be eligible to make this designation. It was estimated that the payments to political parties with respect to the 1968 Presidential election campaigns would approximate $60 million.

The new subsidy received an unfavorable reaction in the media; partly because of the way it passed, as an amendment to an unrelated bill—without consideration by elections or appropriations committees; partly because it was not accompanied by a revision of other laws affecting political finance, but merely added money without achieving reform; partly because of constitutional and practical questions about the plan itself, including the question of fair treatment of minor parties. There were few guidelines as to what expenses could be reimbursed. As enacted, it could have changed the balance of power within the major parties by infusing large sums of money at the top of the party structure, previously dependent to some extent upon state and local funds filtering up to the top. And the advantages this could give to the Presidential wings of the parties could be significant.

Before the subsidy plan had a chance to operate, strong pressures developed for Congressional repeal or modification of the law. The White House appointed a study group to recommend modifications that would strengthen the law, but before these were digested and proposed by the President to the Congress, several Senators undertook to repeal the new subsidy. The Senate occupied itself for six weeks during the Spring of 1967 debating what to do with the new law, and after several reversals—first preserving the law, then seemingly repealing it—finally made the law inoperative but charged the Senate Finance Committee to recommend a new approach. The subsidy law had been on the books only seven months and surely would never be revived in its original form.

By the time the Senate Committee held hearings leading to a new approach, President Johnson sent his proposals supposedly based on the study group recommendations. The Senate Committee on Finance than reported out a new bill, different from both the original law and the White House proposals. This included both tax credits for political contributions and a subsidy formula for both Presidential and Senatorial campaigns. However, while Republicans and Democrats supported the tax credit, no Republicans supported the subsidy provisions. In addition to the lack of bipartisan support, by the time the Committee report was made, pressures on the federal budget and other factors operated to prevent the passage of any new bill.

But the aborted subsidy law and its attendant publicity did help to bring the issue of political finance to the fore and may yet serve as a catalyst to bring pressure for more fundamental reforms. The pressure was evident in the Senate passage of the election reform bill, though as noted, has not yet built up enough steam in the House to assure action on that measure. And beyond those reforms, actual dollar assistance in the form of tax incentives or subsidies or some combination will still be needed.

While the legal framework is important, much must be done privately if political contributing is to become—as it should—as habitual as voting. The effort for a financial breakthrough must be made by the parties and candidates, by individuals, corporations, labor unions, trade associations, civic societies, and other groups.

But legal provisions cannot be wholly successful in the field of political finance. Enforcement has been lax, partly because of lack of respect for the existing system. Many politicians who have been successful under the present system are reluctant to change the rules under which they have won. Also, laxity exists because of partisanship and a reluctance to crack down upon members of one's own party or even of the opposition for fear of retribution when the opposition wins.

American attitudes toward political money are relevant. Some tend to view all politics as "dirty." Some view money in politics as "dirty," or potentially so, because it is sometimes used to "buy" elections, appointments, and influence. On the other hand, there is a growing tendency to regard participation in politics as commendable. A person is recognized as being public-spirited and civic-minded if he takes part in community decisions, or works for a favored party or candidate, or runs for office. If too few contribute, and a number of those who do are well-to-do, many say that their "money talks" and that he who pays the piper calls the tune. Like so many other attitudes toward money in politics, this may be true in some cases, but certainly it is not the whole truth. Other similar generalizations contain only partial truths. The candidate of wealth or the one with most financial support does not always win the nomination. The side with more money in the election does not invariably or even often win. All the money does not come from a few "fat cats," or a few labor unions. And the great majority of politicians cannot be "bought."

CONCLUSION

Since the American party system is characterized by lack of effective leadership control over the process of nomination for public office, problems of political finance are compounded because they are present at both the nomination stage and the general election phase. As noted, the parties came to compete in the political arena without full legal or constitutional status. Campaign abuses brought legislative remedy but mostly of a negative and restrictive kind. Little thought was given to the role of the party in society, and little long-range planning went into proposed remedies. As problems occurred, efforts were made to legislate them away, but in a piecemeal fashion. No comprehensive attack on problems brought about by the role and influence of money in politics occurred. The electoral process generally was not re-shaped to cope with the growth of political parties, nor the expansion of the electorate, nor the high cost of campaigning.

Public concern about the practices and regulation of political finance is not often articulated. One can point to the Report of the President's Commission on Campaign Costs as a model, or to other models, but attempts to adapt and initiate comprehensive model systems cannot readily be found. Florida has had some success with its disclosure and publicity law. Massachusetts is seeking improvement of its public reporting provisions. Oregon finds the publishing of publicity pamphlets useful. Minnesota has pioneered the tax deduction for political contributions and for candidate expenses. But no state has attempted a major overhaul of election law including all facets of disclosure and publicity, limitations, and positive assistance to parties and candidates.

Exposure of political funds to public view need not entail the imposition of complicated restrictions which invite evasion and raise serious constitutional questions. An effective pattern of public reporting can promote public confidence in the party and electoral machinery and contribute toward a more informed and enlightened electorate without infringing upon guaranteed rights or impeding free participation. Legislation should seek to achieve a minimum of inhibition of political activities while shedding a maximum of light upon them—which is now not the case in the U.S.

Publicity has a value quite apart from limitations on expenditures. It can help to enforce legal limitations upon amounts contributed or spent; but its power is independent and in principle, willingness to make public disclosure may well prove to be the best test of a proper maximum limit.

The purposes of publicity are informational and educational, to bring solid news and data about the operation of the American political parties and the political process. The healthy functioning of a democratic form of government rests upon public understanding and broad approval. It is axiomatic that citizens must have access to information about government in all its socioeconomic implications. Ignorance and misinformation about political finance processes hinder efforts to improve the regulatory system, particularly efforts to remove limitations or to provide more forms of direct or indirect governmental assistance to parties and candidates.

Unless new approaches to reporting and governmental assistance and other related laws are found, public officials will continue to be subjected to pressures from special interests, from lobbyists, from large contributors. In American society, such pressures manifest themselves frequently; large contributions tend to reinforce special interest representations, a combination which public officials often find compelling.

The restrictive and inadequate character of most legislation, combined with the lack of enforcement, has done little to raise the standards of American political life, and in fact, may contribute heavily to widespread cynicism toward American politics. The citizens' image of political money as something to be restricted, rather than as an act of political participation to be encouraged, tends to inhibit favorable responses to broadly-based political fund appeals.

The lack of enforcement, combined with public indifference, has another effect: there are few legal cases—other than those dealing with the prohibition of labor union activity—dealing with political finance. The challenge to improve the quality of American political life rests ultimately with the people, but the governmental and party leaderships, and the courts, must share responsibility for manifest failures to date.

Only as political finance becomes better understood, and attitudes toward political finance change, will attempts at its regulation and more salutory management in the political system have a greater chance to succeed. The electorate—indeed all Americans—has responsibilities to that end.

part
five

A COMPARISON

COMPREHENSION of the American political process is enhanced to the degree to which one has the opportunity to compare it with those prevailing in reasonably similar, yet significantly different societies. Thus Chapter 12 provides as benchmarks a description of the political mores of Scandinavia and Great Britain.

Much criticism of American political parties is based upon relevant or non-relevant comparison with parties abroad. The final chapter is addressed to the evaluation of our parties of today.

SVEN GROENNINGS

Sven Groennings studied at Stanford University (A.B. 1956), The Fletcher School of Law and Diplomacy (M.A. 1957), and again at Stanford University (Ph.D. 1962). He was a Woodrow Wilson Fellow, an American-Scandinavian Foundation Fellow, and in 1964 a NCEP Republican National Convention Fellow. In 1968–69 he is serving as a Congressional Fellow of the American Political Science Association.

A member of the faculty of Indiana University since 1962, Groennings teaches primarily about politics in Western Europe. He was the 1964 winner of the Brown Derby Award, presented annually by Sigma Delta Chi to Indiana University's most popular professor. Groennings has been studying political parties and interviewing political leaders in Norway during parts of several years. He is preparing a book on the coalition politics of Norway's non-socialist political parties, is co-editor of *The Study of Coalition Behavior* (1969), and is the compiler of *Scandinavia in Social Science Literature: an English-language Bibliography* (1969).

MARK SPROULE-JONES

Mark Sproule-Jones studied at the London School of Economics (B.Sc. 1964) before coming to the United States on scholarship to specialize in American government and politics. He holds an M.A. (1966) from Indiana University, where he is writing a Ph.D. dissertation on American public employee unions.

Sven Groennings and Mark Sproule-Jones

12. How Others Do It: Britain and Scandinavia

INTRODUCTION

In all democracies the political drama is normally at its height in the election campaigns. It is through elections that we decide who shall govern, and it is through campaigning that the candidates seek the support of the electorate. Most of us are aware that in the United States both the nature of the campaign and the nature of the campaigner have changed with the advent of television. We know also that the style of campaigning varies within the United States, that Democrats in New York City and rural Mississippi, for example, behave differently as campaigners, following different strategies in different political cultures and systems; they campaign according to their environment. Yet campaigners across the United States observe one another and learn from one another. Likewise, other countries learn from us, particularly nowadays with regard to television technique. Perhaps we can learn from other countries; at minimum, by comparing what we do to what others do we can better understand why we do the things we do.

It is perhaps particularly useful to look at what goes on in Britain and the Scandinavian countries, for they have much in common with the United States. They are stable democracies with long traditions of competitive party politics. Also like that of the United States, their political cultures are predominantly secular, rational, pragmatic, and participant; the proportion of the electorate turning out to vote is consistently greater in all of these countries than in the United States. Britain is more like the United States in that it has essentially a two-party system, the main actors being the Labour party and the Conservative party. On the other hand, each of the Scandinavian countries has a multi-party system, and in each case the main parties are similar: Communist (very small except in Finland), Labour (the largest party), Liberal, Agrarian, and Conservative. In Norway, the country we will use as our Scandinavian example, there is also a Protestant religious party, the Christian People's party. In all of these countries, as in the United States, the parties are basically middle-of-the-road; few people would consider it a drastic misfortune should a party other than their favorite win the election. The Labour parties, which are socialist, are all widely accepted democratic parliamentarian, anti-revolutionary, moderate in program, and experienced in governing, led by and large by people not much more radical than Norman Thomas. In each of these countries the Labour party is either a governing party or the largest party of the opposition. For Americans it may be particularly interesting to note the campaign style associated with the Labour parties.

THE CONSTITUTIONAL STAGE

It is the constitutional system itself that largely determines what form campaigning takes. Britain and Scandinavia have unitary systems, not federal systems; fusion of powers, not separation of powers; elections for all the members of parliament at one time, not staggered terms. All power has a national focus, and all power is in parliament. Britain, Denmark, Norway, and Sweden have no separately elected president. Instead, the majority party in parliament names the prime minister, who is the chief executive and who remains in power only as long as he retains the support of the majority in parliament; it follows that members of parliament enjoy influence only as long as their party controls the executive. In this circumstance, there is a payoff to having highly disciplined parties, much more so than in the United States, where a party's congressmen have a local power base, run for office independently of their president, and usually do not all stand together in party blocs when voting in the Congress. In Europe the stakes for winning are so high—all governmental power—that one must be above all a party man; indeed, there is no split-ticket voting. The voter feels that he is always voting for or against a governing party. In effect, the constitutional system dictates that the candidate for parliament campaign on the basis of centrally determined party policies.

There is one significant constitutional way in which the Scandinavian systems differ from the British: they adhere to the principle of proportional representation in awarding parliamentary seats, i.e. a party receives that proportion of seats which corresponds to its share of the total vote, and each district sends several representatives according to this principle. Britain, like the United States, elects one representative per district (constituency). Under proportional representation, however, each party has a chance to win more than one seat per district. Therefore every district party presents a list of candidates. Nominating conventions establish the ranking of these candidates and list them in the preferred order; so, if a party then wins that proportion of votes which will entitle it to three seats, the three candidates whose names appear at the top of that party's list will be sent to parliament. From the standpoint of campaigning, the proportional representation-with-lists system has two effects: the number of candidates campaigning for a seat in parliament on any one district party's list will range from three to a dozen, and the characteristics of the candidates will vary because of the desire of nominating conventions to widen their list's appeal by having it represent a variety of skills and interests. The campaigns are too well managed to give an impression of chaos; nevertheless, the candidates collectively are relatively heterogeneous and numerous. As in all political systems, constitutional provisions affect not only nomination strategy, but also the candidates' campaign behavior and impact.

The timing of elections is quite significant. Whereas in Norway there is no power of dissolution and the parliamentarians may sit snugly in office during the four years between elections, in Britain members of parliament may not enjoy any such luxury. The prime minister may request the dissolution of the House of Commons at any time prior to the expiration of the five year term.[1] Elections may then be held three weeks after dissolution, and are always timed by the prime minister to give the greatest election advantage to his own party. With only weeks in which to prepare and conduct a campaign, a British party cannot fully dismember its campaign machinery. It must be able to revive it on short notice. In effect, the parties campaign at all times. Electioneering is continuous, and the formal campaign period may be considered the climax of this continuous process.

The purpose of the last several paragraphs has been to introduce the relevant differences between the systems and to set the constitutional stage for campaign behavior. In quick review, these European systems are parliamentary, unitary, and characterized by high levels of consensus and voting participation. The parties are quite tightly disciplined, and in each country there is a very strong socialist party. For the Scandinavians we add three closely related complications: multi-party systems, proportional representation, and the list ballot, three factors which cause there to be a great number of candidates. For Britain there is one significant complication, namely that elections may be called at any time.

We turn now to the two main organizational divisions of this paper. First we will consider the process by which one becomes a candidate. Thereafter we will examine the campaign itself, focusing both on the role of the party organization and on the behavior of the candidate. In part we will proceed from the viewpoint of the candidate, exposing you to some of his various sources of concern and headache.

---

[1] The members of the House of Lords—the weak upper House in Britain—are not elected, but succeed either by birth or are appointed by the prime minister.

NOMINATING POLITICS
HOW TO BECOME A CANDIDATE

The first task of any aspirant to elected office is to become a candidate. In the United States one decides to "go into politics" and to "run for office." One usually enters a primary election and, upon winning it, becomes a party's candidate. Nowhere in Europe are there primary elections having the purpose of permitting the voters to select their party's candidates;[2] instead, nominating organizations perform this crucial function. In Britain, one can be quite aggressive in seeking nomination. In Scandinavia, for cultural and institutional-systemic reasons, one cannot be so aggressive; ideally, one should be "pushed into" candidacy. We shall first examine the process in Britain.

While becoming an independent candidate is possible in Britain, it is hardly worthwhile politically because of voter tendency to vote for or against a party government and to vote primarily for his party as such rather than for any particular candidate; indeed he usually votes for the same party throughout his life. Therefore, in order to stand a good chance of being elected, the aspirant should secure a party nomination. Quite obviously, if he is to be nominated, he must develop a nomination strategy, a strategy of action.

The strategy must take into account several considerations: the nearly "continuous electioneering," which affects timing; the provisions of the election law, which affect eligibility; the party's decision-making structure, which may indicate alternative nomination strategies and affect procedure; and the eventual appeal to the people, which will affect the nomination decision. We will first consider the election law.

THE LAW IN GREAT BRITAIN

It is unlikely that the law will offer our aspiring politician any problems in his quest to become a Member of Parliament (M.P.). Any person over 21 years of age who is a citizen, a naturalized citizen, a citizen of a Commonwealth country or a citizen of the Republic of Ireland can offer himself for candidacy unless he is debarred for any one of the following three reasons: First, the candidate must not be a certified lunatic, a deaf mute, a Peer who has not renounced for life his title (and thereby his seat in the House of Lords), a priest in the Established or Roman Catholic Church, a bankrupt or a member of the armed forces. Secondly, he must not be a felon still serving his sentence or a person guilty of election malpractices such as bribery. Finally, he must not hold an office of profit under the Crown; this provision disqualifies most civil servants. In France and Italy, to the contrary, civil servants

---

[2] The primary is an American device developed in an effort to prevent party boss/machine control.

are eligible, frequently are nominated, and constitute major occupational groups in their parliaments.

Rarely would a prospective candidate be disqualified by law. The majority party can, of course, change the nature of the disqualifications if it so pleases. For example, in 1963 the Conservatives changed the law to enable Lord Home to renounce his peerage, thereby making him eligible to seek election to the House of Commons and making it possible for him to become prime minister. Occasionally the disqualifications provoke unintended incidents. In 1962, for example, it was possible for a serviceman to be discharged should he wish to enter an election, and a rush of servicemen decided that this would be the easiest form of "release." At the Colne-Valley and Rotherham by-elections in that year, no fewer than 667 servicemen applied for nomination papers (by-elections are held should an incumbent M.P. resign or die between general elections). The government appointed a panel to interview and decide who were genuine candidates. As a result, only one was discharged, and then, once out, this one changed his mind and did not enter the race after all!

Provided our candidate has not been disqualified, he must present a properly completed nomination paper to an official appointed as "returning officer" for the constituency. A "proper" nomination consists of a number of steps including the submission of papers setting forth, among other things, the names of ten qualified sponsors, and the deposit of about $400 which is returned should the candidate win one-eighth of the votes. The purpose of the deposit is to discourage freak and propaganda candidates, but this discouragement is not always sufficient. A "pop" singer with shoulder-length hair by the name of "Screaming Lord Sutch" has managed to obtain publicity by frequent candidacy at by-elections and in general elections too.

In comparison with many countries and with most American states, the law in Britain is only a minor obstacle. Yet few persons independent of the three major parties run for office, and even fewer are elected. Discounting the Speaker of the House of Commons (who once selected from the body of M.P.'s becomes a strictly neutral chairman of parliamentary proceedings and who usually is not opposed in his constituency when he stands for re-election), only nine persons have been elected to Parliament between January 1950 and October 1966 who have not been first selected by one of the three leading parties. Consequently, it is imperative that our mythical aspirant gain the support of either the Conservatives, Labour, or Liberals. It is to this headache we now turn.

PARTY SELECTION IN GREAT BRITAIN

There are 630 parliamentary constituencies spread over the United Kingdom. There are, on the average, 50,000 eligible voters per constituency (less than one-fifth the number in the average American district). Seats are often redistributed to keep this ratio, occasionally with significant consequences: for example, the 1948 redistribution was the most important single factor in the Labour party's loss of 76 seats in the 1950 election. A candidate can choose to stand for office from any of the 630 constituencies, i.e. he need not have resided in "his" constituency. "Carpetbagging" is the rule rather than the exception and M.P.'s have few if any local connections when they first enter parliament, though the nature of representation is such that M.P.'s must keep at least a home in their respective constituencies.

About two-thirds of the seats are "safe" in the sense that a majority of voters in two-thirds of the constituencies will favor a particular party in every general election; in these districts the personal qualities of candidates count for only a few hundred votes for or against his election. Again, the point to be underscored is that party selection normally is crucial for our aspiring M.P. Because party primaries in the American style do not exist, politicking for nomination involves appealing to key influentials within the party apparatus. Our candidate has to weigh in considerable detail the relative importance of each of the various influences at each stage in the selection process. We will now review those stages of selection.

Application. Both the Conservative and Labour parties require applicants to be party members.[3] This requirement is only a minor burden. In the Labour party, for example, it involves little more than an annual subscription of six shillings (about 80 cents) to a local party or a weekly contribution to your labor union's political fund if it happens to be affiliated with the party. Let us now assume that the membership requirement is fulfilled. From this point the selection processes of the two parties differ. We will therefore adopt two aspirants, one Conservative and one Labour.

Our Conservative aspirant has several options as to how he may submit his name for consideration. He may submit his own name to the local Constituency Association (district party), have it submitted by any other party member, be invited to apply by a local party officer, or be suggested by the vice-chairman of the national party organization. The options suggest procedures. First, he may lobby party members. Such practice is less noticeable than in the Labour party because in the Conservative party a contender may readily submit his own name and

---

[3] Lack of space precludes any discussion of the methods and strategies available to any aspirant to gain the nomination of the Liberal Party. However, it is necessary to point out that Liberal candidates receive only a small fraction of votes in each election (8 per cent in 1966) and an even smaller fraction of seats (2 per cent in 1966). As a result, the number of aspirants per seat is small. The Constituency Associations themselves are small in membership and limited in funds, and they have a large measure of discretion in whom to select. There is very little pre-selection campaigning on behalf of the candidates. The prospective candidate who emerges is usually a dedicated party man. In political attitudes and social background he tends to be very similar to Conservative candidates.

because many Conservatives have an ingrained dislike of politicking. Secondly, he may have his cause advanced by an interest group which will adopt him as a "favorite son": successful contenders tend to be favorably predisposed toward business or farming. Finally, he may seek to have his name placed on the national party's list of possible candidates. This last important option needs elaboration.

The Conservative Headquarters maintains a Standing Advisory Committee on Candidates. This committee, having part-time, amateur membership, keeps a list of Approved Candidates which the local parties are urged to consult. Heading the committee is a full-time professional, the vice-chairman of the party, who can often secure the decisions he desires. Our applicant may apply for a place on "the list." If so, he fills out a form which includes questions on personal data, social class, political and non-political experience and views; and he provides the names of three sponsors. These sponsors must usually be an M.P., a constituency chairman, and a party agent (the coordinator of a constituency's campaign activities). The contender is then interviewed by the vice-chairman and two or three M.P.'s, and if deemed suitable, is recommended along with some others on the list when a constituency is vacant.

In the Labour party, a contender may not submit his own name. He must be formally nominated by one or more of the affiliated organizations of the constituency party (such as trade union branches, cooperative societies, branches of the tiny Cooperative party, or branches of socialist societies), by a ward (precinct) committee or by the party's National Executive Committee, which is the leading decision-making organ for Labour. In addition, he must accept his party's constitution, program, and present policy. Application is the most crucial stage of selection in the Labour party.

Within Labour, one can often secure selection by lobbying. There are informal bodies of members, like the Campaign for Democratic Socialism of the early 1960's which campaigned for adoption of right-wing candidates, and such groups frequently are successful. Also, there are interest groups, in the form of affiliated organizations, which have a formal chance to enter the political arena at its very base. Among these, the trade unions are especially significant. Certain trade unions, along with some socialist societies, originally established the Labour party at the turn of the century. Today, out of a total of some 660 unions with membership reaching almost ten million, 86 affiliate their 5,500,000 members to the party. These unions keep a panel of members they will sponsor if a local party, with permission of the union, wishes to adopt one as its candidate. The unions place an aspirant on their panels if he shows prospective ability (some unions require written examinations and evidence of ability in public speaking) or if they wish to reward a loyal, yet undistinguished member. Union panel listing is a stringent qualification for any hopeful aspirant. Trade union leaders, however, nearly always prefer not to be sponsored as they rarely are able to in-

crease their power by becoming M.P.'s. In close parallel, the Cooperative
party also maintains a parliamentary panel. This party, an offshoot of a
consumers' movement, has affiliated its local parties to local Labour
parties since an agreement in 1927. Provided the Headquarters of the
Labour party agrees, any constituency Labour party can choose a candidate from this panel.

As in the Conservative party, our Labour aspirant may make
application through the national party headquarters, known as Transport House. The National Executive Committee (NEC) has super-
visory powers over the selection of parliamentary candidates, but its
Organizational Sub-Committee actually deals with these matters. Transport House keeps two lists of candidates. List A comprises the names
of persons nominated by national unions and approved by the NEC.
Unless our aspirant possesses the informal qualifications necessary for
sponsorship by a local union to a local party, he is unlikely to be placed
on List A. List B, however, includes names put forward by local parties
for recommendation to others. Before being put on List B, a candidate
is asked to complete a "Candidate's Form of Particulars" which inquires
about length of party service and other personal facts. The inquiry
omits those questions about rank, title and nationality which the Conservatives ask. The contender also gives the names of two well-known
party members as referees and agrees to accept the Rules of the Party.
He is then interviewed by a panel established by the Organizational
Sub-Committee and if successful is recommended to the NEC to be
placed on List B. The NEC rarely objects.

It may appear, at this stage, that seeking placement on Transport
House's Lists is a favorable strategy, but we should note that, as in the
Conservative party, Headquarters' support can be "the kiss of death"
for success at later stages in the selection process. Now let us assume
that our Conservative and Labour aspirants have by some method successfully achieved application, i.e. their names are now on the list of
those to be considered. We approach the next stage.

The short list.   When deadline for applications has passed, special
committees of both local Conservative and local Labour parties draw
up short lists of contenders. From these, the eventual candidate will be
chosen.

In the Conservative party, the initial list of applicants is screened
by a special selection committee appointed by the local constituency
association's executive council. The committee reduces the total number, ranging between 100 for a safe seat and two or three for a hopeless
one, to a shorter list of about ten in the average constituency. The
committee interviews each person in turn and submits a final short list
of three or four to the executive council.

The selection committee is composed of the most active and influential members of the local party. They are skilled in running a political

machine and are rarely challenged in their decisions by other members, for most members are inactive and display strong deference and loyalty to their local leaders and notables. The committee's chairman, who is also the association's presiding officer, is the dominating figure. He usually secures "cooperative" members on the committee, while he also calls and chairs its meetings, prepares its agenda, and communicates with Party Headquarters.

Consequently, if our aspirant appeals successfully to the local chairman, he is within sight of success. The chairman and his loyal supporters demand reliability and loyalty to the national leaders and, if possible, a political ideology that is more consistently right wing than that displayed by the bulk of Conservative voters. So it is that although the national party has for years wanted trade unionists to be selected so as to show the voter that the party is representative of all classes in society, the local associations continue to select candidates of high social position.

In certain constituencies, and especially in the more marginal or "swing" districts, the financial support of a patron or interest group can prove decisive in being placed on the short list. Before 1949, it was even possible for a wealthy aspirant to buy a seat:

> Mr. Macmillan (Party Leader from 1956–1963) was fond of regaling younger members (of Parliament) with an account of a selection committee he attended in the Twenties at which the chairman simply asked each applicant to write his name on a piece of paper together with the amount he was prepared to donate to the association's funds. The highest bidder was adopted forthwith.[4]

Today, stringent party rules limit direct annual contributions to $60 for a selected candidate or $120 by an actual M.P. to his constituency party. Nevertheless, patrons and certain businesses do contribute funds (much is concealed by the party as to sources of income). In 1963, for example, Fisons (producers of chemicals) donated about $6500 to the Conservative Associations in those constituencies in which they had a branch factory, but as far as we can discern these and similar funds are rarely used to promote the selection of a particular contender.

As has been noted previously, the national organs of the Party try to secure the placing of their favorites. The local chairman consults the vice-chairman of the national Conservative party and indicates to him what type of candidate his selection committee is looking for. He may, for instance, stress the need for someone with strong local connections, high social status or even, in some cases, not being Jewish. The national vice-chairman is circumspect about promoting any one man; he will usually proffer the names of ten or so from the List of

---

[4] David Watt, "Picking and Choosing," *The Spectator*, May 1, 1964, p. 573. Quoted in Austin Ranney, *Pathways to Parliament*, (1965), p. 52.

Approved Candidates. The local chairman and his associates are jealous of their local prerogatives.

In the Labour party, it is the local executive committee of the constituency party that compiles the eventual short list. Because of the politicking that has already taken place, this committee has less discretion than its Conservative equivalent. Consequently, they interview an average of twelve aspirants who have succeeded this far and then reduce the number to four or five.

The active party members, as in the Conservatives, have significant control at this stage in the selection process. These activists vary in ideology from constituency to constituency, some being more consistently left-wing and some being more consistently right-wing. However, because an aspirant must have commanded support from a considerable number of members to have reached this stage and because the committee does not like to rule out candidates with a large body of support, the contenders placed on the short list are often persons whose ideological views do not match the views of the activists making up the committee. As a result, this stage is not as crucial for our Labour aspirant as its equivalent is for our Conservative aspirant. On very rare occasions Transport House has exerted pressure on local leaders to remove an undesirable from the short list or to add a special favorite of the national organs, but Transport House has to be extremely careful not to offend local sensibilities. At any rate, it is the more formal selection process to follow that, along with the initial lobbying, largely determines who is to be chosen.

The selection conference. After the short list has been drawn up, the eventual candidate is selected by an appropriate body in each local party. But between these stages, the Labour party differs from the Conservative party in that the list is subject to two intermediate processes.

First, the short list must be submitted to Transport House for validation. This is only a technical procedure to ensure that the nominees possess the formal qualifications of membership and acceptance of party constitution, principles, program policy, and standing-orders.

Secondly, the validated list is then submitted to the General Management Committee of the local party for approval and for fixing the date of the selection conference (itself only a special meeting of the GMC). The GMC is composed of about 100 local members and is similar in political views to the executive committee which compiled the short list. This intervening stage is usually only a formality, but if the short list is not representative of the leading factions in the local party then the GMC may add names. In 1960, for example, in the Welsh constituency of Ebbw Vale, certain members of the local party who were also members of the Mineworkers Union were able to enlarge the list to head off an attempt by members who were also Steelworkers to secure the selection of their "favorite son." Eventually a compromise candidate was selected.

We turn again to the Conservative party. By the time the contenders for a Conservative nomination have reached the stage of the selection conference, they have gone through a rigorous process of screening. All important interests in the local party have been accommodated. From here on, it is a matter of considerable chance whether our mythical aspirant will be selected. Each contender addresses the conference for about fifteen minutes in turn on political and/or personal matters and then is subject to questioning for another fifteen minutes. The best any candidate can do in this short time is to convince the selection conference (which is a special meeting of the local party's executive council) that he is a dependable Conservative. On one occasion, a selection conference did invite its short listed contenders to address a crowd on a street corner to see who was best able to appeal to Labour voters, but this political ingenuity has never been repeated.

The selection conference then names the candidate it wants, and the decision is passed on to a general meeting of the entire meeting of the local party. The members ratify the decision; only very rarely have they been allowed to choose the candidate themselves (doing so would be the closest approximation of an American primary in Britain). The national organs likewise have the right to veto, but this veto has been used only twice since 1945 and only when the selection conference itself was widely divided over its choice.

In the Labour party, the aspirants also speak to the conference for fifteen minutes and answer questions for another fifteen. However, for several reasons this stage is much more important in the Labour party than among the Conservatives.

First, the lobbying that occurred in the nomination stage continues unabated. Our aspirant has to solicit votes from ward committees, affiliated organizations and individual members. All he can offer in return is a favorable political ideology, for no spoils system exists in Britain.

Secondly, there is the complication within the Labour party of having "sponsored" candidates (trade union or cooperative). Each delegate knows who they are and how financial considerations may be important to the local party's funds. Each sponsoring union is limited to a maximum of about $1000 on annual maintenance grants in urban parties and some $1300 in rural parties, as well as a maximum of 80 per cent of the campaign expenditures of the chosen candidate. Perhaps surprisingly, this is not enough to induce the adoption of many union candidates, and the unions are increasingly complaining that many of their nominees are being passed over. Many unions, and especially the Mineworkers, only sponsor candidates for safe seats, for this practice allows them to limit expenditure on campaigns. Between 1945 and 1964, there have been 790 union sponsored candidates, and 80 per cent of these have been elected to Parliament.[5] The Cooperative party is limited to thirty sponsorships and they face much competition for safe seats. In all, only about half of them succeed to Parliament.

Thirdly, Transport House lobbies on occasion for candidates it thinks will strengthen the parliamentary positions of the leaders. Rarely are the central offices successful. In this regard, much depends on the competition for the nomination and whether the person they advocate is nationally renounced (such as a cabinet member who was defeated in a previous election and is looking for a safe seat). Only four times in its history has Transport House been able to place members of its own staff in districts from which they have eventually been elected to Parliament. Our aspirant will have a much better chance of nomination if he can persuade the national organs *not* to advocate his candidature.

Under the impact of these influences, the conference chooses its desired candidate. The nomination is not subject to ratification by the members of the party as happens in the Conservative party. But, unlike the Conservatives, the local party has to send its nomination to Transport House for endorsement. This again is usually only a technical formality, because the National Executive Committee does not have the facilities for investigating every candidate, and it wishes to keep on good terms with the local parties so that a maximum effort may be exerted for the eventual candidate at election time. Since 1945, there have been only ten instances when Transport House has denied locally adopted candidates the right to stand as candidates, and all these cases involved the adoption of candidates considered politically too far left. Even this limited use of the veto has been discriminatory, for ultra-leftists have often been endorsed. Transport House has to weigh the effects of refusal on local parties and, in addition, on other national organs for whom a refusal may be the "last straw" in a political controversy.

Incumbents. Our Labour or Conservative aspirant may have to face the burden of challenging an incumbent M.P. for the nomination. Normally each local party re-adopts the sitting M.P. if he wishes to be re-elected. In usual practice, the incumbent need only indicate this wish and he is re-adopted without question. Consequently, if a constituency has a sitting M.P. who wishes to continue in office, then our aspirant is seriously limited in where to seek nomination. About 90 per cent of the candidates in safe seats are incumbents, and aspirants have to wait for their voluntary retirement before having the opportunity of open competition for nomination. There have been instances, however, when re-adoption has been challenged.

In the Conservative party, incumbents seeking re-adoption have been challenged some thirty times since 1945. In all these cases, the challenge has come from members of the local party and not from the

---

[5] This percentage is inflated by re-elections.

national organs. The national party is unable to deny local re-adoption even if the M.P. has deviated in public from the agreed-on party line (a cardinal sin in British politics!). The constituency party, on the other hand, may be dissatisfied with its M.P. because of some personal failing, because he has failed to "nurse" his constituency in terms of providing adequate local services, or because he has espoused a deviant political viewpoint (often he can win extra esteem from his local party by deviating toward the right). Dissatisfaction is rare, and if the M.P. is both popular and comes from a marginal seat, there is an even greater constraint on the local party. Our aspirant would be foolish to gamble solely on being selected instead of an incumbent.

He would be just as foolish to follow such a strategy within the Labour party. There have been only thirty-two challenges since 1945, and they all originated in either personal failings, inadequate local servicing, or political deviations. When the local party has taken the drastic step of eliminating an incumbent, the national organs have occasionally opposed its decision. Such opposition, however, has resulted only when the local party has challenged an M.P. who has properly followed the *national* political line. In those instances in which the M.P. has deviated from the line of the parliamentary leaders, no opposition has been raised to a refusal of local re-adoption. Unlike the Conservatives, however, there have been five cases in which the national party has expelled an M.P., thereby automatically disqualifying him from re-adoption; expulsion is a drastic power used only with great circumspection. If the local party is strongly united around a deviant M.P., as in the case of colorful renegade Aneurin Bevan and his Ebbw Vale Constituency in the 1950's, the national party will not expel. It will not interfere unless it has a good chance of winning a contest with a local party.

It is an asset of the British system (and in effect a partial compensation for not having an American-style primary), that a capable man faces no residence barrier as he seeks nomination in a district other than the one in which he and an incumbent reside.

Characteristics of the successful. If our contender has been successful through all the stages of party selection, he has overcome the toughest hurdles on the way to parliament. He is now officially known as the Prospective Candidate of the Conservative or Labour party for a particular constituency. He has weighed the necessities and strategies of gaining support of local party members and activists, interest groups and sponsors, and even the national party organs. He has in most cases taken a political position neither too far right nor too far left lest he offend crucial groups within the party. Above all, he has had to show that his attitudes will strengthen his party in the national elections and in the day-to-day business of parliament. He will have become aware that there are more conflicts within the Labour party than within the Conservative party, because within Labour there are perpetual disagreements as to what ought to be the aims of a socialist party. Even if he has encountered disagreements within Labour's ranks, however, the great intensity of our aspirant's feelings and advocacy may have been sufficient to convince fellow members that he has his party at heart. Loyalty will have been the watchword in both parties.

The typical candidate will be male and in his forties, scarcely 5 per cent will be women. Local connections will have helped aspirants in each party, and high social status (in terms of occupation and attendance at a prestigious private school) will probably have been of extremely great value to a Conservative contender. A long record of party, trade union, "Cooperative," or radical devotion, on the other hand, will have been almost a prerequisite for our Labour aspirant. We have some statistics on candidates' occupational background which demonstrate the differences in party orientations. Our statistics are from the the 1964 elections, in which the Conservatives presented a candidate in each of the 630 districts and Labour presented 628. From business occupations came 245 of the Conservatives and 88 of the Labourites; on the other hand, 152 of the Labour candidates and only 11 of the Conservatives were classified as workers. In each party great numbers were drawn from the professions: 272 Conservatives and 268 Labourites. Americans, who elect a greater proportion of lawyers to their legislatures than do any other people, may find it curious that only 99 of the Conservatives and 44 of the Labourites were lawyers.

Our aspirant has now completed his campaign to become his party's candidate, but he has yet to carry on his own and his party's campaign against the other candidate and other party. Although most constituencies are safe for one party or for the other, a candidate still faces the headache of being elected to parliament.

SCANDINAVIAN NOMINATING PRACTICES

As indicated, our Scandinavian example will be Norway, a country not as well-known as Britain to Americans. It has only one-twelfth as many people as Britain and fewer than 2,500,000 eligible voters. Unlike highly urbanized Britain, Norway is a country of small towns and hamlets. Including their suburbs, only five cities have populations exceeding 60,000; in ten of the twenty electoral districts the largest city has less than half that number. In Norway, local newspapers are numerous, and many of the families within a district know one another by reputation. Nevertheless, there is some feeling of isolation, for the topography is rugged and even neighboring towns seem far apart. Where there are few people and everyone reads, it is easy to become known. On the other hand, where people are few and they are far apart in rough terrain, it is difficult for a campaigner to arouse masses. Unlike in Britain, even the outlook of the urbanites is very rural. Geography and settlement patterns will dictate campaign style.

Each of the twenty electoral districts sends from four to thirteen representatives to the 150 member parliament in Oslo. There is, we repeat, a multi-party system with proportional representation and the list ballot. There is extraordinary stability in the share of the vote received by each of the parties; a 5 per cent shift would constitute a "landslide" change. In this situation each party knows its share of the vote, and most of the seats are safe seats. These considerations are crucial in nominating decisions, and they permit very precise calculations.

The nominating process has three stages. First, in the various party locals, there is informal discussion of possible candidates. At the second stage, each community party chapter holds a meeting to select its delegates to the district nomination meeting. At the third stage, this district committee, which may have from a dozen to more than 100 members, selects the candidates. It normally does so without interference from the national party headquarters. The central officers, however, may informally suggest that certain possible candidates might be very useful in parliamentary roles; there is often close exchange of opinions between the local and national levels. Nevertheless, the nominating process is decisively and jealously de-centralized. The procedures are the same for all the major parties.

Each nominating committee knows how many seats its party can hope to win and thus how many of the nominees on its list may be within striking range of a seat in parliament. It may then assign the positions on its list in such a way as to maximize appeal to crucial groups of voters. Among the delegates there may be bargaining and compromising as well as advocacies. The final list will most likely represent a balancing of geography, occupation, age, sex, and political skills. Possibly cultural differences in matters of religion, alcohol, and language also will be represented. The party activists tend to be rewarded, but occasionally people with particular personal appeal and skills will be coopted. It can be decisive to be from a certain important town, to have a particular occupation, to speak the urban language rather than the rural one or vice versa, to be able to balance someone else on the ticket, or perhaps to be attractive to the Young Conservatives or Young Liberals or the trade union affiliates of the Labour party. It is almost always decisive to be an incumbent. It is a marvel of the system that one can nominate an ugly man with useful subject matter competence and leave the most visible campaigning to others on the list. What is crucial, obviously, is to be placed high enough on the list to stand a good chance of being awarded a seat. In such a political system, as in those parts of Britain where there are safe seats, a person with political interests could almost afford to be indifferent to the processes of campaigning and electing if only he could do the nominating!

The lines between the parties are sharp, and candidates can hardly deviate from the policy positions of their parties. To an overwhelming extent, voters vote for the party, not the man. Therefore the painstaking construction and balancing of the party list affects the decisions of very few voters. A survey conducted in one of the country's largest cities at the time of the 1957 elections established that almost half the people could not name a single candidate on the ticket of any party. Yet there were altogether nearly 100 names on the parties' lists, and 83 per cent of the eligible voters did vote.

Norwegian elections offer choices between relatively anonymous parties, not powerful individuals. Political endeavours tend to be viewed not as egotistical games but rather as loyal contributions to party causes. Necrologies frequently proclaim, by way of tribute, that one "has been much used by his party." One who wishes to become a candidate should behave modestly, playing down ambitions. It would be considered brazen were an aspirant to follow the British practice of writing to indicate his availability.

In terms of occupational background, the overwhelming majority of Norway's candidates are functionaries, journalists and editors, teachers and professors, farmers, labor union people, and housewives. At present, there are only four lawyers in the Norwegian parliament. As elsewhere in the western world, politicians have become professional, making life-time careers in politics. The same men campaign in election after election. Between 1945 and 1961, hardly more than 300 individuals occupied the parliament's 150 seats. In Britain's more than 600 districts, the three major parties presented as candidates fewer than 7500 individuals across all the general elections and by-elections from 1918 through 1955. We may say that Britain is a country of veteran campaigners. In Norway the overwhelming majority of the candidates sufficiently high on their parties' lists to stand a chance of winning will likewise be seasoned campaigners.

SOME CRUCIAL QUESTIONS

While we have been quite descriptive in treating stages and strategies, we have intended that our presentation satisfy the reader's curiosity as to what we conceive to be the crucial questions in determining who is to be the candidate and thereby the central campaigner. In our minds the following have been the crucially important questions. What are the prerequisites for nomination? By what processes does nomination occur? Who does the nominating or what is the relative power of the groups involved in the nominating process?

As we turn to the campaign itself, we have in mind another group of questions. How will the campaign be managed? What will be the roles of the candidate, the party bureaucracy, television and other mass media? What will be the relationship of local and national campaigns? What political styles will be appropriate for the candidates and the others involved in the campaign?

THE ELECTION CAMPAIGN

The men who plan campaign strategy in Britain must be able to organize a campaign on short notice. Elections do not have to be held every four years on a specified date as in the United States and Norway. Except when suspended by agreement in wartime, elections must be held at least every five years. Peculiarly, it is the prime minister alone who decides on what date within five years the election will be held. He does not hesitate to fix the date so as to favor the return of his own party with the largest possible majority in parliament. He can even keep concealed the date he has in mind until three weeks before the election takes place. Consequently, his party's election strategy may begin years in advance of the actual date; the opposition parties must also plan ahead and try to guess when the election will be held.

Once our aspirant has gained party nomination, he is enveloped by the electoral strategy of his party. There is little he, individually, can do to secure his election. The parties have been looking ahead at the best ways to appeal to the voters, and so the national strategy and the efforts of the individual candidates are geared to the peculiarities of the British voter.

The typical voter, as we have already stressed, votes for a particular party rather than for a particular candidate. An M.P. who changes his party or who is expelled from one has little chance of being re-elected. As we have already stated, it is thus of the utmost importance that our aspirant gain the nomination of a major party. Personalities do not count in most constituencies. Occasionally the voter will discriminate slightly against Labour left-wingers and Labour women candidates and in favor of Conservative rebels, and occasionally an incumbent M.P. can influence up to 1000 votes in his own favor. Given the number of votes cast for a party within a constituency, however, these exceptions are only important when the fight is evenly matched.

As a rule, voters are strongly guided by their appraisal whether the party they vote for can win locally and nationally and so form the government. This rule about voter motivation suggests that small or new parties will be pushed aside. It is said, however, that every rule has its exceptions. Some exceptions occurred at the time of the rise of the Labour party to the exclusion of the Liberals, but the fledgling Labourites were facilitated by a pact with the Liberals in 1903 not to compete with each other against the Conservatives in the succeeding election. The Liberal party, small today, has indeed been able to win from six to twelve seats in recent elections, but largely because it augments its hard-core vote with defecting Labourites and/or Conservatives. Of course, each of Britain's parties has retained the loyalties of quite a few traditional supporters even when there was little chance of winning. Finally, exceptions to the rule often occur in by-elections because the voters realize that their vote will not determine which party is going to govern, and sense they have greater latitude; indeed, they often use the by-election as a way to protest against the two major parties. It was no doubt in large part because of "by-election irresponsibility" that the Welsh Nationalists won a seat in the summer of 1966.

Taken nationally, there is an almost equal division of voting strength between Labour and Conservatives. No party since 1880 has secured as much as 60 per cent of all the votes cast. We have noted, however, that two-thirds of the seats are safe, and so both major parties gain many surplus votes in these constituencies which, if somehow redistributed, could make significant differences to the outcome of the election nationally. The Labour party won more popular votes than the Conservatives in 1951 and still lost the election due to disproportions in the size of the electorate in varying districts. In 1966, the Liberals averaged 190,000 votes per M.P. elected, while the winning party, Labour, finished with 50,000 votes per M.P.

Persons are rarely induced to switch their support. Changes in government come about through the maturation of new voters, variations in the turnout for the election (ranging between 75 and 90 per cent since 1945), any redistricting between elections, and the decisions of third parties to compete in marginal constituencies. In 1951, for instance, the Labour Government was ousted mainly because the Liberals did not repeat their great effort of 1950 and most of their supporters switched to the Conservative party. The great power of party loyalty at election time is not so surprising when one remembers that almost one in every four voters is a paid-up member of either the Conservative, Labour or Liberal parties.

Class in particular, and, to a lesser extent, age and sex are the most important determinants of party choice. At the moment, the staunchest Conservative supporters are likely to be women over 65 years of age from the wealthiest strata of society. On the other hand, the strongest Labour supporters are men under 25 who are poor and unskilled.

We have depicted the voters in terms of their perspectives, loyalties, and other determinants of voting behavior. It is toward these people that the parties direct their strategy. Compared to American parties, Britain's parties have tended to frame voting appeals intuitively and by traditional methods; they have been tardy in developing appeals based upon inferences from statistical analyses, in utilizing psychological knowledge, and in making the most cost-effective use of the media.

The campaign itself is conducted at two levels, the local and the national level. Our Prospective Candidate takes part in action at the local level, yet it is at the national level that the most important decisions are taken. These national decisions help to establish the party image by which the voters characterize the attributes and deficiencies of the parties competing for their support. The images are, of course, never entirely those the parties would most like. The following remarks made just before the 1966 election are not atypical of the conclusions voters arrive at:

> "Wilson is a crook but he knows it, bless him."
>
> "Wilson. Have you noticed him when he's talking to someone. He don't look them straight in the face. Crafty eyes he's got if you ask me."
>
> "Heath wants to get married. Imagine a Prime Minister going out on dates with his bird (girl friend)."
>
> "The Conservatives are much higher class. Decent living men and all that."
>
> "Grimond's (The Liberal Leader) the only one with any sex appeal. Not that I'm going to vote for him."
>
> "I'll say this for the Labour Party, the libraries are very good. And there's a very nice young lady down there. She got me 3 very nice books this week. How much would they have cost me to buy them?"[6]

The electorate over its years from childhood develops a frame of reference in which to view politics and political parties. The actions of the parties are then fitted into this frame and thereby given meaning. We have already seen that this framework is so strong for each voter in Britain that the parties can indulge in hosts of practices which will not destroy the fierce party loyalty that each voter feels. Consequently, party strategy for winning new votes has the purpose of altering this framework; it must do so in competition with the strategies of other parties and in the face of the often more important non-political forces in society. Thus, for example, television programs that tell of a good society and the importance of changing oneself to change the society may well help that party (in Britain, the Conservatives) which uses a similar theme in appealing to the electorate.

METHODS OF THE BRITISH PARTIES ON THE NATIONAL LEVEL

The next few paragraphs examine the degree of emphasis which the parties place upon policies and platforms and upon advertising through the media as they seek to promote their "images." Both major parties in Britain rely on exposure to their policies and platforms more than on any other strategy of image-building—much more than the effect on the voter warrants. Only within the last ten years have the parties engaged in other public relations techniques. Both parties have overstressed the importance of rational argument on maximizing votes.

---

6 "The Man on the Clapham Omnibus," *The Sunday Times* (London, March 13, 1966), p. 9.

There are three bases for the parties' rational arguments: their long-term party programs, the specific policies they have pursued, and their immediate election manifestoes or platforms. The platform is specifically aimed at the voter, but the voter is more influenced by the other two. In the Labour party, the overall long-term program is determined by the Annual Conference (convention), while the parliamentary leaders have a large measure of discretion about which policies to pursue. In the Conservative party, no formal dichotomy exists between program and policy; the parliamentary leaders have even greater discretion. Both parties establish a platform committee which, with the help of a Research Department, draws up the specific appeal to the voters. Hardly any of the voters are influenced by the parties' platforms.

For several strategic reasons, the government of the day stands a much better change of being re-elected than the opposition has of defeating it. The governing party enjoys legitimacy as the government and can more readily gain the attention of the media; it can promote its own policies and program to the near exclusion of those of the opposition. As a result, the voters tend to know these policies and program, while the other parties, especially if they have been out of power a long time, face a continuous struggle to promote their preferred image. Added to these advantages, the governing party also has the opportunity to promote its leaders as national rather than partisan figures. Thus, for the 1966 election, the Labour party was able to capitalize upon its publication of "White Papers" (proposals of future government legislation) and the successful "fireside-chats" of Wilson as prime minister. The Labour Manifesto, "Time for a Decision," was published very near the election date (itself kept secret by Wilson as long as possible), indeed so late as to pass unnoticed by the average voter. Party literature, including manifestoes, has the sole function of confirming the faith of the already loyal party supporters; it is electorally insignificant.

A second and related method by which the parties promote their images on the national level involves the highly developed techniques of public relations: publicity through advertising, the press and television. The majority party tries to promote the impression of wise past and future policies, and the opposition decries the achievement of the government and puts forward its alternative plan.

Advertising is a relatively modern innovation in British electoral strategy. Until 1957, the parties relied on image promotions through the press, broadcasts, literature, public meetings, and especially word-of-mouth communication. In 1957, however, the Conservative party hired an advertising agency which spent almost $1,500,000 on a national poster and press advertising campaign in the eighteen months prior to the 1959 election. The theme was "You've Never Had It So Good," and it had significant electoral success. The Labour party found such a public relations technique repugnant, not so much because of its concern for undermining the rational behavior of democratic man as because of its tradition of being unfriendly to the world of business and therefore also to its advertising techniques. Labour made a financial profit on the 1959 election, but it lost! In the five years before the 1964 election, however, the Labour party was converted to the necessity of such methods and even exceeded the Conservative party in its use of market research and public relations professionals. The Labour party spent about $900,000 on press advertisements, posters, market research and production costs of their national campaign. The campaign included a slogan, "Let's Go With Labour" with a thumb's-up sign, a series of solid text advertisements aimed at particular groups of voters, posters displaying Wilson's photograph and a short message, and plenty of hard hits at the Conservative government. The advertising was coordinated by a specially appointed publicity officer who drew upon commissioned surveys conducted by a well-known political scientist. The surveys were of uncommitted voters in marginal constituencies.

The Conservative party spent over $250,000 on similar techniques in that two years before the 1964 election, yet they made little use of market research. The advertising campaign had no one theme as in 1959, but stressed the achievements of the party in the previous thirteen years and attacked the Labour alternative. This latter tactic boomeranged as the newer voters could not be influenced by a spectre of a Labour holocaust likewise, business associations and firms were unable to evoke many fears by means of their anti-nationalization advertisement campaign, despite the fact that the steel industry alone contributed $3,500,000 for this purpose. Voters were not stampeded by seeing posters of a frowning beer drinker with the caption "What if they decided to nationalize your pint?" The Conservatives pitched much of their advertising (but with little success) to swing groups such as prosperous workers, housewives, and young people.

Although figures are not yet available, it is apparent that the advertising efforts of 1964 were not repeated on such a scale in 1966. The Labour party, in particular, relied almost solely on its advantage as the incumbent government and its slogan "You Know Labour Government Works." When the advertising campaigns of the two parties are evenly matched in professional preparation, neither party can afford to concentrate on this tactic alone.

Broadcasting, as another method, makes little impact on the result other than increasing turnout on election day.[7] The campaign reaches the voter's screen in three ways. First, the three parties are allowed a

---

[7] The discussion here is of television. Radio broadcasts tend to duplicate the presentations made on TV. Both radio and TV in Britain are national in scope; there are no local stations, although some regional programs are transmitted. Hence, the campaign on the local level, which we will discuss next, includes no broadcasting. In 1964, half the population saw at least one of the party TV programs. About 80 per cent of British homes have television.

certain amount of free time (at present in the ration of 5:5:2 for Conservatives, Labour, and Liberals) based on the number of candidates that the party sponsors in the election. This free time provision is biased against small and growing parties, although the Liberal ration is overgenerous in proportion to the party's national voting strength. These political broadcasts are mainly straight, hard sell party propaganda, which makes few converts but helps arm and encourage the faithful. The parties themselves admit that only the first and last broadcasts are likely to have significant impact. However, if a party needs to make a new leader known, it may be able to establish his profile in the public mind by giving him frequent and depth exposure. Usually the Liberals put on the most polished broadcasts, even though the other parties painstakingly attempt to train politicians in these arts. Both the Conservatives and Labour suffer from having too many senior politicians who consider themselves experts in television presentation. In 1959, however, Harold Macmillan was expertly coached by Edward R. Murrow!

The second way in which the election reaches the voter's screen is through the ordinary news bulletins. Here the voter is often susceptible to image-making. In 1964, Wilson made sure that the early evening news contained something from his daily press conference and that the mid-evening bulletin could include extracts from his main speech that day. On the other hand, Douglas-Home, the Conservative prime minister, planned his campaign without reference to the TV schedules and was often shown at his worst. In 1966, both Wilson and Heath aimed at securing the best possible coverage in these bulletins.

Finally, party images reach the voter through current affairs programs and nightly special campaign reporting. Although no confrontations or debates of the Kennedy-Nixon sort have ever occurred between the leaders of the three parties, in 1966 leading party spokesmen were involved either in interviews or studio discussions. This was a new departure, for the national networks previously felt too constrained by the election law. Any candidate could veto release of an interview or discussion with any of his constituency opponents if he were not provided with and did not accept equal time for presentation of his own views. This new 1966 departure, nevertheless, probably had little effect in actually swaying voters.

Parties also use the press to present their preferred image to the voters. In contrast to the United States but like most other European countries, there are national as well as local newspapers. The overwhelming majority of newspaper readers read the national press. The pattern of election coverage includes front page reports by political correspondents (often based on the daily press conferences held by a prominent party spokesman, usually the party leader), a page or more of campaign news, and a similar amount of constituency or regional reports. The "quality" newspapers also include constituency surveys, statistical analyses of the parties' prospects, and feature articles on the course and tactics of the campaign. Most newspapers have Conservative leanings, but nowadays newspapers tend to limit partisanship to editorials, cartoons, and occasional imbalances in the selection and presentation of news. The partisanship may, of course, boomerang. In 1959, for example, some Labour cartoons cynically portrayed Prime Minister Macmillan as "MacWonder" and even "Supermac"; naturally the Conservatives were quick to utilize these epithets to their own advantage!

But as is true of public opinion polls, newspapers normally have a much greater impact on party leaders and workers than on the electorate. Except for "The Guardian," which has Liberal leanings and whose readers are mostly Conservative supporters, the newspapers all cater to the preferences of the majority of their readers. Like other mass media, the press rarely sways any voters and only succeeds in making the public aware of the coming election.

METHODS OF THE BRITISH PARTIES
ON THE LOCAL LEVEL

The local campaigns are conducted with the prime air of winning the support of the uncommitted voters. Partly because there are so few such voters in Britain and partly because the election law severely limits the expenditures of the candidates, the local campaigns are not as important as the battle on the national scale. Nevertheless, the tactics at this level include various traditional public relations techniques such as political meetings, some more modern ones like advertising, and the occasionally crucial functions of helping to "get-out" the vote.

The national party leaders all make provision for barnstorming meetings throughout the country, but increasingly these local appearances are being concentrated in the marginal constituencies. Moreover, the party leaders are limiting their local speechmaking when either they are not good speakers (for example, Douglas-Home in 1964) or they desire to direct the national campaign from London (as did Wilson in 1966). Public meetings raise the morale of the faithful party workers and have the effect of encouraging them to seek out supporters and get them to the polls; however, they have a minimal impact on the voters themselves. It appears that one of the functions of public meetings is to provide a means whereby the agility of leaders in coping with hecklers may be duly appreciated by the committed party supporters. The 1966 election was no exception:

> QUINTON HOGG (a Conservative leader): "If we buy a picture for the British Museum it is pinched. If we are given the custody of the World (Soccer) Cup someone snatches it away from beneath our noses."

HECKLER: "What about Profumo?"
HOGG: "That gentleman paid a very high price for something which
    some of you have probably done in your lives. What I say is let
    him who is without sin cast the first stone."
HECKLER: "How dare you talk to me like that?"
HOGG: "I exclude you. You're not good looking enough."

When a schoolboy flung a stink-bomb which, shattering, put a sliver
of glass into Wilson's eye, Wilson replied: "a boy who can throw like
that should be in the English cricket team."[8] It is indicative of the
electoral impact of public meetings that the doctor who attended
Wilson's cut eye came to the hall from his home nearby where he
was watching television.

The local press has even less importance electorally The overwhelming majority of local papers are Conservative, and their political
support is manifested in far more ways than in their national counter-
parts. Small in size and staff, few carry sophisticated electoral analyses.
The parties, however, place a large proportion of their advertisements
in the newspapers of the marginal constituencies, and, as we have
already noted, across the years these advertisements may significantly
alter the party image in the eyes of the uncommitted electorate. Often
local advertising attempts to capitalize upon local controversies. Local
issues are of two kinds. The first are those that, originating in nationally proposed policy, have an untypical reaction in a particular
constituency. The second type of issue is generated within a constituency or region and is one which its inhabitants feel can be solved
by one of the national parties. An example of the first type of local
issue arose in the 1964 election, namely whether to substitute comprehensive schools on the American pattern for the system whereby
the brighter students were sent to separate schools. Labour did badly
in Bristol because of this issue, but did well in Liverpool where the
Labour-controlled local councils were embarking on a similar change.
The effects of such issues generally balance themselves out across the
whole country.

The second type of issue, constituency-generated, is more important electorally. The foremost example in recent years was the
colored immigration issue in the 1964 election, in which the "white
backlash" cost Labour three seats. One of these constituencies, Smeth-
wick, swung to the Conservatives by a margin of 20 per cent more
than did adjoining constituencies. In 1966, however, these voters all
returned to the Labour fold, in part because the Labour government
lowered the annual limit on the number of immigrants from colored
countries. In the 1966 election, the issue of prominence in certain
constituencies was the recent abolition of capital punishment. In

___
[8] The quotations were included in Karl E. Meyer's "British Politicians Quip to
Win," Los Angeles Times-Washington Post Service, syndicated in *The Courier
Journal*, Louisville, Kentucky, March 28, 1966, p. A7.

spite of the raucous campaigning of some individual Conservatives, the issue nowhere affected the outcome of the election. Like so many other features of British electioneering, local issues rarely play a significant part in establishing a new government. In fact, although few voters see many substantive differences between the parties, their voting preferences remain remarkably stable.

But why do the candidates not raise local issues for their own advantage? Part of the answer is that the voters perceive elections as contests between national parties; exceptionally, the Liberals have picked up some votes in recent years because of local dissatisfaction. In addition, however, candidates are subject to a legal maximum of election expenses and are obliged, following the election, to submit their financial balance-sheet. The ceiling was set in 1949 at about $1200 per candidate, plus an allowance of two and a half cents an elector in rural constituencies and two cents an elector in urban districts. Candidates are also allowed to spend up to $280 in personal expenses. Most candidates overspend. "Free" services, like printer's bills, are, for example, often paid after the election. Parties do not challenge lest they be caught also. There have been unseatings in the past because of overspending, although in 1964 one elected M.P. was excused. But candidates cannot grossly overspend their limit, and so they cannot indulge in most of the modern public relations techniques.

All three parties make use of party agents, who serve as campaign managers but may almost be better classified as traditional public relations people. These full-time professional party workers are assigned by the national party to individual constituencies. At election time party agents in safe-seat districts take on additional duties in marginal constituencies. The Conservative party has an agent in nearly every constituency, but because of lack of finances there are only some 190 Labour Agents and 80 Liberal ones. Fortunately for Labour and the Liberals, these agents are being increasingly deployed in marginal constituencies. The agents help to coordinate and direct the local organizations in their quest for electoral victory. The organizations aim at securing an up-to-date electoral roster which notes who are their supporters, and which can be checked off on polling day so that laggards may be chased down and taken to the polls in the final hours. Similarly, organizations attempt to secure the names of voters who cannot vote on election day because of sickness or absence from the area so that they can provide them with absentee ballots and postal votes. The parties employ great numbers of volunteers to help fulfill these functions by, if possible, knocking at the door of every eligible voter. Upper-class women, who have free time, are of great help to the Conservatives in this regard, in effect no doubt compensating for the ability of the union leaders to transport groups of their members from the work place to the polls in support of Labour. Although a continuous organization effort is called for and often achieved, much of it is in vain. Apart from elections like that of 1964 in which the outcome was nearly a tie and in which the always better organized Conservatives won nearly twelve seats because of having harnessed more of their postal votes, the impact of the local organization is small. Presumably they stimulate turnout on election day only to a very minor extent.

The campaigning on both local and national levels is generally ineffective unless it has begun some years prior to the actual date and is aimed at the uncommitted voters in marginal constituencies. All three parties are now realizing the importance of these tendencies. However, a rational and expert calculation of actually where to direct party strategy costs money. In that the Conservatives have more money, they have advantages over the other parties, especially as the limits on local expenditures only occasionally affect the ultimate outcome. This Conservative advantage also explains, at least in part, the strenuous efforts by Labour to raise funds from various sources including bingo and other gambling (comprising half the income of the local parties), and increased contributions by affiliated unions. None of the three parties has enjoyed a sufficient income, and financial inadequacies have reinforced the prejudices of the leading politicians in favor of relying on their political intuition. Thus, in 1964, Wilson insisted on controlling overall campaign strategy for the Labour party, and his supporters were often unable to deduce the planned course of action.

The paramount, basic difference in campaigning between Britain and the United States lies in the response of the voter to the maneuvers of the parties and candidates. The British voter is far less susceptible to campaign strategy. Most constituency fights, and in many years the national outcome as well, are decided long before the election date is even announced. Once our mythical aspirant has gained party nomination, he may as well relax. His own efforts in the campaign are hardly ever rewarded, even if he attempts, as some candidates do, to meet most of the voters. The elections are national in scope and, to the extent that their outcomes are determined by campaigning, they are determined at the national level.

SCANDINAVIAN CAMPAIGNING

As in the case in Britain, Scandinavian legislative campaigns are planned principally in the national headquarters, which determines both the election themes and the manner of their presentation. Elections are national in focus, most voters have strong party commitments, and the party candidates play but minor roles in achieving their own election. We will treat the Norwegian example largely in terms of the organization of the campaign at the local level, advertising tactics, and the use of the media at the national level. Norwegian national elections are held every fourth September, the last time in 1965.

Nomination meetings are held during the spring, and interest in the coming elections becomes active around the turn of the year. Membership drives are then accelerated, the number of party meetings increases, and the speculations, assertions, and demands of the party press become steadily livelier. Information campaigns are well under way several months before the election.

In the spring the district parties establish election committees representing as many as possible of the various interests and areas within the district. Next established are sub-committees with limited area responsibility, corresponding perhaps to the school districts. Also named are special committees on campaign finances and on absentee ballots, which are of particularly great importance in a country having a large merchant marine. Other committees are appointed to secure the availability of automobiles to drive voters to the polls. The coordination at the district level is the responsibility of the district party secretary, who, like the British agent, is a paid party official and maintains an office containing district records and rosters. He also serves as a liaison officer for the national headquarters, and is the chief campaign and public relations planner of the district party.

The district parties hold campaign meetings of several kinds, normally at times which do not coincide with the television campaign. Many of these meetings are designed to be small "cozy" get-togethers in homes. A few are evening discussion meetings. In 1965, a Labour party brochure on how to conduct a campaign suggested that there be meetings for various special groups and further suggested that there be coffee and music for older people, films for housewives, and dances for young people. The Labour party holds meetings for union members during coffee breaks or at lunchtime. Prior to the 1965 elections, the Conservative party met with groups of those soon to be released from military service. There has been a general decline of election rallies, the principal exceptions being, in the last election, two immense rallies in Oslo held by the Labour and Conservative parties and featuring top party leaders; such rallies have been a tradition in the Labour party. The appropriate political style for most candidates involves quiet handshaking and attendance at meetings of small groups consisting mainly of party workers and adherents. It does not involve demagogic appeals at mass rallies. Norway has produced very few demagogic or charismatic leaders.

The national headquarters release a great many publications. Platform brochures are distributed widely, but much greater emphasis is placed upon circulation of materials tailored to specific audiences such as seamen or retired people. Most of the parties make a great effort to reach first-time voters. Naturally, greatly disproportionate attention is devoted to the districts in which either a seat is endangered or it may be possible to win an additional seat. Posters and advertisements often have programmatic themes, focusing on such issues as education, pensions, and inflation; otherwise, or in addition, they depict a national leader or the first man on the local party list. Public relations firms assist the parties in composing posters and advertisements. Some parties even send postcards bearing symbols and slogans.

Most of Norway's newspapers are associated with the parties, and the political press aids the campaigns with editorials and advertising. There are full page advertisements; in the Labour papers these are often in striking red. Moreover, the papers publish special campaign issues. The party locals circulate these editions to those whose votes they consider it possible to attract. To avoid wasting expensive copies, party volunteers carefully compose the circulation lists.

The Norwegian party leaders confront one another on television and, simultaneously, on radio. There are series of these confrontations, and they are organized topically. Each party tends to present its member of parliament considered to be the most expert on the topic of the particular evening. Therefore each party has several television figures; all attention is not focused on the one top party leader. Because topographical conditions have limited the spread of television, however, the radio audience is larger than the television audience in most parts of the country.

In the final days of the campaign, as in Britain, there is door-to-door canvassing. In Norway, the party workers usually approach the same door at least twice. First they do so in order to deliver brochures and to talk politics. Later they return to deliver a ballot, which they usually place in an envelope showing the voter's name and address. While this practice may seem strange to modern Americans, the Norwegian, like the Nineteenth Century American, votes by dropping the ballot of the party of his choice into the ballot box. Thus, in the Norwegian system, as in the British system, there is much less emphasis upon the role of the candidate than in the United States.

CONCLUSIONS: PARALLEL TRENDS AND CONTINUING DIFFERENCES IN MODERN DEMOCRACIES

The essential ingredients of campaigning are similar to all democratic systems. It is the emphasis and the style that differ. What affects the style, above all, are the constitutional circumstances and the dimensions of party loyalty. The European countries differ from the United States in being unitary and parliamentary. All power has national focus and there are disciplined national parties. Therefore far more of the campaigning is determined at the national level; and thus there is a lesser role for the individual candidate. Because party loyalties are so very strong, the function of the campaign is in large part to remind the voters of their party identification and to encourage their participation. Having a national press, and in Scandinavia a party press, affects the way in which the parties publicize. Significant differences between Britain and Scandinavia are to be found in nominating practice; these differences may be attributed in large part to variation in the form of ballot. Among the many democracies, those variations in campaigning which stem from constitutional and institutional differences will no doubt endure.

There are, however, some parallel trends. There is increasingly careful preparation for campaigns. There are rising costs associated with increased staffing, increased and more sophisticated advertising, and an accelerating tendency toward computer data processing and support of survey research. In all democracies we are moving into the age of television and of public relations campaigns. The difference between the American and the European systems lies here in the emphasis on what is to be presented for the public's discernment: in the United States, it is more the individual campaigning candidate; in Europe it is more the campaigning party.

CORNELIUS P. COTTER

13. An Evaluation of American Parties

The first chapter raised the question whether we can afford to remain satisfied with a decentralized party system in which party and policy are pretty much divorced, and party government, as understood in parliamentary democracies is not attainable. Implied, but not stated in much of the criticism leveled at the American party system, is the premise that its adequacy can be measured against the standard of the British parliamentary model described in Chapter 12—a system in which "all power has a national focus, and all power is in Parliament."

In one of the superior comparisons of "The Parliamentary and Presidential Systems" yet to see print, Don K. Price has pointed out that the phrase "all power is in Parliament" means for all practical purposes that all power is in the executive, who controls the legislature and the party, using the latter as a disciplining mechanism to keep the former in line.[1] Questions of public policy and party position merge, the only policies considered in the legislature are those which are majority party policies, defined by the party and parliamentary leadership, which is the executive. Each policy proposal introduced in the Commons is the object of monolithic, if frequently *pro forma* opposition by the minority party, and similar support by the controlling party, no matter how contrived or lacking in enthusiasm.

The presidential system, accompanied by federalism, is more free-wheeling. "The United States has a constitutional series of Four Year Plans, during each of which the President can assure his subordinates of a chance to make a record for themselves."[2] Lacking the tradition of a neutral civil service, and the constraint to select his department

---

[1] Public Administration Review 3 (1943) 317–34.
[2] *Ibid.*, p. 325.

heads from the legislature, the President is able to exploit the policy (as distinguished from party) zealousness of the higher echelons of the civil service, and to range freely in business, the professions, the universities in search of top leadership which is likely to produce policies consonant with the President's preferences.

It is true that he is confronted with the problem of selling his policies to an independent legislature where he cannot count upon party votes alone to accomplish his ends. But he is not at the mercy of Congress. Since the Second World War, the concept of the President's legislative program has taken hold, and Presidents of either party consistently have presented coherent packages of policy proposals to Congress, following the presentation with varieties of bargaining activities toward securing enactment.[3] Presidents Truman, Eisenhower, Kennedy, and Johnson have contributed to institutionalizing a legislative liaison function on the White House staff; and the President today has a chief legislative assistant to birddog his program.

The American chief executive is not fastidious in collecting legislative votes for his program. He inclines to take them where he can get them, without regard to party lines. This frequently means that the transitory majority forged to enact one piece of legislation could not have carried the day without votes from the party in opposition to the President. To Eisenhower's initial consternation, it means that there will be significant occasions upon which the President will win or lose with a majority of his party voting against him and a majority of the opposition party supporting him.

Aesthetically lacking as this system of policy adoption may be to the advocates of "responsible party government," it not only works but also may have certain advantages. As Price points out, the President frequently has the flexibility to "make progress piecemeal, without waiting for a whole program to get approval in principle," and, in seeking congressional majorities, he "can get a majority from these groups on one issue, from those groups on another. The party discipline can be relatively loose; groups that oppose the administration on one issue for local or special reasons need not oppose it on the next."[4]

I have argued in another context that

Today the President is commonly regarded by public and Congress alike as the principal initiator of important legislation; and his party's leaders in the House and in the Senate are commonly regarded as *his* leaders. Indeed such has been the relationship between the President and the Congress that it has even transcended party lines. One is reminded of the Herblock cartoon commenting upon the Democratic majority leadership in the first session of the 86th

[3] See Richard E. Neustadt, "Presidency and Legislation: The Growth of Central Clearance," *The American Political Science Review*, 48 (1954) 641–71.

[4] Price, *op. cit.*, p. 329.

Congress. Speaker Rayburn and Majority Leader Johnson are depicted standing before the President's desk at the White House. Eisenhower is put in the ungrateful position of quoting to the legislative leaders Grant's words to Lee at Appomattox, "Tell the men they may keep their horses; they will need them for the Spring plowing." In effect, of course, Herblock was attributing to Eisenhower the feat of having cowed the Democratic leadership of the House and Senate in that session of Congress. In reality, however, for a substantial portion of the President's program, the Democratic leadership . . . had willingly chosen to be the President's spokesmen or at least to cooperate with the President in ushering his program through Congress.[5]

Available evidence suggests that we have achieved in the United States at least the minimum—indeed, somewhat more than that—capacity for purposeful response to the economic, social, and political problems which beset us, and that the party system has been functional rather than dysfunctional toward equipping the nation with that capacity. The elements of political extemporization and decentralization in the party systems reflect, and in so reflecting, render more stable the pluralistic democracy which has evolved in the United States.

This argument by no means satisfies critics of the American party system. Writing in 1951, Samuel Lubell, one of the more astute observers of the American political scene, expressed concern at the pattern of politics he found to exist at that time. Two "rival coalitions" confronted each other over the issue of "the proper limits of government" as a force in the economic and social life of the nation. "Currently the balance in this struggle over the so called Welfare State is held by a sizable segment of the voting population." This segment comprised the "moderates" in American politics—a coalition of "farmers, urban middle class and other independent voters." While he was satisfied with the degree of governmental stability which had been achieved, Lubell feared that coalition politics would make for a "blind process" of policy-making. The "balancing role" of the "moderates" was "evidence, not of an orderly direction of traffic, but of a traffic jam, so thoroughly besnarled that little can get through." The appearance of stability in American politics obscured the essential "political stalemate" which left the nation rudderless.[6]

At about the same time David Riesman was offering an interpretation of American politics cast essentially in stalemate terms. "Power in America seems to me situational and mercurial; it resists attempts to locate it the way a molecule, under the Heisenberg prin-

---
[5] "Legislative Oversight," in Alfred de Grazia (editor), *Congress: The First Branch* (Garden City, N.Y., Doubleday Anchor Book, 1967), pp. 25–26.
[6] *The Future of American Politics* (Garden City, N.Y., Doubleday Anchor Book, 1951, 1956), pp. 259–60.

ciple, resists attempts simultaneously to locate it and time its velocity."[7] In this context, Reisman asks "who really runs things?" His response is essentially negative:

> . . . What people fail to see is that, while it may take leadership to start things running, or to stop them, very little leadership is needed once things are under way—that, indeed, things can get terribly snarled up and still go on running. . . . At any rate, the fact that [things] do get done is no proof that there is someone in charge.[8]

These expressions of distaste for the gloss of disarray which coats American politics are echoed in James MacGregor Burns' *Deadlock of Democracy*, published a decade later and discussed in Chapter 1.

Riesman's question was put in slightly different form by Robert Dahl in *Who Governs?*[9] His answer was not cast in terms of stalemate or drift. Rather, he concluded, upon the basis of a study of politics and policy-making in New Haven, Connecticut, that the dominant voices in policy-making will vary from time to time, from situation to situation, from policy area to policy area. And, in the specific context of the study, the politically elected mayor appeared to have a more widely ranging and intense influence upon policy-making than any other person.

Even Britain and Scandinavia fall short of what Staebler and Ross call "monolithic" parties, if the term is taken to connote a monopoly of the initiation, consideration and adoption of public policies by political parties performing within the framework of a responsible party government model. All retain wide scope for private non-party group activity directed toward influencing public policy. The chief distinction from the American system of pluralistic democracy is that within these party systems access to decision-makers is much more centralized than in the United States and the majority party leadership has great control over selection of candidates, formulation of party policy and, if victorious, translating that policy into program.

In short, American parties are shifting, opportunistic coalitions, operating within a system in which non-party groups can be fully as effective as parties in influencing public policy—indeed, more effective than parties. Parties provide the American people a vehicle for effecting peaceful changes of governing personnel at many levels, and to aspirant public decision-makers, umbrellas under which to run for public office. Conceding that parties perform such relatively limited functions in the American democracy is far from admitting the existence of "stalemate" or a "snarled up" state of political affairs.

---

[7] *The Lonely Crowd* (Garden City, N.Y., Doubleday Anchor Book, 1950, 1953), p. 257.

[8] *Ibid.*, p. 255.

[9] (New Haven, Yale University Press, 1961.)